THE BEGINNER'S GUIDE

TO

ATHEISM

THE BEGINNER'S GUIDE

TO

ATHEISM

Edward Trillian

END OF THE UNIVERSE PUBLICATIONS

Published by
End of the Universe Publications
Dallas, Texas 75248

Cover Design by Edwin Isaac Mullins
Front: La Vérité, (The Truth), Jules Joseph Lefebvre
Rear: Mona Lisa Black Death Print, Edwin Isaac Mullins
Copyright © Edwin Isaac Mullins

ISBN 978-0-692-56832-3

END OF THE UNIVERSE PUBLICATIONS

For my one and only father.
(In case anyone is wondering... I have no heavenly or satanic fathers.
But I feel sorry for those that do.)

TABLE OF CONTENTS

INTRODUCTION

As a child, I was quite the religious little fellow. Right around the age of nine or ten, when I would pray, I would ask God for one thing and one thing only. I told God I wanted to be as wise as King Solomon – the wisest man that ever lived. The Book of Ecclesiastes, authored by the King himself, was the only book of the Bible that made sense to me then. I figured it must be true. So, every night I prayed the same prayer in the hope that the sought-after wisdom would come. I didn't want money, or fame, or toys, or anything else I could imagine – just wisdom. I figured if I could be wise, the other things would follow, or if they did not follow, they wouldn't matter to a wise man anyway.

As time went on, I was struck with the epiphany that I must already be wise simply because I had been wise enough to ask for wisdom and nothing more – and that certainly was noble (and humble) of me! As I entered my early teen years and thought of this even further, I realized no prayer was necessary. It never had been. Something (God perhaps?) was taking care of me. I seemed to be getting all I needed before I even asked. So, the questions began to filter in... Was I "chosen"? And, then a bigger question arose: maybe all this time I had been praying and talking to no one. Maybe I was just lucky!

Now, all of this may sound a bit arrogant or even a bit narcissistic, but in all honesty, the desire for that kingly wisdom came from an innocent (if not a bit delusional) mind, and I hope it is somewhat excusable on those grounds. I would never presume to be a "wise man" today. I have some years left and a lot to learn. But this little anecdote brings me to another ecclesiastical epiphany: As the elderly preacher, King Solomon said, "All is vanity and vexation of spirit." And, I conclude, what is more vain and vexing than believing in something – anything – for which you have no evidence?

And from that, a little book was born...

The Purpose of Books and People

This book has a purpose. And so does everyone else reading this book. I say that because I hear many believing Christians, Muslims, and others, tell me that atheism means you have no purpose in life. Of course, nothing could be further from the truth. And, at least one purpose for this book is actually to help you find that purpose in your own life, and do so without having to rely on an illusory and supernatural belief system.

I wrote this book mostly for the beginning atheist – someone that has only recently consciously become aware that they don't accept the tenets of any religion and are curious about where that puts them in the spectrum of belief. However, veteran atheists can also benefit from this book's content. They can find some rather unusual perspectives and allegorical explanations about non-belief that have previously been unpublished. Actual on-line conversations with theists are printed here and can be quite entertaining and palpable. (See the chapter: **Comments from Hell**.)

If your life is headed in the direction of free-thought, logic, and reason, this book will help you get there a little faster. It will define what atheism is and what it isn't. It's quite amazing how the majority of people don't understand its actual definition. But this book will clear that up for you, and give you the tools you need to help others finally "get it."

Reasons for Reasoning

One of the main motives for writing this book came from my astonishment, after talking with others, in person and on-line, that so many people had never heard of the terms: *burden of proof, argument from ignorance,* or the *God of the Gaps,* (along with many other logical concepts). My assumption was, if religious persons had never heard of these terms, atheists were probably in the dark about them as well. Because both sides can benefit from knowing a little more about these things, writing this book went to the top of my "to do" list.

Despite all that, it should be noted here what this book *isn't.* It is not a dissertation, it is not a science book, and it is not a tome or an opus. It's not even a scholastic reference. It is however a thoughtful and reasoned look at the current trend, in this hemisphere at least, toward an atheist viewpoint. It is mostly a simplified explanation and a forthright conversation on this issue. Although it may appear rude or funny at times, it is intended to be a well-reasoned discussion, using a myriad of allegory, metaphor, and logical observations to make its points.

The Philosophy of Epistemological Tautology or Something Like It...

For the most part, this is a serious book with only a smattering of humor (where humor is irresistibly called for). And, admittedly, it contains some atheist bias. However, there is no need to be a philosopher or even know very much about philosophy to read this book. Some basic logic is presented, but there is no need to know who Heidegger, Hegel, or Kant were. (You won't even have to feel sorry for Schrödinger's cat!) Socrates, Plato, or Aristotle are only given a few lines when needed. Basic ideas that have their roots in philosophy are naturally implied because these concepts have been with us for a very long time, given to us by our culture throughout our history.

And, although you may not find specific philosophers on every page, you will find some hard-earned common sense. I heard someone say, "You have to believe in your tools." Atheists, for the most part, use logic and reason as the tools for determining what's real and what's not. And our belief in those tools is not based on faith. We have past evidence that logic and reason work very well in our pursuit of truth. And on the other side of the aisle, we know faith fails in determining reality, and for that reason, you'll find that faith of any kind does not fit into our toolbox.

It should become obvious that this book is a bit biased toward atheism, as you would expect, because it is, well... a book for atheists, written by an atheist.

It is **not** the "Totally Neutral Compendium of Things Regarding Atheism that I'm Not Sure About and Can't Discuss Because It Might Make My Grammy Scream." This book makes no claims of neutrality. It is not simply a journalistic observation that says, "Take a look at both arguments, and then you decide." As atheists, we have already made our decision, and this book explains a lot of the *why*.

To be fair, despite the intended bias, this book is not attempting to bludgeon god-believers over the head with a horseman's pick. And it is not an attack on any specific group of believers. It's not aimed solely at Christians as some might suggest. It is, for the most part, a defense against those who would unfairly misjudge others that don't believe in the supernatural, and against those that would do so without knowing anything about their quarry. It may appear as though I am "picking on" Christians, but Muslims could just as easily say I'm doing the same regarding their beliefs. (See the chapter on **Islam**.) Admittedly, if this book does focus most often on Christianity, it's only because Christianity is the majority religion in North America. If I lived in a Muslim nation, I would most likely, if allowed to speak, be defending atheists against Islam the majority of the time. If in India, the defense would be against Hinduism, and so on.

What this book does quite well is present ideas with as much logic as is humanly attainable... at least as much as the capacity of the author's brain will allow. Yes, some religious people will be offended, but you would be as well, if everything you thought was true turned out to be not so very true after all!

It's All About the Content, Baby!

As you'll soon see, this book touches on a multitude of topics: Jesus, Yahweh, Allah, Mohammad, Resurrection, Evidence, Faith, Dogmas, Burdens, Miracles, Presuppositions, Heaven, Hell, Myths, Objective Reality, and dozens of inter-related ideas, and it attempts to do so with unusual angles and examples that you may not have heard before. Whatever your belief, hopefully the words within will help you clarify some long-held misunderstandings about what is possibly the most shunned and avoided concept on earth – non-belief.

You'll find this book is not a hard read. Most everything is in layman's terms, and things a bit more complicated are explained as thoroughly as possible without turning the subject matter into a college textbook. And if you are already well-versed in the areas of faith or atheism, you can probably skip around from one chapter to another. Most chapters can stand on their own as a guide to the subject at hand. There is no need to start from the beginning unless you just like doing things that way. One thing readers might like to do is head to the back of the book first and read some of the definitions in the glossary section. It may make a difference.

Enjoy and learn. (Enjoying and learning are, by the way, at least two of the many purposes of life, but that's just my opinion.)

- The Author

CHAPTER ONE

Atheism Defined

"I contend that we are both atheists. I just believe in one fewer god than you do. When you understand why you dismiss all the other possible gods, you will understand why I dismiss yours." – Stephen Roberts

"Every human being is greater than any of the gods because we can prove we exist and the gods cannot do the same of themselves." – Edward Trillian

DECONSTRUCTING ATHEISM

Brace yourself. You are about to embark on a roller coaster ride full of unfamiliar definitions, overlapping sub-definitions, controversial interpretations, and on-going debate – all about this one seven letter word: atheism.

Most people don't know what atheism really means, and atheists themselves can't altogether agree on a definition. But, once someone has reached the conclusion that their view is that of an atheist, most people will try to refine and redefine what it really means for them personally. It's sort of like a juror deciding someone is "not-guilty" and then telling you exactly why she came to that conclusion. It will likely be different for different jurors, but it doesn't change the outcome.

So, let's go ahead and define atheism. We can *refine* it later.

Atheism is based on the original Greek word *theos* meaning "god." The "a-" prefix means "without." Together, atheism means "without a god" or without a *belief* in a god. Therefore, atheism is not a belief, but rather an *absence of belief.* This is an important distinction because most people that do believe in a god will tell you atheism is a belief or a belief system, but they simply don't understand the subtle difference.

For example, no one would bother to steadfastly affirm their non-belief in a modern-day, living minotaur (a half-bull, half-man mythical creature), unless someone else had first declared one actually existed. No one would walk into a room and discuss their lack of belief in such a thing, nor would they build a belief system, culture, or religion around such an absence of belief. Non-belief requires no participation in belief other than the rejection of some other person's belief.

Before digging deeper into the layered definitions of atheism, there are two other words we must use, consistently and in context, if we are going to put any of this in proper perspective. Those two words are *belief* and *knowledge.*

Knowledge is often referred to as a *subset* of belief. Generally, people act on their beliefs despite not having full knowledge of what they believe in. Belief comes first, then comes the knowledge that either confirms or disproves that belief. We alter, refine, or quantify our beliefs with the added knowledge of something, as a way to strengthen or discard those beliefs.

Theism is a statement of belief. In its most basic definition (before qualifiers are added), atheism is a statement concerning some *other person's* belief. Neither atheism nor theism (in their most basic forms) are statements of *knowledge.* The difference between belief and knowledge is essential because you don't have to know something to believe it. You can believe all the puppies you gave away ten years ago are still alive, but until you actually discover and know that to be true, it is still only a belief.

With regard to atheism, the most basic definition is the *rejection* of another person's claim that a specific god exists, or the rejection of another person's claim that *any* god exists. This is, generally speaking, the modern definition. If you get an old enough dictionary you will find the following words associated with the term atheist: pagan, heathen, heretic, doubter, and infidel. And those are just the nice ones!

The word *rejection* is important to note here, because atheism, by using the most basic definition, makes no claims. Although, an atheist could do so, he or she simply takes the claims of others and rejects them for a variety of reasons – reasons which are decided by the person doing the rejecting. The most common reason is due to a lack of evidence. This rejection of the claim is the first step taken before any refinements can be made or any qualifiers can be added to the definition. And the rejection itself is not a claim. It's a declaration of non-belief. It's simply saying, "I don't *believe* you." Can an atheist make a claim of knowledge that goes beyond simply rejecting the god-claim? Yes, of course. An atheist can say, "Not only do I not believe you, I *know* there are no gods!" That's a *claim of knowledge* and a refinement to the basic definition of atheism and, as we'll see later, it has a very specific label.

Whenever we accept or reject the claims of others, we get into the logical process called the *burden of proof,* which is simply this: It's up to the person making the claim – in this case, the person claiming a god exists – to prove that claim. It is not the burden of the person listening to this claim to prove it isn't so.

As is often the case, when the god-believer is incapable of meeting their burden of proof, that is, they cannot come up with evidence that their god exists, or cannot even articulate *why* they believe what they believe, they will often try to shift the burden of proof back to the atheist. Perhaps the god-believer's most common response to the atheist position is: "Well, you can't prove God *doesn't* exist."

Such a blatant attempt at shifting the burden of proof onto the person who, previous to hearing the god-claim, had simply been sitting there minding his own business, drinking his coffee and eating his bagel, is disingenuous on the part of the person making the claim. There is no reason for the person listening to the claim to do the work for the claimant. The listener does not have to prove or disprove anyone's claim about anything. Evidence-gathering is always the requirement of the person making the claim.

If the burden of proof was on a person *hearing* a claim, we would have to spend all of our time disproving things we may not even care about, such as UFO abductions, The Abominable Snowman, Loch Ness monsters, Elvis still being alive, Hitler living past 100, dragons being real, and other rather extraordinary claims. But, that's not our job. If someone believes Elvis is still alive, that person should present their evidence and we, as listeners and observers, will accept or reject that claim based on the strength of that evidence. This process is the only way of getting to the truth, and exceptions to this process cannot be made for any claim. And begging and pleading for such an exception will get zero results.

Atheism can also be viewed as a conversation. One person says, "There is a god." And a second person responds, "I don't believe you." The first person says again, "There is a god. I have proof." And the second person, after viewing the evidence says, "I reject your evidence as insufficient. Therefore, I *still* don't believe you." And so on.

The default position (or starting point) in this conversation is "no belief in a god." Many religious persons would like to argue that the default position is a god existing, but it cannot be so, because it's not self-evident. Something self-evident would be your own existence, or the existence of the universe – something for which you have no doubt. Plus, you immediately get into questions such as "Which god?" and "Can you define 'God?'" If such questions arise, the obviously highly debatable idea of a god existing automatically reveals itself to be a claim, and therefore, cannot be the default. The default position has to be neutral. You must begin at zero. The "no god" position is a position of zero belief and zero knowledge regarding this idea or concept. It is, therefore, the default position.

This process is quite simple:

1. Begin with a default position (zero belief or knowledge,
   a vacuum, emptiness, space, nada, a big shrug)
2. Listen to, read about, or process a claim of truth
3. Accept or reject that claim based on the evidence presented

It's actually a process that works well, not only with religious ideas, with but just about any concept that offers a significant amount of doubt.

Atheist Epiphany

Can anyone convert to atheism in the same way someone converts to Catholicism, or Islam? Well, the answer is no, not in the same way. Atheism is not a religion, as you will see below. But, the word convert (as a verb) simply means *to change,* as with its original meaning: "to turn toward something." And that can mean turning toward an idea, belief, concept, or conclusion. That means you can change, and turn toward atheism. If you're reading this book, chances are you already are an atheist, you just haven't found a good way to express or define your new way of looking at things.

How do you make that turn complete, and how does one become an atheist? Lots of atheists will say, in all sincerity, the best way to become an atheist is to read the holy books of any religion with a logical, reasonable, and open mind. That, they say, will guarantee you a free ride down Atheist Avenue. Others have said, just open up a science book, or just watch a few episodes of *The Universe* on the History Channel, get a perspective on the vastness of space, and how insignificant we are by comparison, and that will turn you into an atheist faster than the speed of light. That may certainly be true to one degree or another, but everyone's journey is different, and everyone has different reasons for becoming an atheist.

But before we get much further, we really should look first at what atheism *isn't.* This may sound like we are trying to prove a claim, going against what we just said was not our job to do, but this is not the case. No claims are being made about atheism in this next section. We are simply debunking claims *others* have already made about atheism.

HOW ATHEISM IS DEFINED BY OTHERS

People that don't understand atheism are also just as confused about atheists. Besides being called many horrible names (epithets that would ordinarily get the name-caller sent straight to hell, if hell existed), an atheist appears to be some sort of mysterious anomaly to those that believe in a god. One of the best ways to know what atheists believe is to look at many of the mistaken ideas god-believers have about atheists and atheism. For example:

"Atheism is a religion!"

Atheism is spelled with a little "a" for good reason. It's not a religion, although many very religious people desperately want to claim otherwise. There are no special obligations to fulfill in order to qualify as an atheist. There are no synagogues, temples, churches, mosques, or any other special holy places that atheists go to get another weekly dose of atheism. There are no special songs atheists sing in praise of atheism. There are no threats of eternal damnation for not doing certain things only atheists would do. There are no holy books that atheists are required to read (including this one). There are no special rites or rituals atheists have to perform to be atheists. There are no magical words atheists have to say to something unseen, to be atheists. If you curse using the word "atheism," nothing happens.

Atheists don't sprinkle blood over doorposts, march around giant black cubes, clutch special beads, always face east, bow, kneel, or lie prostrate. They

16

don't flagellate themselves, refuse to work on certain days of the week, or tell men in robes all the bad things they've done.

Atheists have no cultural ties, no hierarchy, no special laws, no body mutilations, no holidays, no sacred lands, no forbidden foods, no stories, no miracles, no apparitions, no prophets, no saviors, no demons, no angels, no supernatural testimonies, no invisible entities, no special hats or underclothes, no belief in things based on faith, and most importantly, no deity to worship. Atheism just isn't that complicated, or anywhere near that unnecessarily obsessive.

All anyone needs to be an atheist is to not believe in *a* god. And, as you will see, any god will do. And, in contrast to religious claims, an atheist does not have to be a scientist, know anything at all about science, or even care about science, to be an atheist. An atheist does not have to accept any scientific theories to be an atheist, and that includes the Theory of Evolution. And, lastly, and perhaps most importantly, a person does not have to "hate religion" to be an atheist.

In almost every dictionary around the globe, when you look up the word religion you find words like *cultural, worship, faith, devotion, institutionalized, traditional, sacred, holy, supernatural, spiritual, deity* and so on, all used collectively to make the definition of religion complete. None of these words apply to atheism in a singular form, or in any sort of coherent combination. Atheism simply is *not* a religion, no matter how often religious people may parrot the notion, in any sort of ill-defined obsession with bringing atheism down to their level.

"It requires more faith to be an atheist than it does to believe in God!"

It doesn't require faith to *not* believe something. Faith is believing in something without evidence to support that belief. But, if an atheist doesn't have faith, what evidence does an atheist have *against* the belief in a deity? An atheist has this: ample evidence that the god-believer has failed to demonstrate that a god exists. The claim that a god exists has not met its burden of proof. This fact doesn't require faith on the part of an atheist. We can clearly see from the evidence presented that the god-believer has not done his job of demonstrating that his belief is real and true. For an atheist, no other requirements are needed. It's not about disproving God, it's about getting the believer to show evidence for his assertions.

"Atheists just want to sin!"

That's it! You caught us! We only become atheists because we have an uncontrollable urge to rape and pillage! Uhm... No. Not even close. The people that think this of non-believers are guilty of not thinking things through.

What sane person would say: "I want to steal that car. But Jesus says that's wrong. So, I'll just stop believing in Jesus right now, and he'll no longer exist! Then I can steal that car!" It doesn't work that way. That would be the thoughts of a simpleton or a child. Atheists don't reject the notion of a god so they can go out and do horrible deeds. Horrible deeds are done by all kinds of people with all kinds of beliefs, and their beliefs in deities, or lack of beliefs in deities, with a few infamous exceptions, are usually quite irrelevant.

The idea that anyone can suddenly, consciously, decide to *not* believe in a deity because they have a passionate need to sin, is a concept that is so far off the scale, it would surely break any *illogic meter* on first contact. This is true, even if you ignore the fact that sin is subjective, depending on which religious sectarian you talk to, and true even if we were to agree to the flawed concept of moral absolutes as prescribed by religionists.

No one can force themselves to *not* believe what they already believe. It's not possible for a person to decide to stop believing in gravity just so they can fly. Getting to the point of unbelief involves a process that includes acquiring information over time. A person may have a sudden epiphany about a concept, but it's always preceded by new information, or a new way of looking at old information. It cannot be self-coerced.

Of course, it should be noted, atheists do not believe in the existence of Satan either. Using the bizarre logic of the theist, it would mean that anyone who wanted to do good, could simply decide that Satan didn't exist, and this would automatically make them stop sinning. Deities either exist, or they don't. And people either believe that, or they don't. The only middle ground is their own immeasurable degree of doubt.

"Atheists Worship Satan!"

That brings us to one other quick note about what atheists *aren't*. Atheists are not "worshipers of Satan" by default. This rather naïve statement is often made by immature theists that sincerely believe, if you are not aligned with their god, you must somehow be aligned with that same god's opposition. It's the "you are either with us or against us" mentality. This fallacious "logic" has atheists worshiping Satan without even being aware of it! Sorry, but that's still not atheism. Any thinking and sane person knows that belief, or non-belief, requires a conscious awareness of their position on the matter. Otherwise, even dogs could worship Satan, and hyenas could worship Jesus, and do so unawares!

"You Hate God!"

Known properly as *misotheism,* the idea that atheists "hate" God, is the one accusation that is the most common, and the one that is, from an atheist's perspective, the most illogical.

Believers often think "some false Christian must have done something bad to you to make you stop believing and start hating god..." In their minds, it could not possibly be the very straight forward response that the believer's position simply does not appear to be valid to the non-believer. It *must* be some traumatic event from childhood where "god" or one of his representatives "did you wrong."

Although, if you look at the number of preachers, priests, and other religious folk who have the inglorious habit of being arrested for child molestation, you can find plenty of atheists that *are* created through harm done to them by religious persons. But, most people become atheists through peaceful means, simply rejecting the ideas of the theist. In fact, many of the persons damaged by religious organizations and their minions, often continue to believe in God, long after the horrible event, and for a lifetime. Like most atheists, these religious persons don't "hate God." They despise evil deeds.

And of course, the most obvious response to the silly notion that atheists "hate God" is simply this: No one can hate something that doesn't exist. Only believers in God can hate God. The very definition of atheism makes it impossible for an atheist to hate any god. Once you start hating something, you believe it exists.

Clearly, atheists don't hate gods any more than they hate Santa Claus, the Easter Bunny, Spider-man, Jabba the Hutt, or any other non-existent character.

Most atheists do hate stupid beliefs, however. And, in frank discussions about god-concepts, atheists do get frustrated and angry when they encounter perfectly intelligent people that hold beliefs in some sort of deity. Atheists *are* guilty of this sort of impatient arrogance, and should, when appropriate, take this bit of ancient advice: "When you see an opportunity to keep your mouth shut, take it!" To the believer, the atheist's anger regarding the notion of an invisible, unproven, and un-testable god often makes it appear that atheists are "angry at God." But the god isn't the target, and neither is the believer. The target is the concept, the idea, or premise. Bear in mind, most atheists don't really want to offend the religious, we just want to make them think!

"Atheists Refuse to Acknowledge the God They Know Exists!"

If there existed any creature, thing, or power, that could squash people like a bug in an instant (like a god supposedly could), would anyone really *not* acknowledge it? If you're eating lunch and someone threatens your life by holding a gun to your head, and then tells you to drop your sandwich, would you keep on eating just because you don't want to "acknowledge" the person that has power over you? The reason people don't acknowledge a deity is *not* because they stubbornly refuse to face the truth, but because they don't believe that the god in question actually exists.

"Hitler was an atheist! And so was Stalin!"

Yes, and they both had mustaches. Does that mean all men with mustaches are atheists, or that all men with mustaches are evil dictators? What about Karl Marx? He had a beard. Jesus had a beard. Does this make Jesus a communist, or Karl Marx a Christian?

This is nothing more than a *non-sequitur*. The clumping of one trait into another, and drawing a conclusion without calculating the variables or the exceptions, simply *does not follow*. It's a way to shoot from the hip and hit nothing. Even a quick read of history will show that there have been "evil-doers" across the entire political, social, religious and ideological spectrum.

Real maliciousness and wrong-doing on a massive scale comes from psychopaths. And psychopaths will use whatever is available at the time to gain the power they so desperately covet. As conduits for their misdeeds, Torquemada and Hitler used Christianity. Stalin and Pol Pot used Communism (which included an atheist tenet), Caligula used polytheism, Constantine used a combination of Christianity and paganism, and Osama bin Laden used Islam. But psychopaths can barely be called human. They are wired in such a way that they cannot feel empathy. And empathy is what makes us care for one another, no matter what our religious or non-religious affiliations may be, and thus ultimately makes how we actually act toward one another much more relevant to our survival than our beliefs.

THE REAL DEFINITIONS OF ATHEISM

Now that we've eliminated the most accusatory and false definitions of atheism, and covered what atheism *isn't,* let's look at our original (and very basic) definition of atheism one more time: Atheism is a *rejection* of claims made by others about the existence of all gods, or the rejection of claims made by others regarding a specific god.

For most, that definition will suffice. However, because there are actually varying degrees of how the rejection of god-claims are viewed by individuals, it can get a little splintered. But, the bottom line is this: it's all still atheism as our definition shows.

Here are some refinements to atheism you might encounter:

agnostic atheist
gnostic atheist
weak atheist
strong atheist
negative atheist
positive atheist

The most important thing to know about these definitions is that gnosticism and agnosticism address *knowledge,* whereas, atheism and theism address *belief.*

Now let's look at how these words can be paired:

agnostic atheist (also known as an **atheist agnostic**) is someone that does not believe in gods, but *does not claim to know* a god does not exist. This belief is also referred to as weak atheism, or *negative* atheism.

gnostic atheist (also known as an **atheist gnostic**) is someone that does not believe in gods, but also *claims to know* a god does not exist. This belief is also referred to as strong atheism, or *positive* atheism.

That word "but" doesn't change the fact that the person, as defined, is still an atheist.

Or course, there is certainly nothing wrong with refining your definition of atheism. But problems can arise when you get deeper into the agnostic-atheist or gnostic-atheist terminology, and it's not just because these definitions are often confusing. You get into a "What I am" type of self-labeling system, and then you're entering the realm of atheism becoming a belief-system, or what philosophers, and even Christian presuppositional apologists, like to call a "world view."

To put it simply, atheism shouldn't be about labels. It's not who you are, it's not your entire belief system, and it's certainly not a world view. It's actually a position you've taken. A conclusion you've made. It's something you've *done.* You have rejected the ideas placed before you about a specific god existing, or rejected the idea of any gods existing. That's it. That's all there is to it. To put it more succinctly, you can't define yourself by what you *don't* believe. Pretty simple, but so hard for a lot of people to understand.

The Quantified Atheist

But, if we want, we can complicate things even further. You can be an atheist and a believer at the same time! If someone comes up to you with what they believe is evidence for the existence of Vishnu and you reject all of it outright as ridiculous drivel, you are an atheist when it comes to Vishnu. However, you can believe in Jesus, and at the same time deny the existence of Vishnu, just like any atheist or Hindu who has similarly rejected Jesus. To followers of Vishnu, you're an atheist. This, of course, is slicing the definition into little pieces and is hardly necessary, other than to express certain disbelief in some other person's rival deity.

Let's suppose further that you've rejected god claims, but still harbor some thoughts that some other god *may* exist, that is, one you haven't encountered yet, so you haven't rejected that one yet. Even if you think this makes you an agnostic, you are still an atheist. You rejected those previous gods, remember? So your atheist status hasn't changed. You've just added a personal footnote to the definition. In fact, any addition to the basic definition of *rejecting a god-claim* is a footnote. It may clarify and focus your point of view, but it doesn't revoke your atheism. Even believers in one particular god, who reject all the other gods, are atheists when it comes to the other gods.

Why Not Just Be Agnostic Instead?

Agnosticism, as you will see, can be both a sub-set of atheism, and a sub-set of theism.

Gnostic means "knowing." Therefore, as with "a-theism," when you add the prefix "a-" to a word in English, it negates that word and transforms it into its opposite meaning. Therefore, agnostic means "not knowing." When used in regard to a god-concept, it means that the existence or non-existence of a deity is unknown and probably unknowable to humans.

(It's important to note here that Gnosticism, with a capital G, which at first glance, may appear to be the opposite of agnosticism, is nothing of the sort. Gnosticism is an ancient set of religious beliefs rooted in early Christianity, and is unrelated to this discussion.)

The term "agnostic" is a relatively new word. The word was invented in the 19th century by Thomas Henry Huxley, a scientist and a supporter of Charles Darwin's ideas about evolution. The modern day definition of agnostic is a bit different than what Huxley intended. For Huxley, agnosticism was a *method* for determining what is true. To quote Huxley: "...follow your reason as far as it will take you.... and do not pretend that conclusions are certain..." A method is not a belief. It's a process. When anyone veers from Huxley's clearly defined concept that agnosticism is a method, by saying instead that it's a belief all its own, they are not using the word as originally intended. Ideally, agnosticism should be used as a way to take a position, and should not be used as a position itself. As such, agnostic can be used when referencing other lines of inquiry which have nothing to do with beliefs in god-concepts.

So we can see, contrary to popular, non-dictionary vernacular, the agnostic position is not a neutral position, at least not by itself. When the word is used in relation to beliefs in deities, it is not a stand-alone word. It must accompany either the word theist or atheist. Everyone is either a theist or an atheist, whether they like it or not. When someone says, "I'm an agnostic." The immediate response *should* be, "Are you an agnostic-atheist, or an agnostic theist?"

Here's how it works: You can say, "I don't believe in a god, but I suppose there could be one, but there's no way to know for sure." This will make you an agnostic-atheist (as discussed and defined previously).

Or, you can say, "I believe there is a god, but I know I can't prove it, so there's no way to know for sure." This makes you an agnostic-*theist.*

Your agnosticism (as a method of thought) is what brought you to these conclusions. To paraphrase Huxley: "You have followed your reason as far as it would take you, and you do not pretend that your conclusions are certain."

Simply put, people who call themselves agnostic, without the accompanying word of theist or atheist, are making a poor attempt at being neutral.

This of course is somewhat controversial among those that call themselves "agnostics." And, it has caused quite a lot of arguments and debates on this subject alone. And you thought Protestants and Catholics couldn't agree! Sitting on the fence (besides hurting your bottom parts), isn't easy to do when it comes to a belief in gods, but those who call themselves agnostic without the qualifying words of theist or atheist, often try their best to balance themselves on that railing anyway in a futile effort to avoid criticism.

There is nothing wrong with using "agnostic" to describe your belief, or lack of belief, in a deity. But, no one can be "just an agnostic." Because atheism and theism address two diametrically opposing beliefs, you can have no middle ground between the two. There are things we don't know, or can't know, but we can never avoid what we *think* we know. We are always on one side or the other. Put more bluntly: You may not know something for certain, but you'll always have a *belief* about it anyway, either for or against. And unless you're unconscious or dead, you can't prevent that mental process from happening. You can change your mind when new information comes to you, but you will never be in the middle, even if you are flip-flopping your position by the day, or by the minute.

These problems arise because people often confuse the words belief and knowledge. For example, you may be asked, "Do you *believe* a god exists?" It makes no sense to reply, "I don't *know*." That would be responding to question about *belief* with an answer that refers to *knowledge*. The correct response should be either, "I *believe* a god exists," or "I don't *believe* a god exists."

In similar fashion, it makes no sense to answer a question about *knowledge* with an answer that indicates only *belief.* Someone could ask you, "Do you *know* God exists?" If you respond, "I *believe* that he does," it does not answer the question properly. The correct way to respond to a knowledge question is with knowledge. The correct response is either: "I *know* God exists" or "I don't *know* if God exists."

It could easily be said that all atheists and all theists are always agnostic to one degree or another because *people know that they don't know, and they know they can't possibly know everything about anything.* No human being is omniscient. This is where your brain begins to assess what it knows based on the *probability* of something being true. This will quickly get you into things like Bayes' Theorem, for example. (See the **Glossary** section, in the back of the book, for that one.) But no matter which side you find yourself on, atheism gets its strength from the god-believer's inability to meet their burden of proof, and until that burden is met, the probability of the theist's assumptions, hypotheses, and assertions, remain egregiously and almost infinitely low, rightly unacceptable, and easily rejected.

One final word on agnostic positions... The view that all theists and all atheists are agnostics to one degree or another does not do a disservice to those that call themselves *gnostic*-atheists or *gnostic*-theists. Many within these two groups will state their knowledge claims as a possibility – that one *can* know, or could know under certain circumstances, if a god exists or not. They are not actually making the claim that they do know. And that's probably the closest anyone will ever get to a neutral stance. But, either way, until the evidence is presented that you *can* or *do* know such things for certain, most people will always remain a little bit agnostic – whether theistic or atheistic.

The Atheist Position

So, in a nutshell, what does the average atheist believe about gods? Can it be summarized? Here's a brief itemized list of what *most* atheists believe. It's a basic inventory, with a caveat that many atheists may want to amend this to their own liking:

- We have determined through logic, reason, and our own limited senses, that there is no good cause to believe anything for which there is no evidence. This includes god-claims.
- We reject all god-claims that do not meet their burden of proof.

- We hold to the logical deduction that extraordinary claims require extraordinary evidence.
- We willfully acknowledge that, as human beings, we cannot know everything.
- We accept the possibility that a god *could* exist, but with the understanding that the likelihood of such a god existing approaches zero, and that the likelihood that any specific human-delineated god is even less.
- We will continue to hold to these tenets until verifiable evidence is provided that demonstrates otherwise.

Note that there are no attacks against any specific god or gods on this list. Atheism isn't about refuting or disproving anything. It's about thoughtfully and reasonably rejecting other people's ideas about gods.

Theists will want to tear apart these simple ideas to protect their god-claim by attacking specific wording, challenging us by asking, "How do you know your reasoning is reasonable?" And, "You can't disprove god." Or, "You admit there is a possibility, so you could be wrong." And more. All of this will be covered in other areas in the book. In these later chapters, we will easily show, in greater detail, that no matter which way the theist turns, he cannot meet his burden of proof. The dizziness caused by the theist's circular logic makes him lose all consciousness, and when he comes-to, he still finds himself made of matter, and living in the real, non-spiritual, material world.

SUMMARY

Atheism, for most, is hard to define. We know it's not a religion, it's not hatred of god or hatred of god-believers. It's not the worship of Satan or evil, and it's not an excuse to do something bad. To be true to ourselves, we cannot describe atheism in terms of what non-atheists think or say.

We can only define atheism as an action or a decision we have made regarding what *others* believe about gods. An atheist rejects the notion of a god existing because those that believe in a deity have not met their burden of proof. The atheist position is simply one conscious decision we've made about one particular subject – the subject of gods.

Because atheism makes a single conclusion about a single idea, it cannot be an all-encompassing world view. And, although your own atheism may influence how you view the world, it's not the only thing that does, and unfortunately for those that like to generalize, each atheist's view of the world is different.

For an atheist, the believer-in-gods cannot simply hand out their belief and expect an atheist to accept it at face value. We demand more. A single step further is required. The believer must meet non-belief with knowledge, not belief with more belief. Extraordinary claims require extraordinary evidence. The believers' cross they have to bear is their burden of proof, a cross which only they can carry.

Most importantly, we can't define ourselves by what we don't believe. Knowing this, we can move towards a better understanding of why we reject the god-claims of others, and we can more accurately define what that means to us on a personal level.

Atheism isn't the bad word some religionists would like everyone to believe. It's just a word that's poorly understood and unjustifiably feared. And the time is way overdue to change all that.

CHAPTER TWO

Defining Faith, Hope, Myth, Belief, Evidence, Knowledge, and Other Things

"A wise man proportions his belief to the evidence." – David Hume

WHAT IS MYTH?

Myth derives from the Greek word *mythos* which means *narrative fiction.* These narratives have mostly cultural, traditional, and usually ancient sources. But many ancient tales and legends, which we now call myths, were once considered true accounts of a society's primordial past. But, why are these accounts accepted today as nothing more than incredibly exaggerated stories that never really happened? When pressed, most people will point out that a myth contains numerous supernatural beings doing some rather extraordinary, often death-defying, unbelievable things. And yet, when you read most holy books, which are still taken as truth by religious followers in our own time, these ancient stories also contain numerous beings doing some rather extraordinary, death-defying, unbelievable things.

For our purposes, as atheists, the general definition for myth is the same as it is for religion. Myth, like religion, is "the impossible becoming possible" – but, as we'll see, this is true only on paper, or imprisoned within the minds of those with rather extraordinary imaginations.

Urban Legends

Just about everyone has heard of, and can recite back, at least one urban legend – a strange, often humorous, and sometimes horrific story about someone or something that leaves the listener shocked, frightened, or reeling with laughter. The tales get told time and time again, despite their egregious lack of evidence for their actual historical occurrence. Often these stories are retold with changes and embellishments, and are usually presented by the one telling the story as if it happened to someone they know. The story teller's claims that they personally know a witness to the event will often lend credence to the tale. But, rarely are any of these stories true, and few are even based on any real events. Telling made-up stories around the camp fire is as old as human language. It's been going on for a long time, and isn't going to stop anytime soon.

These sorts of "ghost stories" and urban legends are fine as entertainment. The trouble only starts when myths are taken as truth. And it logically forces us to ask the following question: How many stories in the holy books of the religions of the world are actually just urban legends? A good solid answer to that question is: All of them that defy the laws of physics, and those that run counter to logic and reason. The cognitive dissonance required to see one set of incredible stories as being false, while seeing another equally incredible set of stories as true, would be palpable for any reasoned mind. But we aren't talking about minds that use reason.

To believe the mind-boggling, outrageous, and often bizarre miracles and occurrences in our earth's holy books requires something called *faith*.

WHAT IS FAITH?

There is a great amount of argument regarding what faith is and how it's applied, so it's necessary to get our definitions lined up in a row.

Definitions of Faith:

1. A religion and/or the core beliefs of that religion. Example: "I am of the Christian *faith*."

2. Confidence in a desired outcome; trust in someone or something's abilities or intentions; loyalty and allegiance to a person or group. Example: "I have *faith* the Americans will win the war."

3. Belief and trust in a deity; belief in the doctrines or dogmas of a religion. Example: "I have *faith* in Jesus."

4. A firm belief in anything which has no proof or evidence; complete confidence in such beliefs. Example: "I have *faith* that there is life on other planets."

In **Definition 1**, faith references the collective whole of a specific religion and its organization, as it pertains to membership within that religion.

As shown in **Definition 2**, the word faith is often used interchangeably with *trust*. When faith is used to mean trust, it normally carries with it some prior evidence to elicit such trust. When a person says they have faith that the captain of the ship will guide them to the harbor safely and on time, it may or may not be because the person has evidence that the captain has done this before. The source of the trust could simply be that other boats have made it into the harbor in the past, and there's no reason to think this one won't make it also. But as always, trust is belief with (at least *some*) prior evidence.

Definition 3 uses both trust *and* belief as a way to express religious loyalty to a specific deity. But the trust derives from others who also believe, not from the trust in the deity itself, despite the fact that religious persons will state that they "trust in god." The actual evidence that elicited trust is your assumption that these others, who haven't lied to you before, aren't lying to you now about their religious beliefs, or that they, at least, genuinely believe what you believe.

Definition 4 is about belief only. It does not require trust or evidence, nor does it apply to religion alone. One can have belief in anything without any evidence and have complete faith that it's true. No need to trust anyone but yourself here. (Examples: Hitler living past 100; crop circles having been made by UFOs; human vampires existing, etc.) Although **Definition 4** does not apply to religion only, it applies to religious belief itself, both precisely and accurately, as the best definition for faith in a religious context.

Faith, when used explicitly as a substitute for the word trust, is *outward* – it is belief directed toward someone else, a god, or even an object, and can be obtained from previous evidence, no matter how insufficient. Faith when used as a substitute for the word belief is *inward* – its source is the Self. As such, it is self-deceiving, self-convincing, and has no need for evidence. Faith, therefore, used in the religious sense is pure. It is pure in that it is devoid of all evidence, proof, or substantiated fact. It is this lack of any testable evidence that distills faith into its most genuine, volatile and dangerous form. In the distillery that produces faith, (the churches, mosques, and temples), the faithful are proud of the nitroglycerin they carry with them. They care not that such blind allegiance to something for which there is no valid evidence can harm themselves and everyone around them.

Faith, in the religious sense, has, and always will be, correctly defined as "belief without evidence." This, despite all the protestations from religious persons who declare that they do have evidence, and yet repeatedly fail to provide any.

Some *Un*believable Things In The Holy Texts that Require Faith

There are quite a number of events in the Bible, Torah, and Qur'an which defy the laws of physics and sensibility. And as we know, extraordinary claims require extraordinary evidence. A few of them are:

Jewish Bible:

- Intelligence enhancing fruit
- Making a woman from a man's rib
- A living person turned into a column of salt
- Wooden sticks turning into snakes
- Every species of animal, insect and plant rescued from a worldwide flood
- The worldwide change of human languages in an instant

- Female bears killing 42 children for mocking a prophet
- A talking snake
- A talking donkey
- A talking bush that is also on fire
- Someone climbing a ladder up to the sky
- Flying through the air on a horse-drawn chariot
- The earth stopping its rotation on command
- Giant pillars of fire that reach to the sky
- A human ascending into space without a space suit
- Fire raining down onto an altar on command
- A God vs. Man wrestling match
- A man losing his super-human strength due to a haircut
- Ready-made food dropped from the sky without the use of airplanes or helicopters
- Various plagues on command

Christian Bible:

- Human parthenogenesis
- Magically turning water into wine
- Bringing dead people back to life by talking to them
- Rubbing mud on eyes to cure blindness
- Killing a fig tree by talking to it
- Walking on the surface of water without falling in
- Transferring "demons" from a human to a herd of pigs
- Mass suicide of a herd of pigs on command
- Magically multiplying fish and bread from nothing
- Coming back to life after being dead far beyond the time needed to resuscitate
- A human ascending into space without a space suit

Islamic Qur'an:

- Turning a stone into a female camel
- A mooing golden calf
- Turning humans into apes
- Turning humans in pigs
- Invisible beings made of "smokeless fire"
- Clay birds coming to life
- Mountains moving like clouds
- Another mountain crashing down in front of Moses
- Splitting the moon in half
- A talking palm tree
- A flying horse
- Talking ants

- Invisible armies
- Tables of food descending from heaven
- Virgins and plentiful shade given to people in heaven
- A human ascending into space without a space suit
- Numerous ludicrous claims that the Qur'an is full of science

Please note that Christianity accepts the Jewish Bible and its fantastic tales as true, (but alters interpretations to conform with the alleged existence of Jesus.) And Islam accepts most of the Christian *and* Jewish tales, (with various changes, meanings, and additions).

With just a little research you will find some rather bizarre logic-defying events and beliefs within many other religious texts, including the various books of Hinduism, and even those of the more recent religious expressions, such as those revered by Mormons, and the books peddled by Scientologists.

The point of listing the above is to demonstrate that believing such things requires total, resolute, and relentless faith. And this is because there is zero evidence for any of these events. They fall into the category of myths and legends. Some may hope they are true and believe they are true, but no one will ever *know* they are true without a massive, phenomenal, mind-blowing amount of evidence. And the probability of such evidence appearing at any time in our future is extremely close to zero.

A Diversity of Faiths

Most believers in deities do not understand the very word they prize the most within their belief system – faith. As shown previously, faith is defined as belief without evidence. This means the belief must be based on a feeling or emotion rather than well-thought-out logic. The believer in a deity makes the emotional assumption that everyone should just *know* a god exists, (and particularly *their* god exists) automatically and without question because this "knowledge" is so obvious to them.

This exact same emotion is present in all believers no matter what religion they claim. Muslims feel the same exuberance for their belief in Allah as Christians do for Jesus, or Jews for Yahweh. This begs the question as to how they could all be right with such differing gods, precepts, morals, cultures and agendas. And, if all these gods are actually the same god, then any laws or revelations that conflict with any of the others become irrelevant, or highly questionable as to whether they genuinely come from this all-encompassing god.

And as any observer might expect, most believers will, in order to defend the culture built up around their god-concept, tell you that Yahweh, Jesus, Allah and Brahma are *not* the same entity – meaning either somebody's wrong, or somebody lied.

A polytheist might jump in here at this point to say they believe in multiple gods, and that all the gods (or the gods they single out) are real and true in their own way, etc. However, the only thing the polytheist is doing is multiplying his or her burden of proof again and again, making the ability to demonstrate their beliefs even more insurmountable. Likewise is true for the pantheist who believes that a divine force thrives within everything, both living and inanimate. What is rarely addressed is the fact that a more complex claim requires a greater burden of proof.

Faith Compared to Hope

A pious religious believer will tell us that religion is good because it offers us hope. But does faith really give us hope? Not exactly. Hope is wishful thinking, but faith is wishful thinking on steroids. Hope admits that you do not know the outcome, whereas faith takes that hope and turns it into an insistence that you *do* know the outcome. And neither has any evidence.

Hope, like worry, is emotional and virtually useless. It achieves nothing. Many baseball fans hope for their team to win the pennant each year, but most of the time a team barely breaks even. The main difference between faith and hope is that hope is anticipation of wished-for future events, but faith is believing something is true without evidence.

So, with faith (and hope) comes the question: Could there still be evidence out there? Yes. But once the evidence is obtained, faith vanishes. It's no longer required. Now you have only truth. Religious people have faith, but they don't necessarily have truth.

Comingling Science and Faith

In making their case for why atheists should turn to a belief in a god, theists will often attempt to reference the beliefs of famous scientists that are also god-believers. The argument is, "If these great minds believe, and they understand science better than we do, then wouldn't you, a person that also supports science, want to believe like they do?"

Besides the obvious assessment that scientists can sometimes be wrong, we also have the incontrovertible fact that scientists, no matter how famous or capable, have the same amount of evidence for the existence of a deity that the average housewife or plumber has: None.

A 6-year old child prodigy, one that can play almost any musical instrument as well as, or better than, any 40-year old professional, can also believe Santa Claus is real. His musical expertise and brilliance are separate from his fantasy world and his knowledge of what is real. Even brilliant scientists have a part of them that wants to imagine things outside the realm of science, even to the point they can hope and wish that such fanciful things were possible.

Faith in *Not* Believing

Quite often, religious persons will state that "it takes just as much or more faith to be an atheist than it does to believe in God." Again, the god-believer fails to take his own assertion to its logical conclusion. The religionist should ask himself how much faith it takes him to *not* believe in Hercules, or *not* believe in Thor, or *not* believe in Apollo. A quick introspection will reveal that it doesn't take much, if any faith at all, to *not* believe in these gods, all of whom were highly venerated in their time, worshiped daily, wept over, prayed to, and sincerely loved, in spite of their now recognized highly unlikely existence. Not believing in a god is so easy that the non-believer hardly ever thinks about it. No "faith" is required.

WHAT IS BELIEF?

It may seem strange to the reader that *belief* comes after *faith* in this discussion when faith is defined as *belief without evidence*. Shouldn't we have defined belief first? Not necessarily. Most people already know what belief is. This section is more about how belief is *used* rather than how it's defined. But for the purposes of clarity, let's go ahead and define it now...

The Definition of Belief

Belief is an assumption, acceptance, or presupposition that something is true, factual, or real. But, simply believing something is true, factual, or real doesn't automatically make it so. Beliefs do not require any evidence to back them up. However, any amount of evidence greater than zero will always make beliefs more believable.

The Motivation of Belief

What motivates the believer in gods to want to believe? Human beings, like most mammals, are motivated through pain or pleasure, which means they can also be motivated through a lack of pleasure or a lack of pain.

Pain: What is the pain, or *lack of pleasure,* that motivates a believer to believe? There are many, but we need to only address a few.

Fear is the greatest motivator of humans. Fear can make a person do almost anything. Many sudden believers come to believe in a god due to a tragic or painful event, or only after living a rather self-destructive life. When a person is cornered, and left with few choices, any escape is a good one. Quite often, we see an individual attempt to make that escape through a personal change. A new behavior is born, even if fear and self-preservation are its progenitors. Trading a life of crime for an culturally-approved lie is way better than dying or rotting in some prison. Hence, the concept of being "born again."

But what keeps the believer believing after their "rebirth"? It's mostly more fear. Some of these fears – fear of going to hell, fear of not going to heaven, fear of displeasing their god, fear of sinning, fear of blasphemy, fear of death, and even fear of disappointing fellow congregants – are designed to keep the believer believing. For the believer, these fears appear to be quite real, no matter how fantasy-based they may seem to an outsider.

And they work quite well, which is why religions survive, and why specific religions have survived for so long. Religion has all the pat answers for alleviating those fears – after, of course, introducing the new convert to many those fears themselves.

Unfortunately, highly religious human beings have a personal relationship with a delusion. In some ways, it's like a self-induced, yet milder form of paranoia. It's like seeing a shadow of a tree but thinking it's a man, or hearing the wind rustle through the trees but thinking it's a predator. But, it's all just human imagination. Imagining the worst in a situation is an act of survival. It's normal and natural. Ancient humans taught themselves to be vigilant. And we have those same instincts today. When the worst doesn't happen, you're still alive. You survive.

The religious believe in a god and a promise of an afterlife because it's comforting, not because it's real or true. Human beings are good at lying. They're even better at believing lies. But they are best at believing their own lies. And to switch those lies to either the truth, or another lie, often takes a catastrophic event – which is one of the reasons there are so many religious people in prisons. Most got that way *after* incarceration. Highly stressful events have a way of shifting, altering, or even destroying a human being's personal perspective – sometimes for the better, and sometimes for the worse.

Believers believe, and continue to believe, for many other reasons which are, to some degree, simply subsets of the fears we just mentioned. One example is unresolved questions of purpose or existence. Not knowing why you're here in this place, on this planet, at this time, can be very daunting and lonely, especially in a culture that presumes that it's not okay to *not know* things.

Pleasure: Now let's look at the pleasure, or *lack of pain,* that motivates a believer.

Self-delusion can be quite satisfying for many. It keeps the fears away. And much like the continuously added "lives" of a cosmic video game character, if you think you've got another life to live after this one, thoughts of death are almost non-existent, or easily suppressed. There is also a social aspect to the pleasure of belief. Camaraderie with other believers who think like you do (more or less), is comforting. It's as if they are saying, "I may be wrong (or delusional, or lonely, or ignorant), but so is everyone else in the room." But, for people who prefer to think for themselves, there is no comfort being on a sinking ship with friends. The ship is still going down.

What's common to these motivations is the lack of focus on reality. None of these motivations ever attempt to address the core issue, the big question that lurks in the room, the one that the believers choose to ignore: "Is any of this real?" Simply asking that question, even only internally, will bring the whole theater production crashing to the stage floor, ruining the self-delusional play.

Now it's time to explore some different aspects of belief...

The "Unseen" World of Belief

Believers in deities often use the words *immaterial, supernatural,* or *spiritual,* to describe the place or "realm" where their god resides. Often, when one of these words is challenged for the inherent lack of evidence for its existence, the god-believer will switch to one of the other words in this trinity of non-existing dimensions. Example: "No, I don't mean supernatural, it's actually spiritual." These are the same thing.

And these hopelessly un-searchable planes of existence are devoid of any matter, while the entities that reside there can somehow float through our existing matter with ease, even influencing our material world, often without any harm being thrust upon themselves, retaining the same powers they possessed in their immaterial world. It's actually a daytime dream world, but those who accept these things as real claim to be awake and aware.

Belief Through Divine Revelation

Talk to any believer and you'll soon discover that gods send messages to humans and they do so quite often. However, private, or personal "divine revelation" is not a justification for *others* to believe in that revelation. Anecdotal evidence is not really evidence and is only useful to the person who claims the experience. Such "evidence" soon becomes hearsay. It is altered and embellished over time, much like children playing the game of "Telephone." The general rule is that the older the hearsay evidence, the more likely it is exaggerated, changed, redacted, or missing some important elements. Few archaeologists would argue otherwise. All holy writ is subject to this rule as well. "Holy" texts do not get a free pass, or less scrutiny, simply because some number or group of people believe that every word within that text is true. When someone says, "God told me..." whatever comes after those three words cannot ever be verified. It's useless information.

Belief as Confidence

A religious person often defines their belief as "confidence in the truth." However, this falls short of being any kind of improvement on the word belief itself. Confidence in the truth isn't truth. It's a perception of what is declared to be truth. Plenty of people have confidence in what they think is the truth and are completely wrong. Much like the entire population of earth who at one time thought the sun revolved around the earth.

It is the highest pinnacle of arrogance for one to assume they are in direct contact with the creator of the universe. This arrogance negates that same creator's insistence that his followers be humble. This rather obvious observation is lost on most god-believers.

In the *real* world, the value of belief should never exceed its evidence.

WHAT IS KNOWLEDGE?

Most dictionaries will tell us that knowledge is the familiarity, awareness, or understanding of facts, information, or skills, acquired through experience or education. Therefore, knowing something means one has the awareness and understanding of those facts, information or skills.

To philosophers, the study of knowledge is known as epistemology and today most scholars see knowledge as "well-justified true belief." And this is where the distinction between simple belief and knowledge is made. The determining factor that transforms a belief into actual knowledge (or true belief) is that which is *well-justified*. And what makes a belief well-justified? Evidence, logic, reason, or some combination of the three. Faith (belief without evidence, logic or reason), cannot be well-justified and cannot qualify as knowledge.

What frequently boggles the mind of an atheist is how a god-believer can say they *know* something and say they have *faith* in that same something, all in the same breath. If someone knows something, it means that person has verifiable evidence for it. If someone has faith in something, that someone believes in something *without* verifiable evidence. But, believers are renown for using belief and knowledge interchangeably.

Believers in deities have a kind of contradictory arrogance that they *know* their god exists, rules the universe, created the earth, saves people from his hell, grants eternal life, judges the wicked, has a place in heaven for good people, and so on. These are all claims of knowledge, but all are made without any evidence. When challenged on this, the response is, "I have *faith* that it's so." The truth is, you can't have both. You cannot *know* something and have faith in it at the same time. You cannot know something through faith, and you cannot have faith in something you already know. Why? Because the true definition of faith is *belief without evidence*. Once you have the evidence, you don't need the faith. You already *know*.

To put it another way, faith disappears when evidence appears. If you had faith that you would own a specific Van Gogh painting someday, and then later, you actually bought that exact same painting, would you still have faith that someday you would own that painting? Of course not. You already have that painting, right there in your house in front of you. Why would anyone have faith they would get something they already have?

By necessity, evidence always supplants faith. And it's irrational to hold beliefs that are not in proportion to the evidence. This supplanting of faith with evidence is parallel to supplanting *belief* with *knowledge*.

More On the Differences Between Knowledge and Belief

You can only *know* those things for which you have evidence. You can still *believe* things which have a little evidence, a lot of evidence, or something in between. For example, ancient man knew a lot about the sun and its movements across the sky, and could calculate its behavior enough to invent calendars and make predictions about its movement. Lots of evidence. What most cultures did not know was that those movements were based on the earth circling around the sun, not the sun circling around the earth. They had lots of knowledge and a little belief. The part they believed in was wrong, and it was a very big and crucial part. All because they couldn't see the big picture.

But most beliefs are not evidence-rich. For example, you can be eating a chicken sandwich right now, but not know if it will soon give you salmonella poisoning. The part you know, (a low likelihood of getting salmonellosis) you base on past evidence of *not* getting a bacterial infection after eating chicken sandwiches. The part you don't know (whether or not your current sandwich has salmonella in it), you *believe*. You think you're basing this belief on past evidence, but in reality, you're basing your belief on absolutely nothing. You don't know if the sandwich you're eating right now has the salmonella bacteria or not. You haven't investigated it. You're taking a gamble.

Knowing vs. Believing is an everyday distinction, and often a conundrum or a puzzle that is acted upon or dismissed rather quickly:

- What you know: *"There is a very small chance I could get salmonella poisoning."*
- What you believe: *"I won't get salmonella poisoning."*

"What you know" is a fact. "What you believe" isn't a fact. Belief is not the same as actual knowledge. Once you have knowledge, you don't need belief. (Most people eat the sandwich and allow belief to override knowledge.)

WHAT IS EVIDENCE?

The word evidence has been mentioned often thus far. It's time we gave some examples of what that really is.

Evidence is knowledge, whether partial or incomplete. It is a way to *know* something. Any good thesaurus will also give you other words like proof, confirmation, data, facts, support, verification, substantiation, etc., all of which will tell you the same thing – evidence is what you use to show or demonstrate that a claim you have is true. It's all about knowing. But not all evidence is equal. And each claim must have its own separate pertinent evidence.

Theists will often state that "no evidence will ever be good enough for you atheists." This is no doubt a convenient way of never having to present any evidence – a way for the believer to quit the debate. After all, according to the theist, whatever that evidence is, the atheist will toss it aside just so he can hold on to his non-belief. Of course, there aren't really many atheists who think this way. Atheists want truth and demand as much evidence for truth as can possibly be expected – that's why they are atheists in the first place.

Ironically, after making the statement that "no evidence will ever be enough for you atheists," they will then ask the atheist, "What would you consider sufficient evidence?" as if the atheist has the burden of presenting the believer's case for the believer. This argument never leads anywhere because shifting the burden of proof is always a useless endeavor for both sides. No one should be expected to define the parameters of some other party's evidence until after it is actually presented. But, as is usual, the theistic drones present nothing at all. One thing we do know... *no* evidence is the one kind of evidence that will never be sufficient.

Books as Evidence

A couple of thousand years ago, strange symbols on a papyrus scroll, or words chiseled in stone, seemed quite magical to most humans. Only a small percentage of people could actually read, so words were like magic figures full of power and might – they could retell the past and predict the future. They were the most powerful instrument man had outside his own mind.

Now, it seems, there's a bookstore on every other corner, full of books that become obsolete within a few years of their printing. And almost everyone can read. Words are no longer magical. Books are no longer sacred. They are easily thrown away and forgotten. (Of course, if treated correctly, they are properly recycled, mashed up, and remade into a newer, different book.) The millions of books in circulation today range from reprints of ancient texts all the way up to massive explanations of quantum mechanics. All the stuff in between – the romantic novels, the science fiction paperbacks, the how-to books, the coffee table books, and books on computers – are all filled with some of the following: opinion, fantasy, trivia, useful information, wild imaginings, contradictions, lies, creative ideas, suppositions, hyperbole, humor, polemics, and occasionally some truth.

Unfortunately for religionists, their piece of the pie when it comes to getting readers attention has been pushed into a smaller and smaller corner. Humans may like their books, but they are rarely amazed by them anymore. Yet a book is all the religionists have. So, they get people to write more books that simply refer back to the original book. Not too amazing either. When a book is your only tool for convincing someone of something so unequivocally extraordinary as the existence of the creator of our inexplicably vast universe, it makes you less than handicapped in that regard. It's like you invented the hammer, and so you've decided that the hammer is the only thing you're going to use to fix everything for the next 2000 years.

The reality is this, and it's been stated before in *this* book: Holy texts are not evidence for anything. Holy books and writings are the *claim* for the existence of a deity, not the evidence for that claim. This is a very real and important distinction that often eludes the believer. Maybe we should repeat that: Holy books are the *claim* for the existence of a deity, not the evidence for that claim.

Breaking Down The "Faith as Evidence" Argument

When the word "evidence" is presented in a discussion about god, Christians like to quote the following scripture:

> Now faith is the substance of things hoped for, the evidence of things not seen. (*Hebrews 11:1 KJV*)

That sounds very poetic, doesn't it? But, it's still poetic nonsense. If we take the word *substance* as meaning *essence* or *basis,* the first part of the above passage is true. Faith *is* the substance of things hoped for. But hope does not equal truth. Hoping for world peace doesn't make it happen. The scientists working to discover the Higgs-Boson particle *hoped* it was there, but they could never know for certain until the evidence proved it was there.

Faith is current, in the here and now, unlike hope which is dependent upon future events. Faith is also belief without evidence. Let's add the second claim in the passage together with the faith definition inserted. "Now *belief without*

38

evidence is… the evidence of things not seen." This is saying no evidence *is* evidence! This is an argument from ignorance and turns logic on its head. Could anyone truly live their lives this way and expect others to do so with any expectation of morality and justice? Could you say, "I have no evidence Don is guilty of murder, but I *believe* he is, so let's lock him up! The evidence against him is unseen. And the very fact that we can't find any evidence should be evidence enough that he's guilty!"

Haven't we moved beyond this kind of primitive assessment of the world?

Simply put, faith cannot be evidence for anything. If that were true, then faith in anything would automatically make that belief true. It would make Islam true simply because the believers in Islam had faith. The faith of the Hindu would make his beliefs true as well. It would even make faithful believers' stories about UFO abductions true. This is why the only true definition of faith is *belief without evidence.*

If you want evidence for things you can't see, you will need a microscope, telescope, or other scientific instrument. Not faith.

Doing Stuff vs. Believing Stuff

Because one cannot know with perfect certainty that a god exists, or cannot know with perfect certainty that a god does not, a belief about such things has no value either way. If certain knowledge of a god is unattainable, then belief in one is irrelevant. What you actually *do* during your short time on earth takes on a greater significance than what you believe. But because most religions are based on belief, the idea that actions overrule beliefs is bitterly opposed by those belief-based institutions.

For Christians, a child-molesting, axe wielding, serial-killer rapist, who believes in Jesus, has a better chance of getting into a paradise-like afterlife than a dear old, generous, altruistic, loving, sweet, but *non-believing,* empathetic grandmother. Yet, because in the real world, doing is more important than believing, (and even on some subconscious level, Christians know this), they will sometimes turn to presuppositional apologetics in an attempt to reverse this reality and claim knowledge and certainty about their god's existence. But in the end, beliefs are still beliefs, and there is no magic formula to obtain unattainable knowledge.

So, we have to ask ourselves: which is better? Believing there is no god, but doing good things anyway? Or believing there is one, and treating others poorly in spite of this belief?

CONCLUSION

The definition of faith, in the religious sense, is belief without evidence. If a religious person has no evidence, this automatically makes that person an agnostic-theist, by default. No one can say they have faith (belief without evidence) and also say they know they are 100% certain of something. If a person has faith, they have doubt. It's an inescapable fact. And they have this doubt because they are not omniscient and not perfect. When religious people say they know their god exists, they are lying. They do not actually know. They believe. As we have stated many times, belief and knowledge are two very different things.

The Purpose of Religious Belief

Stress in life is often very difficult to deal with. For many, there is a ready-made godly construct of personal "redemption" and being "born again" that can reduce stress by putting all of a human being's burdens onto someone else. But, it's all fake. Like any cult (and there is good evidence that all religions should be classified as cults), it's all based on the collective imaginations about a single theme. Because it's counterfeit, it requires the initiate to suspend all disbelief, and suppress all knowledge or evidence that contradicts the fakery, otherwise, the trick of relieving the burden won't work.

Although, here in the Western World, the concepts of redemption and rebirth are mainly the forte of Christianity (and to a degree, the other Abrahamic faiths), we know this is not exclusive to any one religion. Other religions and even other relatively recent therapies (The Human Potential Movement, Gestalt, pop-psychology, various motivational speakers, Neuro-Linguistic Programming, etc.) offer many of the same things, but Christianity has it down to a science (pardon the irony), and in most cases, have had much longer to practice.

It may be appalling to some, but in the real world there are people who have well-paying jobs in the clergy (priests, rabbis, preachers, imams, etc.) whose "job" is to perpetuate this fakery. You come to them with a problem, and they, with a straight face, tell you what their invisible friend wants you do with your life. For the recipient of this "advice," the denial of reality runs deep, and this denial is mostly proportional to the individual's internal stress. This is why religious conversions are rife with anecdotes regarding the covert's "low point" in life prior to conversion. But the entire episode of low point to conversion does not make the invisible god that the well-paid preacher talked about any more real than a tap-dancing pixie.

Final Thoughts

A lot of us wonder, even as children, whether or not *some* of the things our parents have taught us about their religion could be true. For the early doubter, only the most basic ideas are challenged, such as whether or not some*thing* put this universe together, or whether or not a soul or an afterlife exists. But, as adults, it's the details, the addendums to those ideas, that ruffle our feathers. It's the constant defiance of the laws of physics (essentially magic) that permeates every religious story. Religious zealots that hold these desert, rural, and urban legends to be true are like the blind man who holds the tail of a giant beast, and just by doing so, thinks he can tell the rest of us what that animal looks like. It won't do. Hoping for the possibility of a transcendent creative force, or the possibility of a continuous soul is one thing, but believing the contradictory exaggerations of semi-literate desert nomads is something else entirely.

CHAPTER THREE

Religious Arguments and Fallacies

"Science is simply common sense at its best, that is, rigidly accurate in observation, and merciless to fallacy in logic."
– Thomas Huxley

"The aim of argument, or of discussion, should not be victory, but progress."
– Joseph Joubert

"Life is too short to entertain a superstitious thought."
– Edward Trillian

Religious people are guilty of preaching an overabundance of logical fallacies (as are most people). But fallacies aren't created from nothing. They directly reflect the source of one's compendium of knowledge. For the deeply religious, that source is their sacred texts which are often quoted exactly as written – fallacy and all – and the listener is expected to accept all of it without even a whimper of doubt. And that's the problem.

Although, there is an occasional exception, in most of the holy books and writings of the religious world, you won't find a lot of classical logic. The ancient writers most likely didn't know they were scribing logical fallacies, and probably didn't care – much like modern day bloggers, writers, and politicians. The point was (and is) to get people to believe what you're saying without having to explain it much further. What you are told is presented as "self-evident." However, spotting and understanding fallacies is essential for non-believers because fallacies are not a pathway to truth. Fallacies obscure the facts, even if you believe they don't.

(You may even find some unintended logical fallacies in this book, and you are encouraged to analyze them, if doing so aids your quest for truth.)

In this chapter, we will look at some of the fallacies religious people have been known to recite in their quest to convince, either themselves or others, that their religious belief is true.

The place to begin is at the very top of the religious food chain...

41

ARGUMENTS FOR OR ABOUT GOD

Let's define some terms...

What is an Argument?

There are lots of ways to define argument, but for our purposes, it's *not* a heated verbal exchange between angry people, and it's not a shouting match. Those are the everyday, colloquial definitions of the word argument. We have to use the lesser known, but much more civil definition. And the simplest, but most descriptive way, is to say that it's a *supported opinion.* An opinion by itself is just an opinion (which can also be called a *belief*). A supported opinion is an argument for or against something. To support an opinion, you need something else to bolster your claim – facts, evidence, proofs, and even other opinions do this. The more of these you have, the better your argument. But, we should bear in mind, opinions that are only supported by other opinions are usually the weakest of arguments.

An Argument from Ignorance

An argument from ignorance is much worse than just stating an opinion. Opinions are most often stated with at least *some* reference to something else that supports that opinion. However, an argument from ignorance is mostly an opinion where it is obvious that the opinion holds very little reference to facts. A good Biblical example of this can be found in the New Testament:

> For the wrath of God is revealed from heaven against all ungodliness and unrighteousness of men, who hold the truth in unrighteousness; Because **that which may be known of God is manifest in them; for God hath shewed it unto them.** For the invisible things of him from the creation of the world are clearly seen, being **understood by the things that are made,** even his eternal power and Godhead; so that they are without excuse. (*Romans 1:18-20 KJV*) [Emphasis Added]

This passage is used by Christians as a way to present the argument that all human beings "know" a god exists and that they are simply in denial of this "fact." The Christian alleges that he *knows that you know* because of this passage in his sacred book. Of course, this presumes that the statement in the passage is somehow true, despite the fact that the only way to verify such a thing would be for someone to be omniscient, or at the very least, a mind-reader. It even tosses in the God of the Gaps fallacy, stating that because you can see a tree, for example ("the things that are made"), their god did it!

So, the Christian and non-believer alike cannot present any evidence that any of this scripture is true. And, as we've said elsewhere in this book, if you *can't* know, you *don't* know. Therefore, the argument in Romans 1:18-20 is simply an unsupported opinion, not an argument for god, and can be ignored.

In addition, it can be accurately stated that *all* axioms, presuppositions, premises, or syllogisms about a god, whatever their source, are arguments from ignorance. No one has yet to demonstrate sufficiently the existence of any god, at any time, in any place. A person arguing the attributes of a god that cannot be demonstrated to exist may the prime example of an argument from ignorance. What a god does, knows, thinks, wants, states, and where a god lives, are all arguments from ignorance, all of which spring from a previous argument from ignorance. Two arguments from ignorance do not create an argument from knowledge.

The "Is-Ought" Fallacy

The "Is-Ought" Fallacy is exactly what one would expect – it is moving an argument from what *is* (facts), to what *ought* to exist (not a lot of facts). This necessity within an argument – to start with facts, and progress to what *should be,* is used mostly in reference to questions of morality. But we can use it to debunk god-claims in general and show that moral precepts from a god-source are unfounded.

Because the claim that a god exists is unproven, it cannot be accepted as fact. When discussing any particular moral topic, we could make the statement that moral proclamations from a god is an "is-ought" fallacy (depending on the specifics of whatever is presented in that moral argument itself, but there is no need to get to that point). The facts are this: For example, we cannot verify the "is" part, so if we jump ahead to the "ought," we don't really have an argument to begin with. We cannot consider a statement beginning with "God says..." and conclude with "...therefore we should..." because we simply do not know if this God-thing is real.

In other words, because the theist cannot provide demonstrable evidence for a god, and can only provide faith, or wishful thinking, their entire argument automatically defaults to the "ought" position – but without any real moral authority to back it up. The argument, in reality, is more of an "ought-ought" position. "God ought to exist, therefore these moral ideas ought to exist as well."

The presumption of the believer is that a god exists and therefore a whole list of moral precepts can spring from that presumption. But if this god is non-existent, the supposed morality that comes from that god has little value, unless and until it coincidentally lines up with what humans already innately know to be right or wrong. Theists thrive on this weak position of the presumed existence of a god, which is often followed up with claims of what this god knows, does, says, wants, etc., as if the existence of the god is an evidence-rich fact. This presumption, in turn, leads to a overabundance of moral precepts that are, in truth, based on nothing.

The Appeal to Authority

The Appeal to Authority is a common and often desperate attempt at making an argument stick. The most common way a religious person uses this tactic is to quote their sacred scriptures. As stated before, the weakest arguments are those that use opinions to bolster other opinions.

A scriptural reference is a poor one for a variety of reasons. Even if you ignore (or even successfully refute) the idea that most scriptures are contradictory, poorly constructed, poorly translated, written by ignorant men, or even redacted over time, you are still left with a reference source that has, as its own backing, an unfounded claim. In other words, claiming a god exists and then referencing a source that simply says the same thing, is not much of an appeal to anything. The Bible is not an actual authority on God. If the theist wishes to appeal to an authority to prove his god, he should appeal to an authority *higher* than god. To prove God, you'd have to ask the only true expert on God, and that would be who or whatever created God.

The Appeal to Pity

This sort of fallacy is also known as an *irrelevant emotional appeal.* And, as you can surmise, it does very little to get to the facts. The Beatitudes are good example of this. Here's Jesus giving his famous Sermon on the Mount speech:

> Blessed are the poor in spirit: for theirs is the kingdom of heaven. Blessed are they that mourn: for they shall be comforted. Blessed are the meek: for they shall inherit the earth. Blessed are they which do hunger and thirst after righteousness: for they shall be filled. Blessed are the merciful: for they shall obtain mercy. Blessed are the pure in heart: for they shall see God. Blessed are the peacemakers: for they shall be called the children of God. Blessed are they which are persecuted for righteousness' sake: for theirs is the kingdom of heaven. Blessed are ye, when men shall revile you, and persecute you, and shall say all manner of evil against you falsely, for my sake. – (*Matthew 5:3-11 KJV*)

The above are all promises, similar to any you would hear a politician make in an effort to get re-elected. It all sounds wonderful, if true. But what is this "heaven" thing he keeps talking about? Jesus never adequately explains what or where that is. (Not just here, but a clear definition or location can't be found anywhere in the New Testament.) And how about some comfort, inheritance, peace, mercy, and ending of hunger *right now* instead of in some unknown future time? And how about keeping that persecution part out of the scenario?

Jesus is acknowledging that poor people exist, and that peace and mercy are hard to come by for some, and we should all feel sorry for those people, but instead of doing something about that right now, he'll promise a future heaven for them *someday* – after they've all been resurrected from the dead.

It's hard enough to keep a promise based on reality, but when you've got a captive audience that has voluntarily suspended all disbelief, you can say anything you want and no one will be able to prove you wrong.

The problem with this should be obvious.

The Appeal to Force or Threat

This fallacy is, of course, another type of irrelevant emotional appeal. Trying to persuade others of your position by threatening them is probably the least successful way to win them over to your side in the long run. But the main western religions use this with wild abandon. And the threat they use is Hell. The threat of ending up in an eternal fire, for not believing what they've told you, is often the final comment in any discussion or debate with a god-believer. It is their closing argument. If you cannot be convinced with other emotional pleas, the fear of Hell is the last resort. It's also a sign that the believer has given up. It's often just a dismissal tactic directed at the atheist, as if to say, "I'm done with you. You're going to Hell anyway. What do I care?!"

...And the love of [*insert your favorite god here*] abounds.

The Appeal to Common Opinion

Can 2 billion people all be wrong? That's the number of Christians on earth. Could another 1.6 billion people also be wrong? That's the number of Muslims on earth. How about the almost 900 million Hindus? Obviously, someone is wrong. They can't all be right. The fallacy that derives from an Appeal to Common Opinion is also very common, but not very appealing.

Just because a large group believes something to be true, that doesn't make it so. Once upon a time, every human being on earth believed the sun revolved around the earth (whether flat, round or spherical). It took a long time to discover that *every human being on earth had been wrong.* This fallacy is also referred by its Latin phrase: *argumentum ad populum.*

So, yes, everyone could be wrong about God, gods, and goddesses. And probably are. As atheists, we must assume they are wrong, until sufficient evidence is presented otherwise.

The Genetic Fallacy

This fallacy is the Christian religion in a nutshell. It also applies in copious amounts to Islam. Christianity, with its establishment of the New Testament canon, vainly attempted to make the Old Testament writings match their dogma about Jesus. Islam did the same by grasping on to both the Jewish Torah and the New Testament to create their own holy writ. But, both failed and did so by using The Genetic Fallacy.

Whenever anyone evaluates or bases the merits of their current argument on an earlier context, and uses that to make their case (without considering whether or not the original context is relevant to the current situation), they are engaging in a form of The Genetic Fallacy.

The centerpiece of Christian dogma is the alleged prediction of the Jewish Messiah in the Book of Isaiah, and the contention that Jesus matches this prediction perfectly. (Many of the details of this wayward assumption can be found in the chapter, **Jesus and the New Testament**.) As fallacies go, this one is a little tricky.

However, it is important to note that the Isaiah prophecy, from a Christian perspective, is sort of a genetic fallacy gone wild. In most cases, a genetic fallacy is a conclusion based solely on something's origin rather than its current meaning or context, and the original meaning *could have been true* at one time. However, the texts in Isaiah, as postulated by Christians, have a current meaning based solely on an *inaccurate* interpretation of an original text. And when considering ancient religious writings, it's important to not only consider the original context of the content, but whether or not the content ever applied in the first place.

Christianity uses the Book of Isaiah in the Bible to retroactively "predict" the coming of Jesus as the Messiah. Yet, much of what is in Isaiah that is supposed to refer to a future Jesus does not match. And when reading the text in its entirety, it becomes clear that Isaiah was referencing people, places, and things in his own time, in a much nearer future for him, with none of it having anything to do with the person called Jesus, or any Messiah at all! Although these assertions that the Old Testament predicts Jesus have been debunked hundreds of times by many very learned Biblical scholars, the lay Christian continues to hold on to these ideas like a baby to a blanket. And to add insult to injury, even in the unlikely event that Isaiah had been talking about a coming messiah in the referenced passages, how is anyone to know that the few occurrences that "came true" actually applied to Jesus, or weren't deliberately *made* to come true in an effort to follow Isaiah's ill-referenced script?

So, all this leads to the following questions: Why refer back to Isaiah at all? Or, why refer back to any other ancient text? Can a messiah not appear unless someone predicts him first? Couldn't a god-incarnate just show up unannounced and still be the world's savior? We have irrelevance galore.

Here's how the fallacy plays out in this instance:

Person A: "Jesus is here. He's the Messiah. Isaiah and others predicted him."

Person B: "But you've interpreted Isaiah wrong."

Person A: "What if I interpreted him correctly?"

Person B: "That's irrelevant. The guy is either the messiah, or he isn't. What Isaiah said wouldn't change that. Maybe Isaiah was predicting someone else?"

The result? We have a genetic fallacy that is in serious need of a DNA test. The original progenitor Isaiah has very little to do with his alleged descendant (Christianity). Someone's been fooling around with the scriptures, and they've clearly produced an illegitimate offspring.

Islam, of course, commits a similar genetic fallacy by declaring Jesus to be a real person, yet only as a prophet, not the Messiah. But mentioning him as a "good" or "holy" person in the Qur'an is done in an effort to lend credence to the ideas of Muhammad, a prophet who appears six centuries *after* Jesus. But, it's like saying one brand of cigarette is a good one because we know your grandfather smoked it. It's irrelevant. Mohammed was either a prophet of the desert god Allah, or he wasn't. And that should stand on its own merit, if it has any, with or without an endorsement of Jesus. This betting a few shekels on Jesus while putting most of your big bucks on Mohammed was a clever way to hedge your bets – sort of like invoking Pascal's Wager before Pascal was even born. (See further down.)

The No True Scotsman Fallacy

This simple fallacy is based on the following verbal exchange:

> Person A: "No Scotsman puts sugar on his porridge."
> Person B: "But my uncle Angus likes sugar with his porridge."
> Person A: "Ah yes, but no *true* Scotsman puts sugar on his porridge."

Of course, this is just an attempt at asserting something that simply isn't logically true. All Scotsmen are Scotsmen. It's the basic laws of thought: "Whatever is, is." "Nothing can both be and not be." And, "Everything must either be or not be."

Many religionists will make excuses for their fellow believers by saying, "Not all Christians are like that." Or, "A real Muslim wouldn't act like a terrorist." It's a convenient way to distance one's self from a negative aspect of a religious belief, but it simply isn't true. All Muslims are real Muslims. What they do doesn't negate that truth. This is because one could easily make the *opposite* assertion that the Muslims who are engaged in terrorism are the *real* Muslims, and the ones who *aren't* engaged in terrorism are the "fake" Muslims.

FALLACIES SPECIFIC TO RELIGION

The God of the Gaps

The God of the Gaps fallacy basically works like this:

> "The universe looks like it was made for life! Therefore, God did it!"
> "The universe appears to be fine-tuned! Therefore, God did it!"
> "Scientists make mistakes! Therefore, God did it!"
> "Look around you! You can't make a tree! Therefore, God did it!"
> "Bananas fit in your hand perfectly! Therefore, God did it!"
> "There are no missing links in the fossil record! Therefore, God did it!"
> "There's no evidence God *didn't* do it! Therefore, God did it!"
> "Everything *has* to have a creator! Everything! Therefore, God did it!"
> "I can't come up with a better explanation! Therefore, God did it!"

It's simply another argument from ignorance, known as *argumentum ad ignorantiam.** Not knowing something does not give a person a free pass to insert any unproven thing into the blank space, or the gap that is unknown. Anything unknown remains unknown until demonstrated to be existent. For some people, facts, like tacks, are a hard thing to swallow.

*Note how the Latin word *ignorantiam* breaks down: Ignorant + I + Am. "Ignorant I am." Just something to keep in mind when you meet someone who's in love with the God of the Gaps. It's important to let people know when they don't know.

Pascal's Wager

"Yep, place yer bets, folks! Pick a god, any god! Only one dollar per god!"

For a large majority of true believers in deities, it appears that they only believe based on a wager, or a bet, not because they actually "love" their angry, vindictive gods (Yahweh, Allah, Jesus, etc.) That fear-based wager is actually understandable to a point. After all, why would anyone want to love an entity that was always angry, expected too much from his own broken creation, and at one point, even thought he had to kill a human version of himself to "forgive" that creation?

Enter Blaise Pascal, 17th century French philosopher who argued roughly the following:

One should choose to believe in God, even if there is little evidence that God is real, because not believing could place you in Hell for eternity. Therefore, it is better to take your chances with belief.

The Wager (paraphrased above) is rife with fallacies. The first one should be obvious: Belief isn't really a choice, at least not in the sense that you can change your belief on whim (or a bet). You either believe something or you don't, and you base it on something you think is true, not on something that's convenient.

And the fallacy of presupposing that a god and a hell exist, without any evidence for such things, negates the purpose for any kind of wager at all.

And further, does Pascal's God accept bets as valid means for getting into heaven, and/or avoiding Hell? Isn't there something *more* to achieving salvation? Certainly just believing that the Christian deity is real couldn't be enough to keep you out of the hell as described by Pascal. If Satan, God's adversary, is real, we would certainly contend that *he* believes, and even *knows* God exists, yet that hasn't opened any doors out of Hell for the red Master of Demons. So, it must be something more. As stated by the requisite dogma of most Christian sects, what keeps a Christian out of an eternal and fiery hell is the genuine and contrite repentance from sin, and the acceptance of Jesus as the payment for those sins. So, placing a bet that God probably exists, or even behaving as if he does, isn't enough. This simple wager has nothing to do with being contrite, repentance, or giving your "soul" and "heart" to Jesus. It fails miserably, and is worthless to the Christian believer, hardly reaching even its face value.

The Wager then, which had no value to the atheist from the beginning, has also failed the believer, and failed the fence-sitter to whom it was directed.

The God Game (Pascal's Wager, Part II)

Religious people are living in denial. Their religious beliefs are based on fear. But when confronted with this obvious-to-the-rest-of-us fact, they say it isn't so. They re-label their fear-based beliefs as "love," or "glory," or "rebirth," or "faith" and even "truth." But nothing could be *further* from the truth. If they love, it's because of fear. If they give "glory" to their god, it's because of fear, if they feel reborn, it's because of fear. And other human emotions become less genuine when fear enters the scene.

So, what do these religious people fear? They fear the wrath of their god, they fear death, they fear the unknown, and they fear living life in the present. And the true believer cannot admit this to themselves. The fear of death and not existing forever is too great. The fear that something bad will happen if they don't believe is too pervasive. The fear that their god will wreck their lives if they don't believe is way too personal to ever let that go. So, in the end, they really *are* exercising Pascal's Wager. They are betting that their god and their Bible are right, and that it's okay to have the fear that accompanies those beliefs, because without fear, all bets are off, and you can't win if you don't play the game. And before long, their biggest fear becomes knowing they will someday no longer be around to play God's little game of "heads I win, tails you lose."

The Euthyphro Dilemma

In Plato's *Euthyphro* dialogue, Socrates asks, "Is that which is good commanded by God because it is good, or is it good because God commands it?"

The answers are not exactly comforting. If the first part of the question is true, God is not all powerful. He has to draw upon something more powerful than he is to determine that which is "good." Goodness is fixed and cannot be altered in any way, not even by God himself. God is impotent to change what is moral.

However, if the second part of the question is true, God can capriciously call anything he wants "good" – things that we as humans might consider horrific and immoral. Murder could be okay one day, and not okay the next.

The religions of Abraham (Christianity, Judaism and Islam) all embrace the second horn of this dilemma. Their god is arbitrary, and morals are simply at his whim. His moral judgments are often wildly capricious, demonstrating that his moral standards are that he has *no* standards. The Bible itself bears this out in Isaiah 45:7 – "I form the light, and create darkness: I make peace, and *create evil:* I the Lord do all these things." The important distinction to bear in mind is that for a god to keep his omnipotence, he *must retain the capacity to be immoral,* and must exercise it at his will.

Because what is "good" cannot be adequately defined, whether the good is sourced from a god, or externally without a god, the dilemma is a false one. There are other choices, with the most logical being that *God does not exist,* or no gods exist. If God does not exist, Socrates has no reason to ask his question. Morality is not defined by that which does not exist.

The Watchmaker Argument

This fallacious analogy is probably the most popular among religious apologists for putting forth what is known as "The Argument for Design," also known as creationism.

First proposed by William Paley in 1802, it goes like this:

> ...suppose I had found a watch upon the ground, and it should be inquired how the watch happened to be in that place, I should hardly think ... that for anything I knew the watch might have always been there... after all the schemes and struggles of a reluctant philosophy, the necessary resort is to a Deity. The marks of design are too strong ... Design must have had a designer. That designer must have been a person. That person is GOD. – (*Natural Theology*)

Paley's "epiphany" is, of course, nothing more than the "God of the Gaps" once again. "God did it." This is another argument from ignorance. In fact, we aren't even given a choice – not even a hoped-for false dichotomy. For Paley, when it comes to the construction of the universe, you have only one choice: God did it. Case closed. And other choices – that perhaps some *other* god did it, or some other entity did it, or no one did it, or some *thing* did it that wasn't intelligent, or the universe has always existed in one form or another, etc. – none of these are considered viable conclusions.

The argument for design may be one of theology's weakest defenses for the existence of a god – especially a specific god, due to the unfathomable lack of human knowledge regarding our rather enormous universe. (For more on a fine-tuned universe, see the chapter: **In a Perfect World**.)

Kalam's Cosmological Argument

This argument for the existence of a creator god goes like this: (Try to spot the hidden premises.)

1. Everything that begins to exist has a cause.
2. The universe (space, time, and everything in it) began to exist.
3. Therefore, the universe has a cause.

This argument makes a lot of assumptions and brings up some rather obvious questions:

The first premise deliberately uses the phrase "begins to exist." Doing this conveniently leaves God out of the equation because religious scholars are implying that God has no beginning. But how is it possible that God has no beginning? The Bible states that God is the Alpha and Omega. The Beginning and the End. Is the Bible lying? Isn't God a part of "everything"? Isn't it *impossible* for something with no beginning and no end to actually exist? Isn't the very definition of such a thing the definition of nothing? To exclude God from "everything that begins to exist" is committing the *fallacy of special pleading*. And why is God immune to the idea that everything has to not only have a beginning, but also a cause? What created God?

Kalam's argument fails immediately, unless one wants to accept the infinite regress of a god having a creator, and the god that created him having a creator, and so on.

But, this is not the only problem with these premises. The argument states that everything "begins to exist," but we know that's not really true, not in the way it's being presented by this cosmological argument. As far as we know, *only the universe began to exist.* Everything = the universe *only.* The things you see inside that universe are not beginning to exist anymore. Their already existing atoms are simply being rearranged inside the universe. We do it ourselves when we turn a chicken sandwich into (mostly) waste matter by eating that sandwich. To support this, all we need to do is reference Isaac Newton and the *law of conservation of energy* which states that energy can be neither created nor destroyed.

Now, let's look at what the Kalam argument is actually saying:

1. The *one thing* that began to exist (the universe) has a cause.
2. The universe began to exist.
3. Therefore, the universe has a cause.

In even more simpler terms:

1. X has a cause
2. The universe is X
3. Therefore X has a cause.

Repeating the first premise and making that your conclusion is viciously circular and concludes nothing. But apparently, the excessively religious aren't paying attention in class.

CONCLUSION

We can safely say that all arguments for the existence of a god, put forth to date, are arguments from ignorance. The theistic world offers a litany of false dilemmas, ought-to's, weak appeals, and poorly placed bets. Believers in deities have had to traverse a long hard road in their efforts to demonstrate the existence of their gods. Had they been successful in doing so, there wouldn't be any atheists.

CHAPTER FOUR

Dogmas and Other Stubborn Ideas

"If you would be a real seeker after truth, it is necessary that at least once in your life you doubt, as far as possible, all things." – René Descartes

"Dude! You need to read Duderomney, man!
That Jesus, he had it all right, man!"
– Anonymous stoned Christian

WHO LET THE DOGMAS OUT?

Dogmas are specific tenets and principles that are deemed true by any organized group, such as a church or other religion. These are the assumed "truths" that are considered unchanging. These are core beliefs. Some religions have more dogmas than other religions, and some have dogmas that are easier to understand than others, but...

How Much Dogma Do You Really Need?

More religion equals...

Intolerance. On any given day, a man or woman, one who is already religious, has a brief internal discussion wherein the conclusion is: they simply are not religious *enough*. This anti-epiphany happens quite often to a great many people around the globe, and it results in a kind of self-destruction that the person imagines to be valuable to himself and everyone he comes in contact with, and yet this is nothing but a debilitating illusion. The more devout a person becomes, the more intolerant that person becomes of others that do not have similar views.

This devoutness and dedication to dogma is what produces abortion clinic bombings, planes flying into buildings, and Westboro Baptist Church members protesting at the funerals of gay soldiers. In other words, intolerance and bigotry. So, how much religion, and the accompanying religious dogma, does anyone

53

need? A whole lot less than one might think. Maybe we should look at some of the main dogmas to see if just one or two is really enough...

DOGMA NUMBER ONE: "I AM GOD" = "DOGMA I"

The first dogma of all mainstream religions is that God exists. But, does he? Well, just ask him! In Exodus 3:14, God takes an existential view of the universe. "I am," he says. (Or, we should state that the Bible writers say it for him.) The hoped for response to this "I am" statement is for humans to say, "You are!" But not all of us do that. Rather, *we* say, "Prove it."

Biblical followers and other monotheists expect their listeners to just accept the existence of their god as self-evident, as if the god's existence should be as obvious to the world as *their own* existence is to us. This delusional thought process is not surprising because, without physical evidence for a god, the only place anyone can find their god is in the minds of the believers themselves. Despite this god being encased only in their own brains, to them, their god's existence is real – and *external.* It is the ultimate case of mental projection. The cognitive dissonance of this is virtually (or perhaps literally?) mind-numbing because believers have a serious problem that is ultimately hard to overcome... there is no way for them to show anyone a real god exists outside of their own skulls.

Of course, the real truth is that their god exists because *they* exist. They – believer *and* god – are one and the same. Each person owns their own delusions and their own fantasies. They, therefore, own their own god and mold him into whatever they want him to be. And when they die, their god dies with them.

DOGMA NUMBER TWO: GOD IS "GOOD"

Can God intervene in the affairs of mankind? If you believe in the holy books of the Judeo-Christian-Islamic god, he can, and does. Occasionally.

If god can intervene and save someone's life, but doesn't, are we to assume that the death was just and moral, no matter how heinous the act, no matter the amount of suffering? And if god intervenes and saves some, but ignores others with a similar plight, how are we to learn justice? It's hard for humans to create a moral compass from such seemingly random acts of mercy, justice, or fortune. Humans operate from the "monkey see, monkey do" mindset much better than the "monkey *read*, monkey do" command. Humans see a capricious, violent, angry god, and read about how "good" he is. How is any of this consistent? Or moral? How could God be the source for such a wishy-washy example of morality and goodness?

If we take a look at the Bible itself we can see how god himself claims to be the author of everything, good, bad, and ugly...

And it actually makes sense within the context of an *all-powerful* singular god:

> I form the light, and create darkness: I make peace, and create
> evil: I the Lord do **all** these things. (*Isaiah 45:7 KJV*)
> [Emphasis Added]

It's difficult to reinterpret something so plain and simple as being anything other than what is directly stated. There is no getting around the word "all." It's a word which implies infinity and it's coming from an infinite god, *the* god, himself – the one and only creator of the universe and everything in it.

So, from this we have to assume that the murderous actions of psychopath Ted Bundy, and the Holocaust event, were created by God. It's not that he simply *allowed* these events to happen, he *created* those events. The cognitive dissonance is self-corrected by the religion-addict by stating that this god "had a good reason" for doing such evil deeds. Any human being, especially one claiming empathy of any kind, agreeing to this line of rationalization, is stepping into a hell pit of inescapable *immorality*. Nothing could be more immoral than thinking that a so-called "loving" god creates evil. Yet, we know religionists will swim through any sewer and wallow in any battlefield of blood to make their god's "words" palatable enough to keep on believing. The charge is, we cannot possibly know god's motivations for things. He "works in mysterious ways!" they say, without ever contemplating that if God can create a Holocaust, he is capable of *not* creating one as well. And how is it that humans are expected to comprehend morality, but not evil, especially when they come from the same source?

What most people rarely consider is this: You can only understand morality when you know *why* something is moral. Ditto for what is immoral. If the answer to why something is moral is "because god says so," and the answer to why something is immoral is "because god did it" (see the above Isaiah 45:7 scripture), then God himself is immoral. If God can be moral or immoral on a whim, capriciously, without explanation, and also ask us to be as he is, then we too can be moral or immoral on a whim, capriciously, and without explanation. Morality is then reduced to "Do as thou wilt."

From the viewpoint of the true believer, God is never responsible for anything bad and never makes mistakes. Although he admits in Isaiah 45:7 that he is the author of evil, no one ever gives him the proper credit for such things. Maybe it's because God himself doesn't think his evil doings are really all that bad. Or, perhaps God himself answers to a higher power and out of fear of punishment, doesn't want to take responsibility for his actions? If anyone does get the blame for God's seemingly incessant historical blunders, it's the poor hapless humans he created. And they get that blame apparently as though it's the very reason for their existence. God is like the guy who has a bad day at work and then goes home and kicks his dog.

So, the story line in the Bible plays out like this: The all-knowing, all-powerful God screws up and makes humans imperfect. Then, when they do imperfect things, like sinning, for example, they are blamed for it by the very God that made them that way. And, the helpless, fear-filled humans accept that it is all their fault, exposing perhaps their greatest defect of all.

DOGMA NUMBER THREE: THERE IS AN AFTERLIFE (I THINK!)

Why would anyone want anything to last forever? Imagine you are on a first date with someone. Everything is going well. You've held hands, you've kissed, you've danced all night, you've had a truly wonderful time. At one point you look into each other's eyes and you almost simultaneously say, "I wish this night could last forever!" But, what if you really got your wish? How long would it take for "forever" to get horribly boring? How long before you begged for it to end? The reason anything has value is because it's *rare*. Time with someone is often short, and scarce. That's why we put so much value on it. The same is true of life. Life is rare and unique and that's why it's precious, not because of its abundance. Too much of anything will make anyone take those things for granted and that lessens their value. Spending an eternity with anyone, including a "god" lessens the value of the time spent. Could there ever be a worse torture?

The Quadriplegic Soul

If souls exist, in the afterlife, they are deaf, dumb, and blind quadriplegics. Or completely comatose.

Believers in a life after death are quite certain their conscious awareness will function in much the same way as it does now. Many will say that they will be given "new" bodies and "new" minds (whatever that is). But the soul by itself is quadriplegic, deaf, dumb, and blind. A soul, if it was real, would have no eyes for seeing, no skin for touch, no mouth for taste, no nose for smell, no ears for hearing, no body to move, no brain for thought. A soul would be living a useless existence, worse than a quadriplegic, worse than a comatose patient. What kind of wonderful life could a soul have under such horrible circumstances and for how long would it have to endure this hardship?

Science is currently attempting to take the entire information in a human brain and make an exact duplicate copy which can be downloaded into a hard drive for the possible later uploading into another brain. This is not beyond the realm of possibility or probability. Imagine waking up and realizing you are viewing the world through a camera lens, but you cannot move your body because you don't actually have one! You and your thoughts are inside a computer! No one would be able to bear living this sort of out of body existence. This is very similar to how a disembodied soul would be, if such souls were actually real.

Unfortunately, those that claim souls are real seem to imagine that a soul can do all sorts of things including magically seeing, hearing, smelling, thinking, and even interacting with the living, and do so without the tools necessary to perform those things.

Living Longer Than the Sun

Religious persons, when speaking of their god, often use nebulous terms, terms without delineation or determination: *forever, eternity, always, never*. Ask any true believer and they will tell you that their god has promised them they will live "forever" or for an "eternity," without ever defining what forever and an eternity really is.

For the Christian, Jew, or Muslim who thinks they will live forever, we should probably put that in perspective. Forever is a long time – infinitely long. And infinity never ends. Our sun still has 4.5 billion years left before it dies, yet the truly religious actually believe they will outlive the sun! (Or, they believe their non-corporeal soul – without the means to think, see, smell, hear, taste or feel – will do so.) They really do think that a human being, who is lucky if they can live past 70 years on earth, is going to live past the age of the sun for another 4,500,000,000 years! And, because infinity is never ending, those 4,500,000,000 years are just a tiny blip in the number of years that come after. A Christian human, who's only core religious belief is that an innocent human was executed for the crimes of humanity, will also outlive all the galaxies, and all the stars in those galaxies, all the black holes, and even outlive the entire universe itself! Where will this human live out those trillions upon trillions upon trillions of years, all in the service of this god? At this point, the answer to that question should be absurdly irrelevant.

One More Thing About The After Life...

No one is stopping anyone from dying in their delusion, and a great many do arrive at their final moments of life believing all sorts of lies and half-truths. But living in the past (because of former sins), or living in the future (hoping for Jesus to get back from his break), is wasting precious present moments here on earth. This life has value because it's rare. Religious people take it for granted because they think they have another one coming. No one can prove an afterlife until they've lived an afterlife. Carpe Diem.

DOGMA NUMBER FOUR: GOD IS THE SOURCE OF ALL MORALITY

What is morality, *really?*

From a religious standpoint, morality is doing good, and doing what your god tells you to do, all rolled into one. Morality, for the theist, always has that element of obedience to a deity. This means, of course, that morality can be altered on the whims of the god. Or, more accurately, morality can be altered on the whims of someone who thinks he's in communication with that god. Either way, a person's morality becomes muddled from the outside – it isn't sourced from an individual's own sense of right and wrong. It removes a person's innate sense of what is good, and can often dilute a person's empathy.

Religionists consider morality to be *objective* – that is, what is right or wrong is pre-existent and wholly independent of human opinion. This notion claims that a god (or creator) is the author and standard for all morality. The flaw is in the questions it raises: Which god? How do we know this god has actually made a determination about what is moral? What happens if the god changes his mind about what is moral? And so on. Naturally, there can be no objectivity if no one can verify the source.

57

From the atheist standpoint, morality is inter-dependent. It is dependent upon how you see yourself, how you see others, and how others see you. Its final judgment about what is right or wrong, good or bad, is sourced from within. It is influenced by a person's own culture, community, pre-existing codes of conduct, as well as a person's own intuitive awareness, knowledge, and empathy. It is *subjective,* but it doesn't live in a vacuum. Morality, therefore, can be perceived to change over time, dependent upon human experience and/or knowledge. This is how a concept such as slavery can be perceived as moral in one era or culture, and later be seen as immoral in others. This concept is known as *moral relativism.* It is also what we actually see as functioning in the real world.

Do-Gooders and Evil-Doers

The religious person, adhering their level best to the edicts of their god, will tell us that if their god didn't exist, it would give everyone the freedom to do anything they want and immoral chaos would ensue.

Of course, quite the opposite is true. Among the religious, moral laws given to them by their god do not appear to deter immoral acts at all. And sometimes these rules increase their frequency. The problem is, of course, in nearly all religious books, you find a god who is capricious with morality – a constantly changing god who alters morality, as well as reality, to suit his whims. And you'd better keep track of the changes, or you'll suddenly become "immoral" again.

And when you scrutinize atheists and skeptics, you do not see a sudden outpouring of heinous acts being committed by them once they are fully committed to their position. Normally, what you see is a gradual learning process – an atheist learning about what *real* morality is among our species, and discovering what it really *should* be. For most skeptics, the decision to become an atheist isn't made on a whim, so neither is an atheist's understanding of morality revealed in like manner. It's a carefully thought out process, and eventually makes an atheist *more* moral than the believer, and certainly more moral that the believer's god.

Truly, if the only thing that held a god-believer from raping, stealing, killing, and doing all kinds of horrific deeds, was his perception of a moral law given to him by his invisible god, we would have to conclude that the person was mentally unwell. If there is such a believer out there, atheists are morally bound to make sure that the believer continues to believe. Better to have religious persons held back from their sick tyrannical minds than running amuck.

What About Evil?

> Men think epilepsy divine, merely because they do not understand it. But if they called everything divine they didn't understand, why, there would be no end of divine things.

That was Hippocrates around 400 BCE.

Soon after the pessimism of Christianity came along, followed by the even more militant Islam, one might have re-written Hippocrates words thusly:

> Men think epilepsy *evil,* merely because they do not understand it. But if they called everything *evil* they didn't understand, why, there would be no end of *evil* things.

And this view, of course, is the world we live in – one where the majority religions find evil in every corner.

When Atheists Do Bad Things

The religious like to cite Joseph Stalin now as their prime example of a murderous atheist. They formerly named Hitler, but Hitler expressed way too much allegiance toward Christianity and Islam for them to make a case. Now Stalin is the bad boy. After all, Stalin was responsible for the deaths of approximately 40,000,000 people, give or take a few million. But, Stalin was a psychopath.

Psychopaths aren't always dictators, but dictators are always psychopaths. It's almost part of the job description. Other historical examples include: Pol Pot, Idi Amin, Mao Tse Tung, Saddam Hussein, Napoleon, Julius Caesar, Nero, Attila the Hun, Caligula, and a long line of Kings, Popes, Imams, and Sultans. Psychopaths are incapable of expressing or even understanding empathy. Religion, like political parties and causes, are just tools for them to attain power. They will say they believe in whatever god you need them to believe in, if it will help them gain control. If not believing will do the trick, they will say that as well.

Stalin and the Communists

So, were communists also atheists, and how much did this matter to their followers? To determine this, you have to look at core beliefs. Was atheism the core belief of communism? Or, was the core belief of communism the establishment of a worker's paradise? We know the core belief of communism was to establish a socialist state in which the working class was dominant. Atheism was a tenet of that ideal, but it was not the primary focus of the desire to create a utopian state for the working man. Atheism did not kill millions of people in an effort to gain the worker's paradise, communism did. A war for a worker's paradise could have easily been full of religious fervor and still have killed millions of people.

In almost every case, we find that dictators, of any stripe, normally do not associate themselves with any religious beliefs, except for expediency's sake. This is due entirely to their self-absorption. If the dictator has a god, it is himself. Atheism doesn't create the dictator. The dictator rids himself of all other gods and declares himself god. He is his own delusion.

It's important to look at this from the religious side for a moment. Theists tend to target anyone who doesn't believe as they do as "atheist." However, many people, whom religious folk categorize as atheist, simply never cared much for the god concept and never gave it serious thought. Or, they had only nominal exposure to religion. They are atheist by default, but not by concerned choice or careful analysis. This is similar to people being born into a household with a particular religious belief, and never questioning that belief. Most "atheist" dictators fall into this category. As do most "religious" dictators.

As we can see, showing a dictator as an example of atheism is a poor argument. Clearly, if we have a world full of kind atheists and murderous religious people, as well as gentle believers and genocidal atheists, then something else must be guiding our moral decisions. And moral laws given by a mixed bag of deities cannot be the source.

Objective Morals

The accusation is that atheists don't have objective morals. But, the reality is, theists don't have objective morals either. Gods can change what morality is on a whim. And the real point is that *no one* can have absolute objective morals simply because we cannot view the universe objectively – and we are all different, with different *subjective* views of that universe. One would have to be all-knowing to be objectively moral. What humans do (all of them, including theists) is rationalize their actions. Some use a "holy" book as a reference for that, some use their own upbringing, some use their internal empathy and empirical knowledge. But none of it is done with any sort of absolute certainty. Therefore, any subjectively moral person, accusing other subjectively moral persons of not having any objective morals, is absurd.

Morality then, cannot be defined with a god in mind. Instead, we can only define morality as an agreement regarding what is just and right, among imperfect people of similar values, all of whom have a subjective view of the universe, and who also have no other choice but to see the universe that way. To put it simply, you cannot have a moral lawgiver who changes moral laws on a whim, calls these laws unchanging, and expects you to behave like him.

Real morality comes from a combination of two sources: personal empathy and collective conscience. It cannot come from a capricious and hypocritical god if human beings are to ever claim to be moral. It follows, if such a god is your ultimate authority on morality, then you too, like your god, would become capricious, hypocritical, and your morals would change over time. Of course, *this is exactly what we see among believers in gods.*

Some Moral History

How is it possible that human beings did not know murder was wrong, or "bad," until they heard a god tell them, or until they read it on a stone tablet? Human beings could not have survived for very long had they thought murder was okay prior to the edict. Having a "god" make the declaration was simply to give tribal leaders a systematic way to inflict punishment for crimes – punishment that had at least some amount of equal justice, and an extra dose of fear as a deterrent.

For all we know, Moses was an atheist and created the commandments as a way to hold on to his power as chieftain of the Israelite tribes. The commandments, whether you read the famous Ten or all 613, are bereft of any knowledge of human anatomy or health, and hold only a modicum of compassion. They are clearly man-made, poorly written, and painfully ignorant – exactly what you would expect from a primitive Iron or Bronze Age tribal leader and his cronies. A god, even passively aware of his earthly "children," regarding how they were made and what they need, would not, and could not, have written them.

There is nothing objective about religious morality. Religious morality is by fiat, and cannot be objective. The religious person is not moral. He is obedient. And, speaking of obedience...

DOGMA NUMBER FIVE: FREE WILL

What is free will?

As a noun, free will has various definitions, often accompanied by syncretic nuances, but generally speaking it goes something like this...

Free will is the power and ability to act at one's own discretion, without the intervention of "fate" or pre-determination from an outside force.

So, where does this free will come from? The theist will tell you that free will is a gift from God. But, wait a second... If you cannot even show that a god exists, how can you know that same god gives out gifts? Putting aside any argument that, like God, no evidence exists for free will either... isn't it just as possible, and even more probable, that free will, if it's real, is just part of our evolutionary progression? Isn't it more likely that we evolved consciousness, sentience, awareness, and realized we had choices? And if anyone gave us such a choice, did we not give it to ourselves – by necessity?

Before we answer that, let's look at this from the religious perspective...

Free Will and Scripture

From a theistic point of view, is free will the most sacred thing in the universe? We must ask this question because those who love deities often declare that their god cannot intervene in our free will. If free will is unbreakable, then free will must be the most powerful thing in the universe. It must be a force that even an all-powerful god cannot challenge. Free will must be *more powerful than God.* However, such a reality would essentially destroy the supposed omnipotence of God. This would make quite a conundrum.

We clearly see in the Biblical text, that God *is* capable of breaking a human being's free will. In order for Yahweh to maintain his omnipotence status, he *must* be able to do this, alter the free will of humans, and he is demonstrated doing so here:

And I will **harden Pharaoh's heart,** and multiply my signs and my wonders in the land of Egypt. – (*Exodus 7:3 KJV*) [Emphasis Added]

And further down he keeps his word:

But the LORD **hardened Pharaoh's heart** and he would not listen to Moses and Aaron, just as the LORD had said to Moses. – (*Exodus 9:12 KJV*) [Emphasis Added]

If human free will was important to God, he would make certain to leave it untouched and unmolested, and do so equally for all. Unfortunately, Pharaoh's own personal choices were taken from him and stomped upon like an unwanted insect.

So, we have to conclude that, at least in the case of free will, Yahweh *is* living up to his alleged omnipotence status, at least in this regard, (even if he fails in other places). We can also see how believers in Yahweh-God are flat out wrong when they attempt to make this god appear as though he doesn't alter mankind's free will. If he's real, and if he's omnipotent, your free will should be his to play with. In this case, the Bible correctly declares God's omnipotence. However, this manifestly makes present-day Christians wrong about humans having an unbreakable free will. Simply put, you cannot simultaneously have an unbreakable free will and have an all-powerful god. If you have an all-powerful god, you must have a free will that isn't really free. Your free will must operate at the behest and whims of that all-powerful god.

Again, it's important to note here that what we see in the Biblical text is a selective, interventionist god whose actions negate much of the New Testament's contention that everyone has a choice of whether or not they can be "saved." When it comes to things like who is "elected" for salvation and who is not, Romans 9 seems to indicate that the Christian god has already decided salvation for you. (See the Chapter: **Jesus and The New Testament.**)

Free Will vs. Obedience

If an all-powerful god really wanted obedience from his creation, he would have it. He apparently has the ability to do anything, and that would include forcing obedience upon anyone. (As Yahweh-God did with Pharaoh, above.) But because obedience is *not* something God gets from his "children" most of the time, could it mean that he really doesn't want it as bad as religionists claim? It's hard to say.

We *can* conclude that if God is real, with only a few special interventionist exceptions, free will does trump obedience in god's universe, despite the fact that this same *all-powerful* god claims to be frequently and horribly disappointed he isn't getting any of the stuff he *really* wants – obedience. Perhaps this is why the act of following your free-will, with God hovering over your shoulder, is always a life or death situation. (See God's death threats against Adam and Eve, the entire world with Noah, the murder of Onan, the killing Job's entire family, etc. The list is rather long.)

These are not the actions of a loving parent, but those of an abusive god. Instead of being parental, as in: "These are the rules. The choice is yours to obey them...," it becomes, "Do as I say, or I'll kill you (or your family)." Perhaps God's own free will is the problem?

Why Do Theists Love Free Will?

Evil, which has its roots in religion, and something that theists believe is very real, is a problem that must be addressed by the believer as to why it even exists. Why does a good god allow evil to churn through the lives of his beloved planet of people? Enter free will! Humans choose to do evil and will have to account for such choices... someday. But, like unsuccessful attempts at showing a God exists, no one can really show that free will exists either.

Under the *deterministic* philosophical view, the universe operates like a finely-wound clock, subject to unchanging physical laws, and everything that occurs is inevitable because all events must happen as they do based on the preceding state of the universe.

This, of course, poses a dilemma when we consider free will:

- If determinism is true, free will is impossible because all events are inevitable. We cannot be responsible for inevitable events.

- If determinism is false, our will is partly determined by randomness, thereby making some of our decision-making outside of our control and therefore outside of our responsibility.

Because our free will is compromised in either scenario, free will is false, i.e., *absolute free will does not exist.* And human responsibility doesn't either. Please note that there are many non-religious sources that will contend otherwise. But let's consider this, for a moment anyway...

If free will does not exist, then there is *no need for a god to pass judgment* on anyone, and there is no need for a god at all. Free will and evil give God a reason to exist. And even if free will was an absolute uncompromised part of our reality, there is no reason to think that it could not operate and exist apart from any god.

Therefore, because the existence of free will is an argument that is mostly irresolvable, the real bone of contention from an atheist perspective, isn't really whether or not free will exists, but whether or not free will has a supernatural source, a non-material beginning. Both sides must consider all the possibilities. If free will (the ability to make one's own life choices), actually *does* exist, there is still no need for a god to exist along with it. Our choices, whether free or pre-determined, could simply be a part of our evolutionary makeup. In other words, human beings could exist in a world with or without free will, with neither necessitating any god. But, a real *redeemer-god,* who passes judgment on your supposed independent actions, can only exist in a world where free will exists.

Without free will, we can even the question the necessity of a Jesus-type figure. The supposed purpose of Jesus is to redeem man from sin (born of free will). If there is no sin or evil, there is no need for Jesus. And one can laughably state, that in order to give the life of Jesus purpose and meaning, people should go out and sin as much as possible!

From this we can surmise that there simply is no scenario within the framework of our universe that necessitates a god of any kind. As stated before, and elsewhere...

The equation is: "2 plus 2 equals 4." It is not "2 plus 2 plus god = 4."

One more thing...The greater gods of earth are mostly know-it-alls. They are all-knowing and all-powerful. If God knows what you're going to do before you do it, could it be that God is a *determinist* as well?

DOGMA NUMBER SIX: THE TRINITY
(CHRISTIANS ONLY PLEASE!)

In Christianity, the Trinity is the triune god – a single god divided into three parts. The three parts are Father, Son, and Holy Ghost, with the Father as Yahweh of the Old Testament, the Son as Jesus of the New Testament, and the Holy Ghost as a vaguely delineated, equal but immaterial persona of the other two, which amounts to being some sort of wormhole communication pipeline from Father and Son to the human soul. Many Christians would object to the accuracy of some of this definition, but that's not really the point of this discussion.

What we have with the holy personhood of god as *F, S & HG* is power – power wielded on three fronts. But what is this power, really? From reading the Bible, and how this triple threat operates on humanity, one can see that the F, S & HG is actually *Fear, Shame, and Horrible Guilt.* This may sound like a humorous parody to some, but let's look at this from a serious perspective for a moment.

In the Biblical account, the common theme, or threat, given by Yahweh is *fear.* It is a generalized fear quite often, but other times it has very specific and varied consequences for those who do not fear their god. Nevertheless, fear is tantamount. Followers are asked and commanded to fear Yahweh at every possible moment.

When we move on to the New Testament, *shame* is added to the fear by Jesus and done so in spades. Humans are asked to mutilate themselves (plucking out eyes, cutting off of limbs, castration, etc.) for the sake of "The Kingdom" and shamed into following Jesus no matter what insane task he demands, or magical thing he promises. And the parables, stories, and examples Jesus gives, whether allegorical or not, are clearly designed to bring out feelings of shame. This is all meant to converge into the *ultimate shame* of killing "God" (Jesus on the cross.)

Enter the Holy Ghost, whose existence is other-worldly and magical, but so incredibly powerful that just saying a bad word about this portion of the Trinity is 100%, completely, absolutely, incontrovertibly unforgivable. In other words, it engenders *horrible guilt.* And what guilt is more horrific than that which comes from an absolute zero chance for forgiveness? With this, the dictatorship of the Trinity is complete. It's a mind-fuck. And people wonder how it's possible that the Christian religion has lasted so long. It's not out of love, but through *fear, shame,* and *guilt.*

Who's Your Daddy?

So, we see from this, that the Trinitarian God is the source – not of fear in general – but of *irrational* fear. Now we can add a letter "I" in front of "Father," as God is an irrational father, and as such is also an *illegitimate* father.* This mostly deadbeat father uses the tools of fear, shame, and guilt to get his dictatorial way and then insists his victims give him love and adoration. But, from a human perspective, there is no rational justification for worshiping that which induces irrationality. God, whether in three parts or as a whole, is unworthy of worship – unworthy of even the slightest recognition whatsoever – properly rejected in the same manner as any abusive father would be for his failure to be humane.

*(Illegitimacy, logically, should be conferred, not from parent to child, but assigned to adults only. Children are innocent and cannot ethically be granted or denied legitimacy for something they had no part in deciding. Only a child's parents can be "illegitimate" if such labels are necessary. But no one should be calling children *bastards* in any pejorative sense. Only parents can be liable – and even they can be forgiven for engaging in an act of procreation that is as natural to them as it is to any living thing.)

DOGMA NUMBER SEVEN: PRAYER WORKS

The idea that prayer makes a difference in people's lives is a dogma that is almost never questioned. It's a "must-have" for just about any truly important religion. Prayer, like meditation, is used by even the smallest of religions. However, the religions with their roots in the Middle East seem to treat prayer like it's a vending machine. Expectations run high, especially in the more developed countries around the world, that any request is automatic, and you will always get what you ask for.

Praying for someone or some *thing* is like a desperate teenager promising to do "anything" and do it "forever and ever" if Mom or Dad would just let them borrow the car "this *one* time." It's an attempt to make a rather desperate deal, one that favors the god more than it favors the one doing all the praying. It's a rather childish act, but there's a reason for this.

As we've discovered in other chapters, it's a really bad idea to make promises or vows you cannot keep. (See the story of Jephthah.) But, maybe it's the gods who should take that same advice...

The Christian New Testament has this verse, a direct quote from Jesus Christ himself:

> Ask, and it will be given you; seek, and you will find; knock, and it will be opened to you. For every one who asks receives, and he who seeks finds, and to him who knocks it will be opened... – (*Matthew 7:7 KJV*)

In fact, there is an abundant number other scriptures that back up this magical way of looking at prayer, as if god is a genie that can grant wishes. Matthew 17:20, Matthew 21:21, Mark 11:24, John 14:12-14, Matthew 18:19, James 5:15-16, Mark 9:23, and Luke 1:37 all basically say the same thing. But, plenty of people have prayed for world peace, an end to famine, a beloved pet coming back to life, or a cure for brain cancer, and all have failed miserably. This, despite a Biblical written guarantee that you can have anything you ask for. Prayer like this, obviously has no effect on the outcome.

Of course this "zero effect" is true across the board with *any* prayer of *any* kind. It doesn't matter who does the praying. It doesn't matter which god receives the prayer. And it doesn't matter what is prayed for. The outcomes are always random – some good, some bad, some a little of both. But, Biblically speaking, an answer of "no" should not be an option – not when you're told you can have anything any time you ask. (A more detailed analysis of the scriptures in the Bible that relate to prayer can be found in the chapter, **Jesus and the New Testament**.)

Yes, prayer makes you feel better, if you're the one doing the praying *for someone else* – it makes you imagine that you've actually done something for someone when you haven't. But what prayer doesn't do, for anyone, is make you more moral or grant you more wishes. Numerous scientific studies, the first one conducted in 1872 by Francis Galton, and much more recently – a double-blind study by the Mayo Clinic in 2001 – have demonstrated that prayer in hospitals makes virtually no difference in the outcome of a patient's survival. The studies show that prayer works about the same as flipping a coin when it comes to praying for people to get well. And here's *one* of the reasons this is true...

Coincidentally... a miracle happened.

Littlewood's Law is a concept coined in the 1980's by Cambridge University Professor John Edensor Littlewood. For our purposes, it is the estimation of the number of perceived "miracles" occurring to any individual during a given time span. In other words, a person can expect to experience a "miracle" type event (with odds of one in a million) at the rate of about one per month. This is because during our waking hours, the average human being will see or hear one "event" per second – each of which may be either ordinary or extraordinary. With all these events occurring in each of us, those events crossing paths with other events are statistically going to generate coincidences that, for whatever reason, we will consider "significant."

At some point in your life, an old acquaintance will seem to appear out of nowhere as you bump into that person at the grocery store. Or, at some other moment, you'll find a $20 bill just lying in the grass, and you'll think that was a small miracle because you were needing some cash that day. (When are you *not* needing some cash?) Or, you'll be thinking about your favorite song, and as soon as you turn on the radio, that same song is playing.

Synchronicity, serendipity, miracles, and answered prayer all come from the same source – an overlapping of billions of "events" and thoughts, all converging and statistically becoming something a human being notices as "special" or miraculous. This phenomenon happens to everyone. Unfortunately, the religious follower thinks coincidence equals the supernatural.

The term for taking this to an extreme – seeing patterns in everyday life that are actually quite innocuous, is called *apophenia.* This is quite common among religious folk – such as seeing the face of Jesus on a slice of toast, or the Virgin Mary's blurry image on a window pane. This behavior is also common in schizophrenics. We aren't saying fanatically religious folks are mentally ill, but it does make us worry...

DOGMA NUMBER EIGHT: GOD IS ALL-POWERFUL

Are Allah, Yahweh, Jesus or any of the gods worshiped today really *all powerful?*

Here are 11 Things You Can Do That God Cannot Do:

1. Lie.
2. Do something "evil." (Ask any Muslim or Christian, they will tell you that their god can't do this – ask even the ones who claim to read their holy books.)
3. Win a battle against an army of iron chariots. (See Judges 1:19 in the Bible.)
4. Forgive someone for blaspheming the holy spirit. (Jesus either can't or won't forgive this one.)
5. Forgive someone without Jesus (or anyone else) having to die.
6. Forgive someone without the "authority" of Jesus.
7. Write a book that has less contradictions than the Bible.
8. Write a book that does not ask believers to kill non-believers. (See the Qur'an for that one.)
9. Write a holy book that, for the first time in history, actually *surpasses* the knowledge and morals of the people it's given to. (Read the final chapter of this book to find out how you can do that.)
10. Appear to someone when they ask you to appear.
11. Prove you exist.

All of these things makes you more powerful than God, proving that "God" is nothing more than an invention of human beings who really hadn't thought their deity-concept all the way through.

MORE DOGMAS

There are other dogmas, such as *divine revelation* (what is it, where does it come from), *who is God* (or Jesus, or Allah), and *what a believer must do to be saved* – but these are mostly covered in other chapters. Certainly, there are many more dogmas than the ones in this book, and they often vary greatly depending on which religion you're investigating.

However, this chapter isn't finished yet. We've only covered some of the bigger and more basic dogmas that the major Western religions cling to. The next section (or two) will cover some additional ideas and concepts that are also common among these religious entities and why some people are so damn dogmatic about them!

THE OTHER STUBBORN IDEAS SECTION

The following are not exactly dogmas, but...

There are numerous ideas and concepts that permeate the monotheistic religions, ones that aren't necessarily official beliefs, but rather tendencies, assumptions, and behaviors – the predictable, and inscrutable, repetitive acts of semi-deluded minds. They aren't really dogmas by definition, but they show up often enough, you could just call them: "things *most* believers insist are true or necessary." Let's go over a few of them:

(Maybe we could call them Catmas?)

Seeking and "Finding" God

Someone attempting to convert someone else will at some point turn to the idea that the path to their god is to "seek" him out, or "search" for him, etc. The implication, of course, is for them to search their "heart" – which really means their "soul." This is kind of a wild goose chase when you consider the heart doesn't actually do any thinking and the soul doesn't exist. But, that's not all there is to this. What's really amazing is why believers think a person should search for a god in the first place. A decent (or real) god would never play "Hide and Seek" with his creation, especially when finding him supposedly has eternal life or eternal death implications. Would you play this game with your own children? And if they didn't find you, would you just let them die?

And lastly, if the actual adventure of seeking out a god is supposed to be "good for you," with the supposed "journey" almost as invigorating as the destination... what happens at the finish line when you discover that your god (your allegorical pot of gold), isn't there? Or, that the god you've found is an evil monster, or an axe-wielding psychopath?

Karma the Chameleon

It may seem a little odd that we're going off on a Hindu tangent here, but the concept of "Karma" has become very much a part of Western culture, even though it has a very different meaning here than it did in its original Hindu form.

Unfortunately, Karma, as it exists in the collective mind of the Western World, does not actually exist. The idea that everything you do will "come back to you" in some form, that everyone pays for what they do eventually, good or bad, is simply not true.

If the western, mostly North American, concept of Karma was true or real, one would be able to kill Hitler or Stalin millions of times to achieve justice for those they murdered. However, we know that simply isn't possible. Bad people do sometimes get away with murder, and sometimes innocent people do get hurt, or die in vain. And there is plenty of evidence to support this. All we have to do is read the news.

This twisting of a Hindu concept is ultimately based on the Western religious belief in "Judgment" – that a god will someday judge the world and condemn the wicked. Unfortunately, what this interpretation of Karma actually does is this: It makes people apathetic towards real injustice. Instead of doing something about a problem, or an "evil" in the world, western religious observers simply say to themselves, "Oh, well! They'll get theirs someday!"

This kind of karma simply isn't real. The only way people get justice is by making sure society carries it out *now,* in the present. It doesn't and won't happen otherwise.

Eat Kosher or Eat Everything!? Which Is It?

Most religions around the world have some restrictions regarding what followers should eat and when they should eat. And each religion has a holy source to base this on. For Jews, the admonition is this:

> Thou shalt not seethe a kid in his mother's milk. (*Deuteronomy 14:21. KJV*)

This one little line has, over a span of thousands of years, led to a myriad of special rules and regulations regarding what, with what, and how often, a Jewish person should feed themselves.

Not surprisingly, for Christians, this was all overturned by the disciple Peter's vision declaring you can eat anything you want, which would, obviously, have to include snakes and cockroaches:

> And saw heaven opened, and a certain vessel descending upon him, as it had been a great sheet knit at the four corners, and let down to the earth: Wherein were all manner of fourfooted beasts of the earth, and wild beasts, and creeping things, and fowls of the air. And there came a voice to him, Rise, Peter; kill, and eat. – (*Acts 9:11-13. KJV*)

Both Judaism, Christianity (and Islam by default) got it wrong. The restrictions or non-restrictions of religious dietary laws are not based on health, but superstition and fear. The only reason you should or should not eat something is health. Only science can tell you with any kind of accuracy what you should or should not put in your body.

A god that worries about what his creatures eat, didn't design his creatures very well.

Sex, Lies, and Circumcisions...

David and the Foreskins. No, that's not a 1960's rock band. It's a Biblical story as shown here:

> Wherefore David arose and went, he and his men, and slew of the Philistines two hundred men; and David **brought their foreskins,** and they gave them in full tale to the king, that he might be the king's son in law. And Saul gave him Michal his daughter to wife. – (*1 Samuel 18:27 KJV*) [Emphasis Added]

It's an odd tale and not just because the act of circumcision was performed, but because it was performed on dead people. (Note, if you read this entire Biblical chapter, it is replete with the idea that the man who would be king should naturally be the one that has killed the most people.)

No one has been able to adequately give a rational explanation as to why any god would request the mutilation of the human body for religious purposes. Circumcision is an odd thing for a god to request of a people.

Is it for cleanliness? Primitive man may have had a problem keeping his "junk" clean, but modern man does not. Is it for aesthetics? They are genitals. How good-looking do they need to be? We don't routinely stick our faces down there like our best friends (our dogs) do, just to say hello.

If this mutilating god was real, the conclusions we could draw, in context, from reading the other bizarre things this same god demands, is that the god is either a sadist, a psychopath, or not all-powerful. An all-powerful god would have the ability to design his people without a foreskin from the outset. A god of such alleged great magnitude could have even made this lack of foreskin a genetic trait that could have separated his people from any other earthling without any blood being spilled. But, it didn't happen that way, and any person, with any old god to follow (and a skillful doctor), can get himself circumcised. Therefore...

It must be for the men themselves – as a spiritual construct. So, is circumcision designed to reduce the pleasure of sex, and force men to do other things, like build civilizations, or at the very least, read books? That can't be it either. Circumcised males love pornography to much the same degree as uncircumcised males. So much for increasing spirituality!

The most likely purpose of circumcision was to show other tribes that Yahweh's people were different, special, powerful, and even mysterious. And in primitive times, with men wearing only sheepskin togas, this mutilation is all they had to demonstrate that difference. Certainly, uncircumcised tribal men viewing a circumcised male would have naturally freaked out a bit. Today, knowing that the circumcision of males does very little good, is there really any other reason beyond superstitious belief to continue such a practice?

FOUR UNRELATED OBSERVATIONS AND CONCLUSIONS

The following four seemingly random ideas should guide the reader to consider why the dogmas of any religion may be completely unnecessary.

1. Ignorant Gods Are Not Real

The reason this matters when it comes to religious dogma is that, whatever your religion's core beliefs are, you still have an alleged omniscient god who behaves as if he has no knowledge of what his "children" will do next.

Suppose you adopt a child knowing it has mental issues, knowing that it's often aggressive and hits other children... if it hits another child and you proceed to beat that adopted child unmercifully, even to the point of injury, how is that logical, moral or sane? Yet, this is how the Gods of Heaven behave with regard to humans that sin. Humanity is punished harshly even when the sinful behavior is pre-programmed and/or inevitable. Most gods are blundering idiots, but the dogma tells you that you must believe and follow anyway because somehow the senseless god knows best. He's just "mysterious" and "he loves me."

(Or, he's an idiot, a tyrant and a liar. Just like the people who invented him. Not to be repetitious, but... ignorant gods aren't real. And they're *all* ignorant gods.)

2. Science and Scripture Are Not Equal

It's often said that quoting scriptures to an atheist is a waste of time for the believer, and a nuisance for the atheist. It is also true that quoting science to a believer is much the same.

Yet, there is a huge difference in the perception of practical reality between the two groups. Atheists *and* believers both use science (or the tools science has produced), every day as a convenient way of getting through life – and atheists rarely use scriptures for anything. On the flip side, true believers use scripture to convince themselves that their beliefs are a fine substitute for knowledge, while simultaneously denying science has any relevance at all – *even while using the tools of science!* (It's helpful to note that it's profoundly absurd when something that is obviously absurd is stubbornly and deliberately not viewed as absurd.)

Perhaps the dogmatic believer should pause and take a look at the scientific realities in their everyday lives. To compartmentalize religious thoughts, so that they never cross paths with reality, effectively makes those religious ideas useless. It's as if a believer is one kind of rational person away from his religious abode, and when he or she enters a house of worship they say to themselves, "Time to be delusional now. Flip the switch from rational to irrational!" At some point those wires will get loose and someone *will* short-circuit their brain.

3. Religion is a form of OCD

Obsessive Compulsive Disorder (OCD) is an anxiety disorder in which irrational fears invade the mind, and the irrational compulsive rituals that follow, temporarily relieve those fears. The rituals used by the person afflicted with OCD can be almost anything, but most common are hand washing, counting and recounting items, re-checking doors and locks, and rearranging objects. The fears that produce these rituals can range from constant worry, death of a loved-one, to the fear of performing violent or sexual acts.

A person with even a mild case of OCD must perform many self-invented rituals, and must do so in a specific way, in a specific order, a specific number of times or, as the sufferer believes, *something bad will happen.* When we look at religious rituals, we see that the performance of these rituals must be in a specific way, in a specific order, and a specific number of times, or something bad (the wrath of God) will happen. We can easily see the parallels.

And it brings up some very interesting questions: Did religion produce OCD, or did OCD produce religion?

These are questions best answered by a coterie of mental physicians, but we can clearly see that the similarities between religious ritual as it pertains to fear, and the similarities of self-performing ritual as it pertains to anxiety, are so closely paralleled that the only differences appear to be in degrees, and the insertion of a god figure.

Superstition, *in any form*, is similar to OCD in both its obsession and compulsion. The debate is on-going as to how all of this is connected in the brain, and why human behavior can be so anomalous at times, but this puzzle has life and death implications. Ancient people thought if innocent blood was spilled, bad things would be averted. Of course, there is no real connection between harming innocents and making things good again. And we know the obvious reason is that harming innocents is bad on its own! It's obsession and compulsion at its worst. One cannot do something bad to make something else good. Life doesn't work that way.

This crazy notion was expanded to the belief that if we "kill" god, that would be the ultimate sacrifice, and that would make the whole world good again. But, as history tells us, it's still a silly superstitious idea that never accomplished anything. The only thing that will make the whole world good again is for the people of the whole world to decide *on their own* to do good things. The world and its people have a long way to travel to achieve that, but the world is a lot better than it was even just a few hundred years ago. We are getting there and we are improving. And we're doing it, in spite of backward religious beliefs telling us to wash away our sins with blood, as though blood was some sort of powerful, magical soap.

4. Religion is Exclusive, Not Inclusive

All religions are like exclusive clubs. Yes, you can join, but you must perform certain specific rites, rituals and tasks before you can belong – and you must say you believe in certain things. Of course, none of the things you are asked to do serve any practical purpose. There is nothing practical about genital mutilation, moving your hands and arms in a specific way when entering or leaving a room, banning certain kinds of foods, engaging in self-flagellation rituals, wearing (or not wearing) something on your head, donning special robes,

72

touching or kissing certain special objects, immersing yourself in water, saying specific words in a certain order, bowing, kneeling, crouching, or lying prostrate – none of these actions are practical in any way and can go from the bizarre to the somewhat silly. The only purpose these actions serve is to tell you, and everyone outside the group, that you are "special" – which actually means *superior* to those outside the group.

Those inside the group will always deny that they do these things to feel superior, but in fact, that is the sole purpose of belonging to any group. To group members, those *outside* the group are never as good as those *inside* the group. Outsiders are the "lost," the uninformed, the ignorant, the unsaved, the infidels, the goyim, the kafirs, the unbelievers, the sinners, the unrepentant, the evil ones, the devil's children, and on and on. There is no getting around this air of superiority, with its disdain for outsiders, and its accompanying denial that such group-think arrogance exists. Yet, no matter how much the insiders swear otherwise, when it comes to religions, there are *no exceptions* to this rule.

But what if you strip away the rites, the rituals, and special duties and focus only on belief – the most important part of belonging to the superior group? Belief, without any real evidence to back it up, leaves you with virtually nothing to hold on to. If you're a true believer, you realize on some level that those tasks, rites, and rituals are a necessary investment, even if they are all "smoke and mirrors." Those rituals make you feel that the belief has value. Even if you feel a growing doubt about your beliefs, you tell yourself it would be crazy to back out of the group after all the time you've put in. Even when the belief is questionable, and the rites, rituals and dogmas seem like nothing more than a strange magic show, you still have the *feeling* of belonging to something or someone, so you quickly suppress those doubts you had, and accept and retain your place in the group. Yes, the religion has captured you and placed you in its cage with all the other cattle (and sheep). Of course, there is a way out. But you wouldn't escape now even if they left the gate wide open. You're so much better than those "losers" on the outside.

Yeah, right.

FINAL THOUGHT

The truth is, whatever dogmas a religion has, they will *all* always be inferior to the real world – the one place you can really be yourself. So, dogmas be damned. Live your life for yourself, not for some group's crazy dogmas.

CHAPTER FIVE

A Not-So-Special Case:
Presupposition and The Apoplectic Apocalyptic Apologetic Society

"Everyone is entitled to their own opinions, but they are not entitled to their own facts." – Daniel Patrick Moynihan

"The way you know someone has learned something is when they change their mind." – Edward Trillian

This may be the most exciting chapter all, if not the most bizarre.

If you're an atheist, there's a rather high probability you will one day encounter Christian "presuppositional apologists," and you will need to know exactly how to respond to a barrage of convoluted rationalizations that, in their world, demonstrate how nothing really is quite *something!*

Please note, this chapter is not everything you'll ever need to know about presuppositional apologetics. It's just the tip of the giant cucumber. Nevertheless, it will introduce you to a few facts that can help you learn more, and aid you in defending yourself against dishonest claims – even those not sponsored by theists!

So, let's get started by defining a few things first:

What is a Presupposition?

A presupposition is an implicit assumption. *And,* it is something, in the course of a conversation, people will take for granted. Whether you are sitting around drinking beer with your friends, or giving testimony in a courtroom, it's something stated that everyone knows and assumes to be true – a declaration that goes unchallenged. An example of a sound presupposition would be "The Boston Red Sox play baseball." An even better one is, "The universe exists." You won't find many people that will challenge this fact. Everyone takes it for granted that the universe exists, whatever it may be, even if our knowledge of it is limited.

What is Apologetics?

Apologetics comes from the Greek word *apologia,* which means to "speak in defense" of one's position. The modern use of apologetics is most often religion-based, but can be used in other fields, such as literature.

Christian apologetics is nothing more than Christians defending their beliefs against criticism. It has nothing to do with the modern usage of the word *apology* or *apologize,* where one might say, "I'm sorry," or "Do you forgive me?" Christians aren't asking for someone to forgive them for their contradictory scriptures as one might think. They are, instead, defending those texts with what they see as inerrant rational thought.

What is Presuppositional Apologetics? Or, *"TAG, you're it!"*

The source of modern presuppositionalism comes from an expansion of an older idea known as "The Transcendental Argument for the Existence of God," also known as TAG. TAG presupposes a Christian theistic world view, and states that not only are you unable to know anything without the explicitly defined Christian deity, but all morals, and all logic can only come from this same specific *Christian* god.

The most often cited proponents of presuppositional apologetics are Dutch-born theologian Cornelius Van Til, a Calvinist from the late nineteenth century, and more recently, American theologian Greg Bahnsen, in the late twentieth century. Both wrote extensively on this subject and their work has become popular among modern day Christians, especially among young believers.

Presuppositional apologetics, or presuppositionalism, is just one branch of Christian Apologetics. Creationist apologetics and evidential apologetics are also a part of Christian philosophical discourse. It just so happens that, currently, the presuppositional arm is the one that is at the forefront of the Christian theistic debate.

Although the concept of presuppositional apologetics is Christian based, it could easily be applied to other faiths, and even other ideas. But from a solely Christian perspective, presuppositional apologetics states that the only real basis for human rational thought is the Christian faith to the exclusion of all others. A natural occurrence, erupting from this seemingly narrow and arrogant statement of belief, is that many who are not Christian take immediate offense. And certainly, the presuppositional apologist argument can be found on blogs and forums, and video sites such as YouTube, and hundreds of other places on the Internet, with arguments pro and con that seemingly never end.

The P.A. Agenda

Modern Presuppositional Apologetics (P.A.) urges Christians to argue with non-believers in an "indirect" fashion, by attacking what is perceived, by the

Christian, as the non-believer's world view. A world view, as defined by Christian apologists, is a person's basic assumptions about reality, knowledge, and morality. The Christian apologist begins with the assertion that atheists cannot make sense out of adherence to the laws of logic due to an atheist's own presuppositions about reality. It assumes atheism (which is simply a rejection of a god-claim) is unable to argue against the Christian faith, philosophically, ethically, or logically. From a practical vantage point, this amounts to Christians asserting their position by way of tearing down a dissimilar position (one which they inaccurately define), and then assuming their own position must be right if the other one is wrong. This tactic is the central core of the P.A. debate, and invokes the fallacy of the *straw man* – an attempt to refute their opponent's position by deliberately misrepresenting their opponent's actual stated viewpoint.

What is the true purpose of Christian presuppositional apologetics? It really depends on which apologist you talk to. For those who have only encountered it on Internet discussion boards, the purpose appears rather unsavory. It's become a hot topic, and many lay Christians have jumped on board the P.A. parade float for a piece of the action. And many really do believe their presentation of apologetics is a way to "prove" their god exists. However, when you talk with some of the people leading this parade, you find a more disingenuous platform. There is a common script and a very specific series of questions that P.A. preachers use to deflect any skeptics who are willing to debate Christian beliefs. And there are plenty of Christian amateur philosophers that are more than willing to spread this style of vitriolic discourse to their fellow clerics.

For informal discussions with non-believers, many P.A.'s are trained to not answer questions, even if it's a question as simple as a request to define the god they are defending. This is because they use interrogation tactics designed only to frustrate the person they are talking to. Only they are allowed to ask questions and give pre-set answers. It has been stated by nameless P.A. internet contributors that the purpose of the presuppositional apologetics argument is to "shut mouths," not convert anyone. Of course, on the internet, because of its ability to reach masses of people of like mind, and its easy access to fact verification, it does quite the opposite. It angers people and gets them talking.

These apologists did get one thing right, it converts no one. Unfortunately, for them, by converting no one, they are actually doing the opposite of what Jesus Christ instructed them to do. Instead of following their messiah, they are following Internet trolls who may or may not be Christian.

As we'll see, the Christian presupposition of their god is a fallacy, and a form of circular reasoning based on absolutes it cannot demonstrate. It draws a conclusion based on premises that presuppose that conclusion. It provides no real verified necessity to accept any of its premises.

Logic of The Gods

To look at the P.A.'s philosophical approach which they believe leads to their god, we have to look at the logic they employ to get there. The method the P.A. uses most often is the *syllogism*.

A syllogism, as first defined by the ancient Greek philosopher Aristotle, is a logical argument, the conclusion of which is supported by two premises. One contains the term that is the *predicate* of the conclusion, and the other contains the term that is the *subject* of the conclusion. Common to both premises is the *middle term* that is excluded from the conclusion. A typical form is:

All A's are C's. All B's are A's. therefore all B's are C's.

It's important to note here that a syllogism is *not* a standard of proof. It's simply a way to reach a logical conclusion based on two premises. The following is the most widely used logical syllogism for the TAG argument:

1. If there is no god (the Christian god), knowledge is not possible.
2. Knowledge is possible.
3. Therefore a god exists.

This is argued in exactly the same way with morality and logic, simply by substituting the word *knowledge* with either one of the other two.

The numerous flaws in this will be obvious to many. But, because the argument frequently drifts beyond the fallacious circularity of their syllogism, we will have to dissect the presuppositional apologist position further. In **Part One** of this chapter, we will expose the flaws of the presuppositional apologist argument one at a time. Ten major flaws are presented here, although there are many, many others, often dependent upon which Christian is attempting to manage the discourse, and what sort of definitions they use for key words. Throughout the course of a debate with the P.A., the definitions they choose are often misleading and can shift in meaning, giving the listener a generous sampling of the *fallacy of equivocation.*

Part Two will provide many of the actual scripted statements made by presuppositional apologists when engaged in a debate with a non-believer.

THE TEN FLAWS

The Flaw of the Unfounded Soundness

The soundness of the presuppositional argument is highly questionable. The premise, "If there is no god, knowledge is not possible," is not sound because it cannot be demonstrably true. It's a presupposition which can easily be challenged. Because the first premise could actually be false, the argument, even though it could be considered valid as a whole, is not sound, and should be rejected.

To make the syllogism sound, the syllogism's author would have to first, more clearly define what "god" is, and second, show some evidence for its existence. If the "who" or "what," or existence of the god in question is unknown, it's fallacious to assume something is true just because it hasn't been proven false. It becomes an argument from (or to, toward) ignorance, also known as, *argumentum ad ignorantiam.*

Of course, there is one other very good and wise reason why one should have to define and prove their god before the syllogism will work. It's because the word "God" could just as easily be substituted with the word "leprechaun" or "wise invisible pancake" and have the same amount of validity. For example:

1. If there is no wise invisible pancake, knowledge is not possible.
2. Knowledge is possible.
3. Therefore, a wise invisible pancake exists.

Obviously, as shown here, you can have a "truth" statement (a presupposition, or premise) which is not based on fact or reality. Let's try one more. This time, one where the characters involved may be recognizable:

1. All Smurfs are blue.
2. Smurfette is a Smurf.
3. Therefore, Smurfette is blue.

Smurfs are not real. Smurfette is not real. However, the statement is true within the context of the fictional story of *The Smurfs.* All the premises are true, therefore it is a valid and sound argument. But the characters are *imaginary.* We must allow that it is possible that the god mentioned in the Christian apologists' syllogism is also imaginary until proven otherwise.

The evidence for Smurfs and the evidence for god are similar. Outside of our own imaginations, we can find the Smurfs and God on paper. And information and images of both can be accessed by additional means such as television broadcasts, books, artwork, and computer pages. For both Smurf and God, there is little substantial access to either, beyond what we mentioned.

We have clearly demonstrated how we can create a syllogism that is both valid and sound, but not based on real persons or entities. It is just as true as any syllogism about any god.

If that was not enough to demonstrate how logical syllogisms were not meant to be a path to certainty (or reality), we can add the following *false* syllogism:

1. All dogs have tails.
2. My dog, Lucy, had her tail cut off.
3. (With no tail), Lucy is no longer a dog.

For the syllogism to work as a part of reality, the dog's species would have to miraculously change, along with reality.

The syllogistic form is easy enough to challenge, but presuppositional apologists will ignore the lack of soundness in theirs and continue on as if their presuppositions are self-evident. But, as we've stated elsewhere, *you cannot presuppose your god into existence.* He either exists or he doesn't exist. And the burden of proof is always on the one claiming he does.

The self-evidence for a god, by observation of "creation," has never been validated by the god who supposedly did all the creating. It's just another leap from "something exists," to "therefore, our god did it." It's one more *God of the Gaps* declaration without demonstrating the god. Our need, as non-believers, to have substantiated proofs could naturally move us into the realm of *evidentiary* apologetics which was mentioned earlier (the evidence, historical or physical, for the Christian god). But, we ask, how can the apologist have one without the other? To attempt to prove your god on paper alone, with philosophy, without evidentiary proofs, is the pinnacle of utter futility and dissonance.

The Flaw of Alternative Religious Syllogisms

This flaw is related closely to the **Flaw of the Unfounded Soundness** (above). This, however, is an important distinction because it deals with other religions that are *real* and which make similar assertions about their own god(s). It demonstrates that you can insert any god, or any mythical character in place of the presuppositional apologist's particular god and get the same result. If the syllogism or world view were sound, that would not be possible. But, with the apologist's presuppositional argument, you can make it state that you cannot *know anything* without Yahweh. Or Allah. Or Brahma. Or your spouse. (How does the presuppositional apologist know, at any given moment, that the person they are talking to isn't God in disguise?)

To demonstrate this, let's try the syllogism with another religion:

1. If there is no Vishnu, knowledge is not possible.
2. Knowledge is possible.
3. Therefore Vishnu exists.

Although, this god of the Hindu Trinity is virtually unknown to the West, he is venerated and adored by Hindu worshipers around the world. There are many holy books that mention Vishnu, with one – the *Shruti* – describing Vishnu as the Supreme Being.

Obviously, the Vishnu syllogism and the Christian syllogism cannot be valid simultaneously unless both gods exist simultaneously. How can the Christian presuppositional apologist make a Jesus-centered claim that his syllogism is valid, but the Hindu one isn't? Vishnu is venerated and loved just as much as Jesus is. Which one is correct?

The only recourse to solve this problem is to prove a particular god exists – and once again we are back to square one, wondering why, if the Christian god exists, why does the proof for him not exist? This also demonstrates how syllogisms cannot be a path to religious truth. The apologist's presupposition rationalizes *all* gods, and in doing so, fails to demonstrate any of them.

The Flaw of Leading Questions

"Have you stopped beating your wife?" is a leading question. You have probably never beat up anyone, but this question implies that you have. And the person asking the question expects a yes or no answer! This is the core tactic of the presuppositional apologist discourse. It's not really an argument, but more of a bullying tactic to throw the non-believer off-guard so the apologist can have his "Gotcha!" moment – thus proving that the presuppositional apologist's argument is not really about revealing truth, but rather about "winning" a shouting match.

We will get into the specifics of what those statements commonly are in Part II of this Chapter, but it's important to know that the core beliefs of the presuppositional apologist are rarely revealed from the beginning of the discussion. That's left towards the end, and only after the non-believer has become befuddled from being inundated by a series of rapid-fire trick questions (most of which contain hidden flaws within each statement itself).

The Flaw of the Backward Existence

When we read the first line of the apologist's syllogism, we see that it comes to a specific conclusion while the rest of the syllogism searches for the facts that fit that conclusion. Whereas, logic (and common sense) demands that you assemble the facts first, then discover how or why those facts are true.

The apologist is looking at the world through *apriorism*. What most normal, thinking, functioning people do, logically, is to allow facts to test our world view. When our facts are gathered first, we can keep or modify our world view based on those facts. But to start out with a world view first, and then accept or reject facts based on whether or not they fit neatly into that world view, is doing it backwards!

Suppose you believe people are being kidnapped by aliens from another planet, and you don't base this on any personal experience with aliens, but only because your cousin told you it was true, or you got it from a story you saw on television. You simply decide to accept the alien story as fact without your own personal investigation. And if you do go looking for any clues, you accept only those that hint at your belief, and reject all of those that don't (a.k.a. *confirmation bias*). You are then engaging the same type of backward (*a priori*) logic. The correct way would be to try to find real evidence, for or against alien abduction claims, and accept those findings as fact, no matter what they conclude – even if those facts are something you don't like.

The Flaw of the Capricious God

The three tenets or requirements of a world view, as presented by the Christian apologist, are comprised of what a person believes about morals, logic, and knowledge. They ask: What is their source? And what is the standard a person uses to determine what they are? Their answer is that the moral standard, logical standard, and knowledge standard is their god – the Christian one, as read about in the Christian Bible.

For some rather odd reason, Christians have come to the conclusion that this standard (God) is flawless, mostly because the Bible says he is. But the Bible also describes a god whose own standards for all these things is rather low. The

"Moral Lawgiver" gives immoral laws, executes immoral edicts, and changes what those moral standards should be on a whim. That in itself negates any "logic" this logical standard bearer might have had. And as for knowledge, this god has no clue when he will win a battle, or how to cope with the enemies of his "children," or deal with an entire planet of unruly humans that he allegedly created himself. It becomes clear rather quick, that the standard the Christian is suggesting as fact, cannot be distinguished from fantasy.

You can get into the specifics of this immoral, unknowing, illogical god via some very revealing Bible verses. These are quoted and clearly demonstrated in other chapters. Suffice to say, it isn't very pretty.

There is a reason why the prophets, seers, and scribes inserted so many public relations comments throughout their holy book, such as god is "great, wonderful, holy, perfect, loving," etc. – it was no doubt to tone down the rhetoric about the insane and capricious nature of their standard bearer.

Instead of apologists attacking the morals, logic, or knowledge claims of non-Christians as having no captain to guide their ship, maybe they should take a look at the holes in their own rapidly sinking dinghy. Perhaps a quick peek at Matthew 7:5 would guide them to at least a tinge of humility.

The Flaw of the Lying God

This flaw is all about not knowing. Or, not *really* knowing. Because humans are not omniscient, they can't know everything about anything. And that's what gets the apologist into trouble...

As an exception to reality, presuppositional apologists claim they get their knowledge, truth, morals, and most everything else, through *revelation* from their god. But, because they have to use their unreliable senses and imperfect cognitive skills, the same way non-believers do, it is impossible to know if what is being revealed to them is accurate, or true.

And that brings us to a lying god, (or perhaps a god who was lied about). What does the Christian really know about his god and how much of it does he know for certain? What is really true and what is only partially true? And what is a complete and deliberate falsehood?

The actual facts on the ground are this: It is virtually impossible for a Christian, or any other theist, to know for certain that anything he has read, heard, or imagined about his god is real or true. The possibilities about the real truth about any god are endless. The Christian god could be lying to his people, or he could be Satan in disguise, giving only partial truths, toying with believers minds for his own entertainment. He could be a fallible alien creature from another planet, a human time traveler who returned to the past to make himself into a god, or he could simply be non-existent. The list goes on and on. If you know nothing about a subject, anything could be true.

Therefore, if a lying god is possible, which it is within the context of any information-giving god, then we can easily presuppose that you cannot really know anything *with* god.

To make matters of *knowing* worse – the Bible writers themselves could have been lying, or telling only partial truths, or exaggerating, or just making up stuff whenever it pleased them. How could anyone really know which parts of the Bible were *not* made from any of those scenarios? Did the writers of the Bible *not* have the free-will to edit the Bible in a way that pleased them?

There is no justification to think that because the Bible says it's true, therefore it must be true. This is purely intrinsic in the statement that *any idea, concept, or belief that is validated only by itself could be false.* That applies to anything in the Bible if the only validating source is the Bible itself. There's really no getting around this. The Bible is not true just because the Bible says it's true. And someone thinking it's true inside their own head (unless you can find a currently living 2000 year old witness), cannot be a reliable outside source.

Every single tenet of the presuppositional apologist's position hinges on this reality. Every accusation made about the non-believer's lack of knowledge, lack of certainty, etc., *disproves* god as much as it proves him. How does the believer in God know he's not in a computer matrix, in an elaborate alien produced dream, or that he's not hallucinating everything he thinks he knows? The script of the matrix, dream, or hallucination, could be making him think a god exists, when a god does not.

The only possible way a Christian, or anyone else, could know if the revelations were true would be if the person receiving them was omniscient, equal to his god, or superior to his god. And, here we can assertively and accurately presuppose that no such human being exists.

The Flaw of Suppressed Knowledge

One of the other unverifiable presuppositions put forward by the Christian apologist is the idea that all non-believers are suppressing their own innate "knowledge" that the Christian god is real. This accusation is acquired from their own Bible, specifically, Romans 1:18-20. Of course, no one can really know anything is true simply from reading words on a page. It usually requires a bit more than that.

Socrates said:

> A text can't respond to a question; it will just keep saying the same thing over and over again, no matter how often it is refuted.

Words, and how they are arranged, are important. You cannot have a correct presupposition without that presupposition being universally held as true for everyone in a discussion. For example, you could be sitting in a room with twelve people, *one of them blind,* and you could have a discussion about the table lamp across the room. You could begin your discussion with the following presupposition: "We can all see the lamp across the room..." Wait! What about the blind person? He, or she, cannot see the lamp at all. The presupposition is rejected. If the blind person touches the lamp, or becomes otherwise aware of the lamp, you can restart with the following presupposition: "We are all aware of the lamp across the room..." That presupposition is now considered adequate.

In this vein, one cannot presuppose a god when that god has not been shown to exist. You may see the god, apparition, or thing, but what about those who cannot see what you see? The Christian apologist claims that everyone on earth already knows their god exists, and those who say otherwise are simply in denial. But, that's no different than telling an actual blind man he's faking it. If you aren't the blind man, you cannot know if the blind man is, or isn't, blind. If you *cannot* know, you effectively *do not know.* If you do not know, and cannot know, you lack all credibility when you claim otherwise.

Because the presuppositional apologist could be wrong about everything he claims to know about his Bible and his god, he is in no position to tell anyone what they do, or do not know, nor can he tell them what they "suppress."

If you can claim you know someone is suppressing some inner belief, why not also claim you're psychic, or can read minds, or that you're really a shape-shifting alien? Christians, or any other group, cannot claim to know what other people think, know, or suppress. They are not omniscient. And to claim they can know this based on a tiny paragraph in an ancient book of writings – which itself is inherently questionable, contradictory, and controversial – is nothing less than laughable absurdity. Why not just declare, "I know everything!" and be done with it?

There is a good reason why we evolved private thoughts – because, as a defense mechanism, you're not supposed to know what other people are thinking. It's none of your business. No one has invented a perfect mind-reading machine, nor has anyone evolved into one. Therefore, it bears repeating: if you *can't* know, then you *don't* know.

The Flaw of the Laws of Logic

The presuppositionalist likes to use the laws of logic (as in the *law of identity, law of non-contradiction, law of excluded middle*) as a way of sounding erudite and intelligent. However, most Christians did not come to their religious belief using any of these laws of logic. Most acquired their beliefs through an emotional appeal at a time of internal vulnerability. Quite often, attaching themselves to the presuppositionalist argument is way to convince themselves that their previous emotional leap into the irrationality of faith was not all for naught. The P.A. argument gives them a way to close the gap between unreasonable faith and the science they see all around them. From this we can surmise that most presuppositional apologists are closeted agnostic-theists. Doubters, no doubt, need intellectual reassurance.

Logic is a human tool in much the same way as binoculars are a tool, or a telescope is a tool. Logic helps us see and understand our universe better, even if it is through the span of our own rather imperfect view of reality. When mankind dies out, his tools will die with him, and the universe will continue to be what it is, whether or not mankind ever perceived it correctly.

Even if the laws of logic are absolute and exist *transcendent* to time and space, the use of logic as a *concept* is simply one way for humans to make sense of the universe. It's our description(s) of what we've observed. The logic that humans use is not the kind of logic that, by necessity, rules the universe, or sits immutable and absolute. We, with *our* logic, could be wrong about how the universe works, in part, or in whole. We observe and use the laws of logic linguistically, and abstractly, in our brains, in an attempt to make sense of our view of reality. Actual objective reality does not have to line up with our analysis.

The presuppositional apologist's position is that the laws of logic are absolute and that the concept (or perception) of these laws in the minds of humans is also innate and absolute. The apologist will not admit that what humans do with logic amounts to nothing more than subjectively observing what already exists. (What's almost funny is how the apologist can believe the laws of logic are immutable, everlasting, and can never be broken, but also believes in a god that could change them at any moment. Of course, the apologist would *have* to believe such a contradiction. If the laws are immutable, and not subject to the whims of his god, his god would be subject to those laws as well, and would lose his omnipotence. Naturally, this contradiction, and exception for God through special pleading, is blatantly ignored by the apologist.)

The apologist's main goal of leading the conversation down the path of logic is to get back to the original presupposition that whatever the laws of logic are, and whatever logic is, their god invented those things and stuck them in your head for you. Besides being a giant God of the Gaps (argument from ignorance) fallacy, it also reveals the underlying flaw that the presuppositional apologist simply does not know what logic *is,* even if he's capable of using it correctly on occasion.

This leads us directly into the next flaw...

The Flaw of the "Immaterial" God

The presuppositional apologist will swear that thoughts, feelings, ideas, and abstract concepts are immaterial – therefore God exists. The line of thinking is that because one immaterial thing exists (e.g. abstract ideas), then this other immaterial thing (their god), must also exist. Of course, this is laughably fallacious and a complete non-sequitur. If fairies exist, would it automatically mean unicorns also exist?

A *thought,* whether it be about logic, sex, or cosmology, still has its existence wholly dependent upon a physical, material thing – the brain. This is so, even if we choose to describe the thought as non-physical or "immaterial." A thought is generated via the firing of millions of tiny neurons in your brain in a very specific sequence. When you change your thought, you change the sequence, but it exists inside your brain as electro-chemical pulses. Your awareness of the thought does not make it any less of a real physically-generated phenomenon.

You can call thoughts and ideas any name you wish, but they can only exist within a physical brain. You can name them immaterial, supernatural, spiritual, or you can call them Betsy. It really doesn't matter linguistically. A brain is like a thought machine – or a thought storage device. Thoughts do not magically exist outside the brain and then search for a brain to inhabit. That only works in horror movies.

85

The fact is, when a person dies, their brain dies. And when their brain dies, their thoughts, concepts, ideas, etc., die with them, and cease to exist (and cessation of existence includes any thoughts about a god). There is zero evidence to suggest that thoughts or ideas live on somewhere after death.

If the presuppositionalist wants to assert that things exist outside of our reality in some form or fashion, and wants to label that "immaterial," they will have to define what "exist" means, and will have the burden of proof to demonstrate that "existence." How does god exist? Does he exist in the same way a thought exists, or does he exist only as a thought?

It must be noted that saying all of this is in no way an endorsement of *materialism*. It is simply a statement of clarification and the rejection of a non-sequitur. Stating one non-material thing exists does not provide evidence that any other non-material thing exists. And for an atheist, this statement refers unequivocally to immaterial gods.

Flaw of the Missing World View

This flaw could also be labeled, "Proving your idea is bad, automatically makes my idea good!"

Perhaps the apologist's worst flaw, which is central to their argument, is a ploy that attempts to challenge the non-believer's world view. Again and again, the presuppositional accusers unswervingly insist that atheism is not only a world view, but the total antithesis of their own world view.

Of course this is often how they lose the debate. By stating that atheism is a world view, they put themselves at odds with a variety different types of atheists whose actual world views are not at all like the excessively generalized straw man views the presuppositional apologist assigns to them.

Atheists are not all materialists, not all naturalists, not all nihilists. Atheists do not collectively follow Dawkins, Hitchens, or Darwin. They do not attach themselves automatically to any specific group, leader, political party, or social media channel. They don't even all drink the same brand of beer.

The only thing all atheists have in common is that they don't believe in deities. Period. End of story.

That final flaw takes us to...

PRESUPPOSITIONAL QUESTIONS, STATEMENTS, AND CLAIMS

The following is a series of loaded questions all non-believers encounter when talking to an over-eager, philosophy-laden Bible thumper. These are often in the form of statements and claims that are formulated to elicit an expected response from the listener. The technique used by the presuppositional apologist, when discussing anything (or informally debating) with a non-believer or skeptic, is called *plurium interrogationum*. Also known as, asking leading or loaded questions, and also known as "The Complex Question." It becomes a fallacy when the one asking the question presupposes something that has not been proven or accepted by all parties in the discussion. By definition, this makes the presuppositional apologist's entire argument a fallacy.

It's not surprising that the word interrogationum and the English word interrogation (in its pejorative sense), come from the same Latin root. Interrogation, using loaded questions, is what bad cops do to badger a suspect.

Here are most (not all) of the major questions and statements given by a presuppositional apologist during a typical discourse, followed by commentary as to why they don't work. Most of these will easily refer back to the **Flaws** as presented and explained in **Part One**, and many of the ideas and conclusions will overlap.

"Could you be wrong about everything you think you know?"

Many people, when put on the spot, will answer "Yes" to this question without thinking, because of the use of the word "could." Yes, even though you *could* possibly be wrong about everything, you probably aren't. But the P.A. ignores probability and tries to get you to take it a step further and say you *are* wrong about everything you think you know. The trick to get you there is in the P.A.'s use of the word "everything." The P.A. has taken a possibility (*could*) to lead you to an absolute (*everything*).

It's a way to get the listener to into the Socratic paradox, which is to say, "I know I don't know anything." Naturally, if you *know* you know nothing, you actually know something. In other words, the only function of the apologist's question is to deliberately confuse you so that more off-putting, pre-scripted, dogma-laced questions can be fired in your direction. Moments after hearing this question from the P.A., many recipients of this nonsense immediately recognize exactly how disingenuous the question is. When the P.A. is called out for his dishonesty, he quickly denies his guilt like a serial killer on death row.

Presuppositional apologists must use these all-encompassing absolutes because of their all-encompassing god theory. With a little thought, there are many things we can know and not be wrong about them. We know we exist. We know the universe exists. We know there are no round squares and no square triangles. We know we are not omniscient. We know we are not omnipotent. We know the name we call ourselves, and on and on. So, no, we can't really be wrong about *everything*. And at the same time we don't need to know everything to a degree of absolute certainty to function in our world. The things we do know, we can know just fine without the necessity of a god intervening in our behalf just so we can know things.

The truth is, all science, knowledge, logic, physics, math, and *everything* else in the universe works just fine without the necessity of any god – and the need for any *particular* god is even less. We know $2 + 2 = 4$. The equation has never been $2 + 2 = 4 +$ The Particular God I Believe In.

(It should be obvious in the preceding equation that god must $= 0$. If god equals zero, then god is 0 in all equations.)

As a side note, after the P.A. has told a person "you could be wrong about everything you think you know," he will later claim that the same person innately *knows God exists*. Of course, if you think you know God exists, but could be wrong about *everything* you think you know (which would have to include the existence of God), you quickly discover that the P.A. has essentially stated that you could be wrong about "knowing God exists"! Oops! The P.A. has just destroyed one of his own presuppositions, as well as his core argument, with his own leading question! It's self-destructive circularity at its worst. But, as we'll soon see, the prime rule for the apologist is that all self-contradictory statements must be ignored.

"Prove you exist!"

Once you have shown conclusively that you really *can't* be wrong about everything you think you know, usually by declaring that you know you exist, you immediately get the above phrase.

Anyone can prove their own existence to themselves, but if you really need to prove it to someone else, it's quite simple. All you need to do is slap the person asking for proof across their face with your hand. Then they will know you exist. There will even be residual DNA evidence of your existence (and possibly a hand print) on that person's face. How much more proof do you need?

As with anything else that requires proof, all you need is to be able to test your hypothesis. And, it follows, if the question is absurd, an absurd answer is adequate.

"You have given up on knowledge!"

This is the presuppositional apologist's declaration that follows once you admit that you are not 100% certain of anything. It does not occur to the knee-bowing apologist that he is also not 100% certain about his god. And he cannot understand that just declaring something (like his god, or a revelation) is certain, doesn't automatically make it certain. The presuppositional apologist is confusing "giving up" on knowledge as being the same as giving up on certainty. But knowledge and 100 % certainty are not the same thing.

Knowledge is justified true belief. And certainty, often called *absolute* certainty, or 100% certainty, is perfect knowledge. It is errorless and doubtless. But having imperfect knowledge is still having knowledge, even if it may be slightly flawed. Therefore, because we all have imperfect knowledge about a great many things, we cannot "give up on knowledge." The only people that have "given up on knowledge" are people that are already dead.

In most languages, many words or terms will have more than one meaning. But using one of those alternate meanings to mislead a discussion is the informal fallacy known as *equivocation*. This is what the apologist does when attempting to make any sort of knowledge and absolute certainty mean the same thing. It is apparent, that for the presuppositional apologist, if you're going to use one fallacy, why not use lots of them!

Of course, the heart of this argument, and the central theme of all of the statements and questions from the presuppositionalist, is to bring you back to the original premise in that original unsound syllogism, as presented at the beginning of this chapter. To the presuppositionalist, if you have "given up on

God" you have given up on "knowledge," because "knowledge can only come from god."

And of course, again we have to stop the presuppositional apologist's horse from any attempt to break through his stall before the starter pistol is fired. Over and over, we have to bring him back to the starting gate. Which God? Can you define your god? How do you know this god? Can you prove he exists? Can you show that the information you're receiving from this god is accurate and true? If he can't, the apologist's metaphorical horse is simply not qualified to run in this race.

Knowing we can never have absolute certainty, does not mean we should randomly attempt to rationalize that which appears impossible. And claiming to have absolute certainty without having the ability to demonstrate it, is reason enough to reject it.

"Your certainty of not being certain is self-refuting!"

As a reasonable, thinking human being, you must take the following personal perspective about your place in the universe: "No certain knowledge exists for me. And even of that, I am not certain." This is known as a true paradox. Worded another way: "We cannot be certain of anything, including the first half of this sentence."

If the Primacy of Existence is true, that the universe exists objectively, with or without us, then certain knowledge probably does exist. It's just unlikely that any human has it. We can be reasonably certain that humans are not omniscient. Therefore, obtaining absolute certainty regarding anything is doubtful. If someone obtained certain knowledge about the universe, the rest of us would need to know how it was acquired. We can be reasonably certain it was not acquired through a contradictory, ancient, misguided holy book. Nor was it likely obtained through a personal revelation by someone claiming to have received it from what they think is their god.

Again, some evidence for any of these sources is required, along with some sort of solid verification that the source is not deceiving us. We can be reasonably certain that these traditional religious sources are not valid because of past experience with these kinds of ideas being un-falsifiable, deliberately deceptive, unreliable, and lacking any tangible evidence.

From our small *finite* view of the universe, most humans that are rational conclude that no one has the ability to possess absolute certainty. Neither do we have access to any source that has absolute certainty, because, even if we *did* have that source, we would not be absolutely certain that the source actually possessed absolute certainty. We can begin to see where this is going. We are entering a field of doubt from which we can never escape. For Christians to actually see the universe through unfiltered lenses, they will have give up on the certainty of their god. That is not the same as giving up the belief in their god. It just takes the claim of absolute knowledge out of the equation. And, if there was a god, who's to say it would want human beings to have absolute certainty anyway – about anything at all?

Those of us who are atheists have and obtain our knowledge about things in our world with the awareness that our knowledge is limited. We do not arrogantly suppose that we will ever have certain knowledge about anything. Understanding our small place in the universe makes our perspective more tenable and believable because we are aware that we know very little. When we look at the universe, we are humbled. Christians, however, as apologists, live in a hubristic fantasy world where they believe they can know everything, already do, and actually have a personal source for all knowledge and certain knowledge. These sorts of egocentric and geocentric notions about reality are nothing less than madness and deliberate self-deception.

The only way we could attain certainty would be to put an end to the infinite questions that arise with each new bit of knowledge we acquire. Christian apologists have neither certainty *about* their god, nor certainty *from* their god. How do we know that? Because apologists are not omniscient. We know apologists use their own often unreliable senses and their own narrow reasoning to come to their conclusions (the same as everyone else), and it is impossible, therefore, for them to be 100% certain of anything, and that includes anything about any god. Even though apologists think their god would never lie, the apologists lack of omniscience means their god could be lying to them about not lying to them. Omniscience is *the* requirement for certainty. If a being does not have omniscience, he automatically does not have certainty. There is no way around this fact. Making statements that you have certainty means you are making statements of your own omniscience.

"If that's so, you can't know what I can know!"

This sentence follows after the non-believer has explained to the god-worshiper that no one can possibly know whether or not his god is lying. He will say that his god has revealed things to him "in such a way" that he knows them to be true. The "in such a way" is never defined or presented, just stated. The presuppositional apologist will protest further by saying that the atheist just doesn't understand his position, and that no one can tell him what he is capable or incapable of knowing.

What the P.A. is claiming is that no one can refute his statements because no one can prove that his statements *aren't* true. This is shifting the burden of proof once again. This is stating "X is real, and you cannot prove that X is not real." And X, of course, is not falsifiable. The apologist is claiming certainty and then claiming that no one can be certain that the apologist's claims are not certain. This is another way for the apologist to say, "I know what I know," without ever feeling the obligation to present evidence for the knowing.

If the P.A.'s degree of certainty (whatever that number may be) is greater than someone else's degree of certainty, they should possess the empirical data to back that up, and do so, at minimum, to the degree that they are certain.

But of course, this entire declaration doesn't really address the point, it just makes a mockery of the debate. The god-believer is making a claim that his god exists *and* that this god never lies. Two claims for the price of one. So, these knowledge claims should have some evidence to demonstrate that they are true.

But, because the presuppositional apologist knows he has no such evidence, he covers up this fact by accusing the opposition of not having his special exempt-from-evidence type of hidden knowledge that only he and other believers possess. This is no better than saying, "Liar, liar, pants on fire!" The presuppositionalist's rapid reduction from initial "philosopher" status to playground bully is a rather stunning thing to witness.

"My world view is right because of the impossibility of the contrary!"

But a Christian presuppositional apologist is in no position to know the difference. The apologist's world view is littered with the impossible. Impossible miracles, talking donkeys and talking snakes, people being dead for a weekend and then coming back to life, people zipping off to "heaven" without a space suit, etc. All these things defy the laws of physics and are impossible. So, the presuppositional apologist expects people to accept the idea that the opposite of impossible is impossible? (!) But, that in itself is impossible. And absurd. The contrary of the impossible is what is *possible.* Therefore, it is quite possible, and most likely, that people did not rise from the dead, did not ascend into heaven, and performed no miracles.

And while we're on the subject of miracles... The P.A.'s beliefs regarding miracles amount to wishful thinking. Statements that their miracles are irrefutable are absurd. The fact is, you cannot refute that which has not met its burden of proof. And the P.A. has never made it that far in the debate.

The truth about "world views" is this: A world view does not have to be correct. It is simply, as one might suspect, an individual's "view of the world" – how one navigates through his or her own subjective view of reality. This world view can be labeled, defined, or delineated with specifics, as we see with these not-so-valiant attempts to do so by the Christian apologetic. But for the P.A., the claim that his world view is the valid or correct one, is simply an expansion, or extension, of the other god-claims he makes, and for which he is never able to meet his burden of proof. All human world views are alterable opinions, subjective by necessity. Therefore, to posit and then accept the concrete and immutable validity of one particular world view above all others, is to assert that facts aren't important. And that is not a good starting point for anyone claiming Truth with a capital "T."

"You use your reasoning to justify your reasoning!"

And so does the Christian. We all, theists and atheists alike, have no other choice. We are all readily aware that our senses are not always reliable and that our cognitive abilities are sometimes flawed.

So how can we know what we think we know is actually real? We could suppose that our entire life is just a long vivid dream, or a computer matrix program, or simply our own solipsistic imagination. Whatever it could be, we can and do know there are certain rules this dream, computer program, or imaginary existence follows. And you have no other choice but to follow those rules in any case. If gravity is just your imagination, or just some alien abductor's projection into your brain, it still works exactly the same from your perspective as it does for every other creature or being you encounter. Until you can peel off the façade of the matrix, the dream, or the imaginary existence, the physical rules of this reality remain universal. The operating system of the universe doesn't change on a whim.

This P.A. accusation of circularity is simply an effort to restate their initial premise that you could not even possess reasoning without a god running the universe – a bare assertion which does not meet its burden of proof. But, to make this clear, let's ask a few questions: How would the *absence of a god* make logic and reason impossible? In a universe without a god, what would we expect the conditions to be? What would a universe without a god look like? Can this be demonstrated? From the theist's perspective, how does understanding something make the *method* of understanding it automatically link to a god?

Any student of epistemology will tell you that understanding something is a process. It's getting from Point A to Point B. The Christian apologist asserts he knows what got him there without actually showing any real evidence of how he knows it. Using reasoning to understand reasoning may be circular, but internally so, within the context and confines of what is known. It is not an absolute. But Christian apologists want to make their position about a god an absolute when, ironically, they also need to use circular logic and reasoning to reach their conclusions.

To put this more succinctly, we must all *go with what we know* (those things that are reasonably certain), whether we want to or not. Possession of a "revelation," or belief in a particular deity does not negate this fact. The P.A. must justify his reasoning in the same manner as everyone else. To tell others "your method of reasoning is flawed," while at the same time coming to that conclusion using the exact same kind of flawed reasoning, is nothing less than absurdity, plus hypocrisy, times infinity.

"How do you know that?"

This question is the one asked most often of atheists by the presuppositional apologist. The purpose is to declare their original presupposition that to know anything you have to also know god. Throughout the entire discussion prior to this we've just been going around in circles, as directed by the presuppositional apologist's leading questions. You've tried to answer their questions, but you only get more questions and more bare assertions. At some point, the phrase "How do you know that?" is repeated by the presuppositional apologist to any statement you make. You could say, "My cat is gray," and the apologist will ask, "How do you know that?" The motive is to get you to admit that you really don't know *anything*, and *any* reason you give is invalid because it doesn't include their god.

Whether or not a non-believer knows anything about anything is completely irrelevant to the topic of how the presuppositional apologist is able to know for certain his god has revealed anything to him, or to anyone else. The presuppositionalist can be talking to a healthy man, a person that is comatose, a dog, or a brick wall, and what those things or persons know (or don't know) is irrelevant to what the apologist is claiming. Either the one presupposing a god can receive true revelations and know they are true, or he can't. Attempting to tear down the knowledge claims or beliefs of others won't automatically make their own claims true. An assertion, claim, premise, syllogism, or presupposition has to stand on its own merits, if it has any.

If presuppositional apologists must ask questions of the person they are addressing before they can demonstrate their god claim, it follows that the existence of this god is *other-person dependent.* That means, the god cannot exist without "correcting" the listener's opinion. If the god claim was demonstrable, it could exist on its own, without attacking any other person's world view. With this tactic, the P.A. demonstrates that their god exists only within the mind of the persuader, as a part of his own imagination.

If someone must rely on another person's answers to loaded questions in order to make the proto-evidence become evidence, the evidence is weak. The P.A. should start with the premise that even if no human existed to confirm their evidence, their evidence would still stand.

Of course, there is an additional hidden reason why the P.A. says "How do you know that?" again and again. It's partly due to non-believers, in their every-day world, encountering statements from deeply religious theists, such as "Jesus Christ is alive!" or, "God has prepared a place for you!" In these situations, the non-believer has consistently used this same line: "How do you know that?" And consistently, the believer has had no way to demonstrate that knowledge enough to satisfy any skeptic, because the only thing the believer brings to the table as evidence is old words – words which are spoken, written, hearsay, often contradictory, wildly extraordinary, and wholly unbelievable – especially in an increasingly more scientific world. Christians have decided to turn the tables on the skeptic. Or, so they imagine.

Thus, because the burden of proof, as always, remains in the hands of the believer, the atheist has no choice, but to turn the tables back, and ask the presuppositionalist once again, how he knows what he knows about his deity. And, naturally, you get the next line...

"God has revealed to me things in such a way that I can know it for certain!"

And we've come full-circle (again). In the above presuppositional apologist quote, several things are missing. We need to know what "reveal" means? How is this transmitted to the presuppositional apologist? Is this what is meant by "in such a way"? What are the specifics? And if you can assert that non-believers have no certainty, then why can't a presuppositional apologist have no certainty? We are all living on the same planet and have the same basic brains with access to the same books and information. Why does the presuppositional apologist believe he has obtained certainty? Because he asserts it to be so?

Now, if reality tells us that we cannot be absolutely certain about anything, including this statement, it does not give anyone a free pass to claim absolute certainty through their god. No one can be certain of their god or what he allegedly revealed to someone. We are all in the same boat of uncertainty no matter what we claim. To say, "God has revealed to us in such a way... etc." is still a statement which carries with it an undetermined *degree of certainty,* not absolute certainty. There is no escaping this. Doubt exists in all of humanity. It's the reality we live in.

Because of the presuppositionalist's known and admitted (and Biblically supported) imperfection and fallibility – that is, anything the presuppositionalist thinks, believes, or claims could be wrong – he cannot escape doubt. If he cannot escape doubt, he cannot claim certainty.

When challenged on this pivotal point, the P.A. will resort to the following...

"God Cannot Lie!"

This is just another unverifiable assertion, amongst the huge excess we've already encountered. A Christian apparently knows their god isn't lying simply because their god says he's not lying, which of course, could be a lie. But, the very assertion stating God cannot lie means he can *never* lie. Therefore, if humans *can* lie, but god cannot, humans can do something their god cannot do, and this automatically negates God's omnipotence. The question then follows, what else can God *not* do? Perhaps he cannot tell the truth?

The reality is this, and it applies to any source of truth: If a source of truth is validated only by itself, it could be a lie, and not a source of truth. There is no way for a human to know. And when dealing with an omniscient being, only another omniscient being could know the truth. And there are no omniscient human beings. Basically, the presuppositional apologist knows virtually nothing about his god, or whether any portion of that god's perceived "revelation" is true. In other words, *everything* he thinks he knows about his god could be wrong.

"You do not have the pre-conditions for knowledge!"

The foundation for human knowledge has already been shown to be consciousness inside a functioning brain. We *know* that works. But, it has never been shown that having a belief in a god is a pre-condition for anything other than membership in a religious group. It has never been demonstrated to be a pre-condition for knowledge.

There are conditions for knowledge, but to have a "pre-condition" for knowledge requires a presupposition. This "pre-condition" is considered normative for the presuppositional apologist view only. Yet, the *presupposer* has one big problem... none of the presuppositional apologist's arguments are sound.

At the outset, the apologist abuses the very definition of presupposition. A presupposition is an implicit assumption for which everyone can easily take for granted, such as: "The universe exists." The apologist's presuppositions do not pass the test. As history tells us, prior to the modern era, rarely was there a time when a god-claim was accepted as an implicit assumption without the use of bodily harm to anyone challenging that assumption. Simply put, the P.A.'s "presuppositions" aren't presuppositions by definition.

Additionally, if we take the apologist's presupposition that the "pre-condition for knowledge is God" just one-step further, we have to ask, what is the pre-condition for God himself?

"You have failed to refute what I'm saying by using a valid syllogism! You are irrational and your world view is false!"

A syllogism is not a path to truth in the sense that the P.A. wants to define truth. The P.A. looks for, and claims absolute certainty. But logic, as used and created by the ancient philosophers did not seek or claim that sort of truth at all. Truth, as logic sees it, is not absolute truth. It is not absolute certainty. Truth in logic is an attempt to find patterns in reason that can help determine if a proposition is true, but only in the sense that it is *correct*.

Using logic, anyone can write a syllogism about God being an invention of mankind. Such as:

1. Without Human Imagination, God cannot exist.
2. Human Imagination exists.
3. Therefore, God exists.

This means the pre-conditions for God is human imagination. Therefore, God is man-made. God is imaginary.

This, of course, has the same "absolute certainty" that the syllogism for God being the source of all knowledge, reason, or morals. This should be enough to demonstrate that syllogisms are not a pathway to absolute truth and were never intended to be such.

The accusation of irrationality has been demonstrated in the P.A.'s argument, not in the atheist's counter-argument. It is irrational for the apologist to ask for another syllogism to counter their own already failed god-syllogism. Doing so is completely irrelevant and unnecessary.

Let's ask ourselves this question... Which idea came first in the human mind, the concept of atheism or the concept of a god? (Hint: The one that came *first* in the human mind is the one that has the burden of proof. The other is the response to that first claim.) If they are opposing ideas, you won't have one without the other, but only one has to prove something because of its order of appearance.

The one that came first, of course, is the god concept. No cave man looked up at the stars one day and said, "You know what? I don't believe in gods!" How could he make such a statement if he had never imagined a god to begin with? How could he, if someone else had not first presented it to him? No one wakes up one day and says they don't believe in something they've never heard of. It's just not possible. And it's absurd.

This reality shows us two things: It shows us which side of the P.A. argument has the burden of proof (the theistic side), and it demonstrates how it is also impossible for humans to be born knowing a god exists. Millions of humans were born and died long before one of them decided gods were in charge of the universe. Someone had to invent a god before anyone else could worship that god.

We do not need a syllogism. We need the P.A. to prove their god exists. And, as we can see, that cannot be done on paper, or in a syllogism, or beyond the minds of those who wish it to be so.

"Can you fill a bucket with a pound of thoughts? No! Thoughts are immaterial!"

Quite often the P.A. will go off on tangents. This is one of them. And yes, actually, we *can* carry a pound of thoughts. In fact, we carry about three pounds of thoughts every day. This three pounds is the approximate weight of your own human brain – which should, if you're reading this, contain thoughts.

Unfortunately, the P.A. cannot adequately define "immaterial" as it pertains to his world view anyway, so their use of the word is meaningless. If you can't adequately define a word, how can you possibly label anything with that word? If one calls their god *immaterial,* without a reliable definition, then they can't define their god, and if they can't define their god, then when they say the word "god," they *literally* don't know what they're talking about.

The only things most P.A.'s can point to that could be called immaterial, by their own vague description(s), are words and abstract concepts in a human brain. That means, god is only a thought in someone's head, nothing more. He is equal to all other thoughts, like geometry, or Batman, or abstract art, or even a "crocoduck." Therefore, god *does* exist – but only as a concept. One can extract their god from their own brain by writing a description of him on a piece of paper, but still, that's not much of a god.

"You presuppose there is no god!"

Wrong. Most atheists are agnostic-atheists, meaning they simply reject the tenets presented by other people claiming there is a god, and do so because of the lack of evidence provided by those believers. Most atheists make no claims that there is no god. We only conclude that the god-claimant has not met his burden of proof.

"You are borrowing from my world view!"

This is just another one of the presuppositional apologist's fantasies, which has rudely sprung from their self-appointed pseudo-philosophy. If an atheist rejects the Christian world view, by definition, the atheist cannot be "borrowing" from it, no matter how many Bahnsens, Van Tils, or bombastic bloggers line up behind that accusation. One cannot borrow what they reject. And Christians do not have the patent or copyright on world views, knowledge, logic, morals, or certainty.

The reality is, the Bible-wielding apologist is borrowing from the rest of the world's world views. For example: Modern Christians think slavery is wrong. Why? Not because their moral lawgiver (God) suddenly told them to stop, but because the rest of the world surpassed the Old Testament God's morals and decided slavery was wrong. There are other examples of modern Christians borrowing their morals from the rest of humanity, which include, and are not limited to, how to treat rape victims. To make the claim that the world, or atheism in particular, borrows from the Christian apologist's world view is profoundly dishonest, if not mind-numbingly ignorant.

And of course, the P.A.'s core argument is through the use of syllogisms, presuppositions, axioms, the laws of logic, etc. Where exactly do they think these concepts came from? They are not outlined in their Bible. The basis of these ideas come from the ancient philosophers, the grand majority of which did *not* believe in their god. Just using the very process with which to argue their case, they are borrowing from a non-Biblical, secular world view.

The fact is, atheists know nothing about any god. And a Christian doesn't really know anything about a god either, so when a Christian does finally know *something*, he or she is the one who is actually borrowing from some other person's world view.

As stated, previously, logic is a tool, and it doesn't care who uses it. However, borrowing concepts from the secular world, and using them to claim others borrow from theirs, does nothing to move the debate forward.

"You use inductive reasoning, and I use deductive reasoning, therefore, I win!'

Human beings use inductive reasoning all the time and it works to get them through the day. It's a part of our reality. Inductive reasoning is simply taking a specific bit of information about one specific thing and then expanding that into a generalization about something else. Here's an example:

> We have found zero poisonous snakes in our region. We can assume that there are no poisonous snakes further out in areas that have a similar terrain.

When, at some point in the future, someone discovers a poisonous snake in the areas indicated, the above statement will be proven wrong, of course, but part of induction is the built-in assumption that such a discovery is possible.

However, when it comes to theistic beliefs, an atheist doesn't use inductive reasoning. No inductive argument or claim is being made. We aren't saying, "We've looked for a god, and so far haven't found one..." We aren't actually looking for one. We simply reject the god-claimant's beliefs due to a lack of evidence. Plain and simple. Furthermore, the deductive reasoning of the god-believer has never been shown to be sound or demonstrated to be valid. The atheist awaits both, and will cheerfully accept them as a part of reality when the criteria have been met.

"You're a naturalist! That means you believe..."

Wait a minute. Who said all atheists were naturalists? Some atheists believe in supernatural things like ghosts, and ESP. They just don't believe in a god. Again, this is the presuppositional apologist erecting a straw man, trying to label the atheist's rejection of their god-claims as a "world view." Atheism is not a world view and will never be one. It can only be a *part* of someone's world view.

This is just another annoying attempt by the P.A. to label some other person's views before such views have even been stated.

"What is your *standard* for morality, (knowledge, logic, etc.)"

This question is tossed about because the presuppositional apologist knows most people have never really thought about it before, and it's a convenient way to catch people off guard. And it's a way for the presuppositional apologist to boldly declare that he gets *his* standard from his very specifically delineated, albeit, capricious god, a standard for which he is strangely proud.

From the outset, such a question is absurd and redundant. We have already shown that certain knowledge is absolute, perfect, objective knowledge. It's something the P.A. desperately wants, but can't have. No one can. To have it, we would have to be omniscient. The P.A. thinks he has a pipeline to omniscience through his god. Yet this is impossible because any revelation he receives, no matter how it's transmitted, is going into his own fallible, limited, brain – a brain which is *not* omniscient and therefore cannot verify that the transmission it is receiving from the alleged omniscient being is true. The P.A. knows this, but insists that the one transmission he is getting is truth anyway. Because perfect knowledge is not attainable, perfect morals cannot be attained either, because to have a moral absolute would also require perfect knowledge.

For non-believers, our standard for logic, morality, knowledge, and everything else comes from reality. For more on this, see the next, similar question...

"Where is your definition of truth?"

The P.A. uses absolutes and claims absolute truth, and attempts to do this via logic. Yet logic does not deal with truth in the absolute sense. Somehow the P.A. has missed this important fact.

So what is truth?

Truth is information that is correct. It follows that anything that is correct can be verified and tested for its correctness. This is something the presuppositional apologist should apply to the "truths" about their god. Can they be tested?

At the risk of oversimplifying the argument, let's take a look at the difference between presuppositional apologetics and atheism as it pertains to reality. In the end, the P.A. cannot test the reality of any single thing he claims regarding his god. Atheists, who reject those claims for that very reason, live in a world where the actions they take daily *can* be tested. This means that because whatever the apologist claims, asserts, writes, contemplates, wishes, thinks, preaches, or ponders about his god cannot be tested, there is no valid reason to assume the god they refer to is a part of reality. Atheists test their world to find their reality, and though subjective, imperfect, and never absolute, it is still a part of the reality we all share.

"Can you teach me the laws of logic? You can't unless you already know them!"

The presuppositional apologist is attempting to show that "logic" comes from his god without having to go through the step of proving his god exists first. This is another leading question designed to "prove" that the laws of logic, which the P.A. deems as immutable and forever in existence throughout the universe, are imbedded in the soul of each individual by their god, even before birth. The possibility that logic could have been a discovery, made through the progressive evolution of a sentient human mind, is almost blasphemy.

The Christian apologist forgets that he has a self-proclaimed "unchangeable" god that changes constantly, and who, even if he did not change, is apparently omnipotent and *could* change anything on a whim. He could even change the laws of logic, rendering invalid the argument that those laws are "eternal." If the laws of logic are dependent upon an omnipotent god, how could they be immutable and eternal? The absurdity of the apologist's argument is obvious. We know the laws of logic (as we describe them, use them, and perceive them in our universe), do not change, and therefore those laws are not dependent upon any god. From this alone, we could presuppose that there is *no* god.

"My world view can account for the Uniformity of Nature! And yours can't!"

The uniformity of nature, as used by science, is the concept that things in the future will be consistent with things in the past. This scientific device is based on inductive reasoning, and the P.A. likes to point that out when making this assumption, the conclusions *could* be very wrong. They say this despite the fact that science, in making this assumption, has been astonishingly accurate time and time again, and despite the fact that induction allows for error.

The P.A. will further state that if the uniformity of nature *does* exist, only their world view can account for it – having things in the future be consistent with things in the past is the work of their god, so they say. But, beware! Their god could wipe it all out by tomorrow morning! (So much for uniformity!) While denouncing science for using uniformity as a basis for hypotheses (through inductive reasoning), they will often switch sides and claim it for their own, as long as God is included as a part of that uniformity.

The P.A. will argue that if the non-believer viewed the uniformity of nature honestly, he or she would have to admit they could never really know for certain if the future will be the same as the past without a god to guide the universe. For example, a P.A. will claim that within the alleged "atheist world view of randomness," non-believers cannot be certain that their car won't magically turn into a pumpkin by tomorrow morning. And yet, such things never happen, and the non-believer's world remains basically the same, just like the believer's. Ironically, if science, or human beings in their daily lives, could not rely on the uniformity of nature, then no one could make a statement about anything at all. No one could ever know anything. And that "anything" would have to include religious ideas as well.

If the uniformity of nature, without a god, is the realm of the atheist, skeptic, or scientist, then constant unpredictability must be the world of the god-believer. Things falling out of place, or defying the laws of nature and physics is the expectation of the believer, not the non-believer. Atheists don't claim miracles happen, believers do. The P.A., with his anticipation of potential miracles, cannot know whether the future will resemble the past. An interventionist god could change things in an instant. In such a world, the P.A., with a god who predicts the dead will no longer be dead, or that stars will fall from heaven, is in no position to know much of anything about uniformity, and could hardly be expected to define it for anyone else.

By claiming miracles that defy the laws of physics, the P.A. is not actually claiming the uniformity of nature for his side, but rather advocating for a *non*-uniformity of nature. Non-uniformity of nature *could* imply a god because it implies a destructive force, one that would defy, alter, or even destroy the laws of physics and nature. Such a model requires a creator, simply because it demands that you cannot have one (a destructive force) without the other (a creative force), even though these two forces could have the same author (a god). And yet, whether he realizes it or not, this non-uniformity is precisely what the P.A.'s position infers, even though within the real world we never experience nor observe such *non*-uniformity.

Up to this point we can see how having doubts about all observed reality doesn't contribute much to the conversation, and the proposed alternative – believing in ancient unproven texts instead of that observed reality – does even less.

The biggest problem the P.A. has with the uniformity of nature is that it works. And the non-uniformity of nature (the anticipation and expectation of physics-defying miracles) does not. From this we can conclude that the uniformity of nature implies the Primacy of Existence model – the Universe is what it is – it contains consistency and uniformity within itself, and as such, does not presuppose or necessitate a designer whatsoever.

"Your argument is viciously circular!"

If so, how does that make the Christian theistic argument true, right or correct? Admittedly, sometimes circular reasoning is unavoidable. Science, for example, uses the scientific method to judge the scientific method, and that's circular reasoning. But, because science cannot be proven inductively by empirical evidence alone, we have something called *falsification*. Falsification, in the scientific method, is another term for the ability for which something can be tested. Additionally, science is not a tool to determine absolute certainty. It simply establishes the best current explanations for evidence at hand.

But, can we test anyone's theory about the existence of an invisible, other-dimensional, immaterial god? We cannot, obviously. Therefore, within the presuppositional argument for a god, no falsification is possible, therefore we can dismiss the circular reasoning about a god as unworthy of consideration. In other words, there is no justified reason to believe anything that has no evidence, proof, or testability.

The P.A. can use any kind of reasoning or logic he desires. But, as we mentioned before, the premises must be true and the conclusions must be sound for any consideration to move forward. In addition, we have already shown how deductive reasoning through classical logical concepts is not a pathway to the absolute truth the apologist claims.

Can the presuppositional argument get any worse? Well, yes it can...

"You have a chance world view and cannot account for _____!"

The blank could be anything (reality, knowledge, counting, breathing, pooping, etc.), but this is a setup to presuppose a god, and is simply another presuppositional apologist talking point, and it has nothing to do with real philosophy (or reality).

The assertion that atheists have a "chance" (often substituted as "random") world view, is nothing more than a straw man argument, and an argument from ignorance. The word "chance" actually implies possibility, not probability. And probability is what most atheists use to determine their system of belief.

The other word the P.A. uses, *randomness,* means a lack of predictability. Can we predict the outcome of anything in the universe? Perhaps. But, what *can* be predicted vs. what we are *able* to predict are very different. We are limited in our knowledge, so our ability to predict outcomes is limited. Knowing every variable in a possible outcome would make us able to predict things rather efficiently. But none of us has achieved omniscient status yet.

Fortunately, we do know, even with our limited subjective view of the universe, what appears random may not be random at all. Often, we simply do not have enough information to make a proper assessment. The fact that things *may* have order, does not imply that they *came* from order. Order can come from chaos, and chaos can come from order. Therefore, no designer can be implied or known from either scenario.

Without getting into evolution (which is *not* random) or astrophysics, or quantum mechanics, we can plainly see that the accusation is merely a feeble attempt at chopping off someone else's legs to make themselves look taller.

Living under the specter of a god who could change the entire world tomorrow, alter the laws of physics in an instant, and bring the whole universe to a stand-still, means that if there is anyone living within the bounds of a "chance" or "random" world view, it is the presuppositional apologist and anyone who believes in such a wildly capricious god.

"You know God exists! You're just suppressing your knowledge of him!"

Yes, atheists are suppressing this knowledge in the same way we all secretly know Elvis is still alive.

Sure. God exists. On the pages of books. And in the minds of men. And that's where it ends.

Little green men from Mars, the Yeti, the Loch Ness Monster, the chupacabra, and Hitler living past 100, all exist in those same places. Yet, these last few mentioned have a better chance of being demonstrated to be real than the god that Christians insist others refuse to acknowledge.

If the Christian god was an *innate knowledge* for all humans, you would see millions of Muslims, Sikhs, Hindus, Jews, and people from all religions, of all ages, suddenly converting to Christianity out of the blue, and do so without ever needing another Christian to tell them about Christianity. But, what we actually see is Christians begetting Christians, Muslims begetting Muslims, Jews begetting Jews, Hindus begetting Hindus, and so on. And the vast majority of those people remain as such their entire lives. There isn't ever a spontaneous combustion of the Holy Spirit waking up the alleged innate knowledge of the Christian god in those that know very little about Christianity. It simply does not happen. You need missionaries for that.

With this newest bare assertion from the P.A., we can refer back to **The Flaw of Suppressed Knowledge.** Tacking on this unfounded presupposition to an already non-falsifiable (and nonsensical) one about the existence of an unproven, inaccessible god is either the height of arrogance or the depth of ignorance. It is acutely necessary that the apologist demonstrate the first one before adding the second. The addition of more presuppositions to the original presupposition actually *weakens* the P.A. argument rather than enhances it.

One additional comment should be made on this point. The presuppositional apologist's view is refuted within the same Bible that they claim announces its validity:

> In flaming fire, taking vengeance on *them that know not God,* and that obey not the gospel of our Lord Jesus Christ: Who shall be punished with everlasting destruction from the presence of the Lord, and from the glory of his power... – (*2 Thessalonians 1:8-9 KJV*) [Emphasis Added]

Apparently, the infallible Bible made a boo-boo. It clearly states that there *are* people who "know not God," thus contradicting, and rendering useless, any preposterous claim that no such human exists.

"My Axiom Proves I'm Right!"

You can call it an axiom, you can call it an assertion, you can call it a presupposition, or you can call it Uncle Dave. It really doesn't matter. Such a statement, in whichever of these forms it takes, if it is to be used as a starting point for reasoning, still has to be something that yields no controversy, and no challenge. It must be something that the people concerned with what you say can take as a given – as self-evident. When has Christianity ever existed in such a privileged state? Of course, the answer is never. This is true for any god claims.

The fact that Christians, and other theists, want to get a free pass on this requirement through *special pleading,* simply demonstrates their own awareness of the fact that they cannot prove anything whatsoever about their god-claims. Once again, with every argument, every protest, every declaration by the theist, it gets back to this one basic necessity: You must prove your god claims. Prove your knowledge assertions about this thing, or re-declare what you really possess – beliefs and only beliefs. *Beliefs without any evidence.* In another word, *faith.*

"My beliefs are justified true beliefs!"

At some point, if the tables have been turned sufficiently enough that most of the conversation has the P.A. talking about his own position instead of haranguing about everyone else's, the P.A. will state that their god claims are "justified true beliefs." This is part of the standard script used by most P.A.'s. Yet, most don't understand what the world *justified* means. Justification requires at least some verification, and they have already demonstrated their inability to provide any at all. In the absence of actual justification, the phrase, "justified true belief" rings hollow, and we are back to the beginning, having now come full circle on this laboriously lumbering and broken merry-go-round.

"Have you ever lied or been lied to?"

This is the final interrogative in their attempt to lead you to their conversion speech. It's a final gasp. It gets deep into why lying is a sin and why you're destined for hell, etc. However, the presuppositional apologist should be asked this same question as well. And this brings us back to the possibility, that if their god is real, he could be lying. (And we can refer back to the presuppositional apologist's vacant assertion that **"God Cannot Lie!"** See further up.)

"There is no proof or evidence that will ever be sufficient for you atheists!"

This is said by the P.A. when he (finally) realizes he cannot meet his burden of proof. But, of course, his declaration is wrong. There are plenty of ways the P.A. could bring evidence to the table. Physical evidence of any miracle in the Bible would help. Of course, this gets us into evidentiary apologetics, which is another world where Christians attempt to use paper as evidence. We won't go into that here. But, suffice to say, physical evidence of any kind would be the extraordinary evidence an atheist requires.

One other way, of course, is for this "immaterial" god to appear to us. Certainly, if we go by the Bible, which the P.A. insists we do, asking for Jesus to appear is not a problem. Anything you ask, according to the Bible, can and will be done, like any magic genie would provide. (James 1:5) And certainly, Jesus appearing to people after his resurrection means if he did it once, he can do it again. The Bible says he did so to several persons after his alleged reanimation. (John 20:11-17) And, should we really doubt the abilities of an all-powerful god? Appearing to anyone should be easy for such an entity. And, because this god claims he wants everyone to be saved, appearing to atheists should be top priority for him. (1 Timothy 2:3-4) So, we leave it up to the P.A. to help in giving us this appearance. They should be obeying their Master's Voice and praying night and day for him to appear to atheists, for the goal and command of the follower of Christ is to convert others.

The Debate is Over

After going around and around in circles with the P.A.'s insistence upon destroying other people's beliefs in an effort to prop up his own, we find ourselves back at square one. There really is no need to argue further, as the P.A., from the start, has never met his burden of proof. But, now that we understand the tactics, the circularity, and the motive, we can more easily deal with such arguments in the future.

Let's take a breath and review....

Presuppositionalist Contradictions

Now, we can review some of the P.A.'s misguided thoughts for a moment. There are numerous contradictions throughout the P.A. argument, but here are the ones that matter most:

- The P.A. refuses to justify presuppositions, but claims his presuppositions are *justified true beliefs*. This is a contradiction.

- The P.A. admits to being limited, but claims to be able to identify, with absolute certainty, a limitless being. This is a contradiction.

- The P.A. claims knowledge of revelation while simultaneously rejecting human ability to reason as a basis for *knowing anything*. This is a contradiction.

To put it another way, the P.A. claims human reason alone is not sufficient to justify *any* beliefs to be true, then claims certain knowledge of some specific truth. The P.A.'s core claim is a contradiction. If human infallibility is truly universal, there can be no exception to this rule, and no special revelation which is transmitted to that universally fallible mind can be regarded as an absolute truth. A fallible mind cannot know if a revelation is a truth or a lie. And a magical god giving a brain a moment of infallible understanding of truth cannot be falsified any more than the magical god itself can be falsified.

These contradictions reveal how the P.A. refuses to acknowledge the logical impossibility of a restricted, fallible, human justifying, or even identifying, something as omniscient without the necessity of invoking faith alone.

The presuppositional apologist fails to admit that *claiming* knowledge of something isn't enough in the real world – you have to actually *have* it.

Summary of the P.A. Conversational Agenda:

- To immerse themselves in metaphysics and ignore everything that came after it, including modern science, the scientific method, and the concept of falsification.

- To employ dishonest debate tactics, such as asking leading questions again and again, in an attempt to misdirect and control the conversation.

- To have at the ready, a preconceived notion of any other person's world view, and to blatantly declare that whatever it is, it's the opposite of their own, and the "wrong" one.

- To attempt in every possible way to shift their own burden of proof away from themselves to whomever they can, and to deny they even have a burden of proof.

- To borrow logical concepts from the secular world, and then accuse their opponent of borrowing them from theirs.

- To swear that those borrowed logical concepts they use, when challenged, or shown to be fallacious, don't apply to them or their world view.

- To deliberately confuse and intertwine the concepts of *belief* and *knowledge*, using the definitions of these words as if they were one and the same, and stating their beliefs as claims of certainty.

Please note, these are the common tactics of the average Christian apologist preacher, teacher, and counselor that is prevalent in North America today. There are other more lucid, erudite, and thoughtful apologists who will discuss these concepts in a rational way, but they are currently few and far between.

The Proper Way to Discuss Apologetics with a Presuppositional Apologist

Here's what the P.A. must do to satisfy the non-believer:

1. The P.A. should offer his best syllogism, presupposition, axiom, or other statement regarding his god-claim.

2. The P.A. must then define "God." Who or what is the P.A. talking about? The definition should be understood by all parties to the discussion.

3. The P.A. must acknowledge his burden of proof. He must be made aware that his presupposition, axiom, or other statements about his defined god, requires that the P.A. and the P.A. *only*, provide the adequate evidence or proof that the god he is claiming is actually a part of reality. The P.A. must do this *without* asking the listener any questions whatsoever. If the P.A. insists on asking questions, it follows that the existence of

the god must be dependent upon the listener's existence, or is dependent upon what the listener thinks. If so, the god-claim cannot include an omniscient god, and the P.A. should start over.

4. In the very likely *absence* of the P.A. meeting his or her burden of proof for a god-claim, the discussion is over. There is no need to go any further. There is little reason, beyond verbal entertainment, to continue a discussion about a thing that cannot be shown to be a part of reality.

For anyone new to atheism, it's imperative to have a way to counter the P.A. agenda without having to go through a long worn out verbal blitzkrieg. The non-believer should use the following, or some semblance thereof, when a presuppositional apologist attempts to corner him or her in a one-sided debate. It should go something like this...

> "I am obligated by the rules of the logical concepts you use – which you borrow from the secular world view, (because they cannot be found in the Bible) – to *not* answer any of your questions about my world view until after you have first defined the object (God) in your premise, and demonstrated the existence of that object. Your god-concept is an extraordinary claim and requires extraordinary evidence. As such, it should stand on *its own* merits, have *its own* evidence, *its own* proofs, and it should be easily explained without any attempts at understanding or misunderstanding the world views of any other person on earth. I make no claims. I remain silent. I wait for your burden of proof to be met..."

CONCLUSION:
NOTHING FROM NOTHING LEAVES NOTHING

The presuppositional apologist hates to think that all he really has is *faith.* He wants to claim *knowledge,* but can't. And he has a tough time understanding the difference between the two.

We can safely say that believing in something doesn't make it real, and not believing it does not negate its possibility. But, to pick your world view based first on what it comfortably concludes, rather than determining your world view by gathering the facts based what you know to a reasonable certainty, is inherently blind and capricious. However, this is exactly the course taken by the Christian apologist.

When all is said and done, the only thing believers in deities have is assertions. It's one assertion piled up on top of another assertion. No evidence, just talk. Just hearsay. It's written down? Still hearsay. If you're a religious person, you start out with a "creator" of everything. Then you tell everyone you know where he lives. Then you assert what he's made of. Then you claim to know what he thinks. Then you are certain you know what he said. Finally, you assert you know what he's going to do in the future.

But in reality, it comes down to this – the true believer has virtually *nothing*. An argument or presupposition isn't proof or knowledge. Rationalizing yourself into a paper bag full of god assertions isn't evidence either. God-claims can only arrive at *nothing*. And, according to believers, something cannot come from *nothing*. So, if that's true, no god can ever come out of an argument made from *nothing*.

When analyzed carefully, the P.A. doesn't actually have a world view. He has *an obscured view of the world.* He has placed the blinders on his own eyes by throwing imagination, delusion, and stubbornness into his field of vision, and has done so with very little justification.

By contrast, the non-believer's position is consistent because it acknowledges the imperfection of the subjective view of the universe that each human has, while also acknowledging the perfection of the objective universe existing as a whole. The universe is perfect in its own way, and we view it through a limited lens. Through this lens (our minds and bodies) we see consistency in the universe, but we can't see all of the universe. This is why we are only partially right about things – because we have a partial view. This reality applies to everyone whether they acknowledge it or not.

The bottom line is this: You cannot assert your god into existence. You cannot philosophize, presuppose, preach, pray, hope, wish, or write your god into existence either. If you could, it would be one hell of a magic trick. That, or by default, you would be your own god's god.

And as with all theological arguments, the circle always comes back around to the theist having to prove his god exists when he makes a knowledge claim about that god. And it's a responsibility he quickly shirks as he slithers back into the shadows and returns later to say "All you really need is faith" – meaning, no evidence is provided, so no evidence is necessary. So, what were those claims of "I *know* God exists" all about?

A Final Word

Christian presuppositional apologists are the lost souls of Christianity, trying to prove their god's existence on paper, as if the paper their own Bible is written on is not enough, and they need more.

Jesus never used syllogisms. He either ignored, or was unaware of, classical Greek logic. If he existed in any form, and was versed in such concepts, he must have felt these sorts of arguments unnecessary, even if his modern-day followers think otherwise and work counter to his message.

Christian theists who use classical Greek logical concepts will have to choose between the triumvirate of Socrates, Plato, and Aristotle – or Jesus. It's up to them. Concern yourself with proving something on paper, or concern yourself with compassion, empathy, love, and the physical welfare of your fellow man. For both the secular world view and the Christian world view, it's the only choice that matters.

CHAPTER SIX

Yahweh and The Old Testament

"The God of the Old Testament is arguably the most unpleasant character in all fiction: jealous and proud of it; a petty, unjust, unforgiving control-freak; a vindictive, bloodthirsty ethnic cleanser; a misogynistic, homophobic, racist, infanticidal, genocidal, filicidal, pestilential, megalomaniacal, sadomasochistic, capriciously malevolent bully." – Richard Dawkins, *The God Delusion*

"Yahweh or the Highway!" – Stephen Colbert

WHOLLY, HOLEY, HOLY SCRIPTURES?

Holy scriptures are the sacred, venerated, sacrosanct, admired, sanctioned, honored and revered written works associated with the god of a particular religion. And those are just a few of the adjectives we could associate with the officially approved texts of most religions in the world.

But, no matter what they are called, or how they are described, the one thing we must acknowledge again and again is that Bibles, Torahs, Qur'ans, and other holy writings are the *claim* regarding a god, not the *evidence* for a god. (We would not make this statement so boldly if we were discussing things that were not supernatural, or if they contained the words written by the self-assigned prophets or messiahs themselves.) When you read any group's holy book, for the most part, you are not looking at hard evidence, you are looking at a compendium of divergent claims. Evidence on paper should at least be written contemporaneous to the claim, and if it isn't, the evidence will have to be outside of that claim and overwhelming. As astronomer Carl Sagan once said, "Extraordinary claims require extraordinary evidence."

The religious zealot will try to conflate these two (claims and evidence) by stating that his claim (the scripture itself) is the evidence. The true-believer will even go so far as to state that his claim is *self-evident.* But, we all know, words on a page are just words on a page. And when it comes to words on a page, there really isn't anything that is self-evident.

Worshiping the Bible (and other holy books)

Pointing out a flaw or contradiction, in the Bible or Qur'an, to a true believer in deities is probably the quickest way to anger said believer. You can make any kind of terse and foul remark about the god itself, but saying that the holy script is convoluted, contradictory, confusing, or flat out wrong, is grounds for expulsion from planet earth. What these scripture bouncers, or Word of God police, don't quite see is that they are *de facto* worshiping the words themselves rather than their god. They are putting preference for the sanctity, the holiness, and the accuracy of those words ahead of the deity that those words reference. It has not occurred to them that the words about their god could be false, but the god's existence could still be true. For the believer, the holy writ *must* be linked to the holy god, or the holy god somehow disappears.

As (the alleged to exist) Socrates said: "A text can't respond to a question; it will just keep saying the same thing over and over again, no matter how often it is refuted."

And this is why atheists are quite certain gods *do* exist outside the imagination of mankind – but only on paper.

The Future: A Papyrus-less Society

Imagine being accused of murdering your neighbor. You're hauled off to court to stand trial and your defense attorney tells you he has a fantastic, amazing, unbelievable way to get you acquitted. So, you ask him what it is, and he shows you a piece of paper. Written on this paper are the words, "He didn't do it." You look at him aghast. "That's all you've got?!" you scream. You're justifiably angry. "That's all I need." he replies. You ask, "Where did you get it and who wrote it?" He says, "I found it, and I don't know who wrote it, but it looks pretty old, so I believe it must be a prediction from the past, and based of the neat handwriting, it was written by a very wise man. It's a prediction that you and I would be standing here one day and I could use this to get you acquitted!"

You'd think he was crazy, right? And you'd fire him on the spot. But, this is the same amount of "evidence" that the Bible, Qur'an, and other holy books have for their gods, and the sellers of these books expect you and everyone else to accept them without critical thinking. They have pieces of paper, written long ago, by supposedly wise men, telling you something that in many cases is irrelevant to your life. And in cases where it could be relevant, it is often immoral, and in cases where it definitely *is* relevant, you could have discovered that relevance through any number of other sources. And none of it gives any real evidence for a god's existence. To put it bluntly, a piece of paper is just a piece of paper. It doesn't *do* anything.

"But, atheists are taking things out of context..."

The biggest complaint believers have about non-believers is that atheists are "taking things out of context" – meaning that atheists are misinterpreting or misrepresenting what the holy writ really means. However, when you step back from the debate and look at the Big Picture, you will see that it's actually believers who are taking things out of context, especially if the context is reality.

All religious claims (which includes all holy texts) can be criticized and even ridiculed at any level, and to any degree, within the context of reality. This is obviously due to the fact that the claimants have zero evidence for their claims. Therefore, "taking things out of context" is quite irrelevant for the critic, if not rather audacious hypocrisy on the part of the believer. There is a valid reason why some people ridicule others who think Elvis Presley is still alive, or who think Sasquatch is a real creature, and it all comes back to a lack of credible evidence.

As critics of unfounded claims, we are allowed to take anything we desire "out of context." For example, if someone claimed the earth was a cube, and was subsequently challenged and ridiculed for that statement, and further, as critics, we had to look at this claim within the "proper context" of a parallel universe, we would have to demand evidence for that parallel universe. And without evidence, we would have no reason to believe the claim, and every reason to deride or dissect the claim in any manner we chose. This is the same for all holy writings. The claimant should show evidence, or stop making the claim.

Having said that, we will attempt most often, for reasons of clarity, to keep our criticisms within the context of a religious narrative fantasy (in this case, the Bible). However, it will be necessary to point out that while religionists themselves have great difficulty discerning proper context (often deliberately obfuscating facts), such an expectation from critics is a bit irrational, if not disingenuous.

Staking the Claims and Making Them Stick

The most important thing to do, before we look at whether or not there really is a "Moral Lawgiver" (in this case, Yahweh), as proposed by Christians, Muslims, Jews, and other followers of a single all-powerful deity, is to study the actual (alleged) behavior and interaction of this entity with human beings.

To do this, we will need to first look at the Old Testament Bible and what it claims God (Yahweh) actually did, said, condemned or condoned.

This examination will concern itself with mostly the Christian view. The Muslim view, and to a lesser degree the Jewish view of God, will be addressed in other chapters. We do this because Islam does not have the entire Old Testament as a part of the Qur'an (although it references its content and supports many of its tenets). And, Judaism has other writings such as the Talmud, that attempt to support the Old Testament (also known as the Tanakh). This additional scripture helps Judaism interpret, or reinterpret, what the Tanakh allegedly means. Having these extra-Biblical sources helps Judaism, as much as Christians *not* having them hurts Christianity. Yet, how much any sort of after-the-fact interpretation helps or hurts either one is irrelevant for this discussion. What we will be perusing is the exact wording of what we will call the 'middle ground' between Judaism and Islam – and for the Western world, the majority version of this god – the Christian Old Testament Bible. We will set aside Talmudic and Qur'anic references, for now. After all, when reading any novel, or even a book of non-fiction, should we go by what someone else says about that book? Or, should we simply read the actual words of the book ourselves and make our own judgment?

To do that, we will introduce the God of the Old Testament by dividing his narrative into four parts: A Desert War God Arises, The Actions of Yahweh, An Analysis of Yahweh, and The Laws and Commands of Yahweh.

A DESERT WAR GOD ARISES

Who is Yahweh?

Yahweh is the great and only god of the Jews, Christians, and Muslims, but you could easily find large populations of believers in all three that would tell you the other two branches of these religions are not actually worshiping Yahweh, or they're doing it all wrong. Of course, the name(s) of Yahweh, depending on which religion you ascribe to, or even which denomination of religion you adhere to, is different for each group. For Muslims, he's Allah. For Jews, it's Adonai, or HaShem – not actually names, but names of reverence, because within Judaism, you're not allowed to speak or even write the name Yahweh (because something bad might happen if you do). For Christians, it's God, or Lord, or Jehovah, or Jesus, and various other ethereal epithets.

All of this is rather superfluous, as we shall see, because how Yahweh is used and seen in modern times is a bit different than it was way back when Yahweh was first discovered.

The Invisibility Cloak

This new god, Yahweh, really was different from all the rest. He was invisible. He was the unseen god, a spirit god, incorporeal and supernatural with no physical body, but possessing all power, and all knowledge. Although this invisibility, along with other attributes such as singularity and omnipresence, developed over time (with an early version of Yahweh only being visible as pillars of smoke, burning bushes, etc.), the idea of an intangible, wholly invisible god was quite revolutionary, at least in the minds of primitive man.

The Sudden "Appearance" of Yahweh the Great

The ancient archeological record, with the epigraphy therein, shows no sign of a Yahweh until the end of the Bronze Age and the beginning of the Iron Age which is, at its earliest, around 1400 BCE. For all intents and purposes, prior to this, Yahweh simply didn't exist! He's only been around for approximately 3400 years. If the earth is only 6000 years old, as creationists claim, then who were humans worshiping for the 2600 years before Yahweh showed up? Why is there a history of humans on earth that is older than the god they worship?

Many creationists continue to argue for 17th Century Irish Archbishop James Ussher's contention that the Exodus of the Hebrews from Egypt occurred around 3500 years ago. According to the Bible, those same Hebrews had been worshiping Yahweh for a minimum of 430 years prior to the Exodus – the duration of their enslavement in Egypt (and before). So, let's do the math... 3500 + 430 = 3930 years ago. Archaeological sources, however, show that Yahweh became a god much later, at around 3400 years ago, at the earliest. How is it possible for any tribe to worship an unknown god for 500 years before anyone, including the Hebrews themselves, had ever heard of him?

More recent creationists, called Young Earth Creationists, have revised Ussher's calculations, and have increased the estimate for the earth's age to as much as 10,000 years ago. This, of course, allows for even more humans to be born and die without ever knowing anything about the Yahweh-god who created them.

(It's important to note that no matter how you do the math, accurate or otherwise, none of it demonstrates that Yahweh is real. A religious believer's calculations lining up with an archaeologist's assessment regarding when human beings first acknowledged Yahweh as a deity, does not magically invoke that deity into reality.)

However, it is nothing less than astounding how much importance has been placed on a god that was completely, absolutely, irrefutably unknown to the entire world until about 1400 BCE, and then, in the beginning, only as a lesser war god in a pantheon of other Semitic Middle Eastern (specifically Canaanite) gods. Yahweh, with his female consort, Asherah, rose to power in the Middle East, in part, because his followers killed, via total genocide, anyone who didn't follow him. For example, if you cannot find anyone alive who believes in Hathor, and you know all of Hathor's followers have been ethnically cleansed from the region, Hathor naturally died with them. It's one of the ruthless ways gods can die, and how rival gods survive.

Had the followers of Moloch (or Chemosh) had better war strategies, better weapons, or perhaps had more psychopathic leaders than the ancient Israelites, the Bible you read today might be all about Moloch, or some other currently insignificant, or unknown god. History is written by the victors and credit for that victory always goes to the winner's god. Yahweh, apparently, was blessed with a string of brutal victories and became a dominant force in the minds of the Iron Age tribes of the day, at least for a time.

Numerous decades later, when Yahweh began to lose his battles on the ground, he began to shrink into the pages and scrolls of ancient texts as simply *bigger* than all this petty fighting, quickly becoming a god of the entire universe, one who was suddenly concerned as much with your soul and moral stature as he was with a restoration of nationhood. This would later transform into almost no concern for nationality, and instead, a fanatical concern for the soul, culminating with the fast-growing personality/death cult of Christianity, leaving the old version of Yahweh still stuck within the pages of the ancient scrolls, no longer able to free himself enough to do the special, *high-end production value* miracles for his chosen people.

Later, as Yahweh slept beneath the soft pages of the Jewish Tanakh, his neglected and illegitimate children would eventually fray into broken strands of belief, including the cultish angry fanaticism of Islam, the suicidal gullibility of the People's Temple in Guyana, and the bizarre paranoia of the Branch Davidians, just to name a few. However, with all tragedies aside, to understand Yahweh fully, we need to understand, not only how, but *why* he evolved...

Fifty Shades of God

As stated earlier, in order to get a better picture of the Yahweh character, you have to go back to the believers' preferred source – the Bible. But this raises the question as to why are there so many texts outside the Bible to explain the Bible? Why are holy words not sufficient enough to understand what was being said? Should the text itself, if wondrous, holy, and correct, need someone to explain what it "really" means?

There is a valid reason why Jews don't study the Torah only, and it's because Judaism has numerous other sources which define and defend Yahweh's actions, such as the *mefarshim* through the Mishnah, the Gemara, and the Midrash. It could be said that within Orthodox Judaism, over-analysis is a way of life. And, when it comes to Yahweh, the real reason for such over-analysis is this...

Yahweh is a terrible god, and that is not a reference to his power, but to his job performance. For Jews, it is essential to have these other sources, to tone down Yahweh's constant need to over-do everything, and for the learned to rationalize his numerous mistakes. This process is, on some level, admirable. The last thing we need is someone actually taking too many of Yahweh's misadventures and bizarre rules and rituals too *literally*. That's where the other two main branches of the Yahweh cult come into play...

Christianity, the first orphan of Judaism, doesn't have the benefit of the same pre-Christian extra-Biblical writings that Jews have. Yahweh looks kind of evil at first glance, so Christians draw on the New Testament for solace and quickly declare that all that stuff in the "Old" Testament no longer applies because Yahweh's son came down from the heavens and fixed everything. And, besides, it's not about your body any more, it's all about your soul. It's no big deal if the unchanging god decided to change things, right? And this is why, for Christians, most extra-Biblical writings are about Jesus, not Yahweh.

(One interesting side note is the schizophrenic attitude Christians possess about the Old Testament. Any Christian will tell you that the Old Testament laws no longer apply to the Christian, yet these are the same people that insist the Ten Commandments be displayed in public buildings in the U.S., as if they have no clue that the Ten Commandments, in their entirety, are in the Old Testament *only*. If the Old Testament laws no longer apply, then why display these few? Christians should be the first in line to demand their removal, declaring loudly that Jesus took their place!)

...Let's get back to Yahweh. Muslims believe in him too. And Muslims have even less written *eisegesis* to reference in order to conceal the atrocities of Yahweh, (renamed "Allah") than the Christians do. And unfortunately, Islam has yet to enter into any era of reform. Judaism and Christianity have evolved somewhat, with the former having done so much more than the latter, due to Judaism's lengthier time on earth. With age comes wisdom, and Islam is a vile teenager with no parental guidance. In raw form, Yahweh (as Allah) is the perfect war god for a warrior people.

So, what are we left with? We have one god with many evolutionary strands. With all the different views and uses of Yahweh, we are forced to look at the Bible in one of its oldest, barest, basic forms, without referencing any outside commentary from any particular group.

And now that we know who Yahweh was, and where he came from, we can finally look at what he (allegedly) did...

OOPS! HE DID IT AGAIN: THE ACTIONS OF YAHWEH

The Garden of Needin' (Some Logic)

As they say, to begin with, you need to "begin at the beginning." This must be with the first book of the Bible, Genesis...

There are quite a number of flaws in the Biblical story of creation. These are mostly contradictions in the timeline and quite a number of scientific impossibilities. For example, after light from the sun and moon is created, stars also appear, and their light is instantaneous, even though we know that the nearest star sending that light our way would take over 4 years to reach earth, and every other star would take even longer. Even the light from our nearest galaxy would take over 2.5 million years to reach us. This childish reckoning of how the universe formed is astounding, but not unexpected from primitive human beings. Naturally, the creation story, for many believers, is defended as an allegory, not to be taken literally. Allegory or not, it is clear, this is not a story written by an all-powerful, all-knowing supernatural being.

The Genesis story jumps from pseudo-scientific astronomy, to bizarro-world creationism in just a couple of chapters. There are plenty of addled events within the Garden of Eden story, but one of those that stands out the most is the unjust punishment our alleged God gives to his first "children," Adam and Eve – a nice, rather earthy couple who were created by God as full-sized adults.

When the first pair of humans are contemplating whether or not they should eat fruit from the "Tree of the Knowledge of Good and Evil," they are completely innocent – having no clue what knowledge is, or what good is, or what evil is – and God certainly hasn't provided them with a dictionary. Despite this, after the First Couple eats the fruit, and God discovers this, he punishes them by kicking them out of their garden home and condemning them to die (eventually).

Strangely, God somehow expected Adam and Eve to *have* knowledge of good and evil before actually *acquiring* it (by eating the fruit). This is just one of the first of many moments where the sanity and intelligence of God are virtually non-existent.

This logic-defying act is enough to condemn these scriptures as nonsense. (And we don't even have to get into the absurdity of how a snake was able to speak without vocal cords to the First Woman, and was able to convince her to take a bite out some fancy *nootropic* fruit.)

In this story, God the "father" has zero parenting skills. If a small child, who knew nothing about electricity (and was incapable of understanding anything about electricity), put his finger in an empty light socket, and did so even after you told him not to, and even after you explained the consequences, would you punish him, or would you be happy that he wasn't injured? And wouldn't you also blame yourself for not watching your child more closely, or for not putting barriers in place to prevent such possible tragedies? Is this really as it appears – that the cruelty and neglect of the omnipresent Father-God was entirely intentional?

The conclusion we must draw, if we are to understand this first of many farces on the Bible's pages, is that when it comes to the mostly absent and wholly negligent God of the Universe, the blame for anything always rests on the shoulders of the tiny humans he's created, never on God himself. Does this alleged God fear responsibility? Does God have a creator of his own who is watching God for mistakes? If so, God should have been, demoted, fired, or removed from his post a long time ago.

The Human Experiment, Take Two

It didn't take long – only a few chapters in the Bible, for Yahweh to get upset with his new creation. After creating a man (Adam) from clay, after building a wife (Eve) for him from Adam's own rib, after punishing them for their curiosity, and after they reproduced themselves into a large population (something Yahweh *told* them to do), Yahweh starts to regret the whole thing:

> And God saw that the wickedness of man was great in the earth, and that every imagination of the *thoughts of his heart* was only evil continually. And it repented the Lord that he had made man on the earth, and it grieved him at his heart. And the Lord said, I will destroy man whom I have created from the face of the earth; both man, and beast, and the creeping thing, and the fowls of the air; for it repenteth me that I have made them. – (*Genesis 6:5-7 KJV*) [Emphasis Added]

So, Yahweh decides to kill everyone and everything. But, he makes an exception – he is merciful after all. 18 million people dying by drowning is okay, as long as we can start over with Noah and his family of 8. At this point, you're probably thinking, "How is it possible for an all-knowing, all powerful god to be displeased with something he created?"

Noah:
Zookeeper, Meteorologist, Boat Captain, Heavy Drinker and Family Man

The Story of Noah reads like a rather long children's book – the kind you read to your child before he nods off to sleep at night. Exaggeration and fantasy are a given. (Often, the Noah story *is* a favorite among North American children, replete with colorful cartoon pictures of cute but exotic animals boarding boats in the rain.)

The story begins with Yahweh regretting he had ever created man, because the only thing humans were concerned with was "evil thoughts." If this sounds like "victim blaming"... well, it is.

(NOTE: These evil thoughts apparently emanated from their physical hearts, not their brains. Primitive man, and Yahweh too, didn't know what a brain was for. Humans, even the few who suspected that the brain was for thinking, wouldn't know for certain, scientifically, until the 18th Century.)

Deus ex Machina

The Noah story is so non-scientific, it's either a wild-ass exaggeration on the part of some primitive know-nothing, or every event is a miracle from that loving God, Yahweh. For God's sake (literally), let's call 'em miracles...!

Somehow, Noah, who is nearly 600 years old (a miracle!), builds a boat that is as big as Yankee Stadium out of trees and pitch (a miracle!), gathers over 16,000 "kinds" of animals, times two or more, from all over the world into that boat (a miracle!), manages to feed all those animals their specialized diets (a miracle!), keeps the predatory animals separate from their prey (a miracle!), manages to shovel all the massive piles of animal excrement off the boat through a single on-board window (a miracle!), prevents cold-climate animals from heat stroke (a miracle!), and did this through 40 days and 40 nights of constant rainfall which was the equivalent of *360 inches of rain per hour* (a miracle!)

Wait! There's more! When the rain stopped, and the waters receded some *five to seven months later*, and they finally made it to dry land, the animals didn't eat each other (a miracle!), and the meat eaters, without any other animals to eat, somehow still survived to reproduce more of their kind (a miracle!), and even though all the vegetation had been destroyed, the plant eaters somehow also survived, (a miracle!), and Noah was even able to offer Yahweh a burnt offering on an altar, sacrificing one of the now possibly extinct birds (a miracle!), and was even able to find some grapes to make wine, (a miracle!), enough that he was able to get drunk and naked soon after all these events occurred (a miracle!)

Perhaps it was all a drunken nightmare?

There is zero scientific evidence for a world-wide flood. No evidence in sea-floors, no evidence in tree ring data, no evidence in ice cores, and that's just the tip of the scientific un-melted iceberg. Science has shown that the story of Noah is a complete impossibility. *It simply did not happen.*

Those Frustrating Iron Chariots

As if an overly exaggerated rainy season wasn't embarrassing enough, many hundreds of years later, the hapless Yahweh, the great and powerful creator of all things, had a really tough time fighting a battle for his people. Remember, this was the Iron Age, and iron is the most powerful element of the Iron Age. So powerful that Yahweh couldn't defeat an army that used it:

And the LORD was with Judah; and he drave out the inhabitants of the mountain; but could not drive out the inhabitants of the valley, because they had chariots of iron. – (*1 Judges 1:19 KJV*)

This ignominious incident was like Yahweh's Viet Nam. This was one war he simply was destined to lose. So, he withdrew – without honor. We can be happy that Yahweh isn't fighting for us today. What would he do against *tanks of iron,* or nuclear weapons?

Yahweh Likes It When You Barbecue

According to the Book of Leviticus, a most important need for Yahweh is savory aromas. Here are just two examples:

And the priest shall sprinkle the blood upon the altar of the Lord at the door of the tabernacle of the congregation, and burn the fat for a *sweet savour* unto the Lord. – (*Leviticus 17:6 KJV*) [Emphasis Added]

and...

And the priest shall burn them upon the altar: it is the food of the offering made by fire for a *sweet savour: all the fat is the Lord's.* – (*Leviticus 3:16 KJV*) [Emphasis Added]

Well, who doesn't love fat? Especially burning fat? This "sweet savour" is expected to reach the giant (invisible) nostrils of Yahweh, up in "heaven," and melt his heart, apparently so he'll take a break from being angry, and play nice with his humans. This "burning by fire" of animals is seen as very powerful by the primitive believers in Yahweh. This may seem laughable to modern man, but there are plenty of followers of "The Lord" who want to see the world begin this practice once again, and forever.

Yahweh, the Poor Poor Pitiful Astrophysicist

Yahweh may have trouble with iron chariots, but his Star Wars capabilities are top-notch! This is one amazing intervention:

Then spake Joshua to the Lord in the day when the Lord delivered up the Amorites before the children of Israel, and he said in the sight of Israel, Sun, stand thou still upon Gibeon; and thou, Moon, in the valley of Ajalon. **And the sun stood still,** and the moon stayed, until the people had avenged themselves upon their enemies. Is not this written in the book of Jasher? So **the sun stood still** in the midst of heaven, and hasted not to go down about a whole day. And there was no day like that before it or after it, that the Lord hearkened unto the voice of a man: for the Lord fought for Israel. – (*Joshua 10:12-14 KJV*) [Emphasis Added]

We see from the Bible that Joshua is alleged to have commanded the Sun (and Moon!) to stand still in order to prolong the day's length. This is simply not possible, no matter how your wildest imagination wishes otherwise. To prolong the day's length, you need the Earth to stand still, not the Sun. Perhaps God doesn't know how to make a universe, or Joshua is woefully ignorant of astronomy? Either way, it should be obvious that this God character (and his "power") is nothing more than someone's primitive ponderings about how the stuff in the sky works. Or, maybe someone was hallucinating, or just outright lying. To add potential injury to an already intelligence-insulting story, do we need to mention how entire continent sized chunks of the earth would go sliding off the edge of the globe, and how massive tidal waves would ensue, killing everything on the planet, if the earth suddenly stopped its rotation, just so a tiny herd of Israelites could win a minor desert sword fight? Somebody's lying, and it's not physics that's doing so.

However, you needn't be concerned about such things if you are a man who has been damaged between the legs in the aforementioned sword fight. In fact, you need not ever talk to God again...

If You're Missing Your Bat or Your Balls, Don't Come Crying to God

In the Bible, Deuteronomy 23:1 references genital damage as being a condition that makes a person unworthy of worshiping god:

> He that is wounded in the stones, or hath his privy member cut off, shall not enter into the congregation of the Lord. (*KJV*)

Any male human being would consider such a thing cruel, especially if the injury was no fault of his own. But then, the claim of mercy from Yahweh is often fraudulent. For a god who claims to value "spirit" and to *be* spirit, his morbid obsession with the physical realm, especially the genitalia of humans, is rather odd.

God's Holy Backside

A god more sheer than pantyhose! Every modern believer in a supernatural monotheistic god will tell you that God, the creator of our universe, is invisible, spiritual, and immaterial. He cannot be seen. Certainly, the convenience of invisibility cannot be underestimated. It's a big deal. It's powerful. But for whom is it most convenient? Which side gets the better deal – the god, or the believer? A group of worshipers with an invisible god has the advantage of never having to produce that god. And a god that is invisible never has to be accountable to his creation. But, is *this* particular god, Yahweh, truly invisible?

119

And he said, Thou canst not see **my face**: for there shall no man see me, and live. And the Lord said, Behold, there is a place by me, and thou shalt stand upon a rock: And it shall come to pass, while my glory passeth by, that I will put thee in a clift of the rock, and will cover thee with **my hand** while I pass by: And I will take away mine hand, and thou shalt see **my back parts**: but my face shall not be seen. – (*Exodus 33:20-24 KJV*) [Emphasis Added]

The problems with this passage are extensive. To begin with, if God is supposed to be always invisible, seeing a god that is three-dimensional, with a face and a back, makes little sense. And if this god is all-powerful, then would he not be able to let anyone see him and allow them to live anyway? Would he not have the power to resurrect anyone who actually did die from the encounter? Is this just another one of Yahweh's lies? Or, did Moses see something else? In any case, whether the protean Yahweh is a spiritual god, an invisible god, or a less-than-powerful 3-D god, a loving and responsible god shouldn't play Hide-and-Go-Seek with his creation, especially when the outcome of this ethereal game could mean death for the participants.

Scriptures, like the one above, that pose too many unanswerable questions are virtually useless to the reader. So, why write them to begin with? The answer is, of course, that Yahweh's identity, his abilities, and his demeanor, developed over time. He is a conglomeration of ancient gods, primitive ideas, and numerous interpretations, all fused into one. The above scripture is just a window into Yahweh's personal *evolution.*

God Is Mysterious

As we have shown, if the Bible is true, and God (Yahweh) exists, in whatever form, he obviously doesn't want to be seen much. He deliberately makes himself mysterious and hidden as much as possible. If this is so, atheists must be God's best friends, and religious people must be God's greatest annoyance.

Theists spend a great amount of energy telling everyone to go out and find this hidden god, in a kind of celestial game of hide-and-go-seek, as mentioned above. Yahweh clearly doesn't want to be seen, other than his "backside," or perhaps a little piece of him in the form of Jesus. (Is Yahweh's backside and Jesus one and the same?) In any event, atheists are saying he doesn't exist, thereby helping Yahweh, the perpetual hermit, hide!

This is all ridiculous speculation, of course, but it has as much value and weight as any other hypothesis brought forth from the religious crowd. And, as we've mentioned in other chapters, all *unfalsifiable ideas* are equal.

* * *

120

Bible Liars

Most well-intentioned religious folk will tell you that lying is "wrong," if not a full-blown sin. But is it? The Bible has a few well-respected liars and God is one of them.

God lies to his people almost from Day One. In Genesis, he tells the first people they will die *the same day* they eat of the forbidden fruit. That was a lie. They died many years later after being cast out of their Garden. Here's the passage:

> But of the tree of the knowledge of good and evil, thou shalt not eat of it: for **in the day that thou eatest** thereof thou shalt surely die. – *(Genesis 2:17 KJV)* [Emphasis Added]

Later, God sends a spirit to make his prophets lie:

> And the Lord said unto him, Wherewith? And he said, I will go forth, and **I will be a lying spirit** in the mouth of all his prophets. – *(1 Kings 22:22 KJV)* [Emphasis Added]

He does it again here:

> O Lord, thou hast deceived me, and I was deceived; thou art stronger than I, and hast prevailed... – *(Jeremiah 20:7 KJV)*

God finally admits to being the primary deceiver of his own prophets:

> And if the prophet be deceived when he hath spoken a thing, I the Lord have deceived that prophet... – *(Ezekiel 14:9 KJV)*

This isn't just Old Testament stuff. He continues with this deception even into the New Testament, proving that God *can* be consistent at some things.

> And for this cause God shall send them strong delusion, that they should believe a lie... – *(2 Thessalonians 2:11 KJV)*

As for other "respected" people in the Bible: Abraham lies, Sarah lies, Rebecca lies, Jacob lies, Isaac lies, Rachel lies, King David lies, and so on. The Biblical liars are mimicking their lying god and doing so quite well. Can we really blame them?

As the character Dr. Gregory House, M.D. (from the television show, *House)* says,... *"Everybody lies."*

Perhaps the Bible should be renamed, *The Pseudologia Fantastica,* which roughly translates into "The Fantastic Lie." It's also an alternative phrase for pathological lying. Certainly many of the various Biblical authors could easily be accused of *mythomania.* Compulsive lying is the implement of those with antisocial and/or borderline personality disorder. And these traits can clearly be seen in the behaviors of many of the players and characters in the Bible.

Do All Lies and Deception Come From Yahweh?

Maybe. But how could we possibly know? The reality is, no believer in any god actually knows a single thing of truth about that god. No believer actually knows where their god is, or how to find where he lives. They don't know what he looks like, or even if he's male. They don't know if he dead or alive, or whether or not he's an habitual liar.

In fact, what a person *doesn't* know about their god approaches infinity. Anything a believer might say about their god is probably a lie. And as such, that lie could easily border on blasphemy, if blasphemy mattered. If you say you *know* God has white hair, when it's possible he's completely bald, that's a lie. You don't have to *know* you're lying when you tell a lie. You simply have to open your mouth and speak something you know nothing about. And acting "innocent" won't help your case.

If you tell a questionable story, even if you believe it to be true, you're still telling a lie. If you begin to tell others that former U.S. President Millard Fillmore was gay, and research discovers he was not, even if you believed at the time that he was gay, you passed on the lie anyway. Should you be held accountable? Yes, of course. The correct solution would have been to keep quiet and/or do some research on the matter to discover the truth either way. Ignorance is no excuse. After you've run away from a police officer, and after he catches you and places the handcuffs on you, try telling him you didn't know there was a law against resisting arrest.

Contrary to Vladimir Lenin, a lie told often enough does *not* become the truth. It may always be believed, but a lie is forever a lie.

Yahweh and Genocide

Many have often wondered, and even children have asked, why this god of the Bible did not simply cause a virus to wipe out the Israelites' enemies? If he was all powerful, why didn't he just vaporize them? Or make all of them sterile? Why did he command the Israelite tribes to slash them to pieces instead? Where was his imagination or inventiveness? Could this god not be merciful, even to the condemned? And what about the mental trauma of the Israelites themselves when they had to slice open a pregnant woman with a sword? Did they not feel any guilt or remorse? Or, was everyone in the tribe a psychopath? If the genocides were meant to teach the Israelite tribes to have mercy on their enemies, or to somehow "learn" empathy, it didn't work very well. God's children continued to rape and pillage with great abandon for centuries onward.

This, of course, does point to a god that is no wiser and no more powerful than the guys on the ground with the iron hatchets. Or, it points to the real fact that there was no god leading this tribe. It was covetousness, and greed that was in charge of the raping, slashing, and killing of other people – other people who may have reached the choice, grade-A tract of land first. This was real genocide and ethnic cleansing, glossed over and sanctified with heavy and continuous doses of religion, premised solely on the fear of an imaginary invisible killer whose very name was supposedly unspeakable.

(When reading this, keep in mind, that during the Iron and Bronze Ages, it was not just the Israelites who were engaged in brutal wars and ethnic cleansing – so were just about every tribe near and far, and all around the globe. Wars with swords, knives, axes, hatchets, horses, and chariots was *normal*. The Hebraic tribes were just better at writing it down!)

Justifying Genocide

In the Bible, whenever God or God's people commit genocide, whether through ordering bears to kill children, or armies killing entire cities including their livestock, the absurd justification for such action is always the same: those people murdered were so vile and so wicked that they had to all be eradicated from the earth completely and forever. This would include their children and unborn children who were genetically also so vile and wicked that God knew they would all grow up to be horrible, vile, and wicked people without exception. This is, of course, is not too different from the justifications used in many of the more modern acts of ethnic cleansing. (See: Pol Pot, Hitler, Stalin, Idi Amin, Mao; See also the locations – Yugoslavia, The Ukraine, Rwanda, and the Americas prior to the 20th Century, etc.)

What you end up with is a psychopathic god using his psychopathic people to kill other whole tribes of future psychopaths. This ridiculous rationale never seems to get the job done completely, however.

One famous instance has Moses, and his warrior sidekicks, killing mass quantities of Midianite men and boys, but leaving all the virgin women and girls alive for their own, obviously highly dignified and non-lascivious, personal needs, right? How long these young women remained virgins, or how long it took for them to get pregnant soon after capture, is anyone's guess. This act, naturally, would not exactly qualify as the most brilliant way of getting rid of an evil people who were genetically prone to lead your people astray. (Numbers 31:1-15)

The truly odd part of this is story is *why* the Midianites were ordered to be slaughtered. Apparently, some Israelite men had earlier been sexually cavorting with Midianite women. Moses somehow connected their unsavory fooling around to a plague that was affecting Israel at the time. Strangely, the resultant punishment meted out against the Midianites was to kill all the Midianite men and sexually cavort with even *more* (albeit virginal) Midianite women!

In another Biblical place and time, Saul, the hapless king preceding the bloody King David, is commanded by God to totally mass murder an entire people, the Amalekites, including their evil, psychotic cattle, and other mentally deranged donkeys and sheep. Yet Saul somehow manages to screw things up and miss a few of these tumultuous tribesmen, and they apparently go on to breed again, like the cockroaches they are, and evilly harass the poor Israelites and their descendents forever and ever. Of course, *not* killing every living thing in the Amalekite camp was considered a terrible "sin" against God because God really needed everything that was even remotely Amalekite, totally, wholly, absolutely, 100 percent *dead.* (1 Samuel 15:1-34)

Saul was only human, so no one could really expect him to be the perfect genocidal maniac. The perfect genocidal maniac could only be God himself. Yet, as we saw in the story of Noah, even God couldn't get rid of all the evil that human beings have deep down in their genes, even after killing everyone on the entire planet, with the exception of a family of eight, in a terrifying flood. As we know, many of Noah's descendants have killed, and are still killing other humans in much the same way as they always have. So much for the genius policy of having psychopaths kill off all the psychopaths.

The next time a god wants a certain people to live a certain place, perhaps he should just put them there to begin with, instead of ordering them to slaughter the people that are already there. Why have your "children" move into a blood soaked land? Why is there a need for continuous war, generation after generation?

God, The Destroyer of Free Will

Not only does God lie and kill, he destroys the free will of human beings whenever it suits him. See the following:

> And the LORD hardened the heart of Pharaoh, and he hearkened not unto them; as the LORD had spoken unto Moses." – Exodus 9:12 (KJV) [Emphasis Added]

Pharaoh, the evil ruler of Egypt who was keeping the Hebrews as slaves, was not allowed to be the good guy, even if being one had been what he wanted. He was going to be the enemy of Moses, no matter what! It's wonderful that God has time to take care of this stuff, especially when there are other important things going on in the universe, such as black holes at the center of the galaxy sucking up stars like a pig eats his dinner.

But, while we're talking about trying to live your life on your own terms, without the intervention of crazy people or gods, there's this...

The Special Story of Job

In English, Job is pronounced with a long "o." But, we could pronounce it with a short "o" – when you consider that Job's *job* was simply to be God's pawn. Or, perhaps his lab rat.

The Biblical Job was "a perfect and an upright man, one that feareth God, and escheweth evil." He was also the richest and greatest "man of the east." He had seven sons, three daughters, 3000 camels, 500 oxen, 500 "she asses," and a house full of servants.

But they were expendable.

God (Yahweh) makes a bet with Satan (the lesser god of Hell), that Satan could do anything he wanted to Job and Job would never curse God. So, Satan takes that bet and soon arranges to have all of Job's servants brutally murdered, has a house fall on his children (killing them), and even has Job's sheep burned to death and his camels stolen. Job is childless and penniless, yet still refuses to curse Yahweh. Yikes! At least he has his health! Oh, but not for long...

Satan ups the ante... The devious duo, Satan and God, toy with poor Job again. Satan claims that if Job has his "bone and flesh" touched, then he will curse God. So Satan gives Job boils from head to toe, and still Job doesn't curse God. (Obviously, poor Job has no idea what a jerk his god is.)

Yahweh wins the bet. And Job enters into a deep funk, full of grief and self-reflection. Finally, Job has a long series of conversations with his friends who conclude that Job's fate must be due to some horrible sin he committed. Job knows he's done nothing wrong, so he then turns to Yahweh himself for answers. Not surprisingly, Yahweh brags about himself and then convinces Job to start again. Yahweh gives Job twice as much as he had before, ending up with 14,000 sheep, 6000 camels, 1000 oxen, and 1000 of those she-asses. Plus, he gets a brand new set of seven sons and three daughters! (We can assume they were not clones of the previous set.)

Of course, Yahweh has no remorse for his brutish behavior. Messing with people's lives and minds is no big deal for Yahweh. Sort of like a psychopathic child pulling the wings off butterflies. No big deal, right?

...Unless you're the butterfly.

IDEAS AND CONCEPTS: ANALYZING YAHWEH

Is God Evil?

If Yahweh was a real entity, could he be considered evil?

> Is God willing to prevent evil, but not able? Then he is not omnipotent. Is he able, but not willing? Then he is malevolent. Is he both able and willing? Then whence cometh evil? Is he neither able nor willing? Then why call him God? – (*Epicurus, 4th Century B.C.E.*)

Those are good questions to ponder. But how many god-followers ever take the time to actually consider any of them? What follows is a passage that doesn't come from an ancient Greek philosopher, but rather from the Bible itself:

> I form the light, and create darkness: I make peace, and *create evil:* I the LORD do all these things. – (*Isaiah 45:7 KJV*) [Emphasis Added]

There it is, in black and white – God admits to all of it. He plays all the parts. It's his show. He's writer, producer, and director. It cannot be interpreted any differently. And how, if God is the creator of the entire universe, could it be otherwise?

125

In the above scripture, the Hebrew word for evil is *rah,* and *rah* always means evil. Always. It never means "calamity" or "disaster" as some Christian apologists will argue. For them, their god actually creating everything, including evil, goes against all the hype about a loving god whose son implores everyone to love their enemies, (although hating one's family is okay. See: Luke 14:26). For this one brief moment, in this one brief passage, the all-powerful god suddenly isn't so loving. But the believer somehow *knows* his god cannot create evil. He cannot create an evil being (Satan). He cannot create evil humans. It's not in his "nature." (?) For the Christian, this word "evil" absolutely *must* mean something else.

We need to ask ourselves, when the word *evil* is used, does it ever mean a tornado just blew through town? No. (At least not to modern thinking homo sapiens.) Evil always means evil. You can wrongly describe or *interpret* a tornado as being evil, but the word evil itself still means what evil has always meant: *intentional* acts of destructive and often horrific behavior, whatever the source. That's what *rah* is. Christians are trying to give the word a new definition, or expand its already established definition. Because of their lack of scientific knowledge, the writers of the Bible often thought unfortunate events had their source in something evil and *deliberate.* Even though they were aware of the distinction between unfortunate and evil, and between calamity and evil, and had separate words for those distinctions, they would never substitute another word for evil when they actually meant evil. The nuance here, from the perspective of the Bible writers, is clear. A calamity can be called evil, but evil isn't just a calamity. Evil is always evil. *Rah* is always *rah.* And God, apparently, is its cause. (For atheists, evil exists, but is always human-sourced.)

More Evil From An Evil God

Is there further Biblical evidence for Yahweh-God being the author of all things evil?

> And it came to pass on the morrow, that the **evil spirit from God** came upon Saul, and he prophesied ... and David played with his hand. – (*1 Samuel 18:10 KJV*) [Emphasis Added]

So, the evilness of Yahweh is seconded, and the motion carries. But, wait! Don't stop there!

> And while he yet talked with them, behold, the messenger came down unto him: and he said, Behold, this **evil** is of the Lord; what should I wait for the Lord any longer? – (*2 Kings 6:33 KJV*) [Emphasis Added]

> Out of the mouth of the most High proceedeth not **evil** *and* good? – (*Lamentations 3:38 KJV*) [Emphasis Added]

126

But he said unto her, Thou speakest as one of the foolish
women speaketh. What? Shall we receive good at the hand of
God, and shall we not receive **evil**?... – (*Job 2:10 KJV*)
[Emphasis Added]

Shall a trumpet be blown in the city, and the people not be
afraid? Shall there be **evil** in a city, and the Lord hath not done
it? – (*Amos 3:6 KJV*) [Emphasis Added]

These texts suggest that the early followers of Yahweh knew exactly what
modern followers refuse to acknowledge – that all evil came from their god. It
was a given. It refutes the modern notion that Yahweh is, or was ever, omni-
benevolent. But that doesn't stop Christians from claiming "God is love," and
nothing else, over and over again. After all, they have God *incarnate*, and he
loves everyone, even his enemies. Why a god of everything would even have
enemies is never explained with any sort of clarity, however.

Killing In Biblical Context

Bible defenders like to accuse atheists of not seeing scriptural passages in
context, meaning atheists cannot discern what a passage "really" means because
an atheist doesn't have the Holy Spirit to guide them to that real meaning.
Apparently, one must have some kind of "special eyes" to see the true meaning
of scriptures. But this is just hokum, plain and simple. When a word says murder
it means murder. For Christian Bible-redactors, slave is reinterpreted to mean
"servant," rape becomes "seduction," and genocide or ethnic cleansing becomes,
"well, somebody had to kill them all! They were all evil!" Exactly *who* is taking
things out of context again? Did we miss something here?
     The idea that an entire city of people, men women and children needed to be
wiped out completely because they were all evil, where even the babies had to
die because they were potentially evil, sounds a lot like The Soviet Union or
Nazi Germany in WWII. Maybe the Bible context doctors need to come up with
a better excuse for all those genocides. That one's not really working for them in
the 21st Century.
     An excellent example of how these kinds of passages simply cannot be
justified, no matter how you spin them, is the now infamous story of the forty-
two children who were mauled by bears for calling a prophet "bald."

And he went up from thence unto Bethel: and as he was going
up by the way, there came forth little children out of the city,
and mocked him, and said unto him, Go up, thou bald head; go
up, thou bald head. And he turned back, and looked on them,
and cursed them in the name of the Lord. And there came forth
two she bears out of the wood, and tare forty and two children
of them. – (*2 Kings 2:23-24 KJV*)

Certainly, the punishment didn't fit the crime no matter who did the name calling, but somehow Christian scholars think that it's important to clarify who actually got slaughtered. Some Biblical double-speakers have reinterpreted the "children" in the passage to mean "teenagers," as if murder for name calling is somehow okay if the people being mauled to death are a little older!

Perhaps Biblical apologists should follow George Washington's advice: "It is better to offer no excuse than a bad one."

Obedience Is Bliss!

Throughout the Old Testament, it is clear that God forgets his own commandment of "Thou Shalt Not Kill." Or, he feels that since the universe is all his, he can do what he wants. So much for setting a good example.

One story that, if true, is rather heartbreaking. It's the story of Jephthah's daughter, and again, it emphasizes the need to *obey* god, rather than use your own best judgment:

Back in "the day," Jephthah was a military leader caught in a desperate battle. In an act of *spontaneous compulsion,* he made a vow to his god, Yahweh, that if he won the battle, he would sacrifice the first living thing to come out of his house when he returned home. Jephthah knew that Yahweh loved it when you killed and burned some living creature for him, and he especially liked "first" things. (See Judges 11:34-40 for the actual story.)

So, lucky Jephthah won the battle and returned home. The first thing to exit his house as he approached was his only child, his beloved daughter. Oops! (Note: She was so beloved and significant that the author doesn't bother to mention her name.) Sadly, Jephthah was forced to tell his daughter about his vow, that he had promised to ritually kill her (murder her) – for Yahweh's kindness in letting him murder his enemies. Makes sense, right?

Of course, the nameless daughter courageously agrees that she must die. (Don't they always in these stories?) Of course, vows were not taken lightly in those good ole days. If you said something, you'd better mean it. And so, Jephthah and daughter, go through with the sacrifice. We cannot begin to imagine how repulsive it would be to stab your own daughter and then burn her body because you think your god needs a "thank you" in the form of a dead child.

This story is supposed to be a real event, *and* a lesson. The lesson is, "don't make vows you can't keep." It's a fine idea to consider, but it's a brutal way to present a lesson.

For atheists in the modern era, this story can only reek of sadness and horror. We know that without any superstition about a god who demands death through ritual sacrifice, and without any concept that killing something somehow makes things better, Jephthah's daughter, and other innocent people like her, would have lived (hopefully) happy lives.

The moral of this story is lacking morality, of course, but the message is clear: Obedience over Logic. Obeying God is more important than thinking for yourself. In the mind of Jephthah, his rationalization was that *obedience to his own vow to God was also obedience to God himself.* And we know from other

Biblical tales, if God tells you to do something stupid or immoral, it's not really stupid or immoral. And you had better do whatever it is, or else God will be horribly angry, and even worse things will happen to you. A running theme throughout the Bible is that the "moral lawgiver" doesn't have to be moral, and can change the definition of morality whenever he wishes. And believers are deliberately blind to this conundrum.

Of course, for those of us who reject gods and the false notions that surround them, the *real* lesson of Jephthah and his daughter isn't "don't make vows you can't keep," but rather, "don't obey your own superstitions."

The Beginnings of Heavenly Public Relations

Any astute reader of the Bible may notice that it constantly reminds readers of how "good" Yahweh is. The question is, "Who are they trying to convince (or kid)?" After encountering numerous atrocities, genocides, immoral acts, and outright mistakes that are Yahweh's own doing, it is not surprising that the Bible is forced to remind everyone that he really is a "good" god despite all those terrible things. Besides, the Bible writers probably figured, if they didn't insert those praises, Yahweh would probably crush them like a bug.

God Is Loathe

God is love, the saying goes. However, there is quite enough evidence from the Old Testament that the opposite is true. If this myth is not a myth, and is a part of reality, how do we know this god doesn't actually hate humans? Yahweh even stated that he despised humanity. This was the reason for the Great Flood. (See Genesis 6:5-7) The final book in the Christian Bible is replete with how disappointed (again) this god is with human beings, and how he has a set plan to destroy the majority of them (again). God only loves humans when they defy their own God-inscribed programming and obey his impossible laws, or when they believe something without evidence. This is a very strange god indeed.

This is why some have postulated that the Bible is a *red herring.* These people contend that God *does* exist, but he only rewards those who do *not* obey any decrees or laws that are clearly ridiculous and/or contradictory (i.e. the Bible). The actual creator of the universe doesn't care about obedience, they say. He cares about your ability to think. That is, the Bible, Qur'an, Torah, and other holy texts are deliberately contradictory and are designed to fail on purpose, and the followers of superstition are weeded out because of their failure to discard those irrational ideas. In other words, the Bible is a test. To pass the test, you must reject the Bible. And this test applies equally to any holy book or text.

Some Thoughts About Morality

Is it really impossible for humans to innately know murder is wrong? Why couldn't humans evolve in such a way to realize this? Isn't injecting a god where one is unnecessary the height of arrogance? And what about mass killers, such as Stalin, Hitler, Pol Pot, and Mao? It is quite logical to assume that these dictators knew innately that murder is wrong and chose to do it anyway. The same is true for all murderers. Knowing something is immoral doesn't stop people from doing immoral things. And facing a moral dilemma, that is, knowing what is moral vs. immoral, can often be subjective depending on the circumstances. No two situations are ever the same. There are variances in time, place, necessity, knowledge, motive, and awareness. All these things can alter what someone generally already *knows* to be moral or immoral.

If I steal your wallet, it's wrong. I know this because I have empathy (something most of us are born with – the exceptions are psychopaths), and I would not want my own wallet stolen. This morality comes from society, from people having to live together, and our innate affinity towards others. There is no "Moral Lawgiver" as written in the Bible or any other holy book. If there was a real, heavenly, moral lawgiver based on the Biblical model, slavery would still be practiced, rapists would still marry their victims, and children would still be stoned to death for disobedience.

Because we are self-aware and aware of our own mortality, we have developed a fear of death and a fear of killing. We evolved empathy in the process. And from empathy comes our moral compass. And there is probably no better example of human beings suppressing that empathy, through the use of religion, than slavery...

For God, Slavery is Moral

It is no accident that the followers of Yahweh, Allah and Jesus are called servants, slaves, and sheep. The relationship between these gods and their followers is a Master / Slave relationship. These gods are wholly dictatorial, and expect total obedience. Is it any wonder that the Torah, the Qur'an and the Bible (and other holy books) endorse, condone, and sanctify the concept of slavery? Aren't the human enslavers of other humans simply behaving in full imitation of their god(s) behavior toward themselves?

When it comes to the Bible, the endorsement of slavery is quite clear. In fact, slavery is one of the few things in the Christian version of the Bible that is consistent in both the Old and New Testaments. This is one of the few times Yahweh-God decides *not* to entirely change his mind on something after becoming Jesus. And while we're on the subject of change...

JUST DO IT: THE LAWS AND COMMANDS OF YAHWEH

In the Jewish Talmud, the following seven laws, known as the Noachide Laws, were supposedly given by Moses to the "Children of Noah," meaning to all humanity. Non-Jews who obey these laws are supposedly entitled to a place in "the world to come," apparently after Judgment Day. How generous!

1.   Do not deny God.
2.   Do not blaspheme God.
3.   Do not murder.

4. Do not engage in incest, adultery, pederasty or bestiality, as well as homosexual relations.
5. Do not steal.
6. Do not eat of a live animal.
7. Establish courts/legal system to ensure law and obedience.

We only mention this list because obviously Yahweh is at the head. (Note the first two.) Some of these have some obvious merit, but these first two mean nothing to an atheist, or even to a believer in a non-Jewish sourced god. Cannot the people of the world choose their own set of basic laws, and have they not already done so? Was the ego of Moses so huge that he had to make commandments not only for his tribe, but for the rest of the entire world?

Gap of the Gods

Reading the Bible, one quickly notices how replete it is with laws, admonitions, commandments, and regulations. But, did someone leave out a commandment regarding slavery? When it comes to the major rules, shouldn't there be *eleven* commandments instead of ten? Did someone deliberately edit the Bible and cross out the one about enslaving others? Humans know slavery is wrong, why doesn't Yahweh? Think of all the misery and hatred that could have been avoided if this kind of commandment had been added:

> Thou shalt possess no one. Maketh thou no man, woman, or child your slave, whether they be of your people, or from other lands, so that ye shall be no slave to others. Such is an abomination unto the Lord. (Author's Version)

Billions of people would have escaped a horrendous and wasted life, were it not for this omission. For this alone, Yahweh is denounced by non-believers. And by default, those who attempt to defend slavery, in any form, and from any source, for any reason, are also condemned by humanity.

Sex – It's the Law!

The Bible contains numerous laws and prohibitions regarding sex, enough of them that a reader gets the idea that this desert tribe is quite obsessed with this topic, although this was probably the norm for most cultures just as it is today. But, the ancient people of the Bible weren't trying to have more unfettered sex, they were trying to have *less*. However, the further back in time you go in the Bible, the more acceptable some practices are:

- (Rape) Genesis 19:5-8 – Lot is threatened with rape, and offers his two virgin daughters to be raped in exchange for sparing himself such humiliation. The Bible seems to think this is okay.

131

- (Rape and Incest) Genesis 19:30-38 – Lot has sex with his daughters, but is barely aware it's happening. The two women get him drunk for the purpose of becoming pregnant. The Bible seems to think this is okay.

- (Incest) Genesis 20:12 – Abraham, and his wife Sarah, have the same father, but different mothers. The Bible doesn't seem to have a problem with this either.

- (Coitus Interruptus) Genesis 38:8-10 – Onan, is guilty of withdrawal from, and ejaculation outside of, a vagina. God kills Onan for this because Biblical law required that he impregnate his dead brother's wife, and he really "wasn't that into her." Not getting someone pregnant? Now *this* is a serious violation!

- (Prostitution) Genesis 38:13-24 – Tamar trades sex with her father-in-law for a goat. Goats were very valuable back then.

- (Adultery) Exodus 20:14 – The seventh commandment prohibits adultery. Of course, this does not prevent a man from having several wives.

- (Adultery, Homosexuality, Bestiality, etc.) Leviticus 18:1-30 – A specific lineup of sexual prohibitions is listed, including having sex with a menstruating woman. It also includes the punishments (from God) for doing these things, such as, "vomiting" them from the tribe, souls being cut off, various iniquities being "visited" upon them, etc. This is when we finally get to some *real* laws!

- (Prostitution) Deuteronomy 23:17-18 – Prostitution is prohibited, defining it specifically by disallowing all "cult prostitutes." Perhaps non-cult prostitution was okay?

- (Adultery, Abortion) 2 Samuel 11:3-5 – King David commits adultery with Bathsheba (after killing her husband), and his act results in a God-ordained miscarriage / abortion.

- (Rape and Incest) 2 Samuel 13 – Amnon, King David's son, rapes his half-sister, Tamar. Two sins in one. Later, Amnon is the victim of a revenge killing – murdered by his half-brother.

- (Adultery) Proverbs 5:1-23 – Adultery with "strange" women is discussed in a long sermon.

So what's going on here? What is the real reason for the initial acceptance of certain sexual behaviors (incest) and then, much later, all the prohibitions of sex by the early Bible leaders? Some anthropologists have suggested that it may have been because they were a small tribe, and any sort of sex which was not concerned with procreation meant the possibility of one less person being born. The people of the Bible were certainly obsessed with a man's "seed," a euphemism for his ejaculate. This could easily be the real reason why wasting it through *coitus interruptus*, bestiality, and homosexuality, was forbidden, and not simply because such acts were not "normal."

A small tribe trying to keep its sovereignty and identity would have a better chance at survival if its numbers were increasing. The Israelites were obsessed with knowing how many of them there were at any given time. A census was important to them because even a small battle with a neighboring tribe could be devastating, even if it was a battle of attrition.

It's important to know *why* these prohibitions exist, especially when they still influence how we think and feel about sex in modern times. Perhaps it is advisable to discard these ancient prohibitions and start anew. A bit of logic would help human beings understand their sexuality much better than the chronicled desperation of some primitive tribesmen. However, it won't be easy. As we know, sex and logic are often like oil and water. They don't mix very well. Even in the 21st Century.

The Modern Ten Commandments

Christopher Hitchens, and others, have come up with their own new and revised versions of the Ten Commandments. These are up-to-date versions which are not about mocking the original, but rather improving the list by including those things that were omitted. Even magician Penn Gillette, with a little help from his fans, has some very wise and revised suggestions in his book, *God, No!*

But, is it really necessary to revise them? Perhaps we should just toss them out and start over? Humanity has matured somewhat. When it comes to doing the *right thing,* we now know what to do, even if we don't always do it. And we're trying harder. Maybe starting from scratch would be a better idea.

CONCLUSION AND SUMMARY

How Holy is Holy?

There is no reason to think any group's religious texts are special, especially not by their own authority. After all, we don't expect a criminal to investigate his own crime. Nor do we expect a scientist to do his own peer review. And, if we're smart, we don't allow a student to grade his own paper. Only outside, neutral, non-partisan investigation can shed any light on what evidence there is for a deity.

How can anyone in the present time know whether the words on a page authored thousands of years ago are true? With numerous individual authors, how can we discern which of these writers were embellishing, exaggerating the truth, or outright lying? The answer is, we don't know. Simply because a place name is accurate, or even a time frame is accurate, it does not follow that the stories alleged to have occurred in that time and place really happened.

The Old Testament, like the vast majority of religious texts, is obviously exaggerated, embellished, skewed, contradictory, illogical and predictably primitive – full of fantastic, logic-defying tales that contain perhaps only an ounce of real truth. To suspend all disbelief and take any significant portion of the Bible as literally true, one has to deliberately and defiantly escape reality and consciously maintain this delusion daily. It's unhealthy, and should be personally morally objectionable.

God and Special F/X

The moment the ancient Hebrews declared their god to be invisible, it changed everything – at least in the minds of humans. Before this, gods could be seen because they were made of wood, stone, or precious metals. But if one god can be invisible, it opens a Pandora's Box of possibilities that hundreds or thousands of things can also be invisible – other gods, angels, devils, jinn, or anything anyone decides *should* be invisible – and magically powerful. It's the invention of the supernatural. And the effect is to bring forth the fruit of fear and to multiply delusion. The world has never been the same since.

God is Good, Man is Bad, Truth is Ugly

By now, you should have a sense of who Yahweh was – a mysterious, war-like, imperfect, often fragile, angry god, invented by primitive tribesmen for the purpose of assuaging their fear of the unknown, and for controlling the fear of others. And Yahweh is written true to form.

When reading the Bible narrative, it appears that God created man fallible on purpose and set things up so humans would blame themselves for the defect. This implies that this infallible god fears that his own created beings could rise up to his level and overpower him. And, paradoxically, this implies his fallibility.

From an atheist standpoint, this Yahweh-God is a failure. Not so in a literal sense, because a non-existent being cannot fail or succeed, but in an historical sense in much the same way that other now-defunct gods were failures. It is clear that Yahweh falls short numerous times within his own narrative – reason enough to believe that this entity is wholly wrought from the imaginations of men.

Yet Yahweh is only one god of many, and like any invention or any story, he's been altered, edited, and reformulated multiple times over the various millennia. Are any of his other versions any better?

Perhaps now we should go to the next chapter, and see if The New Testament, makes any more sense than the Old...

CHAPTER SEVEN

Jesus and The New Testament

"Jesus may love you, but will he respect you in the morning?"
– Anonymous

*"If it takes the threat of hell to make you a moral person, then you are not at all
moral, you are just a coward who responds well to threats."*
– Leo Wolf

Everyone loves a superhero. Messiahs are much like them, but a messiah is a
superhero who presumably saves people from *themselves*. Yahweh's chosen
children were waiting for such a savior for quite some time (and still are), but
Christians say he came and went. And he did so in the body of Jesus.

We won't need to get too deep into the specifics of how and why Jews reject
the notion that Jesus was the Jewish Messiah. Suffice to say, Jews from the very
beginning have been vehemently opposed to Jesus as their Messiah. And here
are a few of the reasons summarized:

- Jesus was not born from King David's male line.
- Jesus was not prophesied to be born of a virgin.
- Jesus did not build the Third Temple.
- Jesus did not gather *all* Jews back to Israel.
- Jesus did not end *all* war, disease, and suffering.
- Jesus did not bring worldwide knowledge of God to everyone
  everywhere.
- Jesus did not unite all humanity.

Christians get out of those last five requirements by saying that Jesus will do all
these things *when he gets back*. So, as long as Jesus stays gone, fulfillment of
prophecy really doesn't matter much – meaning there really is no reason to
believe in Jesus based on prophecies you can't verify.

Jews also contend that the Messiah *cannot*:

- Be a demigod.

And, that God (Yahweh) *cannot:*

- Be a human being.
- Be divided (as in The Trinity)

How many mistakes do you need to be disqualified? Just one, of course. It's plain to see that the Christian claim simply could not be true, even if the ubiquitous god, Yahweh, did exist.

So, Yahweh is a god that should really be the head of only one religion (Judaism), and yet we have Christianity and Islam claiming him as well. Oops!

Jewish vs. Christian arguments aside, we need to focus on The New Testament itself – to investigate whether or not it is as full of the same sort of contradictions, flaws, and fantasies as the Old Testament.

WHAT IS THE NEW TESTAMENT?

The Christian Version of God

There are 27 Books in the New Testament Bible, with various timelines and authors (mostly *pseudepigraphical*), addressing the life of Jesus and his message. All of these books were written after the death of Jesus, leaving no written record that is contemporaneous with the life of the man who was claimed to be God Incarnate.

Those who wrote about Jesus had various motivations for doing so. Much of these writings were not simply to create an historical record, but to assert the author's own personal view about who Jesus was, or how others should interpret what Jesus said.

As Christianity grew, it became increasingly difficult to discern which texts about Jesus were actually true, accurate, or acceptable interpretations of religious thought. The writings were so disparate, and so dispersed across the Middle East and Roman Empire, that it took over 200 years to get any sort of general consensus of what should be the handbook for Christian belief. (This is a time frame is equivalent in years to the entire existence of The United States of America.) Actual acceptance of these 27 books as the universal canon for Christianity didn't happen until the 4th Century.

It makes one wonder: How could good Christians be good for nearly 300 years without a New Testament Bible?

What Was Left Out and Why?

The many other words and texts written about Jesus that never made it into the Bible are known as the Biblical Apocrypha. Some of the more note-worthy extra-Biblical, early Christian works that did not make it into the modern New Testament canon are:

- *The Gospel of Thomas*, a compendium of the sayings of Jesus from various sources, likely written 100+ years after the death of Jesus.

- *The Gospel of Mary,* another 2nd Century text full of various Christian themes, including the role of women in the church, and inducements to have followers preach. It is still not known if this Gospel was intended to be a narrative by Mary Magdalene, or by Mary, the mother of Jesus.

- *The Gospel of Peter,* a late 2nd Century document containing some rather extraordinary ideas, concepts and occurrences, including a talking cross and enormously tall angels. It is rather docetic in nature, stating that the physicality of Jesus was an "illusion."

- *The Gospel of Judas,* another scripture composed in the late 2nd Century, written as a series of conversations between Jesus and Judas Iscariot. This Gospel shows Judas as being the most knowledgeable of all the disciples and negates the modern mainstream view of Judas as the evil "betrayer" of Jesus.

- *The Gospel of Philip,* a 3rd Century gospel which strongly implied that Jesus was married to Mary Magdalene – a rumor that had gained much credence during the early Christian era.

In leaving these Gospels out of the canon, how are we to know that the first ecumenical councils, when selecting which books were to be kept and which ones were to be discarded, actually made the "correct" choice? Perhaps these extra-Biblical Gospels contain the most truth, and Matthew, Mark, Luke and John are the real heretical texts?

Enter Gnosticism...

Gnosticism

Gnostic comes from a Greek word which means "knowledgeable" or "learned." The Gnostics were early 2nd Century Christians whose beliefs were concerned with attaining oneness with an all-spiritual God, and shunning the physical or material world. It was almost entirely based on Christianity, but sought to emphasize the spiritual aspects of their beliefs to the point of viewing the resurrection of Jesus as a non-event, and choosing to revere Jesus as a spirit being.

Denying the incarnation of Jesus was the epitome of heresy to the mainstream Christians in the first few centuries C.E., and early ecumenical councils sought to remove these "blasphemies" from the early Christian Bible.

However, Gnosticism, despite its many forms, was so pervasive within the early Christian sects, that it could not be purged from the new canon completely.

In both Matthew and Luke, the Bible has Jesus quoting the exact core teaching of Gnosticism – that "The Kingdom of God" was not a physical place, but a spiritual one, i.e., it is "within you." And if this is so, it automatically implies that Hell is not a physical place as well. This further suggests that almost everything Jesus spoke about could be seen as spiritual in nature, negating any need for a bodily resurrection from his physical execution. The non-existence (or non-necessity) of a literal death on the cross, and a subsequent resurrection, is at the heart of Gnostic teaching.

There are many who also contend that Paul the Epistle, a revered founder of what has become modern (mostly) literalist Christianity, was a proto-Gnostic. Elaine Pagels, a professor of religion at Princeton University has written a book, *The Gnostic Paul,* which covers this quite convincingly.

Of course, the solution for the early Christian church was to literalize the incarnation of God through Jesus as a real and physical event, and confer belief in him solely through spiritual means. Unfortunately, this compromise created as many problems as it solved.

Who Wrote What First?

The order of the books in the New Testament is not the order they were actually written. Looking at the actual chronological order of when they were actually composed is quite revealing. Exact dates of authorship are impossible to ascertain, but we can order them by general time frame. The first person to write about Jesus was Paul the Epistle. Paul never met Jesus and never talks about the resurrection of Jesus as a real event, taking a stance that is almost Gnostic in nature. The first of his writings has been dated approximately 20 years after the death of Jesus.

After Paul's rather spiritual approach to Christianity, we find the pseudepigraphical texts of Matthew, Mark, Luke and John written much later than Paul's. It is in these gospels where we find the sayings of Jesus and his alleged miracles. What's most revealing is the fact that the further you go in time from the actual events surrounding the life and death of Jesus, the more fantastic the tales of his life become. It's where the lines between historical fact, urban legend, and outright fantasy become blurred, all culminating in the horrific end of the world nightmare in the Book of Revelation.

It's time now to take a look at the actual text to see exactly how fantastical and hyperbolic these stories really were...

WHO WAS JESUS?

Did Jesus Exist? Excellent question. But if anyone really has to ask, it means there must be some doubt. And, if there is some claim that he existed supernaturally, it only increases that likelihood that he didn't exist at all.

We never hear anyone making statements like, "Did Napoleon really exist?" Or, "Did Julius Caesar really exist?" Why? Perhaps it's because there is a large amount of detailed written record of these people existing, records written *during the actual lifetimes* of these historical figures. If the life of Jesus had similarly been documented, no one would be asking, "Did Jesus exist?" Furthermore, the reality of Jesus loses on one more count because Jesus himself wrote nothing about his own life.

But an idea that is much more important to an atheist is this: Is the existence or non-existence of Jesus relevant? To an atheist, if Jesus existed, he *had* to exist as a man and could not have been a god. Therefore, if an atheist rejects the claim that Jesus was a god, then Jesus existing only as a man has very little meaning beyond an ordinary historical context. If he didn't exist at all, in any form, then any discussion of him serves little purpose other than to demonstrate the never-ending gullibility of human-kind.

Similarly, the lives of Napoleon and Julius Caesar could mean little to an atheist, except as persons that could merit some historical or scholarly study, if a person is so inclined. Jesus could then also merit some reflective historical analysis, as a study in mythology, but this in no way guides the life of an atheist in any greater measure than any other figure of the past.

Jesus simply existing does not automatically make the things written about him true. And any story written after his death has less validity (many times over) than anything said about him during his lifetime. So the reality is, when the question is asked, "Did Jesus exist?" the proper response should be, "Which Jesus?" Is it the one barely mentioned by the historians of his day, or the one that had amazing supernatural powers attributed to him by writers that came much later, many years after his death?

Even if one can prove that Jesus did exist, and someone decides Jesus is their god, they still need to find a way to prove that the magical powers that were attributed to him existed as well. And, if the extraordinary idea is made that Jesus, after 2000 years, is still alive, then it becomes clear that the person making all these claims has a truly monumental task. Is it any wonder that atheists have their doubts?

It gets worse – for the believer. Each new supernatural claim about Jesus since the religion was founded is a new claim and must stand on its own. Bleeding Jesus statues, and images of the face of Jesus on grilled cheese sandwiches, must each stand on their own as extraordinary claims requiring extraordinary evidence. What you get is a snowball effect of odd and trivial claims for the existence of Jesus that, because of their un-provable and un-testable nature, only make the claim of Jesus ever existing all the more unreliable and untrustworthy. If you cannot trust the believer's testimony today, why would anyone *not* doubt the testimony of believers that made similar claims two thousand years prior?

"Lunatic, Liar, or Lord"

A favorite argument Christians like to throw out is this dandy: "If Jesus existed, he was either a Lunatic, Liar, or Lord!" And the corresponding Christian who is presenting this statement concludes that he had to be Lord, of course, conveniently ignoring the first part of the declaration: "If he existed..." The statement is taken as a paraphrase from the sayings of C.S. Lewis, a twentieth century Christian apologist. It's a false dilemma (or more accurately, a false *trilemma*) because it doesn't give the listener any other choices but those three. Other choices could be these: Jesus could be a rewritten version of the life of Apollonius of Tyana (or other mystics of the era, many of whom were also called Jesus), or a concoction of the Roman Empire to assuage the poor, as has been suggested by some, or simply a man for which others made up fantastic stories. *If he existed.*

So, we are back to the beginning again. There isn't much evidence for Jesus and therefore, there isn't much reason to believe he existed as anything other than a man for which much has been discussed and exaggerated. As we've said many times, there is never any reason to believe anything that has no evidence. More importantly, to the average atheist with no belief in gods of any kind, the existence or non-existence of Jesus is only a tiny bit more entertaining than most other historical trivia.

Allegories and Metaphors and Facts! Oh My!

Before going too deep into New Testament waters, we must address the idea that much of the Bible could be allegorical. Or, much of it could be literal. But which stories are which? We know that in order for the modern Christian believer to gain his salvation, the resurrection of Jesus must be literal. If so, much of the rest of what he physically did must be literal as well. What is more likely to be allegorical is what Jesus himself allegedly said to his disciples. Therefore, we have to examine the accuracy of those things likely to be literal, as well as the sensibility of those things likely to be allegorical. What are the errors, if any, in each?

As an atheist, keep in mind, when discussing the Bible with a "true believer," the moment anyone mentions a literal inaccuracy in the Bible record, the Bible will suddenly be described by the Christian as allegorical. However, if one argues the same point as being allegorical and found to be in error, the true believer will state that it's literal! It's a constant struggle for the Bible advocate to make their book fit the puzzle of life, no matter how circuitous the journey becomes just to make things work.

Additionally, deity-lovers will complain any time a non-believer "uses the Bible to disprove the Bible." Yet it is perfectly logical to use the Bible in precisely this way. Scrutinizing Bible errors is simply cross-examining the statements of the believers using the only tool available to any of us. After all, is there a better choice than the Bible to understand the Bible? If the Bible does condemn itself, it's not the fault of the one pointing that out. It's the fault of the Bible writers themselves.

Begat-itudes

Who begat whom to get down to Jesus? There are a lot of questions to ask regarding the genealogy of Jesus, but never an adequate answer: Isn't the non-physical Yahweh the physical father of Jesus? Why mention a human paternal lineage when there isn't one? How can a spiritual being be a physical father?

140

Why are the lineages different when you look at one New Testament book vs. another (Matthew vs. Luke)?

None of these quite legitimate questions have ever been adequately addressed by even the most clever of Christian apologists. The trouble with lies and lying is that the more layers of lies you tell, the harder it is to keep your story straight. When the reality that the genealogical puzzle pieces simply cannot fit, no one wants to step forward to say that perhaps Jesus was just a man with real parents, and that those parents actually had sexual intercourse and thus Jesus was born a human (only).

Jesus Who?

If Jesus did exist, who was he? To answer this question, we must first look at who Jesus was, as presented – through the writings that Christians themselves accept as factual. To be fair, we must look at *their* evidence, and temporarily set aside our own belief, or disbelief. We must look at Jesus through the writings of the Christian Bible and specifically, the New Testament scriptures. But be forewarned, it's rather strange. If someone were to ask us to summarize the life of Jesus in 100 words or less, it might come out something like this:

The spirit god Yahweh impregnates his own future mother with his physical self, and thus becomes his own father and his own son simultaneously. (This is a sort of celestial incest – the Oedipus complex made even *more* complex!) Later, Yahweh/God kills his own son (or allows his own son to die at the hands of others), but because he *is* his own son, he essentially kills himself.

This kind of celestial incest and self-destruction, if it were true, would be nothing less than abhorrent, if not utterly confusing! But before we try to reverse engineer these events to make some sense of them, we really should look at each co-conspirator in the grand plan one at a time, starting with God (the baby-daddy), and the very beginning of Jesus' life – at conception.

Yahweh Performs In Vitro Fertilization

Let's ask this rather sensitive question: If Yahweh-God impregnated his own future mother, how did he do it? If he's an invisible spirit, how did he get the sperm for that momentous event? Magic? What does non-physical (spiritual) sperm look like?

This may sound offensive to some (especially to Christians), but it is a serious question. In fact, the whole doctrine of Christianity hinges on the fact that Mary was impregnated by God, and that Jesus was, *de facto,* God's own son – half man, half god. Are we to just skip over this and say, "God works in mysterious ways!"? Meaning "Poof! There it is!" Isn't this just a fancy way of saying it was done with *magic*? Christian apologists don't seem to have the answer.

Jesus obviously had a physical mother, but how did Jesus get his spiritual heritage? Perhaps there is no spiritual source.

Let's read a section of St. Paul's *magnum opus:*

> Concerning his Son Jesus Christ our Lord, which was made of
> the **seed** of David according to the **flesh**... – (*Romans 1:3 KJV*)
> [Emphasis Added]

You cannot have it both ways. If Jesus was a direct male descendent of King David, as the Old Testament prophecies (and the New Testament scriptures above) require, the "seed" that impregnated Mary had to come from a physical Joseph, not a spiritual God. It must be so, if the genealogies of the New Testament are to be consistent with the interpretations of the prophecies about the Messiah in the Old Testament. And "flesh" cannot be spirit in any context.

Enter the apologists. They assert that it was not Joseph who was descended from King David, but Mary herself. But, for Jesus to qualify as the Messiah, descent of Mary from David would be automatically null and void. According to the Old Testament, the Messiah *must* be descended from King David's *male* line. Genesis 49:10, Isaiah 11:1, and Jeremiah 23:5 all support this requirement.

Trying to make Mary a descendant of David doesn't work, not only because the prophetic words of the Old Testament say so, but because the genealogies of the New Testament both show only the lineages of Joseph. Mary is never mentioned. There is no way to verify what family Mary belonged to. And female genealogies didn't really count in the ancient world anyway. (See Numbers 1:18.) Only men could pass on kingship. Simply put: Women can't be kings.

However, Christianity refuses to relinquish its claim that Jesus had a virgin birth and no earthly father. To maintain the myth, the story flips on its head and it doesn't matter who Mary's daddy was. Suddenly, God's heavenly invisible seed trumps all those Old Testament prophecies, and outweighs any of the New Testament genealogies of the cuckold Joseph anyway.

The reality is, no matter how you slice or splice the genes, David the King is completely cut out of the equation. Perhaps Jesus is an interplanetary alien, but he is disqualified to be the Messiah for the little desert tribe of Jewish people.

Imagine yourself living 2000 years ago, anywhere on the globe. It was quite uncomplicated to believe women could get pregnant by some ethereal magical force. No one had ever had a course in biology. No one knew that sperm cells existed. (In fact, spermatozoa wasn't known to exist until the first microbiologist, Anton Van Leeuwenhoek, himself a Christian, looked at them on a self-constructed microscope slide in 1677.) Human beings didn't know women had eggs either. In the agricultural Middle East, the female womb was soil to be plowed, and the sperm was the seed from which humans grew. In the ancient world, the only thing people knew about reproduction was that sex and ejaculations led to babies. They knew nothing about DNA, fertilization, or the minute details of how reproductive organs actually worked. Leaving women out of the line of inheritance was effortless, and made sense at the time.

It's quite easy to view the world through magical eyes when you're ignorant or uninformed. Ask any 6-year old Christian child about Santa and the magic of Christmas and you can see on his face that same belief, coupled with bewilderment, that adults most likely had about a great many things prior to the scientific discoveries that shattered that magic to pieces.

Modern day adult humans have no excuse. They know a lot of science now, at least compared to their superstitious ancestors. Questions about how Mary got pregnant by an invisible spirit or god should be addressed without the ignorance of magic and wishful thinking. To paraphrase Saint Paul, "Time to put away childish things." Is *parthenogenesis* possible in humans? Maybe. But that doesn't make the offspring from that event a "god."

There's Something About Mary...

Was Mary a virgin when she gave birth to Jesus? For most modern day skeptics and atheists, it's barely a question worth considering. Not only is it highly unlikely, it's irrelevant. A better question would be, "Why is a *virgin* mother so important?" Lack of sexual intercourse in a young woman does not make her "perfect" or "godly" in any sense, any more than having sexual intercourse makes her "bad" or "defiled." And if virginity was the only thing necessary to become the container of the god-seed, Mary herself could have been the worst, bitchiest, rebellious teenager in all of Judea, still be a virgin, and still *qualify*. In other words, virginity is highly overrated. (Although we can see how some highly suspicious human males might have been a little insecure about these things when living back in the days before the DNA test.)

And if God is so perfect and magical, what difference would it have made if he had had himself conceived inside a prostitute? Why couldn't a god who loved all his creatures get past all that? And why would a god need a woman to make himself incarnate anyway? Could he not simply appear as a ready-made baby on anyone's doorstep, and have the people who find him take him in as one of their own? It would have made a great comparable narrative to the Moses character of the Old Testament.

We should also add that the original Biblical adjective describing Mary is *almah* which means *young girl* and in no way automatically assigns her the status of "virgin." Plenty of young girls aren't. This simple ambiguity has been argued time and again over the past two millennia. But, suffice to say, if the word virgin was meant to be understood as such, based on its obvious importance to Christianity, *virgin* would have been specifically stated.

Science shows us that we all arrived on planet Earth via human conception – the union of a human egg and a human sperm, with most of us attaining that union through the sexual intercourse of our parents. But because none of us were conscious of our conception – we really weren't able to judge whether it was a "good" conception or a "bad" one. But we can be reasonably certain that our mother's virginity (or lack of it) wasn't the deciding factor either way.

Joey Loves Cuckoldry

No one ever discusses poor Joseph, the husband of Mary and the step-father of Jesus. What was he thinking about all this? His teenage bride is pregnant by some mysterious entity, and he has to live with this shame the rest of his life? It's not like the rest of the world, or his family, really believed Mary was going to give birth to a god. Only a few of them would figure that out much later, according to the myth. So, those that knew the parents of Jesus either suspected the couple had premarital sex, or Jesus was the result of Mary rolling around in the stables with somebody else other than Joe. Either way, Mary must have been viewed as a slut or Joseph as a cuckold. And this may be the real reason why one version has them running off to Egypt for a time.

What's the moral of the story? Get your story (or stories) straight, *before* you start mythologizing.

Jesus the Sinner

Jesus called himself the "Son of Man," meaning a son of mankind. He had a human mother, and supposedly a god for a father. But, the Bible says, all humans have sinned, with no exceptions. (Romans 3:23) How is it possible that Jesus, whose mother, Mary, was a sinner, could not have received his mother's sinful genes? Being a virgin teenager, as Mary allegedly was, does not exempt one from sinning. Mary could not have been a perfect person just because her hymen was intact.

Very quickly, we can see that this convoluted story has a lot of holes, one of which is the bizarre idea that Jesus, as a human, didn't inherit the original sin from Adam and Eve that Mary was no doubt carrying in her ovaries. Did the invisible god-sperm Yahweh was carrying in his invisible loins zap those sinful genes right out of Mary's egg at the moment of conception?!

Of course, all of this conjecture is silly because the story is twisted and absurd.

THE MINISTRY OF JESUS

The Man Who Imagined He Was God

After the birth of Jesus, very little is mentioned in the accepted texts of the Holy Bible from then until he is nearly a teenager. At the age of 12, we see a Jesus that is, at the very least, intelligent enough to argue and banter with the elders of the synagogue. This is nothing unusual for any *pre* bar mitzvah age Jewish boy who has been immersed in study of the Torah. But for non-Jewish readers, this somehow seems amazing. But, no matter. The best is yet to come.

Little else is mentioned about Jesus from that tender age of 12 until he turns 30. A full 18 years pass and Jesus does nothing? No dating, marrying, carousing with friends – just remaining chaste and perfect for all that time – a man without temptations or ambitions? It seems a bit preposterous, but perhaps the details of that part of his life are left unwritten, uneventful, or lost to antiquity? *The Infancy Gospel of Thomas* does tell about a young Jesus, but one who was less than perfect, as Jesus is shown cursing another boy who later dies, blinding another child's parents, and doing trivial miracles such as turning clay birds into real ones. But this book never made it into the Biblical canon, and not because the stories about young Jesus were ridiculously unbelievable, but because they

144

depicted a more human, imperfect Jesus. However, because of their physics-defying nature, we can easily pass over these early details regarding the life of Jesus, the same as any Christian.

We see in the Bible that Jesus begins his ministry with his baptism, around the age of 30. Jesus is immersed in the water by the appropriately named John the Baptist, and soon after, the Holy Spirit descends upon Jesus.

Any novice reader, at first glance, would assume that this descending Holy Spirit is actually the god, Yahweh – who himself is described as both holy and a spirit – but it isn't. Suddenly, we are introduced to another sub-section of the godhead. It's not just Yahweh playing both the part of a human son and a father god. There is a third piece of this puzzle which for all intents and purposes is no different in function or description that the spirit God, Yahweh. So, we are left with more questions than answers. If this holy spirit comes from God and separates itself from God to do things like descend on earthly gods and men (to improve them, perhaps?), then what is left behind from whence it came? A sectioned Yahweh, by himself? A shell? A less powerful Yahweh? An *unholy* spirit? And if God and Holy Spirit are one and the same, why bother to describe them separately?

It is clear that the Holy Spirit is meant to be a unique entity and an equal one-third of the godhead. (When divided equally, that's 0.33 with an infinite number of 3's after it, which could never actually complete a whole when added together. But the math isn't important right now.) This new Holy Third is somehow special because Jesus introduces a new eternally damning prohibition regarding anyone speaking ill of this extra ethereal thing. So, we have to just accept it and move on. The holy, and wholly spiritual, God has a double, a twin. But a very special twin, apparently.

More on "The Holy Spigot"

The Jews originally did not have a holy spirit separate from God. God was spirit, and holy, therefore God *was* the holy spirit. And God could not be incarnate. God was not a physical material being, and would have no need to become a man. From ancient times, Jews have repeated again and again: "God is One!" Not three into one. And not three out of one. God is indivisible, according to the Jews, and this was the indisputable Jewish dogma prior to the appearance of the dubious existence of the Jesus character.

Outside of Old Testament insistence that Yahweh is a single being, the concept of a triune god goes back much further than Yahweh and the Hebrews. We can find this concept in ancient Egypt with the gods Amun, Ptah, and Re (Ra). These gods are regarded as a trinity who are distinct gods, but together they are One:

> All gods are three: Amun, Re and Ptah, whom none equals. He who hides his name as Amun, he appears to the face as Re (Ra), his body is Ptah. – (*The Leiden Hymns*)

So much for Christian originality.

Jesus gets tempted... finally!

Immediately after his baptism with physical water and spiritual spirit, Jesus goes out into the wilderness – which we assume to be the desert where there are no people to witness what happens. And it is here that Jesus is tempted by Satan. Why Jesus wasn't tempted like this when he was 21 and more vulnerable, that is, without his Holy Spirit to guide him and protect him from temptation, is rather mysterious. Perhaps Satan was on a long hiatus? Satan must be kicking himself for missing such a fortuitous opportunity.

Jesus was in that wilderness for forty days and didn't eat anything the entire time. This would have to be the first miracle of Jesus, because it's highly unlikely anyone could master this feat alone. Nevertheless, Jesus overcomes this and his struggle against Satan's temptation, and despite no one even knowing he had been starving himself for almost six weeks in a row, he returns to Galilee suddenly semi-famous – but the reason for that isn't clearly explained. (See Luke 4:14)

Very soon after this event, Jesus gets busy rather quickly, choosing disciples and healing the sick. He would soon become bigger than The Beatles. (!)

Jesus the Itinerant

We now know what Jesus was allegedly doing in his early thirties – walking from town to town, preaching and teaching to the people, and attracting mostly the vulnerable lower classes with his message. But, to get a greater picture of the preacher Jesus, we need to look at his attitude, his presence, his demeanor, and his apparent state of mind as he traveled across the Levant in search of these followers. And afterward, we can study what Jesus actually said to those who followed.

Word(s) to your Mother!

When reading the story of an adult Jesus in the New Testament, one gets a sense that much of what Jesus says is either an ominous threat, a reprimand, a narcissistic comment, or a story to force the listener to feel pangs of guilt. Beyond this, Jesus doesn't really seem to have much else to offer that is positive other than an occasional reference to peace, love, and charity – but those lofty ideals have to be plucked from between the threats of future violence, torture and damnation. Anyone can talk about themselves, threaten people, and make others feel guilty. Is this really the *raison d'être* for the ministry of Jesus? Perhaps we should ask the following question first...

Was Jesus a Narcissist of the Fanatic Type?

Whatever his purpose in life was to have been, whether for himself or for others, no one ever said Jesus was stupid. His followers could be called that, however – as others often are when they innocently or blindly follow a crazy person into a delusional abyss. Gullible people often make the mistake of thinking that someone with an exaggerated confidence must know what they're talking about and therefore must always be right. This amazingly confident person becomes easy to follow. And the followers become easy to manipulate. And rarely is it for a good cause. It's happened way too many times throughout the history of humanity. And as history tells us, the vast majority of those manipulators were extreme narcissists.

Let's see if Jesus was one of them. This test is based on the definition of Narcissistic Personality Disorder as shown within the Diagnostic and Statistical Manual of Mental Disorders (DSM-IV). Bear in mind, you only need to have five or more of these traits to be considered an egomaniac, a person with NPD.

Traits of someone with narcissistic personality disorder:

1. **An exaggerated sense of one's own abilities and achievements. Has a grandiose sense of self importance, e.g., exaggerates achievements and talents.** (Jesus stating anyone can move mountains by faith in him alone...and to this day no one has ever achieved such a preposterous thing. Most self-proclaimed psychics have trouble bending spoons, much less moving entire mountains. See Matthew 17:20.)

2. **Is preoccupied with fantasies of unlimited success, power, brilliance, beauty, or ideal love.** (The entire New Testament when Jesus speaks. See the discussion further down in this chapter regarding love.)

3. **Believes that he or she is "special" and unique and can only be understood by, or should associate with, other special or high status people.** (Jesus telling his followers they can only "...come to the father through me." And his frequent reminders to others that "My kingdom is not of this world." See John 6:44 and John 18:36.)

4. **Requires excessive admiration.** (Jesus frequently talked about his coming future "kingdom," with him at the head, which he expected would be established at any moment. See Mark 1:15, Matthew 3:2, 10:7 and 4:17.)

5. **Has a sense of entitlement, i.e., unreasonable expectations of especially favorable treatment or automatic compliance with his or her expectations.** (Jesus teaching in the temple at age 12, and rebuking his parents. Frequent attempts to get others to "follow me." The words me and I are used with incredible frequency by Jesus. Rarely does he make a statement without inserting his own ego, and often even does so in third person narrative. See most of the words of Jesus in the New Testament.)

6. **Is interpersonally exploitative, i.e., takes advantage of others to achieve his or her own ends.** (Using his disciples and other followers for his own self-aggrandizement and "glory." A perfect example is Jesus

throwing out the money-changers to make himself look powerful and humble at the same time. See Matthew 21:12.)

7. **Lacks empathy.** (Stating you must "hate your mother and father..." for him, of course! Having no concern for grieving families, stating, "Let the dead bury the dead..." etc. See Luke 14:26 and Matthew 8:22.)

8. **Is often envious of others or believes that others are envious of him or her.** (Constantly quarrelling with the Pharisees. Jesus was not part of the "in-crowd" and it clearly bothered him. See Luke 19:39, Luke 20:21, John 3:2, John 8:3-4, Matthew 22:41-46, and Mark 12:35-40.)

9. **Shows arrogant or haughty behaviors and attitudes.** (Jesus telling entire crowds such self-aggrandizing things as, "I am the way, the truth, and the life." See John 14:6 for just one example.)

And all of Jesus' attempts at "humility," and service to others, were still used for one end in mind – self glorification. No humble act was ever *not* accompanied with the reminder of his greatness, and a lesson on whom credit was due.

Jesus scores a whopping 9 out of 9 on the NPD scale!

To try the same test on the "father" of Jesus, Yahweh, go to the chapter on the Old Testament. You may discover that this NPD is hereditary.

The Seven Faces of Dr. Jesus

Narcissism may be the dominant negative trait in his personality, but for Jesus, it's not the only one. When we read the New Testament all the way through, it appears as though there are many "Jesuses." That is, there is a single Jesus with a vast array of personas, with often conflicting and contradictory ideas, which make it seem as though Jesus is running for office, telling the people what they want to hear, and altering the message depending on his audience. We will try to cover as many of these Jesus-types in this section below:

Love Hurts

Love. Everybody wants it. Everybody needs it. But does everyone agree on what it is? Here's Jesus talking about love:

> 'Master, which is the great commandment in the law?' Jesus said unto him, 'Thou shalt love the Lord thy God with all thy heart, and with all thy soul, and with all thy mind. This is the first and great commandment. And the second is like unto it, Thou shalt love thy neighbour as thyself. On these two commandments hang all the law and the prophets.' – (*Matthew 22:36-40 KJV*)

148

Sounds peaceful, doesn't it? But when we read this, shouldn't we ask what Jesus' definition of "love" is? And is it a good and moral definition? Jesus is talking about commandments from God here. However, in another part of the same book, (Matthew 5:17-20) Jesus says all of the law is to be obeyed and fulfilled (i.e., the law is sacred and holy). So, when one looks at that law and sees how ignorant, violent, misanthropic, and genocidal it is, we must only conclude that Jesus thought those actions represented "love." If Jesus is committed to that law, then his father (Yahweh) killing all his chosen people's *neighbors* was an act of "love" by Jesus' definition of love. Creating an eternal torment for not believing in him is "love," according to Jesus. Approving of slavery and rape is "love" as far as Jesus is concerned. This kind of "love" (for the commandments of God) is the same kind of love psychopaths talk about because they are incapable of experiencing real love. Is this really the kind of *evil persona* anyone would want to follow?

Apparently, a god becoming a man does not make that god more sympathetic to mankind. In fact, it appears that it may make him less so.

A Love/Hate Relationship

The quote by Jesus about love (above) is also repeated in Mark 12:28-31. But, Jesus is also quoted as saying this:

> If any man come to me, and **hate** not his father, and mother, and wife, and children, and brethren, and sisters, yea, and his own life also, he cannot be my disciple. – (*Luke 14:26 KJV*) [Emphasis Added]

Can you have it both ways? Love God and your neighbor, but hate everyone else? Christians make a lot of excuses for their Lord, saying non-believers are taking this out of context, or that "hate" doesn't really mean hate. Should we also assume that "love" doesn't really mean love? As stated elsewhere, if a word doesn't "really mean" something, why use the word in the first place? Cannot the creator of all things come up with a better word than "hate"? And can there be degrees of hate? And if so, which degree of hate is Jesus talking about here? Or, is this just another mistranslation?

There have yet to be presented any adequate responses to this conundrum. One of the key phrases in the above passage refers to hating one's own life. And, as modern psychology has shown, self-loathing indeed does lead to the loathing of others – usually with very unfortunate outcomes. If Jesus simply means "turn your back" on others and follow him, then that's what he should have said. This, of course, is asking people to "sacrifice" their own day-to-day lives for Jesus. And Jesus doesn't really seem to care what is left behind – abandoned wives, children, and others who will suffer without a husband, father, or provider. In any event, an advocate of love cannot also be an advocate of hate – in exactly the same way that "no one can serve two masters." (See Matthew 6:24).

149

Jesus Disqualifies Everyone On Earth

Jesus has some really strict rules and qualifications for having you as a follower. The continuation of the above passage about hate is as follows:

> ...And whosoever doth not bear his cross, and come after me, cannot be my disciple... So likewise, whosoever he be of you that forsaketh not **all** that he hath, he cannot be my disciple. – (*Luke 14:27-33 KJV*) [Emphasis Added]

The final line sums it up well when the word "all" is used. Again, this cannot be altered to mean "some" or "most." All is all. All means everything. A disciple must give up and "hate" everything that is not focused on Jesus. Somehow this is supposed to save you from having that exact same Jesus toss you into an eternal burning torture chamber. What a freak we have in Jesus! It's saying in its most basic terms, "Worship me twenty-four hours a day and nothing else, or I'll burn you!"

Now, we must ask ourselves: Have we ever seen any human on earth do anything close to what Jesus demands in Luke 14:26-33? Of course we have not. We then must conclude, if doing what Jesus demands is the definition of a Christian, then Christians don't really exist, and never have.

Anger Management Jesus

When it comes to anger, Jesus himself is contradictory: In Matthew 5:22 he plainly states that anger is a sin, yet in various other places in the Bible he angrily curses several cities, curses a fig tree in anger, and in one passage, "looks around angrily." His hypocrisy doesn't set a very good example. Although Jesus says "love your enemies," in numerous passages, Jesus is aggressively hurling epithets at his own enemies, and not very lovingly. Ephesians 4:26, written after Jesus' death tries to assuage the commandment of Jesus by stating, "be angry and do not sin" even though Jesus statement was quite clear that "anyone angry with his brother" is subject to judgment and eventual "hell fire."

And speaking of hell...

Firefighters of the Ancient World

Let's talk about the place people allegedly go for not believing all the monstrous things Jesus has to offer: Hell. It's a forever burning fire with no escape. Primitive man may not have known much, but he understood the concept of infinity, or "forever." And to burn forever was exceptionally scary.

If you just sat and pondered for a moment, and thought about primitive man, what powerful thing would he be most concerned about? The answer is fire. It's mysterious. It's both controllable and uncontrollable. And no primitive man knows where it comes from. Is it any wonder that the Bible is obsessed with fire? The word fire appears 549 times in the Bible. There's a fiery sword keeping people out of the Garden of Eden, there are pillars of fire, fiery chariots, fires from heaven, burning bushes, lakes of fire, "strange" fires, altars of fire, when anything bad happens it always gets consumed by fire, and the worst place you could go (hell) is made up of fire. Holy Smokes! This was the motive for creating a place of punishment which consisted of only fire. But, we don't have to fear fire (as much) anymore. Maybe it's time for humans to grow up. There are now other scarier things we have to worry about.

Where the hell did hell come from?

Jesus actually makes things *worse* by introducing his version of Hell to the mind of the Christian believer. Hell is the ultimate threat, the never ending threat, the one threat that just won't go away.

Hell is a sinister place, ruled by a horrible god-like creature known as Satan, The Devil, Lucifer, and numerous other names that are supposed to make the Christian believer shudder.

Hell in the Old Testament, (which has numerous *other* ancient Jewish writings to support it), does not have a Hell with the same meaning as the one in the new Christian book that it spawned. Hell in the Old Testament normally means death, or a graveyard, not a spiritual fireplace where your soul goes if you've been a bad little boy or a bad little girl.

Jesus clearly borrowed the fiery concept of Hell (*Hades,* or more accurately, *Tartarus*) from the neighboring Greeks, as Jesus was living at a time when his country (and his religion) was being greatly influenced by the beliefs of the Greeks and Romans. Jesus makes the egregious mistake of incorporating an alien idea (hellfire and torture in the afterlife) into his own already specious version of Judaism.

Hell is the Reason for the Season

There is a reason why Christianity hasn't fallen into the hole of obscurity like other myths: Fear. Christianity is the only one that has a "blasphemy clause" – an unforgivable sin. It's also one of the ones (the other being Islam) that has the punishment of eternal torment for the finite "thought crime" of simply saying, "I don't believe." Human beings are very fearful creatures. Any religion, with such a cruel concept as hell, is truly harsh. It's this stranglehold on the human mind that keeps these ideas alive. Without the exaggerated fear, such religions would die a quick death.

Living In a Rational Hell

Would you beat your child with a baseball bat for not brushing his teeth? Would you stab your child in the stomach for not doing his homework? Would you toss your child off a cliff for stealing a cookie? Then, why would God torture his children forever for simply not believing he exists (especially if he rarely does anything to show himself)?

What rational God would punish rationality? Bad guys get to heaven by repenting at the last minute, but good altruistic non-believers go to hell? That doctrine in itself is inherently immoral. One more rationale to not believe in the god-concept.

Getting Tortured by the Guy Who's Saving You
(The Heavenly Protection Racket)

Imagine for a moment that you own a thriving business in the downtown area of your home town. Imagine also that one day a guy comes into your store to offer you protection from vandals, thieves, shoplifters, and even from your competitors. The cost for this protection is that you simply have to do what he says, no questions asked. You just have to trust him. Your first question might be, "What happens if I *don't* do everything you say, or what if I want the protection to stop? Then what?" The guy replies, "Well, if you refuse, I'll break your thumbs, your legs, and torture you until I decide to stop torturing you." Sounds like the Mafia, doesn't it? And it's not a very appealing deal at all.

Yet, this is very similar to what Jesus offers. (And why this book often refers to the "Kingdom of God" as a ruthless dictatorship.) Jesus also offers protection, and the fantastical additional offer of "eternal" life with him, but you also have to do as he says. If you don't, won't, or can't, you get tortured forever. (In Jesus-World, everyone lives forever, it's just a small fraction of people who *don't* get the eternal burning sensation.) And the torture chamber is already fired up and standing by for those who don't obey. It turns out, the guy "protecting" you will also be the guy ordering you into the ovens by his decree. And his evil lackey, Satan, will be the one pushing you in. Jesus, it seems, is a thug and a mobster in sheep's clothing. Put a (pitch)fork in you, you're done.

Yahweh's Rival (Satan, The Red God)

Talk to any religious person subscribing to either of the Big Three (Judaism, Christianity, or Islam) and you'll soon see how amazing it is that Satan somehow manages to get his message across to people so much better and clearer than Yahweh or Jesus. And some have even suggested that Jesus and Satan are the same god! (It's not that far-fetched if you suspend all disbelief – as you must if you believe in the fantasy world of gods.) If you're the creator of *everything,* you have to play all the parts in your grand universe-wide game of human manipulation.

However, for an atheist, Satan, whatever or whoever he allegedly is (or was), is just another god – one that is sometimes worse and sometimes better than the other gods, but still just part of some delusional human being's out-of-control imagination.

The condemnations we have for one god apply equally to all the gods: they are nonsense until proven to exist.

The Jesus Police

Here are the "crimes" for which Jesus would terminate you, or send you to a fiery eternal torment:

1. Not believing he exists or existed.
2. Not following his "teachings."
3. Not loving your "neighbor" (as in fellow man).
4. Calling another person a fool.
5. Saying bad things about the elusive and poorly defined "Holy Spirit."

Obviously, freedom of speech does not exist in the Kingdom of God, making it the ultimate dictatorship. And being executed for thought crimes (see number 1) makes the Kingdom of God the most heinous police state in the universe. It's fascinating how Jesus wants you to weep over *his* execution, but he won't be shedding any tears over yours.

Jesus and the Giant Mixed Message

Jesus is a demanding fellow, and is quite consistent with his inconsistencies.

> Be perfect, therefore, as your heavenly Father is perfect. – (*Matthew 5:48 KVJ*)

But, isn't that impossible? Impossible, even with the good and perfect Jesus to make you perfect? So, how perfect is Jesus?

> And he said unto him, Why callest thou me good? there is **none good** but one, that is, God: but if thou wilt enter into life, keep the commandments. – (*Matthew 19:17 KJV*) [Emphasis Added]

Okay, so we aren't good (and that includes Jesus) and we *can't* be good without the non-good Jesus, but Jesus expects perfection anyway? And, all of this isn't really about loving a "loving" god anyway, it's about *obedience?*

> Jesus saith unto him, I am the way, the truth, and the life: no man cometh unto the Father, but by me. – (*John 14:6 KJV*)

So, the only way to be perfect is to believe in Jesus, the guy who admits he isn't good himself, and who also invented an eternal torment for those who aren't good?

> But I will forewarn you whom ye shall fear: Fear him, which after he hath killed hath power to cast into hell; yea, I say unto you, Fear him. – (*Luke 12:5 KJV*)

Will the non-good Jesus eventually toss himself into the fire as well?
Once again, we see expectations of perfection, constant criticism of behaviors, personality obsession, cruel threats of punishment. Is Jesus *trying* to make you get OCD, or social anxiety disorder (among the other problems that could come from all of this)?

Reality Jesus

"The truth will set you free!" This is one of the most oft-quoted lines attributed to the Jesus of Nazareth character. However, there are at least two problems with this statement. First, from reading the other lines attributed to Jesus, we can see that Jesus is not concerned with actual truth, but is rather keenly focused on *belief* instead. And, as shown elsewhere in this book, those two things, belief (wishing, hoping) and truth (knowing something to be correct) are two very different things. What Jesus actually means is, "Belief (in me) will set you free," which is an unfounded statement based on the fact (the truth) that Jesus does not provide anyone with much evidence for his divinity, demonstrating quite clearly on the other hand, that he is a person with delusions of grandeur and likely a person suffering from narcissistic personality disorder.

But, what if the original statement, by itself, is true? Is "the truth will set you free" true? Or, even partially true? Truth is simply something we *know* to be correct, and we know it based on our limited subjective view of the universe. This kind of truth can change when more information is acquired. That's always a possibility that we cannot lightly dismiss. Because we *know* this truth about truth, we can surmise that it isn't really truth that sets us free, but *knowledge* that does so. Once we know something, it's nearly impossible to eliminate that from our minds. The more we know, the less our limitations, and the freer we become. Had Jesus stated *this* truth, "Knowledge will set you free!" – his religion wouldn't have made it out of the first century because, as we happily now *know,* knowledge forever demolishes mysticism and superstition, the two pillars of religious thought.

Jesus Hates Figs!

Below is the infamous passage of Jesus encountering Middle Eastern fruit:

> Now in the morning as he returned into the city, he hungered. And when he saw a fig tree in the way, he came to it, and found nothing thereon, but leaves only, and said unto it, 'Let no fruit grow on thee henceforward for ever.' And presently the fig tree withered away. And when the disciples saw it, they marvelled, saying, 'How soon is the fig tree withered away!' Jesus answered and said unto them, 'Verily I say unto you, If ye have faith, and doubt not, ye shall not only do this which is done to the fig tree, but also if ye shall say unto this mountain, Be thou removed, and be thou cast into the sea; it shall be done.' – (*Matthew 21:18-21 KJV*)

The passage reveals that Jesus was *not* a god. A truly supernatural being would have no need to react this way. (Is the passage lying when it states Jesus was hungry?) If you really are hungry, why not just make the fig tree suddenly bear fruit? Wouldn't it take as much energy to do that as it would to make the plant instantly wither and die? Or, does Jesus prefer destroying life over creating it? Again, quite frequently, Jesus appears to be more evil than good.

What we see here is that Jesus exercises his freedom of choice and chooses the negative, destructive path. What if his choice had been to make the tree bear fruit? The lesson could have been that god is ultimately in control of everything and can turn anything into good. Yet it appears the opposite is true, as Jesus would rather condemn, even symbolically. The Author of Everything chooses to threaten people. Why? Does this mean he's not really in control after all?

Jesus Hates Testicles (Almost as Much as Figs!)

Maybe it's the similar shape – figs and testicles – where Jesus has his problem, but here's the passage:

> For there are some eunuchs, which were so born from their mother's womb: and there are some eunuchs, which were made eunuchs of men: and there be eunuchs, which have made themselves eunuchs for the kingdom of heaven's sake. He that is able to receive it, let him receive it. – (*Matthew 19:12 KJV*)

As if circumcision wasn't painful enough! Now, the god-man is going for your balls! What's ironic is the fact that Yahweh, the alleged father of Jesus, told Moses that anyone with mutilated genitals (circumcision being the only exception) was not worthy to be in God's presence. So much for father-to-son consistency:

> He that is wounded in the stones or hath his private member cut off shall not enter into the congregation of the Lord. – (*Deuteronomy 23:1 KJV*)

Perhaps Yahweh's injunction was literal and the one from Jesus was metaphorical? In any case, the first causes physical pain, and the latter causes psychological pain, neither of which are evidence for a loving god.

Jesus: "The Eyes Have It!"

Will the mutilation ever end? Apparently not. Another set of human orbs are assaulted by Jesus. (Again, there must be something about the shape of figs, eyes, and testicles Jesus just doesn't like.)

The New Testament shows Jesus discussing the idea of plucking out your eye in *two* different passages (Matthew 18:9 and Mark 9:47). This is for the sin of lust, so by the end of the gospels, you're completely eyeless! We should mention that it's not just eyes that are guilty, hands are evil as well. (See Matthew 5:29.) If people took Jesus literally (and some have), every male over the age of 13 would be completely blind and disfigured.

Here is one of the *eye* passages:

And if thy **right eye** offend thee, pluck it out, and cast it from thee: for it is profitable for thee that one of thy members should perish, and not that thy whole body should be cast into hell. – (*Matthew 18:9 KJV*) [Emphasis Added]

Here's the other involving your hand:

And if thy **right hand** offend thee, cut it off, and cast it from thee: for it is profitable for thee that one of thy members should perish, and not that thy whole body should be cast into hell. – (*Matthew 5:29 KJV*) [Emphasis Added]

Is the cutting off of hands a prohibition against masturbation? Apparently, lust (a creation of God for reproduction in humans) was so offensive to Jesus that a man ought to *choose* to remake his body without hands or eyes – not in the image of god, but in the image of a pathetic mutilation?

Even if this was all meant metaphorically, it still fails. The problem is that Jesus doesn't understand that the mind controls the body, not the other way around. If you have no eyes or hands, what is stopping you from fantasizing about the opposite sex? Nothing, of course. Your eyes are not controlling your brain, your brain is controlling your eyes. The same is true for the hands. The only way to remove lust is to remove the portion of the brain that controls lust. But in the time of Jesus, most people, Jesus included, thought the brain was a useless organ, and that the heart was where all emotion and thought came from. If primitive man had known the truth, children of today would be using construction paper to cut out the shapes of *gray brains* on Valentine's Day instead of red hearts. (!)

Obviously, Jesus had an ignorant and primitive way of looking at things – which is a predictable reflection of the culture in which he lived.

Jesus Didn't Heal Enough People

Matthew 27:51-52 states that the moment Jesus died, many saints from the past were resurrected. How many is many? That's anyone's guess. Apparently, while Jesus was alive, he didn't heal or resurrect enough people to prove his worth, so he added a few more at the moment of death.

This is what we can call the Miracle of the Winged Monkeys because it is just as plausible as the flying chimp-like creatures in *The Wizard of Oz*. In the Wizard story, the Winged Monkeys were smart enough to obey commands but could not speak. This is similar to the people who were supposedly resurrected about the same time Jesus died. They too were able to obey a command (from God) to pull themselves out of the dirt soon after their re-assembly and make-over. But, apparently, being dead awhile affects your ability to *tell anyone* you were resurrected! Why did no one interview these newly reanimated people? Or, why did no one interview these perfected zombie's relatives about how amazing it was to see a *non-dead* Uncle Wally after all these years?

156

The Limitless Limbless

Oddly enough, Jesus was able to resurrect entire human bodies, and make "sick" people well again, but amputees are conveniently ignored. We never hear in the Bible, and haven't ever heard since, of any person losing a limb and then becoming physically healed by Jesus or his minions. If you can restore an entire body back to life, why not a limb? It's less work. Not as much supernatural energy is needed for a body part. But, alas, it never happens. What does Jesus have against limbless people? If you're missing a limb, your pleas for healing are ignored? Yahweh, when transformed into Jesus, finally accepts men without testicles, but those without arms or legs will have to wait another 2000 years?

The suspicion grows. When a "powerful" being is suddenly discovered to have such obvious limitations, we begin to suspect that all the "healing" of the sick, and the "rising of the dead" were all magic tricks designed to make Jesus the precursor to Houdini in both fame and fortune. Should we try to guess how much Jesus paid Lazarus for his acting skills?

Jesus Tells Stories Around The Campfire

God the Son, is still a "Father." Does that make the followers of Jesus, Yahweh's grandchildren? Without being any more facetious than necessary, we have to ask, why does a father make his instructions so ambiguous? If he wanted his "children" to exercise their free will and have a real clear choice, wouldn't he want to be more specific or obvious, and not hide his instructions in mystery or parable, especially when his own disciples are having such a hard time following his line of reasoning? Wouldn't he just say, "You do this, and this will happen. You do this other thing, and this other thing will happen. But, it's still your choice." Wouldn't this sort of direct approach be more like a *real* parent talking to his children? And if the hidden meanings were meant to show that sometimes you have to figure things out on your own, then why is Christianity so opposed to science – that realm of learning that requires humanity to do exactly that – figure things out on your own?

The Christian faithful will say that the reason Jesus relates all these philosophical stories with hidden meanings is simply to test his followers. So, Jesus is a scientist after all! But, this experiment cannot hold water (or wine) if Jesus is more than just a messiah – if he is also a god. As the all-knowing, all-powerful creator of the universe, Jesus would know whether or not someone will pass a test of faith before it ever happens. And he allegedly does so when he accurately predicts his apostle, Peter, will deny him three times in one night. No need to test anyone when you already know the outcome. And it cannot help the "testee" if his fate is already predetermined by the all-knowing god. Any way you slice this herring, it's still a dead fish. The Christian apologists are wrong.

To Save or Not to Save

The Christian pulpit will also pitch the more accurate idea that God/Jesus spoke in parables because he didn't want certain people to know about his "Good

News." He wanted these contemporaneous "closed-minded" people to be condemned. (See Matthew 13:10-11 and Mark 4:10-13.) In fact, Jesus even admits that if he did not intentionally talk in parables, those people might listen to him and *not* perish in his cruel metaphysical torture of fire. So, Jesus deliberately, actively, and consciously, keeps his supposed secrets about the universe from others, and lets them die without knowing his alleged truth. If the story of Jesus were a real one, the analogy of Jesus' decision would be the same as seeing your child drowning while you're standing on the shore with a lifeline, but due to *your own anger,* instead of throwing the lifeline to your child, you go hide behind a rock. How's that for a parable?

More *Not* Saving by the Savior

Early on in the New Testament, Jesus makes the following rather revealing statement:

> Not every one that saith unto me, Lord, Lord, shall enter into the kingdom of heaven; but he that doeth the will of my Father which is in heaven. Many will say to me in that day, Lord, Lord, have we not prophesied in thy name? and in thy name have cast out devils? and in thy name done many wonderful works? And then will I profess unto them, I never knew you: depart from me, ye that work iniquity. – (*Matthew 7:21-23 KJV*)

This is one more of the many scriptures that reinforce Jesus' determination to only let in a very tiny number of people into his "Kingdom" while letting everyone else get dumped into the fiery pit he created.

Matthew 7:21-23 has Jesus saying that not all that call on the Lord will be saved. And, yet we clearly have a problem of consistency when we read the later apostles, who are not quoting the actual words of Jesus himself: Acts 2:21 and Romans 10:13 claim that *anyone* that calls on the Lord Jesus will be saved. Are these just more examples of Christians *reversing* the exact words of Jesus to fit their own interpretation or agenda? It appears so. Christians started this habit pretty early on it seems. A pattern that continues to this day.

Yet, when you think about Jesus saying a large number of his own followers would *not* be saved from his torment, it makes sense, at least within the entire convoluted context of Christian dogma. Matthew 7:13-14 is another dire passage where Jesus gives another (even earlier) warning that not all will be saved:

> Enter ye in at the strait gate: for wide is the gate, and broad is the way, that leadeth to destruction, and many there be which go in thereat: Because strait is the gate, and narrow is the way, which leadeth unto life, and few there be that find it. (*KJV*)

Even if Jesus had not clearly stated his intent, simply being a creator of infinite fears and threats, he reveals himself to be someone who does not want everyone to be saved. Why build an eternal fiery torture chamber if you're not going to use it? If Jesus did want everyone to be saved, as an all-powerful god, he could, and would work it out so that *everyone would actually be saved*, one way or another, and would not make such a noticeably threatening statement as shown in Matthew 7:21-23 (above).

So, is somebody lying? Once again, we see another apostle-generated about-face recorded in 2 Peter 3:9, stating that Jesus *does* want everyone to be saved. (Remember, if a real god wanted something, a real god would get it.)

> The Lord is not slack concerning his promise, as some men count slackness; but is longsuffering to us-ward, **not willing that any should perish,** but that all should come to repentance. (*KJV*) [Emphasis Added]

It appears Peter is denying Jesus again! Or, at least contradicting him. Maybe there's not enough room in heaven for everyone, or the alleged Lord thinks certain people smell funny, but in any event, Jesus is certainly *willing* that people will perish, and the author of Peter is covering for him. The whole "plan" (burning in hell for an eternity) is a vicious way to eliminate people (or "souls").

At least one of the early Christian apologists is willing to reiterate that the alleged messiah does *not* want everyone to be saved. Paul, in Romans 9:22-23 says this:

> What if God, willing to shew his wrath, and to make his power known, endured with much longsuffering the **vessels of wrath fitted to destruction**: And that he might make known the riches of his glory on the vessels of mercy, which he had **afore prepared** unto glory... (*KJV*) [Emphasis Added]

"Vessels" – if you read the entire chapter, are *human beings*. Romans 9 is saying that God has created some humans for destruction, for the single purpose of demonstrating his power and glory and nothing more. This negates free will (by deciding for the human beforehand who will be "saved" and who will not), and shows the Almighty God to be the Almighty Psychopath. It's the "I brought you into this world, I can take you out!" philosophy all abusive parents say to their children, *plus* the actual means and premeditated guarantee to carry out that threat. Again, an almighty god who really wanted everyone to be saved, would just wave his magic wand and everyone would be saved. In the end, it's his ballgame, his rules, his outcome. And his lies.

Although the great majority of self-proclaimed Christians do believe what they believe out of fear, according to most Bible scholars, fear is not the "correct" motive for believing in Jesus. Love is. And yet, it is Jesus himself who created the fear factors (i.e., hell, and blaspheming the Holy Spirit.) If the only thing Jesus wanted is your love, threats would not be unnecessary. Threats of death are not a very effective way of getting someone's love. Of course, as we mentioned previously, perhaps Jesus' love is a bit skewed, or he simply has no concept of what human love really is.

Apparently, it never occurred to Jesus that people might actually love him, his message, and one another, *without* any sort of highly exaggerated threats looming in the background.

Hairy Jesus and the Goblet of Fire

While we're on the subject of saving people... Why isn't the living Jesus daily lamenting and weeping over the souls of atheists, crying his eyes out non-stop? If Jesus really wanted everyone to be saved, wouldn't he physically intervene in their lives?

Christians say, "God will talk to you if you only open your heart and mind!" Yet Paul, a Jewish Pharisee, known for his murderous zealotry against Christians, and *not* an atheist, didn't have to do any personal soul searching. He was supposedly zapped with a light from heaven and blinded. Who wouldn't convert after that kind of trauma? Apparently, the all-powerful god stopped conking people on the head with a spiritual sky hammer a long time ago. So, to Jesus, either other people don't matter as much as Paul, (especially atheists) or he only reserves the in-your-face, here-I-am type of conversion for believers in God who also happen to kill Christians!

The Prophecies and Predictions of Jesus

One of the reasons given by Christians as to why others should believe that Jesus is "The One," is Jesus' amazing ability to predict the future. But, Jesus wasn't exactly Kreskin when it came to predicting things, as you'll see in a moment. In fact, Nostradamus, the 16th Century alchemist was much more accurate and specific than Jesus ever was. On that basis, maybe we should consider that Nostradamus was the Messiah!

The "prophecies" of Jesus are not a valid reason to believe Jesus was a god, messiah, or even a good con man. His predictions were so trite and ambiguous, you can be certain, were he alive today, many would advise him to not quit his day job as a carpenter.

Here is one of Jesus' most famous predictions:

> Immediately after the tribulation of those days shall the sun be darkened and the moon shall not give her light, and the stars shall fall from heaven and the powers of the heavens shall be shaken... – (*Matthew 24:29 KJV*)

There isn't really an "up" or "down" in space, so stars "falling" from heaven makes no sense. Where are they going to land? On earth? When the stars are millions of times larger than the earth? If he meant meteors, comets, or asteroids, why didn't he *say* meteors, comets, or asteroids? Could the truth be that Jesus and his followers knew virtually nothing about astronomy?

As for the sun being "darkened" – that would mean certain death for all life on earth, and that would include the magical Jesus as he's coming through the darkened clouds without a flashlight. Furthermore, the "powers of the heavens" would not be shook. A tiny planet like Earth, disappearing from the vastness of the universe, would hardly be noticed.

In Matthew 24:35, Jesus predicts that "heaven and earth will pass away, but my words will by no means pass away." He predicted his words would last forever, even beyond the death of the sun, apparently, and even beyond the death of the universe. Jesus' narcissism runs deep. This is a "prediction" that no one can ever verify. When the universe is about to take its last metaphorical breath, and no life forms exist, who will be there to witness whether or not the words of Jesus were right or wrong, or if they still exist? Anyone can make such impossible, unverifiable, non-falsifiable predictions. It doesn't take super powers to do this.

Other contemporaneous predictions allegedly made by Jesus about himself, how or when he would die, who would betray him, etc., are all inadmissible as they are not profound, or amazing, or any other ethereal adjective one might want to use. Yet such "predictions" can easily be placed in the record after the fact and claimed as true by anyone who lived after Jesus. And, as we can see, the Biblical canon, and the writings included in that canon, were all declared factual long after the death of Jesus. Anyone can be an editor. And zealous religious editors have the most to gain through exaggeration.

Back to the Future Jesus

In Matthew 24:2, Jesus predicts the destruction of the Temple in Jerusalem. However, the Temple had been destroyed once before, and Jesus was living in a time of constant war and devastation. It wasn't a stretch to predict that anything at all would no longer remain standing.

Further on, in Matthew 24:6, Jesus predicts "wars and rumors of wars." War was the constant life of the Bronze and Iron Age human being. The area Jesus lived in was in constant upheaval. Resistance to Roman rule was everywhere. To predict a war in that region would have been easy, especially when you're standing right in the middle of it. This is not a very specific prediction and such rumors were already in place.

Jesus also predicts the people of Jerusalem will be scattered. Yes, that's what happens to people during war when their city is ransacked. Who doesn't know this? Today, we call these displaced people *refugees.* And certainly, Jesus understood that the paltry Jewish resistance was no match for Roman rule or even the outlying countries beyond Roman rule. Anyone could have predicted that the Jewish people would lose a battle over Jerusalem.

Jesus predicts the Jewish people would be persecuted. Yes, that's what happens when you're the loser in a war. Once again, Jesus is Captain Obvious.

Jesus predicts Jerusalem would be trampled by Gentiles. Wasn't that *already* the case, with the entire Levant being ruled over by Romans? Aren't Romans gentiles? How is this a prediction? A better prediction would have been to give the exact date when Israel recaptured Jerusalem in 1967.

That would be impressive.

Lord of the Promise Rings

After the predictions, come promises. So, what are the promises of Jesus? Eternal life, answers to prayers, incredible faith?

No one has ever received eternal life, so that promise is out the window. No person living at the time of Jesus continued to stay alive to see the return of Jesus from heaven and the establishment of his "Kingdom" as Jesus predicted, so that promise is an obvious failure. No one has ever been able to move a mountain (or even bend a spoon) with faith alone, so that promise is also bogus. People don't actually get anything they want through prayer (as will be explained further down), so that one is also worthless. In the end, as always, Jesus and the subordinates who worship him, will put all the blame on the humans. In the world of gods, it's always the mortal's fault.

Jesus and His Heavy Yoke

Once again, Jesus makes things worse for the poor believer. Now, not only must he follow the laws of Moses (see Matthew 5:17-20), Jesus puts even more of a burden on the human being. Now, humans are suddenly guilty of thought crimes and are constantly being watched by the totalitarian God of the Hebrews. Castration, plucking out of eyes, cutting off of hands are actually "choices" on the road to being righteous.

But, does anything Jesus said in Matthew 5:17-20, about adhering to the old Jewish Law, overrule anything said by Jesus in any of the chapters that follow? How do you discern which of Jesus' sayings take precedence over another when they are so often contradictory?

Part of this problem is that not all works of fiction are automatically readable or understandable, and in the case of the Bible, you actually have a compendium of different books from different authors. We must concede the possibility that at least some of the writers of the Bible were rather poor at their craft. That aside, the Bible does have a sort of consistency, when you consider Jesus was simply adding more demagogic injunctions to an already heavy slate of ridiculous demands for which humans were expected to comply. Religion is totalitarianism, although totalitarianism isn't always religious. But The Dear Leader, in any such regime, is always insane.

The Anti Free Speech Zone

The definition of blasphemy from original Greek suggests hurtful, evil, slack, impious derogatory speech. Jesus tells everyone to shut up about it:

> And whosoever speaketh a word against the son of man, it shall be forgiven him: but whosoever speaketh against the Holy Ghost, it shall not be forgiven him, neither in this world, neither in the world to come. – (*Matthew 12:32 KJV*)

162

This is more suppression of thought and speech by the alleged creator of free will, thought, and speech. The supposed defective "sinful" human is expected to attempt perfection, and when he fails, as we know he will, he's condemned to death. This is the exact cardboard cut-out design of every dictatorship that has ever existed. Too many laws that cannot possibly be kept are enacted, so that the citizens can be arrested for any possible reason, to control them, imprison them, or kill them at will. It is the Dictatorship of the Kingdom of God – and evil by definition and design.

Asking For a Loan at The First Bank of Jesus

There are two very important passages in the Bible which address prayer and just how powerful it is *supposed* to be. One is Matthew 17:20 which reads:

> And Jesus said unto them, Because of your unbelief: for verily I say unto you, If ye have faith as a grain of mustard seed, ye shall say unto this mountain, Remove hence to yonder place; and it shall remove; and **nothing** shall be impossible unto you. (*KJV*) [Emphasis Added]

And the other is:

> I can do **all** things through Christ who strengthens me. – (*Philippians 4:13 KJV*) [Emphasis Added]

The words in these two passages are quite clear and absolute: *all things,* and *nothing is impossible.*

Christians will often alter the words of Jesus, and the words of the Bible, and declare that "sometimes" you get what you pray for. And Bible believers will tell you that what you pray for isn't instantaneous, you have to wait for it. Yet, the Bible plainly declares *anything* you want you can get because *all* things are possible. It doesn't say "sometimes" and "some things," or "occasionally." All things being possible would also have to include anything instantaneous. So, we must ask, has any Christian ever moved a whole mountain by faith alone? Instantaneously, or otherwise? Are they still waiting for it, perhaps? Apparently, Jesus thought this was a clever statement, but that was before dynamite and bulldozers, which as we know, is the *only* way anyone has ever moved a mountain (not with faith, but with hard work and innovation.)

Readers of the Bible should note that Jesus rarely gives a caveat for anything he says. He certainly never adds any qualifiers to his statements about prayer, such as "Oh, by the way, it isn't instantaneous, you have to wait for it." Or, "...Oh, as far as the mountain moving thing, you'll have to also use dynamite..." Qualifiers and exceptions are added, long after the statement is made, hundreds of years later, by Christian followers, as a way of making these outlandish and embarrassing claims fit the belief system.

Jesus, rather than allowing for exceptions to his rules, makes statements that are to be taken as absolutes. There is no hint that anyone is supposed to read between the lines and assume something different. Either that is the case, or he's deliberately trying to obfuscate his message.

Other passages in the New Testament seek to support the previous ones mentioned: Matthew 21:21 reiterates Jesus' claim that faith can cause humans to lift up entire mountains. He does this after mysteriously killing a fig tree. So why didn't Jesus just move a mountain himself as a demonstration of this faith? Destroying a fig tree is rather insignificant by comparison, is it not?

James 5:15 states that prayer heals the sick. Yet, as science has shown, healing occurs with or without faith, making prayer irrelevant to the outcome.

John 14:13 again has Jesus stating that he will do *anything* you ask.

Then, of course, we have 1 John 3:21-22 – the actual loophole for Jesus to get out of having to grant any of your wishes, as John simply states that Jesus can only help you if you do not sin. And because *everyone* has sinned, as it says in Romans 3:23, it means *no one* can be helped by Jesus through prayer!

> ...if our heart condemn us not, then have we confidence toward God. And whatsoever we ask, we receive of him, because we keep his commandments, and do those things that are pleasing in his sight. – (*1 John 3:21-22 KJV*)

If it takes a pure heart to get God to do anything for you, how long does a human being actually possess a "heart that condemn(s) us not"? A millisecond? And how many milliseconds of doing things "pleasing in his sight," will get a mountain to move one inch? As it turns out, Jesus cannot actually help anyone, just as the evidence has shown. Christians want to make these passages pass muster, as a part of their confirmation bias, but they simply fail, as they usually do.

Jesus and His Magic Lamp

Jesus makes the claim that faith can alter reality, that faith can defy physics, and change the molecular structure of things. Yet, faith is nothing more than a belief *without evidence* for that belief. It's equivalent to wishful thinking. Thinking or wishing really hard about something, for a specific outcome, does not make it happen. Reality doesn't change because we want it, wish for it, or pray for it to change. Jesus, along with every person that prays, got it wrong. Prayers that get "answered" in the affirmative are the result of millions of praying people converging with the natural occurrence of coincidence, or inevitable outcomes.

Statistically, somewhere, someone's request will come true. Kids praying for their baseball team to win the World Series exist in every city in the U.S. The kids who prayed for the actual winning team got their prayers answered and the kids rooting for the other 29 teams did not. It's a massive case of confirmation bias gone haywire. But, prayer is a selfish act. When people pray, they don't think of the people who might be harmed if, or when, they actually get what they want. As the saying goes, "No good deed goes unpunished." But no one really wants to be on punishment's receiving end.

Gays, Rapists, and Slaves! Oh My!

We know Jesus whole-heartedly and energetically supported the Old Testament and the various laws it contains:

> For verily I say unto you, Till heaven and earth pass, one jot or one tittle shall in no wise pass from **the law**, till all be fulfilled.
> – (*Matthew 5:18 KJV*) [Emphasis Added]

And because of this endorsement, some people confidently declare the following:

"Jesus Hates Fags!"

The above line actually appears on placards carried by members of the Westboro Baptist Church when that pernicious congregation protests against gay marriage, or the very existence of gay soldiers. This, despite the fact that Jesus himself never discussed homosexuality in any way at all. Christians have to reach back into the Old Testament (a book the Christians themselves say "no longer applies," despite Jesus' own personal endorsement of its laws) in order to make this assumption about the degree to which Jesus dislikes homosexuals.

The Old Testament verse reads as such:

> If a man also lie with mankind, as he lieth with a woman, both of them have committed an abomination: they shall surely be put to death; their blood shall be upon them. – (*Leviticus 20:13 KJV*)

It's a good thing the majority of Christians *do* believe the old laws of the Old Testament "no longer apply," or there would be a lot of unnecessary killings going on, made possible by "true believers" in Jesus.

Of course there are passages in the New Testament (not the words of Jesus himself) that *hint* at homosexuality being frowned upon, but never the kind of wholehearted condemnation that would be considered hatred, and never anything leading to death. And yet, even this is enough for the many followers of Jesus to judge other human beings for a lifestyle that was not chosen for them, but rather given to them *in utero*.

A 2010 study, aptly titled, *"Sexual Hormones and the Brain: An Essential Alliance for Sexual Identity and Sexual Orientation"* by Garcia-Falgueras and Swaab states:

> ...the fetal brain develops during the intrauterine period in the male direction through a direct action of testosterone on the developing nerve cells, or in the female direction through the absence of this hormone surge ... our gender identity ... and

sexual orientation are programmed ... into our brain structures when we are still in the womb.

In other words, before you are ever born, not enough of a very specific male hormone (testosterone), or too much of it, determines whether you will eventually become heterosexual or homosexual.

This means a gay person is *made* to be exactly the way they are. And because of this, we have to ask the Christian: Weren't they made this way by the very God that is condemning them? How is being gay anyone's fault but God's?

Semi-Raping for Jesus

The most famous Biblical passage regarding rape is as follows:

> If a man find a damsel that is a virgin, which is not betrothed, and lay hold on her, and lie with her, and they be found; Then the man that lay with her shall give unto the damsel's father fifty shekels of silver, and she shall be his wife; because he hath humbled her, he may not put her away all his days. – (*Deuteronomy 22:28-29 KJV*)

You might find it difficult today to find anyone who would advocate for a woman being forced to marry her rapist. (However, for even more vile religious commands like this one, see the chapter on **Islam.**) Christian apologists will argue that it really doesn't say rape. It's really just "forcing" her or "coercing" her. Of course, that is *still rape* by any compassionate human being's definition, and the apologist loses on all counts. It's very disconcerting to the believer to admit that their holy book is backward and primitive.

And then you have slavery...

Jesus and the Slave Trade

In Matthew 18:21-35, Jesus gives the Parable of the Unforgiving Slave. It's clearly a story about being grateful for what you have and not complaining about what you don't have. Nice. But what a grand opportunity to speak against *owning people* in the first place! Jesus fails at this task again and again. His stories normally end up admonishing human beings for their disobedience. In other words, Jesus is more likely to tell humans to obey laws, rather than tell them to change laws, or get rid of bad laws. It's no surprise then, that he never tells humanity to stop owning slaves.

Within other parts of the New Testament you find numerous passages that refer to slavery, but none that preach against slavery itself.

You would think a truly compassionate god-man's first *mission,* before walking on water, killing a fig tree, or turning water into wine, would be *manumission* – the emancipation of all slaves. If Jesus had come with all his power and all his followers at the ready, and had died in much the same way as it is said he did, and his only focus had been this one idea – the eradication of real, physical slavery, how much different would the world be today? Instead, we are told, he came to free your "spirit" and yet he, and none of his followers today, can adequately determine or define what spirit is. Jesus, *again,* got things backwards.

The correct way? First, free the man's body. Then he can sit with you man-to-man and talk about the freedom of mind. If you've put him in shackles, how likely is he to listen to your ramblings about god's mercy? Truly, Jesus, the *god-as-human-being,* appears to have a great amount of difficulty understanding human nature.

The fascinating moral dilemma is that modern Christians seem to be against slavery, despite the fact that Yahweh and Jesus never condemned it. In fact, the God and his son gave some rather detailed instructions on how to treat slaves without ever commenting on the abomination of slavery itself. And from that, we can easily observe this truth: If you're all-powerful, not condemning slavery is the same as *endorsing* it.

And why are modern Christians almost 100% against slavery, despite the holy writ which chooses otherwise? Could it be that the morality of humanity as a whole has now surpassed the morality of the imagined god?

And to the apologists who insist that Bible slavery was "different" or "not as bad" as the kind of slavery humanity practiced in the 18th and 19th centuries... there is only one humane and correct way to regard slavery: It is immoral at *any* level.

Is There an App for Inconsistency?

So, here are the big trio of dilemmas for Christians:

1. In regard to homosexuality, if the Old Testament law does not apply, now that we have the precious Jesus to take its place, then homosexuality isn't something to get upset about. If O.T. law *does* apply, then homosexuality deserves a death penalty, and gay people need to be rounded up by Christians and stoned to death as soon as possible.

2. When it comes to rapists, if the Old Testament law does not apply, then thank modern man's rationality! Why would anyone follow *any* set of laws that included one that said rape was okay, even in special cases? However, if the Old Testament law *does* apply, a Christian father needs to make sure that whomever rapes his daughter gets a chance to marry her. Don't forget to register her at "Bed, Bath and Beyond"!

3. But when it comes to slavery, it really doesn't matter if the Old Testament law applies or not, Christians and Jews *can* own slaves. Both Yahweh and Jesus support it!

Now, this may seem, on the surface, simplistic in its argument, but Biblical scripture *is* the driving force of the Christian belief system. And scripture is all we have to use to make these judgments as to what a Christian is supposed to *do* to be "right with God." Therefore, we observe that the inconsistency of the basic Christian belief, as to what law does or does not apply, now that Jesus has arrived, is mind-numbingly capricious and insidiously invasive, and it ought to be stopped.

Christians need to make up their collective minds about whether or not the Old Testament applies in the modern world. They need to pick one. This is an all or nothing decision. Even Jesus said so. The Old Law either applies and you can own slaves, stone defiant children, allow rapists to marry their victims, kill homosexuals, et al. Or, it no longer applies and you can skip it *entirely*. No need to protest the removal of the Ten Commandments from court house buildings if those ten Old Testament laws no longer apply. In the 21st century, the convenience of selective condemnation is no longer acceptable.

SACRIFICING JESUS

A Jesus to Die For!

Christians will often ask what is, to them, a rhetorical question: If Jesus wasn't God in the flesh, why would/did so many die for him? This actually demands an answer, and history gives us many more than just one.

People die for all kinds of foolish things. And the further back you go in history the more foolish reasons you find. People died for the cause of Nazism, and Communism, and various American war adventures. People died for Muhammad and his fanatical followers. They died for Gandhi, they died for Mao, they died for Kings, Popes, David Koresh, and many more. The list of people dying for irrational causes and psychopathic leaders is a rather long list. Those people who followed those leaders were also tricked into believing their cause was right. Perhaps Christians should not act so smug about Jesus being "the right one" to die for.

The Binding of Isaac and the Execution of Jesus

In the Old Testament story of Isaac, Abraham is about to sacrifice his own son on an altar, when at the last second, a ram appears from the bushes and Abraham sacrifices the ram instead, sparing Isaac from having his throat cut. Without getting into the horrific psychological trauma Isaac must have endured, we can see that Isaac was not killed. Although, some Christians like to compare this to Yahweh sacrificing his own son, Jesus, it's not exactly comparing apples to apples. Abraham didn't go through with it. Yahweh apparently *did*.

Christians will tell you, "God does not want sacrifices!" The Abraham and Isaac story seems to bear this out. This concept comes from the heart of the Biblical passage, Matthew 12:7:

168

...I will have mercy, and not sacrifice... (*KJV*)

That's a good thing. Human sacrifice is wrong no matter how you slice it, (or slice the person being sacrificed).

But, this should make anyone stop and think... If god *didn't* want human sacrifice, then Jesus was a fraud. There was no need for God to do the very thing he didn't want his people to do. If there was no need to sacrifice Isaac, there was no need to sacrifice Jesus.

If the deal between God and Man had been God saying, "I'll sacrifice this one man, if all of you will stop sacrificing each other," then it would have been an endeavor worth some merit, in spite of its cruelty to that one man. But, this is not the message we hear. Christianity was not about ending human sacrifice. In the area where Christianity sprang up, that had already been drastically reduced or abolished, as it had in most cultures. Instead, Christianity was about glorifying the killing of a god, which would in turn create human guilt, and would hopefully keep those rebellious humans in a very, very, straight line.

The Unbearable Lightness of Being Jesus

When stepping back and looking at the bigger picture of the Jesus myth, perhaps as a visitor from another world, it makes one wonder what was the point of the crucifixion of Jesus? If one accepts the divinity of Jesus, with Jesus being God, the creator of the universe, we have to ask, did Jesus really sacrifice anything? Was it a sacrifice to give up a human body he didn't really need in the first place? Was it a sacrifice to suffer excruciating pain for a few hours, a time frame which would be the equivalent of less than a trillionth of a millisecond to an eternal god? Was it really a sacrifice for Jesus, knowing that in the end he would be promoted to King of the Universe?

So, if there was no real sacrifice, what was the real purpose of the crucifixion? Was it to make humanity feel unfathomable guilt for killing their own creator, and was this guilt supposed to control the human mind – to blame humanity for this god's own mistakes – mistakes he made when he created humans, and the mistake of not ridding the world of humanity's adversary (Satan)?

The story all so convoluted that it has taken generations of apologists to work out all the excuses for the sea of holes that wash over this whole myth.

Vampire Disciples Eat the Flesh of Zombie Jesus

The following passage is in the Bible and it sounds a lot like something out of a flesh-eating zombie novel:

> ...Verily, verily, I say unto you, Except ye eat the flesh of the Son of man, and drink his blood, ye have no life in you. Whoso eateth my flesh, and drinketh my blood, hath eternal life; and I will raise him up at the last day. For my flesh is meat indeed, and my blood is drink indeed. He that eateth my flesh, and

drinketh my blood, dwelleth in me, and I in him. As the living Father hath sent me, and I live by the Father: so he that eateth me... – *(John 6:53-57 KJV)*

This is getting rather physical when the message of Jesus is supposed to be spiritual. Critics of those of us who are critics of the Bible will say we are taking this out of context, that this is a metaphor, not something to be taken literally. Yes, we know. But not all metaphors are sound, or worthy of consideration. And this is just one of many that are primitive-based and superstition derived.

So what is this passage all about? Because it is a metaphor, we know it's not really about cannibalism, vampirism, or flesh-eating zombies. That's a relief because, whatever message is being conveyed, it is somewhat lost in the savage imagery. Like the other metaphors of Jesus – the plucking out of eyes, the cutting off of hands, and the castration of men for his "kingdom," this additional morbid metaphorical request is hard to swallow. And we are beginning to think Jesus is obsessed with extreme, physically macabre images within his parables, sayings and allegories. Is it any wonder that this is the same person who introduces the concept of eternal torture to the world?

This passage from John is supposed to mean that you must have the (self-proclaimed) man-god, Jesus, inside you, and you must choose to do this yourself, if you want to live forever. But, this cannibalistic reference to represent a spiritual process is actually quite sickening. Apparently, Jesus has no other way to demonstrate this idea without forever ruining the imagery of a Jewish Passover Seder or a Shabbat Kiddush.

The Christian's Favorite Verse

This is the verse that every perfunctory Christian knows by rote:

For God so loved the world, that he gave his only begotten Son, that whosoever believeth in him should not perish, but have everlasting life. – (John 3:16 KJV)

A rather maudlin passage. But, if the Christian god *really* loved the world, he could have sent his son to teach us some real things (about germs, math, space, science), some things that would not divide us (rules on diplomacy and freedom), some words to set slaves free (instead of endorsing slavery), some real miracles that would make us more likely to believe (instead of useless magic like walking on water, killing fig trees, and making wine out of water). But, the weak and woefully mindless Yahweh decided to focus all his energy on killing his son and using a primitive human construct – blood sacrifice – as the method, instead of coming up with his own more god-like plan to save mankind.

Whatever this god could have done otherwise, it would have been an improvement over killing an innocent person and threatening non-believers with eternal torture. What Yahweh/Jesus *didn't* do for human beings says as much about the dubious reality of his godhood as anything else.

Forgive Jesus, For He Does Not Have a Clue

The type of forgiveness promised in John 3:16 (above) is a rather ridiculous and cruel way to pardon someone. The idea that a bloody sacrifice of a human being somehow magically makes sin go away is a bit of a stretch for even the wildest imagination. It's a primitive, cruel, malevolent concept based on nothing. The only way to create real forgiveness is for the person doing the forgiving to actually mean it. That's all there is to it. You don't have to kill yourself, or do anything violent to "prove" you mean it. If you're sincere, the other party will probably know it. And, if not, there's not much you can do about it.

It is actually immoral for a god to create human beings as sinners and then blame them for the sin. Why would any thinking person have a genuine, *non*-fear-based interest in being forgiven in such way by any god?

For most parents, when their own children do bad things, they can usually tell if the child is contrite or not. If the child is truly sorry, most parents just forgive them. No one has to die, no one has to be tortured, no one has to be threatened. Something close to unconditional love is possible, but the Jesus-god does not appear to have any thing of the sort. Not even close.

Blood and Sacrifices

Christians will often refer to the death of Jesus as the "perfect sacrifice." But there is no need for a "perfect" sacrifice, because there is no need for *any* sacrifice. There never was. Killing something, whether it's a lamb, a calf, or a Jesus, has never been necessary to make someone else innocent, or to remove a person's sins. The Christian insists on this nonsense so he can be "born again," but it doesn't actually do anything except put a person in a delusional state. It's sort of like women who get their hymen surgically restored so they can be "virgins" again. None of it is based on reality.

A *New* Parable About Sacrifice

Let's say, Larry, Tom, and their friend Jack go camping. Around the campfire, Jack confesses that he recently cheated on his wife. Larry and Tom have never cheated on their wives, so being innocent in that respect, they're appalled by Jack's behavior. But they can see that Jack regrets his "sin." Jack says he doesn't know if his wife will ever forgive him. Then Tom gets this great idea. He gets out a knife and slits Larry's throat. As Larry bleeds to death, he tells Jack, "See! Larry never cheated on his wife! His innocent blood will guarantee that you, Jack, are forgiven! Innocent blood makes guilty people become *not* guilty!"

The man bleeding to death in the above scenario is similar to what Jesus attempts to do on the cross – use his blood to wash away the sins of the guilty. There is no way to make this sort of illogical and gruesome idea work for anyone. Some may say that the concept of God dying for Man did away with human sacrifice in every culture in which Christianity came in contact. However, there could have been a better, wiser, more humane way of dealing with the concept of blood sacrifice. A simple, six word commandment: "Thou shalt not kill the innocent." But, such a rule would have left out all the blood, gore, and drama. And for a psychopathic god, that just won't do.

Blood is just blood. It has no magical powers. You can get a blood transfusion that will save your life, and as long as the blood type is the same as your own, it won't matter if that blood came from a serial killer or a saint.

The entire scenario of "innocent" blood making guilty people not guilty is the product of primitive and ignorant people. In modern times, such an idea almost appears as if it was made up by a simpleton. No god is needed to set up such a monstrous "plan." This would only be useful for a limited, primitive, man-devised god. It is totally unnecessary for an all-powerful god to do anything so vile. Why would any god use such a method? An all-powerful god would just forgive with the wave of his hand and be done with it.

Those poor idiots killing birds and lambs on an altar and sprinkling the animal's blood around them were highly superstitious. It's important for the believer to step back and see this for what it is: primitive superstition, no different from any witch doctor doing basically the same thing in other ancient cultures. There is no scientific connection between killing innocents and the re-institution of innocence upon the guilty. It doesn't exist. It didn't exist back in the Bronze and Iron Ages, and it doesn't exist now. If you rob a bank, someone else killing an innocent child won't make up for that. But, that's the same concept the Christian uses as the basis for his belief system.

The Superior Forgiveness of Our Imaginary Friend

Christians will sometimes ask an atheist the following question: "Would you forgive someone if they murdered your family member?" This is asked with the expectation that, for most people, the honest, albeit hypothetical, answer would be no. The Christian will cite the "fact" that Jesus would forgive that person and therefore the forgiveness of Jesus is far superior to that of any human.

And yet, this question assumes Jesus was actually a real person, then also assumes Jesus had the power to forgive anyone outside of the three decades he allegedly existed on earth. It also assumes that we *should* forgive people simply because the accused is fully contrite. Do all murderers deserve or need forgiveness? Is it somehow a sin for a person *not* to forgive a killer? In most cases, forgiveness does more for the one doing the forgiving, in an effort to gain closure for being a victim, and less for the one being forgiven, especially when no one can ever really know the degree of the accused person's sincerity.

Human beings don't claim to be perfectly all-loving, all-forgiving, and all-merciful. The Biblical god does. That's supposed to be his big claim to having the job. Whether or not a person forgives someone for murdering their family member is irrelevant. What *is* relevant is why anyone thinks Jesus had to die in order for human beings to be forgiven. There are plenty of people who have the power to forgive others who have wronged them, and who also don't believe in Jesus. And there are plenty of people who choose not to forgive, and who also claim to have the "love" of Jesus permeating their every pore.

172

So, what does the execution of Jesus actually do? Does it make God feel sorry for us and change his mind about us? What was necessary about slaughtering a man in order for God to do his job and be forgiving? Particularly when he allegedly created us with his full knowledge of our sins in advance? How is it that a loving god can't simply say, "I forgive you" and move on?

THE RESURRECTION OF JESUS

Zombie Jesus Comes Back to Life

Everything in our universe has a logical scientific explanation. Someone not knowing what that is yet, doesn't change that fact. We know that people do not come back to life after being dead for three days (time enough for their body to begin to decompose). To become fully alive and reanimated after such a lengthy death would require a major suspension of all natural and physical laws. It just doesn't happen. To come back to life even after being dead a few minutes requires some serious CPR and often a medical team armed with at least a defibrillator, or the ability to administer an intracardiac injection.

The Cloudy Ascension of Jesus

After all the convoluted mystical stories, unimpressive miracles, threats of torture, vague predictions, ego-centric behaviors, Jesus zips off into heaven! To primitive man (a term that accurately applies to the people Jesus was preaching to, and to Jesus himself), heaven was somewhere beyond the clouds. In order to get to heaven you had to pass through those clouds. For Jesus to come back to earth, he would have to pass through them again. Stars, their size, distance from earth, and their purpose, was something for which human beings had almost zero information. Now, of course we know plenty. And we know about the limitations of the atmosphere and we know that humans cannot get past the upper reaches of the atmosphere (past the clouds) without first putting on a space suit and getting into a space craft. Otherwise, they would risk dying a horrible death from extreme changes in temperature, or from a lack of oxygen, or from the UV rays of the sun. But, somehow, believers in Jesus (and Allah) think the Messiah (and the Prophet) managed to survive all that, and made it past the clouds to some invisible heaven, and did so without any protective gear.

So, what you have is one impossible fantasy (the resurrection) stacked on top of another impossible fantasy (the ascension), and the people who claim this as fact have "lots of 'splainin' to do!" A believer, however, is just supposed to believe, and not question anything. But reality is getting so far "in your face" now that it's irretrievably jammed between your frontal lobes. It's hard to ignore the facts, and the number of facts which contradict the fiction of the Bible are increasing exponentially. This is why so many are quickly learning that all religion is based on fantasy, delusion, and primitive paranoia.

The Fear Factor

Man's fear of death is the creator of religious belief. Because God is born from human fear, fear created God. Fear gave birth to God. And fear is used copiously throughout the Bible text, as shown:

> But the mercy of the Lord is from everlasting to everlasting upon them that **fear** him, and his righteousness unto children's children. – (*Psalm 103:17 KJV*) [Emphasis Added]

> Praise ye the Lord. Blessed is the man that **feareth** the Lord, that delighteth greatly in his commandments. – (*Psalm 112:1 KJV*) [Emphasis Added]

> And fear not them which kill the body, but are not able to kill the soul: but rather **fear** him which is able to destroy both soul and body in hell. – (*Matthew 10:28 KJV*) [Emphasis Added]

However, the same Bible says this:

> There is no fear in love; but perfect **love** casteth out fear: because fear hath torment. He that feareth is not made perfect in **love**." – (*1 John 4:18 KJV*) [Emphasis Added]

From this last passage, can we conclude that love destroys any need to fear God, and one who fears God is not made perfect in love?

THE CONCLUSION OF JESUS

Jesus was not the perfect person his follows imagine him to be. His obsession with his followers self-mutilation (even as allegorical tales), his heightened narcissism, his adaptation of the Greek Hell, his indifference to slavery, his poor predictive skills, his incessant need for martyrdom, and his often contradictory statements, are all glaring examples of an imperfect human being – imperfections which are ignored to satisfy some humans' need to assuage their own fear of their personal demise.

How Great Thou Aren't

As we have seen, there are three main myths associated with Jesus: The Existence Myth, the Divinity Myth, and the Resurrection Myth. The existence or non-existence of Jesus is irrelevant to most atheists because it does not address anyone being, or not being, a god at all. It's no different than someone debating the existence of any other questionably historical figure, such as King Arthur, or Socrates.

However, atheists do object to the Divinity and Resurrection Myths. Was Jesus, if he existed, a god? We say no. There is no evidence to back that up and hearsay is not evidence. Did Jesus, whether a god or not, come back to life after being dead for three days? We say no. There is no evidence to back that up, and again, hearsay is not evidence. Therefore, we ask, where did these myths come from? Clearly, they are exaggerations by those who had some kind of interest in creating a religion or at least a following – whether to unite a group for war (or peace), or to make a profit, or from simple self-delusion, or some other completely unknown reason. Whatever the reason, which is still undetermined and up for debate, it could not have happened the way the Bible describes.

We can spell out our objections in more basic terms. Here are events in the life of Jesus that are attributed to him, followed by how atheists view them:

- Jesus being conceived by a virgin? This is a problem. Parthenogenesis is extremely unlikely in humans.
- Jesus being born? Fine. No problem. Lots of people are born every day.
- Jesus living to adulthood? Fine. No problem there.
- Jesus preaching? Fine. Not a problem. Lots of people were preaching during Jesus' lifetime.
- Jesus doing miracles? Can only be accepted as an event if they were well-planned magic tricks.
- Jesus being crucified? Fine. Lots of people were crucified.
- Jesus coming back to life? No, not after being dead three days. Negating the laws of nature and physics make it unacceptable.
- Jesus ascending into heaven? No, not without a rocket and a space suit.

As we can see, the birth, the adult life, the preaching, and crucifixion of Jesus are not a problem for atheists. These are all in the realm of possibility. However, his alleged virgin birth, miracles, resurrection, and ascent into "heaven" *are* problems. Big ones.

The Christian will state, without reserve, that the Bible is the inerrant, infallible revelation from the Christian god. The atheist will not ever agree with this, even when acknowledging that some portion of the Bible could be accurate, true, or even useful. This is because, as we've clearly seen, the Bible frequently contradicts itself, contradicts history, contradicts the laws of physics, and contradicts logic. It does all of these things much too often to be called "inerrant."

Biblical Contradictions

Are there too many flaws for the New Testament to be believable? There are certainly too many to list here, but a few are noteworthy:

- Contradictory genealogies for Jesus.
- Contradictory dates for *when* Jesus was born.

- Historical contradictions regarding *whether or not* a census was taken around the time of Jesus' birth.
- Contradictory interpretations regarding Jesus' alleged virgin birth.
- Contradictory reasons *why* Jesus was born in Bethlehem.
- Historical facts that contradict King Herod's alleged "slaughter of the innocents."
- Contradictory statements regarding *how many* donkeys Jesus was riding when he entered Jerusalem.
- Contradictory statements regarding whether or not John the Baptist knew Jesus was the Messiah.
- Contradictory statements as to *why* a perfect sinless God-Man (Jesus) had to be baptized to wash away his sins.
- Contradictions about *how long* it took for Jesus' accursed fig tree to die.
- Contradictions regarding *when* the Last Supper actually occurred.
- Contradictions regarding *who* prophesied the death of Judas Iscariot.
- Contradictions regarding *where* Jesus was taken after his arrest.
- Contradictions as to whether Jesus did or did not speak to Pilate.
- Timeline contradictions regarding *when* priests and scribes met to interrogate Jesus.
- Contradictions as to whether or not Jesus carried his own cross to his crucifixion.
- *Three* contradictory versions of the final words of Jesus before his death.
- Contradictions regarding *how* Judas committed suicide.
- Contradictions regarding *who* purchased Judas' Iscariot's "Field of Blood."
- Contradictions regarding *who* put a robe on Jesus, and what color it was.
- Contradictions regarding *who* found Jesus' empty tomb.
- Contradictions regarding *who* the alleged witnesses claim to have encountered at the empty tomb
- Contradictions regarding the actual location *where* Jesus ascended into heaven.
- Contradictions regarding *what* the witnesses to Paul's conversion were doing when it happened.

Over time, all the edits and redactions, mostly to force Jesus' life to conform to Old Testament prophecies, took a toll on the facts. Had there been only a tiny number of contradictions, these could possibly been excused on some level. But in this case, there are just too many to ignore.

Context or Conned Text?

For everything we say here, for all we condemn, scrutinize, criticize and analyze, the believers in the New Testament will accuse us of taking scriptures "out of context." Perhaps this is true to some degree, but even that is subjective. Isn't it possible, however, that it's the follower of Jesus who is taking things out of context? Could it be that the believer in scripture is taking *reality* out of context? Reality doesn't allow people to walk on water, turn water into wine, or wither fig trees without some kind of magic – without some kind of human, hidden manipulation of the real world. Magic is deceit. Believing that kind of deceit to be real is taking reality out of context. The context of reality also says that no one can come back to life after being dead for three days (and in the case of some people in the Biblical background, dead for decades!) At some point, reality has no context to the believer. The lines are blurred and they are lost to their delusions, wishful thinking, and the hope of more demonstrations of magic.

Excuses, Excuses!

Most religions have it backwards. They slavishly blame themselves for all the evil in the world and excuse their god of any responsibility. Fear of death will do that to you. But, the reality is this: if there is a god, or if there are gods of any kind who know everything and can do anything, humans, being a frail species, knowing very little, and living only a short time, have an excuse. After all, humans are *not* perfect. Someone, especially a god, should be obligated to forgive them for those imperfections – on the spot, and without reciprocation, and should understand and empathize with those human frailties.

And on the flip side of that coin, shouldn't a perfect, all-knowing, all creating, all-loving god take at least *some* responsibility for making this mess of humanity? The confused, fearful, imperfect, religious humans don't think so. Or, they at least *say* their god is blameless. And, as mentioned before, fear will make you do (and say) some rather strange things.

Jesus and the Woozle Effect

What's a Woozle? The word Woozle comes from an imaginary character in A. A. Milne's 1926 children's book, *Winnie-the-Pooh.* "The Woozle Effect" itself was first used by William Bevan, as a condemnation of faulty methods in psychological research, citing it as far back as 1953. Since then, Woozle effects have multiplied and seeped into other areas of investigation.

When someone, or some group, continuously cites past publications of false, or non-evidentiary information to the point that people start to believe there *is* evidence for those things, these erroneous ideas begin to be accepted as fact. Those are Woozles. Some develop into false trivia, or even urban legends. Others evolve into religions.

The Bible and Qur'an, along with many other holy books, are rife with physics-defying stories, legends, miracles, and flagrantly false ideas, and these are daily cited as fact again and again, and all without any evidence whatsoever.

And millions of human beings accept these Woozles as "facts." What is frowned upon in other fields as near-criminal science, or at the very least, bad journalism, is accepted as a form of warped reality when it comes to religious beliefs.

But, as we have seen, Jesus is not only a Woozle, he's a son of a Woozle.

When a story dies... what is left?

The End of Forever

A god who invented a fiery eternal torture chamber (Hell) to punish human beings (that he made imperfect), and who places them in that chamber for the simple reason of not believing he exists, isn't really interested in saving anyone. At any angle we view the disenchanted horror story that is Christianity, a god allowing the bulk of his creation to the wiped out, so only a few can be saved, is inherently immoral, and would be so, even if he decided to leave out the element of eternal torture. If such a god was real, he could only be called evil.

The Christian New Testament and Muslim Qur'an promote a Hell that has a beginning, but no end. And so, we ask: "What could be more cruel?" Any person with compassion knows that nothing is more inhumane than unnecessary cruelty. Recognizing that truth is how we discover the source of evil. And, now that we know where evil lies, it is our obligation to ourselves to live without it.

CHAPTER EIGHT

A Modern Parable

A famous painter made a portrait of his best friend without his friend's knowledge. He wrapped it in paper and gave it to his friend as a birthday gift. The friend took it home, and as he was bringing it in his house, he dinged one corner of the frame against the door entryway. The friend unwrapped the gift and noticed that the painting was indeed an accurate portrayal of him and was actually quite beautiful. But, that ding in the frame was blatantly noticeable. He thought that maybe he could change out the frame, but it was also quite lovely otherwise and appeared to be too difficult to remove. So, the friend hung the painting on his wall in spite of the blemish on the frame.

Many years passed and the painter and his friend lost touch with one another. The painter had moved away to the East, while the friend himself had moved out West. Many miles separated them, but they always kept the memories of each other alive. One day, the painter, now old and gray, had to make a trip to the West to receive an award for one of his other works. Despite his age and depleted health, he felt it was his obligation to go. He decided while he was there, he would look up his old friend. He went to his friend's house and was immediately invited in with hugs and handshakes. Surely, this would be a great time to reminisce.

The artist looked around. There in the center of the living room was the painting he had given his old friend. It looked nothing like what he had created. It was ripped and had various large and small holes in the canvas. It was stained with all sorts of liquids where someone had thrown bottles at it, in perhaps some violent rage. Even darts were stuck in the cloth. And someone had written obscene words across the center of the image. The artist was appalled. "What have you done to my painting!" he demanded.

"*Your* painting?" answered his friend. "You gave that to me as gift. I can do what I want with a gift. Besides, you're a painter. I figured I could always get you to paint another one for me if I needed it."

"That painting was a rare and unique work of art! It took me many, many, hours to complete and perfect! What's wrong with you?!" The artist was beside himself with anger.

The friend tried his best to explain. "Look, it had this one blemish on the side of the frame there, and it bothered me for years. I hated that blemish. So, because I couldn't fix the blemish, I guess I sort of made the rest of the painting match the blemish. So what?"

"You idiot! I just sold a painting of another friend, very similar to the one you trashed, for $600,000! And it had numerous blemishes in the frame! In fact, the blemishes are there on purpose! They add character to the painting!"

"Oh,...well maybe we can fix this one?" said the now hapless friend.

"No! It's ruined! And I'm too old to remake another one. This friendship is over!" And the artist stormed out, never to return.

Just in case anyone missed it, in this modern parable, God is the artist, religious people are the careless friend, the painting is a human life (or it could represent the earth itself), and the "blemishes" are sins.

Whether we were put here by a creative force, or grew here from a happy accident, those of us who have no belief in a god or gods, are fairly certain this life is the only one we have – even with all its fortunate blemishes. We take this very seriously. We see it as our duty to take care of this life, by living it with as much eagerness and vigor as possible. Life's rarity necessitates that we do. We don't know if there is an afterlife. If there is, we'll see it when we get there.

CHAPTER NINE

Islam: Illiteracy and Illusion

"It does surprise me that intelligent people in the 21st century could claim that if you respond to the terrorists with force, you spawn terrorism, but if you appease them, you somehow tame them. This argument, as I said, is very interesting, and very surprising." – Meles Zenawi

"Those who can make you believe absurdities can make you commit atrocities." – Voltaire

"Beware of false prophets, which come to you in sheep's clothing, but inwardly they are ravening wolves." – Jesus Christ

THE BASICS OF A BASE RELIGION

Muhammad was born in Mecca (in modern day Saudi Arabia) in the year 570 C.E. Due to his parents untimely deaths, he was raised by an uncle. Despite having been illiterate throughout his life, Muhammad went on to become the prophet and leader of a new religion – Islam. Adherents of this now 1400 year old religion call themselves Muslims. (Muslim means "one who submits to God.")

Send Me An Angel!

When Muhammad was 40 years old, he claimed he was visited by the angel Gabriel who gave him a revelation from Allah (God). What were these revelations all about?

The first revelation was that "God Is One." This monotheism was a direct rejection of paganism and mirrors exactly what Judaism had been claiming for almost 1800 years prior. Muhammad was also told that Jesus Christ was not the son of God, but merely a prophet, to be revered like Abraham, Moses, David, and other Biblical leaders, but not worshiped. Muhammad's stated goal was to restore the "original" monotheistic religion to the world – a religion that had been corrupted over time. Muhammad was to be known in the Muslim world as God's "final" messenger, and last prophet. (This, of course, makes reform of Islam virtually impossible, because anyone coming after Muhammad would be seen as false.)

The Descendants of Ishmael

The Jewish Torah and the Christian Old Testament, state that Abraham had two sons, Ishmael and Isaac. Ishmael was born first from a handmaiden named Hagar, who was in the service of Abraham's wife, Sarah. Isaac was born from Sarah herself, around a decade and a half later. Muslims like to suppose that Ishmael is the ancestor of all Arabs, including Muhammad, in the same way that Judaism claims Isaac is the ancestor of all Jews. Such lineages are almost impossible to prove. Nevertheless, this has given these two groups their religious identities and heritage. They both claim the same patriarch, Abraham, and both claim the same creator god, Yahweh/Allah. They just differ on which ancestral son they come from – plus a few other things we'll get into.

Although Muslims are proud of the alleged genetic link to a son of Abraham, we're not sure they are all proud of God's own prophecy regarding Ishmael and his descendants:

> And he shall be a wild ass of a man: his hand shall be against every man, and every man's hand against him; and he shall dwell in the face of all his brethren. – (*Genesis 16:12, KJV*)

Okay, so sometimes prophecies *do* come true!

But, Islam doesn't always accept the content of the holy books that preceded it. Those books have, supposedly, been "corrupted." Therefore, we should look at the holy book of Islam, the book all Muslims revere more than life itself: The Qur'an...

THE QUR'AN, ISLAM'S HOLY BOOK

Because Muhammad couldn't read or write, the Qur'an was written down by a coterie of his fellow companions. Luckily, for Muhammad, many of his closest followers memorized many of his revelations, and after his death, the Qur'an was compiled and put into a codex. However, there were differences in the exact wording coming from the various scribes. Around 650 C.E., the caliph at the time, Uthman ibn Affan, ordered the creation of the first standard copy of the Qur'an. This final version is what is used by Muslims today. Most other variants of that era have been destroyed. Some of these contained significant differences from the current version. (But no matter. This is apparently how Allah has his "exact" words promulgated to the masses.)

Even so, Islam has other sources for its beliefs that are outside the Qur'an...

The Hadith and The Sira

Hadith means "tradition." The Hadith is, for the most part, a collection of sayings, teachings, and deeds of the prophet Muhammad. This includes Muhammad's actions and conversations as reported by those who knew him. Although these sayings and opinions attributed to Muhammad are not found in the Qur'an, most Muslims consider the Hadith to be an important adjunct to the Qur'an and as a conduit for clarification of the Qur'an.

Another source for Islamic religious thought comes from "Sirat Rasul Allah" or the "Life of the Messenger of Allah." Usually referred to as simply "the Sira," collectively, they are the various traditional Muslim biographies of Muhammad. A hadith is more concerned with a story that conveys an interpretation of Islamic law, whereas the content within the Sira is supposed to be about actual historical events in the Life of Muhammad.

Both the Sira and the Hadith have strongly influenced the interpretation of the Qur'an, and in doing so, also influenced the behavior of Muslims.

The Five Pillars of Islam

Islam is a religion, but one unlike any other. So, we have to ask: what are the most important tenets of Islam? Most Muslims will tell you the answer is contained in "The Five Pillars of Islam"... They are as follows:

1. Faith
2. Prayer
3. Giving Alms
4. Fasting
5. Pilgrimage to Mecca

What we immediately notice is that only one of these is actually doing something beyond the Self. Faith achieves nothing, as faith is simply belief without evidence. Prayer, as we've seen in other chapters, is non-productive. Fasting can be cleansing, but is something anyone can do without a religious incentive. And pilgrimage to Mecca does nothing for your fellow man or woman. Only giving of alms, or helping the needy, has the compassion and empathy you would expect (and hope) a religious sect would want to promote, and yet it's number 3 on the list!

But, what does it really mean to give alms to the poor? The Qur'an says:

> Worship Allah and associate nothing with Him, and to parents do good, and to relatives, orphans, the needy, the near neighbor, the neighbor farther away, the companion at your side, the traveler, and **those (slaves) whom your right hands possess.** Indeed, Allah does not like those who are self-deluding and boastful. – (Qur'an 4:36 *Sahih International Translation*) [Emphasis Added]

Obviously, like the Jewish and Christian texts that preceded the Qur'an, slavery is totally acceptable. Wouldn't freeing those slaves be the best alms they could ever possibly receive? Why wasn't Allah, whose words were no longer "corrupted" due to the genius of the illiterate Muhammad (and his angel), able to banish the concept of slavery once and for all?

Then, there's this in the Qur'an:

> Do ye make the giving of drink to pilgrims, or the maintenance of the Sacred Mosque, equal to those who believe in Allah and the Last Day, and strive with might and main in the cause of Allah? They are not comparable in the sight of Allah: and Allah guides not those who do wrong. – (*Qur'an 9:19, Yusuf Ali*)

The phrase "strive with might and main" is *jihad* – holy war. In other words, helping the poor is not as important as believing in Islam and fighting in holy wars. Holy war, apparently, trumps the third Pillar of Islam.

Oh, well. Slaves and alms don't really matter. Holy wars are way more important anyway!

Reading Outside the Lines

For Muslims, the Qur'an is literally the word of Allah-God, but only when it's written or spoken in Arabic. This is actually making the Arabic language itself have much more significance than it deserves. Logically, the sayings of a creator of the universe would be special and holy in any language, but not so with the Qur'an. When you speak or read the Qur'an, you are (allegedly) speaking the exact words of Allah, in its purest form, with zero errors. And in any other language, you aren't. This is why Muslims insist that the Qur'an can't be understood unless read in Arabic. Of course, this says nothing about people who *can* read the words, (because they know the Arabic alphabet and how the words sound), but don't know what the words actually mean – like a young child just learning how to read. Simply reading the words of a god doesn't mean they automatically make sense. And that's true even if you *do* know what the words mean.

Historically, in the field of proselyte-seeking religions and their holy writ, the Qur'an is a late-comer. And Muslims have always viewed it as the "final" revelation from God. However, this last message from God is much more violent than the previous one, making one wonder why this God, after preaching peace-through-guilt for over 600 years, suddenly decided that conversion by the sword was somehow a better idea.

In the modern era, we can look back and see how civilization might have prospered just fine without this new religious weed growing in the desert.

> The fact that the majority of smokers do not develop lung cancer does not negate the fact that smoking is the main cause of lung cancer; likewise, the fact that the majority of Muslims

184

do not develop terrorism does not negate the fact that Islamic ideology is the main cause of terrorism. – (*Tawfik Hamid a.k.a. Tarek Abdelhamid, Egyptian author and former member of the militant al-Gama'a al-Islamiyya*)

It doesn't get any clearer than that.

What's Really Inside...

The Qur'an contains over 100 verses that call for violence against unbelievers, making the Bible and Jewish texts look like a pair a sleeping kittens by comparison. These texts are brutally obsessed with the judgment of the *kafir* (unbeliever, infidel). There are many verses detailing how non-Muslims will be tortured, flogged, burned, and so on. With these verses, a Muslim is quickly indoctrinated into a swirling cloud of hatred for anyone who is not following the Islamic faith. It's a doctrine of *Us* vs. *Them*. You are either with us or against us. Dualistic. Black or White. And filled with rage:

> The punishment of those who wage war against Allah and His Messenger, and strive with might and main for mischief through the land is: **execution, or crucifixion**, or the cutting off of hands and feet from opposite sides, or exile from the land: that is their disgrace in this world, and a heavy punishment is theirs in the Hereafter; – (*Qur'an 5:33, Yusuf Ali*) [Emphasis Added]

There's more...

> But when the forbidden months are past, then **fight and slay** the Pagans wherever ye find them, and seize them, beleaguer them, and lie in wait for them in every stratagem (of war)... – (*Qur'an 9:5, Yusuf Ali*) [Emphasis Added]

> They but wish that ye should reject Faith, as they do, and thus be on the same footing (as they): But take not friends from their ranks until they flee in the way of Allah (From what is forbidden). But if they turn renegades, **seize them and slay them wherever ye find them**; and (in any case) take no friends or helpers from their ranks; – (*Qur'an 4:89, Yusuf Ali*) [Emphasis Added]

> Fight those who believe not in Allah nor the Last Day, nor hold that forbidden which hath been forbidden by Allah and His Messenger, nor acknowledge the religion of Truth, (even if they are) of the People of the Book, until they pay the Jizya with willing submission, and feel themselves subdued. – (*Qur'an 9:29, Yusuf Ali*)

(Note: "People of the Book" are Jews, and "jizya" is a tax unbelievers must pay for their unbelief, and supposedly for their "protection.")

> O Prophet! strive hard against the unbelievers and the Hypocrites, and be firm against them. Their abode is Hell,- an evil refuge indeed. – (*Qur'an 9:73, Yusuf Ali*)

> Muhammad is the messenger of Allah; and those who are with him are strong against Unbelievers, (but) compassionate amongst each other. – (*Qur'an 48:29, Yusuf Ali*)

> Allah hath purchased of the believers their persons and their goods; for theirs (in return) is the garden (of Paradise): they fight in His cause, and **slay and are slain**: a promise binding on Him in truth, through the Law, the Gospel, and the Qur'an: and who is more faithful to his covenant than Allah? then rejoice in the bargain which ye have concluded: that is the achievement supreme. – (*Qur'an 9:111, Yusuf Ali*) [Emphasis Added]

> O ye who believe! **fight the unbelievers** who gird you about, and let them find firmness in you: and know that Allah is with those who fear Him. – (*Qur'an 9:123, Yusuf Ali*) [Emphasis Added]

As you can see, if you don't believe in Islam, a Muslim believes he has every right to kill you. Of course, in practice, if you and he are living in a relative peaceful place, he likely will not. However, the idea that he may do so, if things get bad, is a specter no free-thinking non-Muslim wants to live with. Certainly, there are Jews, Christians, and non-believers currently living in Muslim countries, as they have done so throughout the history of Islam. However, from the beginning, as it is now, they are often persecuted and treated as less than fully human by Muslim authorities.

(Please note: Christians, Jews, Hindus, pagans, atheists, and any other person who does not believe wholly in Islam is considered a *kafir*. However, the word *kafir* to a Muslim has pejorative connotations that go beyond simply not believing in Islam. *Kafir* is nuanced to mean the lowest, worst form of subhuman a person could imagine, barely worthy of existence.)

Hell In the Holy Book

So, what does a Muslim think happens to a non-Muslim who isn't lucky enough to be murdered by a Muslim warrior or executed by an Islamic court? Well, they go to Hell, of course. (Or, their soul does.)

The Qur'an mentions the concept of Hell and the punishment of eternal fire almost *500 times*. It's quite an obsession. The following is a small sampling of those verses. According to the religion of peace, you can go to hell...

186

For not believing in Allah:

> ...and indeed Hell surrounds the Unbelievers (on all sides). – (*Qur'an 9:49, Yusuf Ali*)

For "opposing" Allah and Muhammad:

> Know they not that for those who oppose Allah and His Messenger, is the Fire of Hell? - wherein they shall dwell..? – (*Qur'an 9:63, Yusuf Ali*)

For wanting to join a different religion:

> If anyone desires a religion other than Islam (submission to Allah), never will it be accepted of him; and in the Hereafter He will be in the ranks of those who have lost. – (*Qur'an 3:85, Yusuf Ali*)

For being a "hypocrite":

> Allah hath promised the Hypocrites men and women, and the rejecters, of Faith, the fire of Hell: Therein shall they dwell: Sufficient is it for them: for them is the curse of Allah, and an enduring punishment... – (*Qur'an 9:68, Yusuf Ali*)

For being wealthy and/or for being opposed to war:

> Those who were left behind rejoiced in their inaction behind the back of the Messenger of Allah: they hated to strive and fight, with their goods and their persons, in the cause of Allah: they said, 'Go not forth in the heat.' Say, 'The fire of Hell is fiercer in heat.' If only they could understand! Let them laugh a little: much will they weep: a recompense for the (evil) that they do. – (*Qur'an 9:81-82, Yusuf Ali*)

For trying to compose a surah (scripture) that is better than those in the Qur'an:

> And if ye are in doubt as to what We have revealed from time to time to Our servant, then produce a Surah like thereunto; and call your witnesses or helpers (If there are any) besides Allah, if your (doubts) are true. But if ye cannot- and of a surety ye cannot- then fear the Fire whose fuel is men and stones,- which is prepared for those who reject Faith. – (*Qur'an 2:23-24, Yusuf Ali*)

For making friends with non-believers:

Thou seest many of them turning in friendship to the Unbelievers. Evil indeed are (the works) which their souls have sent forward before them (with the result), that Allah's wrath is on them, and in torment will they abide. – *(Qur'an 5:80, Yusuf Ali)*

For making friends with Christians and Jews:

O ye who believe! take not the Jews and the Christians for your friends and protectors: They are but friends and protectors to each other. And he amongst you that turns to them (for friendship) is of them. Verily Allah guideth not a people unjust. – *(Qur'an 5:51, Yusuf Ali)*

For having pride in a sin. ("Sin," as always, is rather ambiguous and subject to the whims of the accuser.):

When it is said to him, 'Fear Allah', He is led by arrogance to crime. Enough for him is Hell;-An evil bed indeed... – *(Qur'an 2:206, Yusuf Ali)*

For becoming a Muslim and then changing your mind: (This is also mentioned in Qur'an 2:217.)

On the Day when some faces will be (lit up with) white, and some faces will be (in the gloom of) black: To those whose faces will be black, (will be said): 'Did ye reject Faith after accepting it? Taste then the penalty for rejecting Faith.' – *(Qur'an 3:106 Yusuf Ali)*

For anyone who makes a last-minute conversion to Islam:

Of no effect is the repentance of those who continue to do evil, until death faces one of them, and he says, 'Now have I repented indeed'; nor of those who die rejecting Faith: for them have We prepared a punishment most grievous. – *(Qur'an 4:18, Yusuf Ali)*

(Note how the above is in high contrast to Christianity, which welcomes last-minute conversions.)

For being Jewish:

For the iniquity of the Jews We made unlawful for them certain (foods) good and wholesome which had been lawful for them;- in that they hindered many from Allah's Way;- That they took usury, though they were forbidden; and that they devoured men's substance wrongfully;- we have prepared for those among them who reject faith a grievous punishment. – (*Qur'an 4:160-161, Yusuf Ali*)

For being Christian:

They do blaspheme who say: 'Allah is Christ the son of Mary.' But said Christ: 'O Children of Israel! worship Allah, my Lord and your Lord.' Whoever joins other gods with Allah,- Allah will forbid him the garden, and the Fire will be his abode. There will for the wrong-doers be no one to help. – (*Qur'an 5:72, Yusuf Ali*)

For being a Christian and believing in The Trinity:

They do blaspheme who say: Allah is one of three in a Trinity: for there is no god except One Allah. If they desist not from their word (of blasphemy), verily a grievous penalty will befall the blasphemers among them. – (*Qur'an 5:73, Yusuf Ali*)

It's important to note here that Islam completely misunderstands what the Trinity is to Christians. For Christians, it is the Father, Son, and Holy Spirit, whereas the Qur'an mistakenly thinks Christians believe in Father, Son (Jesus), and Mother (Mary). See the following:

And behold! Allah will say: 'O Jesus the son of Mary! Didst thou say unto men, worship me and my mother as gods in derogation of Allah'?... – (*Qur'an 5:116, Yusuf Ali*)

Not only are all religions not the same (or equal), they also have a hard time understanding what the others are doing and saying.

What Happens In Hell, Doesn't Stay In Hell

Somehow, the Qur'an knows exactly what happens when you go to this place called Hell:

Those who reject our Signs, We shall soon cast into the Fire: as often as their skins are roasted through, We shall change them for fresh skins, that they may taste the penalty: for Allah is Exalted in Power, Wise. – (*Qur'an 4:56, Yusuf Ali*)

How Muslims know this detail about Hell's procedures is anybody's guess. The condemned apparently get their skin burned away and then get a new skin which is then immediately burned away, and so on, and so on, forever. A psychopath's mind is a terrible thing indeed!

(Notice also how Allah is considered "Wise" for being cruel.)

Some Islamic Advice Regarding Hell

If you're a good Muslim, please don't pray for unbelievers, even if they are part of your family:

> It is not fitting, for the Prophet and those who believe, that they should pray for forgiveness for Pagans, **even though they be of kin,** after it is clear to them that they are companions of the Fire. – (*Qur'an 9:113, Yusuf Ali*) [Emphasis Added]

In fact, don't even bother warning non-believers:

> As to those who reject Faith, it is the same to them whether thou warn them or do not warn them; they will not believe. **Allah hath set a seal on their hearts and on their hearing, and on their eyes is a veil**; great is the penalty they (incur). – (*Qur'an 2:6-7, Yusuf Ali*) [Emphasis Added]

Apparently, Allah, like Yahweh did in the Old Testament, has taken over some non-believers free-will and has already decided to prevent them from ever repenting. Instead, he will send them straight to Hell. (Perhaps he created them for that purpose?)

So, where does evil come from, that so many should end up in Hell? Apparently, for Islam, its source is the same as what the Bible states in Isaiah 45:7 – directly from the creator. However, the Qur'an words it like this:

> Say: I seek refuge with the Lord of the Dawn, From the mischief of created things; – (*Qur'an 113:1-2, Yusuf Ali*)

"Mischief" is translated as "evil" in the vast majority of English translations. Yusif Ali's version may be a way of covering up the obvious. The Shakir Translation from the 19th century pulls no punches. The second line in the passage reads: "From the evil of what He has created..." Either way, it looks like we have match between Yahweh and Allah as being the primary creators of evil in the universe.

And it's not just the men-folk who are targeted for destruction, bizarre punishments, or cruel treatment...

Women and Children and Islam

After 1400 years, Islam has still not understood what a great loss it is when one-half of your population is not allowed to fully contribute to society. Female education is severely restricted in nations which have a Muslim majority, resulting in a less than 50% literacy rate (on average) for women and girls. Employment of women is also restricted. Working, of course, is rather difficult when you can't read. (Of course, the job of holy warrior is open to all, even the illiterate. Just ask Muhammad himself.)

190

When talking to westerners, Muslims will claim that Islamic women are "equal" to men and are revered. However, that Qur'an they hold as sacred tells a different story.

Like the Old Testament, the Qur'an is quick to justify the brutal treatment of women during war. Female slaves, even married ones are fair game:

> Also (prohibited are) women already married, except those whom your right hands **possess**... − (*Qur'an 4:24, Yusuf Ali*) [Emphasis Added]

Women as booty, captured in war and raped, and/or taken as wives or slaves, is nothing new, and eagerly repeated in the Qur'an. However, this sick behavior is made worse when it becomes a "decree" or command from somebody's god. Allah is no friend of women, obviously.

When it comes to the subject of women, the Qur'an is full of goodies like this:

> Your wives are a tilth for you, so go into your tilth when you like... − (*Qur'an 2:223, Yusuf Ali*)

Women are crudely considered something that needs to be plowed. It's almost as if a teenage boy wrote the Qur'an. "Tilth" means tilling the soil to plant seeds. You can use your own imagination to figure out what kind of plow they're using. And what about a woman's menstrual cycle? Well...

> They ask thee concerning women's courses. Say: They are a hurt and a pollution: So keep away from women in their courses, and do not approach them until they are clean. But when they have purified themselves, ye may approach them in any manner, time, or place ordained for you by Allah. For Allah loves those who turn to Him constantly and He loves those who keep themselves pure and clean. − (*Qur'an 2:222, Yusuf Ali*)

When it comes to inheritance, women are never equal:

> Allah (thus) directs you as regards your Children's (Inheritance): to the male, a portion equal to that of two females... − (*Qur'an 4:11, Yusuf Ali*)

A woman's value is half that of a man's − even her testimony:

> ...and get two witnesses, out of your own men, and if there are not two men, then a man and two women, such as ye choose, for witnesses, so that if one of them errs, the other can remind her... − (*Qur'an 2:282, Yusuf Ali*)

For a woman, being under house arrest becomes a life sentence:

> If any of your women are guilty of lewdness, Take the evidence of four witnesses from amongst you against them; and if they testify, confine them to houses **until death...** – (*Qur'an 4:15, Yusuf Ali*) [Emphasis Added]

Husbands get a free pass for domestic violence:

> Men are the protectors and maintainers of women, because Allah has given the one more than the other, and because they support them from their means. Therefore the righteous women are devoutly obedient, and guard in absence what Allah would have them guard. As to those women on whose part ye fear disloyalty and ill-conduct, admonish them, refuse to share their beds, **beat them**; but if they return to obedience, seek not against them Means: For Allah is Most High, great. – (*Qur'an 4:34, Yusuf Ali*) [Emphasis Added]

This is one of the greatest problems within Islam. Domestic violence against women is rampant throughout the Muslim world, and the above surah from the Qur'an is one of the main reasons. In deference to Sharia Law, many courts in Muslim-majority nations refuse to even consider cases of domestic violence against women. Among the majority of Muslim nations, between 31% to 90% of women report having experienced domestic violence from husbands or other male relatives at some point in their lives. Most Muslim women accept this as a "normal" aspect of their existence, knowing there is virtually no place they can go for relief or support.

And here is the justification for making women wear a black tent, a.k.a., the *burqa:*

> O Prophet! Tell thy wives and daughters, and the believing women, that they should cast their outer garments over their persons: that is most convenient, that they should be known and not molested... – (*Qur'an 33:59, Yusuf Ali*)

And, in case you were wondering,... how long should a *newly divorced pre-pubescent girl* wait before she gets remarried? The Qur'an knows...

> Such of your women as have passed the age of monthly courses, for them the prescribed period, if ye have any doubts, is three months, **and for those who have no courses (it is the same)**: for those who carry (life within their wombs), their period is until they deliver their burdens: and for those who fear Allah, He will make their path easy. – (*Qur'an 65:4, Yusuf Ali*) [Emphasis Added]

"Courses" are menstrual cycles. The above is clearly discussing the *idda* - the time period a Muslim female must wait before she can remarry after a divorce or death of her spouse. There is no doubt this is including girls who have not reached puberty.

Giving pre-pubescent children away for the purposes of marriage was a common practice among many primitive middle-eastern tribes, and it still practiced in parts of the Indian subcontinent and elsewhere in the Muslim world. In Islam, there is no minimum age for marriage under Sharia Law!

And lastly, there is this. Not from the Qur'an itself, but from an Islamic leader and devout believer in the Qur'an:

> It is better for a girl to marry in such a time when she would begin menstruation at her husband's house rather than her father's home. Any father marrying his daughter so young will have a permanent place in heaven. – (Ayatollah Khomeini, *Tahrirolvasyleh, vol. 4, Darol Elm, Gom, Iran, 1990*)

What?! Not ready to convert yet?!

A Quick Guide to Islam and Homosexuality

There are at least four sections in the Qur'an which discuss homosexuality. Much of this is in reference to the story of Lot in Sodom, but in any event, homosexuals are called an abomination, wanton folk, froward folk, outcasts, lewd, and senseless. These can be found in Qur'an 7:80-81, Qur'an 26:165-166, Qur'an 27:54-55, and Qur'an 29:28-29, and the words in English are subject to translation, but nowhere do you find anything positive. From this, the Islamic State (ISIS), which took over large swaths of Syria and Iraq recently, used these surahs to execute homosexuals, and did so by hurling these men off high cliffs.

And the "religion of peace" becomes *the religion of hate.*

Qur'an and Sharia

Sharia Law is Islamic religious law based on The Qur'an and the Hadiths. Sharia means *path,* as in "God's path." Because Sharia Law is not secular, it often comes in conflict with human rights, freedom of thought, and women's rights, all of which are foundations of law within non-Muslim nations.

Nearly all Muslim-majority nations use some form of Sharia Law. Many of the harsh sentences handed down to women, non-believers, Jews, Hindus and Christians – such as, beheadings, stonings, floggings, and the cutting off of hands and/or feet – all get their power from Sharia Law.

Sharia Law does not only rule over civil disputes or societal crimes, but delves also into private activities, such as a person's individual sexual choices, etiquette, hygiene, diet, and prayer. And despite its oppressive nature (or perhaps because of it), it is considered by Muslims to be God's (Allah's) infallible rule of law.

Many in the West argue that Islam has a secret agenda to take over the first world nations through immigration, and through eventual implementation of Sharia Law. It would seem that this is so when you study the pockets of Muslim communities that have sprung up in various cities in Europe and their subsequent demands that local laws conform to Sharia Law. But, such an agenda is not exactly secret. All you have to do is read and understand the Qur'an:

> It is He Who hath sent His Messenger with guidance and the Religion of Truth, **to proclaim it over all religion,** even though the Pagans may detest (it). – (*Qur'an 9:33, Yusuf Ali*) [Emphasis Added]

The goal of every Muslim is clear: Make every human being into a Muslim. This is the plan (and the path) – a sort of spiritual "Invasion of the Body Snatchers." As you sleep, your culture, your law, and your religious beliefs are transformed into something alien to you and your senses – a debasement and degrading of everything you held in high regard.

> When angels take the souls of those who die in sin against their souls, they say: 'In what (plight) Were ye?' They reply: 'Weak and *oppressed* Were we in the earth.' They say: 'Was not the earth of Allah spacious enough for you to move yourselves away (From evil)?' Such men will find their abode in Hell,- What an evil refuge! – (*Qur'an 4:97, Yusuf Ali*) [Emphasis Added]

The conclusion we draw from the above passage is that religiously *oppressed* Muslims should emigrate to another country if they want to assure their salvation. However, what we see in reality is religious Muslims coming from very religious Muslim countries – places you would assume are "Muslim paradises" – and moving to the West, to nations that are not as welcoming (or not as aware?) We should, therefore, have no reason to believe any devout Muslim is coming to a Western nation because of "oppression" – but rather, for some other (possibly hidden) agenda.

One thing's for sure, they aren't leaving their homelands to covert to another religion. And they aren't becoming atheists...

Wait! What About "Moderate" Islam?

All Muslims can't be like that, can they? There are about 1.6 billion Muslims in the world and they aren't all throwing bombs! Maybe we need to look at this a little closer.

While it's true that not all Muslims are terrorists, what the average Mo on the street *doesn't* do or say, tells us volumes. A huge number of non-bomb throwing Muslims believe in Sharia Law (which advocates domestic violence against women, the non-education of women and girls, a belief in holy war

194

(jihad), the dehumanizing of "infidels" at all levels of society, and even the execution of people who convert from Islam to another faith.)

Out of 23 of the nations surveyed in a 2012 Pew Research Center Poll, 17 of them (74%), had populations in which over half of the people stated they believed Sharia was "the revealed word of God (Allah.)"

In 25 out of 36 countries surveyed, when asked if Sharia should be the supreme law of the land where they lived, the majority of those populations said "yes." That's almost 70% of nations with a significant Muslim population – all containing citizens who would gladly allow a person to be executed for the "crime" of switching religions, or be happy to see all women in burkas without an education or job, or would be fine if someone had their hands or feet cut off as punishment for stealing. And let's not forget *stoning to death* for committing adultery.

And what about Muslims in the United States, (a nation that was not a part of the above PRC poll and which has a low Muslim population)? A 2015 blog poll sponsored by Center for Security Policy, shows that almost 30 percent of Muslims in the U.S. believe it's okay to use violence "against those that insult the prophet Muhammad, the Qur'an, or Islamic faith."

The simple truth is, *moderate Islam does not exist.* Islam is a political and religious system of unbendable dogmas, deliberately set up to be a "you are either with us, or against us" type of tyranny, all based on a myriad of woefully primitive superstitions and beliefs – and with zero chance for reform. Those who are Muslim in name only, who do not fully practice the religion, are (to the vast majority of Islam) hypocrites, infidels, unbelievers, apostates, backstabbers, and deserving of the worst punishments of Islam *and* hell (please pardon the redundancy).

If only half of the Muslim population on earth wanted sharia law to be the law of the land, that's still 800,000,000 people who want to live in the Dark Ages! Certainly, the people of earth have a problem. And it isn't atheism.

ISLAM'S WAR ON EVERYONE

The Divine Language

Any religious Muslim will tell you that the only way the truth of the Qur'an can be revealed to you is if it is read in the original Arabic. This means two things: First, it implies that Allah was incapable of transmitting his great message to people who speak other languages, and second, it is more of a way for the Muslim to deflect criticism about the Qur'an's content. However, as any simpleton can figure out, stating that you want and need to kill non-believers is exactly the same in any language. The phrase "Kill all infidels," when spoken in Arabic, is still going to mean "Kill all infidels" in each and every language. It will not suddenly transform itself into "Give all non-believers a bouquet of flowers." And reading it in Arabic will not give you the sudden epiphany that killing non-believers is more divine than it is in English. You either believe killing non-believers is okay, or you don't. The particular language in your head is irrelevant. And this brings up another question, if The Qur'an can only be truly understood in Arabic, why has it been translated into so many languages? If the reader isn't going to get it anyway, why bother?

The war on the *kafir,* infidel, or unbeliever, is considered holy. *Jihad,* which means "struggle" in Arabic, is used in reference to both physical holy war and/or a spiritual war within oneself. But, within the Muslim holy writ, jihad is often described as an obligation *not* for the old or infirm. Certainly, the old and weak can have spiritual war, therefore, physical jihad is the true and primary requirement for every Muslim, as evidenced here:

> In the Muslim community, the holy war is a religious duty, because of the universalism of the (Muslim) mission (and obligation to) convert everybody to Islam either by persuasion or **force.** – (*Ibn Khaldun*) [Emphasis Added]

But, let us be clear, to a follower of Islam, any *jihad,* struggle or war, is a hostile fight to maintain the religion. It's desperate and it's to the *death.*

Not Reading is Fundamentalist!

How much better could the world have been had someone simply had the compassion to teach the poor orphan boy, Muhammad, how to read! Throughout the Qur'an, we see references to the stories originally told in the Torah or the Christian Bible, and most of them are woefully inaccurate and conflated. This is clearly due to Muhammad's inability to read. Had he actually read the books he both chastised and adored, he would have been better able to make intelligent criticisms of them. Yet, because Muhammad was fated to never be a scholar, there was one thing he could become, and that was – warlord.

Muhammad the Warlord

You cannot be a warlord without war, and a fanatical idea (or religion) to go with it. The Qur'an and the Hadiths give us plenty of examples of Muhammad's lust for violence, and many encouragements to do battle. Here is but a smattering of verses:

Muslims are told to fight for Allah because he's watching them...

> Then fight in the cause of Allah, and know that Allah Heareth and knoweth all things. – (*Qur'an 2:244, Yusuf Ali*)

And killing people might even be good for you...

> Fighting is prescribed for you, and ye dislike it. But it is possible that ye dislike a thing which is good for you, and that ye love a thing which is bad for you. But Allah knoweth, and ye know not. – (*Qur'an 2:216, Yusuf Ali*)

The recruitment for war continues...

> And if ye are slain, or die, in the way of Allah, forgiveness and
> mercy from Allah are far better than all they could amass. –
> (*Qur'an 3:157, Yusuf Ali*)

All warriors go to heaven...

> Think not of those who are slain in Allah's way as dead. Nay,
> they live, finding their sustenance... – (*Qur'an 3:169, Yusuf Ali*)
> [This surah was quoted by Osama bin Laden in his "Letter to
> America" in reference to the September 11, 2001 attacks.]

Dying for Allah in religious wars is profitable...

> Let those fight in the cause of Allah Who sell the life of this
> world for the hereafter. To him who fighteth in the cause of
> Allah,- whether he is slain or gets victory - Soon shall We give
> him a reward of great (value). – (*Qur'an 4:74, Yusuf Ali*)

Religious wars are certainly worth bragging about, aren't they?...

> How many towns have We destroyed? Our punishment took
> them on a sudden by night or while they slept for their
> afternoon rest. – (*Qur'an 7:4, Yusuf Ali*)

There are so many of these types of passages, a pattern emerges that only a
blind man could not see what's really going on. It's the Islamic War Channel,
24/7, with no interruptions and no commercials...

And the Violence of Muhammad Continues in the Hadith and Sira:

Here, Muhammad says killing Jews is okay for the Muslim:

> Allah's Apostle said, 'The Hour will not be established until you
> fight with the Jews, and the stone behind which a Jew will be
> hiding will say. 'O Muslim! There is a Jew hiding behind me,
> so kill him.' – (*Bukhari 52:177*)

Again, Muhammad is after the Jews:

> The morning after the murder of Ashraf, the Prophet declared,
> 'Kill any Jew who falls under your power.' – (*al-Tabari 7:97*)

Of course, killing women and children is okay, too:

The Prophet passed by me at a place called Al-Abwa or Waddan, and was asked whether it was permissible to attack the pagan warriors at night with the probability of exposing their women and children to danger. The Prophet replied, 'They (the women and children) are from them (the pagans).' – (*Bukhari 52:256*)

Muhammad has a female poet (and critic of Muhammad) assassinated:

When the apostle (Muhammad) heard what she had said he said, 'Who will rid me of Marwan's daughter? O'Umayr b. Adiy al-Khatmi who was with him heard him, and that very night he went to her house and killed her. In the morning he came to the apostle and told him what he had done and he said, 'You have helped God and His apostle, O'Umayr!' When he asked if he would have to bear any evil consequences the apostle said, 'Two goats won't butt their heads about her...' – (*Ibn Ishaq p. 675 and 676*)

Muhammad says terror is *good*:

Allah's Apostle said, 'I have been sent with the shortest expressions bearing the widest meanings, and I have been made victorious with **terror**...' – (*Bukhari 52:220*) [Emphasis Added]

Muhammad says forcing others to *convert or die* is commanded by Allah:

Allah's Apostle said, 'I have been ordered to fight the people till they say: **'None has the right to be worshipped but Allah**.' – (*Bukhari 8:387*) [Emphasis Added]

Muhammad burns people alive in their homes for not praying:

The Prophet added, 'Certainly I decided to order the Mu'adh-dhin to pronounce Iqama and order a man to lead the prayer and then take a fire flame to burn all those who had not left their houses so far for the prayer along with their houses.' – (*Bukhari 11:626*)

Apparently, murder creates a rush of endorphins and unmitigated elation as Muhammad says *jihad* (holy war) "elevates" one toward heaven:

He (Muhammad) did that and said: 'There is another act which elevates the position of a man in Paradise to a grade one hundred, and the elevation between one grade and the other is equal to the height of the heaven from the earth. He (Abu Sa'id)

198

said: 'What is that act?' He replied: 'Jihad in the way of Allah! Jihad in the way of Allah!' – (*Muslim 20-4645*)

The wondrous empathy of a warrior/psychopath is on full display, (i.e., the actual words of Muhammad):

> **Killing unbelievers** is a small matter to us. – (*al-Tabari 9:69*) [Emphasis Added]

Yes, but it's not just easy to do. Killing people is "wonderful" (for the Muslim jihadist):

> Thereupon Masud leapt upon Sunayna, one of the Jewish merchants with whom his family had social and commercial relations and **killed him.** The Muslim's brother complained, saying, 'Why did you kill him? You have much fat in your belly from his charity.' Masud answered, 'By Allah, had Muhammad ordered me to murder you, my brother, I would have cut off your head.' Wherein the brother said, 'Any religion that can bring you to this is indeed **wonderful!'** – (*Ibn Ishaq 369*) [Emphasis Added]

The above hadith has become an embarrassment to many Muslim apologists. Whether the above story actually happened or not is irrelevant. The fact that someone, *anyone,* would think that a blind obedience which leads to someone's death is in some way "wonderful," tells us much, when we consider the core values of the religion that inspires such behavior.

None of this comes from a vacuum. It has a source. It's the desert ranting of a Dark Age warrior. A tyrannical psychopath. A terrorist who called himself a prophet.

Verses Used For Beheadings

Are you a *kafir*? Hold on to your hat (and everything under it!)

> Therefore, when ye meet the Unbelievers (in fight), **smite at their necks**; At length, when ye have thoroughly subdued them, bind a bond firmly (on them): thereafter (is the time for) either generosity or ransom: Until the war lays down its burdens... – (*Qur'an 47:4, Yusuf Ali*) [Emphasis Added]

Along with:

> ...I will instill terror into the hearts of the Unbelievers: **smite ye above their necks** and smite all their finger-tips off them. – (*Qur'an 8:12, Yusuf Ali*) [Emphasis Added]

Yes, brutal execution for the simple "crime" of... *not believing in Islam.*

Of course, the Qur'an isn't Islam's only source for beheading. There are 41 references to beheading in the Sira, and 9 in the Hadith. Muhammad and his minions were prolific practitioners of beheading. Here is a fine and blatant example:

> ...Testify that none has the right to be worshipped except Allah, or else **I will chop off your neck**... – (*Bukhari 59:643*) [Emphasis Added]

Nice.

Here, a fellow named Sufyan is being told this:

> [Muhammad] said, 'Woe to you, Abu Sufyan, isn't it time that you recognize that I am Allah's apostle?' He (Abu Sufyan) answered, 'As to that I still have some doubt.' I (the narrator) said to him, 'Submit and testify that there is no god but Allah and that Muhammad is the apostle of Allah **before you lose your head.'** – (*Ibn Ishaq/Hisham 814*) [Emphasis Added]

The other beheading passages are quite similar: Convert or lose your head. The Kingdom of Saudi Arabia currently beheads around 100 people a year for "crimes" that wouldn't get you a day in jail (or even a small fine) in a non-Muslim nation.

Islam Is Not a "Religion of Peace"

Islam dubs itself, "The Religion of Peace" but no one is giving them a copyright on that. Definitions of words don't always translate well when cultures are polar opposites. In this case, Islam is a "religion of peace" in much the same way the Soviet Union was a "democratic republic."

Of course, the word Islam itself means "submission to Allah," an act which is supposed to bring "peace," and is often compared to the Hebrew word "shalom," which actually *does* mean peace. But words and actions are often two very different things.

If Islam was truly a "religion of peace," terrorism springing forth from it would be virtually impossible. (This is true for any religion that claims to be peaceful.) The words of their prophets and from their god would be so clear and strict, that war would never metastasize from their holy writ, no matter how much those sacred words had been twisted. And yet, we see Islamic terrorism worldwide. Again, if there were no *words and deeds of war* from the Prophet and the Qur'an, there would be no Islamic terrorism. The fault clearly lies in the religion of Islam itself. And no Muslim wants to face this truth, or even think about this truth. Facts, for most religions, are more terrifying than bombs.

We can see the aims of Islam from the Qur'an itself, and the translation by Muhammad Habib Shakir says it best:

And fight them until there is no persecution, and **religion is only for Allah.** But if they desist, then there should be no hostility except against the oppressors. – (*Qur'an 2:193*) [Emphasis Added]

Muhammad makes his agenda clear: The whole world must be converted to Islam (or die.)

What Islam Says – It Isn't What You Think

Words have different meanings to different people, properly translated or otherwise. Islam is so inexorably tied to its dogma and doctrine that ideas and concepts rooted in the Western Enlightenment, have no meaning to a Muslim. Here are examples of words that are familiar to people in the West, followed what those words actually mean to Muslims.

- Human Rights – Can be granted under sharia law *only*.
- Freedom – Given *only* when submitting to sharia law.
- Justice – Achieved *only* under sharia law.
- *Jihad* – Struggle and war against non-Muslims.
- Innocent Person – Can *only* be a Muslim (no exceptions).
- Peace – Total submission to Allah and Islam *only*.
- Defending the Faith – Fighting unbelievers, even *offensively*.
- Terrorism – Any terroristic act *not* used for the cause of Allah.
- Learning and Science – Only valid if it agrees with the Qur'an.

This is why Muslims can talk to the media and call for things like *Freedom* and *Justice* and *Peace,* and everyone will nod their heads and agree. But they are speaking words that don't mean what you think they mean.

Ethics Shmethics!

Why does it seem that Islam says one thing, and then does another? The main reason is something called *taqiyya*. Muslims are not allowed to cheat other Muslims, or lie to other Muslims, or steal from other Muslims, and so on. Although the rules are reciprocal between Muslims, they are something else entirely when dealing with a low-life, inferior, kafir (you). Lying to you to further the goals of worldwide domination is perfectly acceptable:

Let not the believers Take for friends or helpers Unbelievers rather than believers: if any do that, in nothing will there be help from Allah: except by way of precaution, that ye may Guard yourselves from them. But Allah cautions you (To remember) Himself; for the final goal is to Allah. – (*Qur'an 3:28, Yusuf Ali*)

201

In other words, a Muslim should only ally themselves with non-believers when it serves Islam. It's okay to pretend to be a non-believer's ally or friend, if it advances Islam. And this is exactly how this verse is used in practice. The following is from one of Islam's greatest scholars:

In this case, such believers are allowed to show friendship to the disbelievers outwardly, but never inwardly. For instance, Al-Bukhari recorded that Abu Ad-Darda' said, **'We smile in the face of some people although our hearts curse them.'** Al-Bukhari said that Al-Hasan said, 'The Tuqyah is allowed until the Day of Resurrection...' – (*Ibn Kathir, from Tafsir al-Qur'an al-'Adhim*) [Emphasis Added]

There is no Golden Rule in Islam that applies to anyone but Muslims. Deception toward non-Muslims is considered the right thing to do. (It's interesting that so many Muslims call the USA "The Great Satan," and Christians call Satan the "Father of Lies," and yet it is only Islam that lies and calls it "good.")

"Je Suis Charlie"

Drawing images of Muhammad should not invoke a death sentence, as it did for the workers of the French satirical magazine *Charlie Hebdo* in January 2015. The attack by Islamic fundamentalists resulted in the brutal murder of 12 people, and injured 11 more, some critically. The French people, and millions of others around the world who knew what it meant to have the right of free speech, began to identify with Charlie Hebdo, and thus the phrase "Je Suis Charlie" (I am Charlie) was born. The attack became a symbol for the divide between the liberal freedoms of the West and the tyranny of all religious belief.

Muslims argue that the memory and image of Muhammad is as sacred to them as the American flag is to Americans, and therefore neither should be mocked. That is only true to a point. If you ask an American which is *more* sacred, the flag, or the right to Freedom of Speech, the flag loses. Better to be mocked and free, than to keep your symbol as a slave.

All you need is to read some of the surahs and scriptures highlighted in this book to know that much of the content within the pages of many "holy" texts around the world could be considered *hate speech*. Perhaps these hapless religions and their legions of intolerance should consider this before any of them begin to propose the banning of criticism aimed at their beliefs. Criticism is a good thing – for everyone and every institution. If a religion doesn't want their words banned, they should consider not making any attempt to ban words they too don't like. Should we not invoke The Golden Rule, or at least an "eye for an eye"? The lesson to be learned is this: *There is nothing on earth more equal than Freedom of Speech.*

However, most of the bigoted words that come from Islam and other fundamentalist religions are immunized via laws protecting religious freedom. Although, Islam can just as easily be classified as a political movement.

Emigrating to a country, then pushing to enact sharia law to usurp laws of the land which are already established, is *political,* not religious. Every time an Islamic terrorist attack occurs, that is a political statement, not a religious one. Perhaps Islam should have its religious status revoked and treated like the political movement it has become. It can then be taxed, and when it gets out of line, it can be sued and its members prosecuted – in much the same way as any political party or movement.

Whatever the future of democracy holds, we do know this: Islam has never had an Enlightenment, and probably never will. Freedom of Speech means feelings get hurt and beliefs get challenged, and from this we learn and grow. Islam and other fundamentalist religions refuse to take the risk of losing an argument, of ever being wrong, and therefore give up their opportunity to expand their possibilities. Those of us in the West understand the difference. The road to being "right" means you suffer scrutiny, investigation, challenged beliefs, and sometimes even mockery along the way.

Je Suis Charlie.

Islam Lite

"Not all Muslims are like that!" is the buzz-phrase used to gloss over atrocities that are directly descended from a religion that believes all the words (including the violent ones) are the actual words of their deity. The fact is, they don't all have to be "like that" to hurt people. Because almost half of all Muslims living in Britain want to see some sort of Sharia Law become part of British Law, we can see clearly how this exemplifies the harm done from those who "aren't like that." They may not be blowing themselves up in a crowded mall, but they are blowing up the way of life of the nations who took them in. And that is nothing less than a travesty.

Clearly, those Muslims who do nothing to promote or oppose jihad are subscribing to a kind of "lighter" version of Islam. When terrorism occurs at the hands of Islam, these are the Muslims who are silent. We hear no condemnation from them until others demand it. Is this silence from the fear of being terrorized themselves, or is it tacit support for terrorist activity? Or, is it a little of both? Either way, few within the religion itself are making moves to stop their religion from spreading terror. It is clear that it will only stop when the people being terrorized have had enough.

A Brief History In the Desert

Let's interrupt this program for a quick history lesson. What was happening in Europe before the Warlord of Allah bought his first horse?

Most persons at least a little familiar with the history of the demise of the Roman Empire and its aftermath are aware of how far Europe had fallen by the early decades of the seventh century. What historians have often debated is why and how it all happened. We do know that Europeans were getting invaded by Barbarians from the north, but those invaders quickly settled down and assimilated into the areas they conquered. Whatever the decline, prior to the seventh century, it was a relatively slow process.

Modern scholars have just now started to discover that the hard fall that happened in the seventh century, the fall that dumped the continent deep into the Dark Ages, wasn't entirely Europe's fault. In fact, it may have been mostly the fault of the invading Arab Muslims to Europe's south and east.

> In Mediterranean Europe ... Arab raiders, fired by the belief that it was legitimate and even righteous to live off the wealth and resources of the infidel, launched raid after raid against the towns and villages on the coasts, plundering both lay and ecclesiastical settlements and destroying crops in the fields. Early medieval documents are full of descriptions of these atrocities. – (Emmet Scott, *Mohammed and Charlemagne Revisited)*

Once Islam had established itself as a religion of war, any nation or people became a continuing target for violence. The constant jihad against Europe happened for literally hundreds of years, and it was still going on unabated by the time of the European Renaissance. The estimation is that Muslim pirates, with their bases in North Africa, kidnapped and enslaved approximately 1.5 million Europeans from the sixteenth to nineteenth centuries. By comparison, the Spanish Inquisition, which spanned a parallel, but slightly greater, time frame, managed only to kill between 2000 to 5000 people. And today, more people are killed by Muslims *each year* than in all the years of the Spanish Inquisition combined.

Modern scholars are finally waking up to the reality that the European Crusades were as much a response to the onslaught of Muslim invasion and terrorist activity, as they were to convert the Holy Land to Christianity.

And not even North America was immune to the *jihadi* virus...

Islam and a Young United States of America

The United States of America was barely a decade old, and already fighting Muslims. Most of them were Islamic pirates who were capturing merchant vessels bound for Europe's ports. The first to fight these battles were the newly formed U.S. Marines. These wars were so significant to the Marine Corps that the first two lines of the Marine's Hymn commemorates their bravery:

> From the Halls of Montezuma
> To the shores of *Tripoli;*
> We fight our country's battles
> In the air, on land, and sea;

Today, Tripoli is, of course, in Muslim Libya and the words refer to the Battle of Derne, in 1805, during the First Barbary War. (Yes, there was more than one!) These terrorist acts were at the behest and approval of the Barbary States (a conglomeration of states in north Africa including modern-day Algeria, Morocco, Libya and Tunisia). The terrorist activity included, in typical Islamic fashion, the taking of slaves. Many U.S. navy men were captured, enslaved, and never heard from again. Of course, the ultimate goal for the Barbary States was to be paid a high ransom for the return of ships, cargo and crew. And they usually got their wish – without a fight. That is, until they encountered a well-armed American Navy.

Over the course of almost 40 years, the United States fought many bloody battles in the Mediterranean sea over their right to move freely into European ports, and during this time their only real enemy in that region was the Muslim states. As U.S. naval might increased, the battles became more in favor of the new nation, and the often cash-strapped young government no longer had to pay tribute to terrorists.

But, early on, the U.S. government was nearly dumbfounded regarding the nature of what was happening to their ships. Letters written by Thomas Jefferson in 1786 to the U.S. Secretary of Foreign Affairs, John Jay, gives us plenty of insight. Jefferson's attempt to negotiate a treaty with the Islamic states, includes the following explanation (below). When he asked the envoy from Tripoli why the Barbary states were attacking U.S. ships, Jefferson writes that the envoy told him...

> ... it was founded on the Laws of their Prophet, that it was written in their Koran, that all nations who should not have acknowledged their authority were sinners, that it was their right and duty to make war upon them wherever they could be found, and to make slaves of all they could take as Prisoners, and that every Musselman [Muslim] who should be slain in battle was sure to go to Paradise. – (Thomas Jefferson, *The Papers of Thomas Jefferson*)

Has anything changed regarding jihad since Islam began? As of this writing, Islam has perpetrated 27,459 deadly terror attacks since September 11, 2001. [Source: thereligionofpeace.com]

If Muhammad were alive today, he would be arrested, tried, and possibly executed for being a terrorist – and remembered as nothing more than a bloody pirate.

THE "GOLDEN AGE" OF ISLAM

With all this killing and hatred toward anyone who doesn't believe in (or follow) Allah's laws, was there ever a time when Islam was not like this? Is all this just the work of a few extremists? Muslim apologists will try to tell you it is, and will often point to Islam's "Golden Age" which ended about 750 years ago.

Of course, it's never a good thing for any nation, culture, or religion to have its "Golden Age" be in the distant past. In modern terms, a Golden Age means a time of prosperity, stability, and peace. Ideally, a civilization's Golden Age should be either now, or in the near future. Islam's Golden Age came and went. But, let's take a good hard look at what it was really like...

The Archeological Record

The Golden Age of Islam is considered to be from about 750 C.E. to 1260 C.E. As you might expect, any great civilization's "Golden Age" should leave behind a massive amount of evidence for its existence, just as Rome, ancient Egypt, and the various Chinese dynasties have done. Yet, when we look at Islam's great era, there is virtually nothing. In city after ancient city, archaeologists dig and dig and find mostly layers of dirt and sand. Where did the evidence for Islamic greatness go? Where are the great libraries, architecture, inventions and innovations? Where is Islam's great mark on our history? Islam must have been busy doing *something,* but there aren't even many mosques being built during this "golden" time. The one thing we do see, without question, is a path of destruction where former great classical civilizations are burnt, destroyed or wiped out completely in virtually every area Islam conquered. And nothing of value replaced what was lost.

Even if we set aside the absence of a glorious archaeological footprint, the historical records that are available show a consistent Muslim rule of orthodox Islamic thought based on strict interpretations of the Qur'an. The surviving ideas of Greek philosophy and science were only employed to further that orthodoxy and to bolster religious oppression.

When anyone speaks of a Golden Age of Islamic "learning," it means exactly that – learning about Islam – studying the Qur'an, and how its religion of repression should rule the world. It does not mean Islam was engaged in the intensive study of classical logic. Theocracies have always tended toward avoiding reason. Islam is no exception. And, like in all cultures dominated by religious belief and superstition, the few interspersed and sporadic decades that showed a glimmer of enlightenment were there in spite of religious dogma, not because of it.

War Against the World

One way to determine if an organization is (or has) a *political ideology* is to observe whether or not it makes war. Few religions do this, and fewer still do it for very long. Yet, throughout its history, going back to its basic inception and establishment, Islam has made war. Only political movements seek to draw political boundaries through war, and war has been the impetus for the existence and survival of Islam all along. Islam is clearly more political than religious.

Although Islamic apologists like to claim that Islam had advanced "science," the historical record shows that the Muslim faithful spent most of their time attacking Europe, India, and Africa, and doing whatever they could to kill Hindus, Christians, and Pagans at every opportunity. And when they weren't beheading non-Muslims, they were burning down libraries, and destroying the art and culture of every city and nation they invaded. These are the facts that anyone can gather from just about any comprehensive history book. But you rarely hear it from the media, and it won't make it into your child's school books.

The Golden Age successes of Islam included this small sampling:

- Massacre of 6000 human beings at Amorium (in Asia Minor) 838 CE.
- Burning of the Monastery at Monte Cassino, Italy, and murder of the monks who worked there, 883 CE.
- Burning of the Library of al-Hakam II, Cordoba, Spain, 976 CE, in an effort to rid the earth of "ancient science."
- Burning to the ground the city of Barcelona, Spain, and the enslavement or murder of most of its inhabitants, 985 CE.
- Enslavement of 500,000 Hindus by Sultan Mahmud, in Punjab, India, 1001-1002 CE. Another 253,000 were enslaved by the Sultan in 1019 CE.
- Destruction of the Hindu Temple at Somnath, India, and the murder of 50,000 people, 1024 CE.
- Burning of the Library in Rayy, Persia, 1029 CE.
- Murder of 6,000 Jews in Fez, Morocco by Muslim conqueror Abul Kamal Tumin, 1032 CE.
- Murder of 4000 Jews in Grenada, Spain by Muslim mobs, 1066 CE. The Jewish vizier was crucified.
- In Spain, the deportation of all Christians and Jews who refused to convert to Islam. (The other option was execution.) 1126 CE and again in 1143 CE.
- Burning of the Library of Ghazna, Ghurid Empire, (Afghanistan) in 1151 CE.
- Beheading of Buddhist monks and burning of the library in the Maldives, 1153 CE.
- Burning of the massive Buddhist and Hindu library in Nalanda, India, in 1193 CE, and the additional enslavement of over 3000 people. The fire burned for days, and the monks were burned alive.
- Enslavement of 20,000 people from Raja Bhim, India, 1195 CE.
- Enslavement of 50,000 Hindus at Kalinjar, India, 1202 CE.

Science and learning is not primary on your mind when you are burning libraries and taking slaves. Of course, we are focusing on Islam's "Golden" Age, making the above list a small truncated cross-section of the "religion of peace." But the historically documented actions prior to 750 CE, and after 1260 CE, are much the same. What we see are forced conversions, enslavement of captives, and the absolute destruction of prior civilizations. This list above is only the tip of the horrific Islamic iceberg. If we were to list the atrocities before and after the "Golden Age," this book could barely contain them. All of these types of events extend unabated from the 13th through to the 19th, 20th, and 21st centuries.

With the proper research, we quickly discover that the religion of peace is actually the religion of war.

The Golden Age of Slaves

To anyone wondering if Muhammad was ever opposed to slavery, or if ever believed in *equality*, here's just one of many references that state otherwise:

> Allah sets forth the Parable (of two men: one) a slave under the dominion of another; He has no power of any sort; and (the other) a man on whom We have bestowed goodly favours from Ourselves, and he spends thereof (freely), privately and publicly: are the two equal? (By no means;) praise be to Allah...
> – (*Qur'an 16:75, Yusuf Ali*)

During their Golden Age of conquest, which continued uninterrupted for 500 years (!), it is estimated that Islamic nations took over one million European slaves back to Islamic lands. In the eyes of Islam, this was perfectly acceptable because Muhammad had never condemned slavery from the very beginning. But, remember, Muhammad was supposed to be the "Final Messenger" of God (Allah), but for some reason, Allah, when it came to the prior revelations of Jews and Christians, never bothered to fix *this* particular corruption.

Europe, India and China were not Islam's only targets. It is estimated that over 110 million black Africans were killed by the policies and beliefs of Islam.

> ...a minimum of 28 Million Africans were enslaved in the Muslim Middle East. Since, at least, 80 percent of those captured by Muslim slave traders were calculated to have died before reaching the slave market, it is believed that the death toll from 1400 years of Arab and Muslim slave raids into Africa could have been as high as 112 Million. When added to the number of those sold in the slave markets, the total number of African victims of the trans-Saharan and East African slave trade could be significantly higher than 140 Million people. – (John Allembillah Azumah, *The Legacy of Arab-Islam in Africa*)

The facts speak for themselves. The idea that Islam is the preserver of science and classical European culture is a myth. Islam has never had a "Golden Age" and probably never will.

One Golden Example: The Astrolabe

The astrolabe was an inclinometer used by astronomers, astrologers, and most often by navigators, to determine the position of the stars and calculate time and distance relative to the user's position on earth.

Muslims like to take credit for this invention, but the first astrolabe was invented about 700 years before the first Muslim was born. Astrolabes were in use throughout eastern Christendom for centuries.

Some Muslims seem to think that writing about something (as various Muslim scientists did about the astrolabe during the medieval era), is the same as actually inventing it. Although, Muslim scientists did improve this invention somewhat, the propaganda isn't anything to get excited about.

Most of the achievements that came out of the Islamic Golden Age were made by conquered non-Muslims under Islamic rule. Some were even made by heretics who held Islam in disdain. There is also an historical correlation between a weakening Islamic empire (militarily) and the lessening of scientific "discovery." As the cannibalization of other civilizations diminished, due to a lack of new lands to conquer, the claims of Islamic greatness began to die.

The Algebra Myth

Many Islamic apologists make a rather weak attempt at giving credit for the "invention" of Algebra to Arabs and Islamists. However, the only real contribution is the word *Algebra* itself, from *Al-jabr,* and even Arab etymologists aren't sure what *Al-jabr* originally meant. Algebra, as a branch of mathematics, has been around since classical antiquity – hundreds of years BCE. The 8th Century CE shows the Islamic empire making an awkward attempt at civilization and somehow managed to translate a large number of ancient Greek mathematical texts into Arabic. But, actual contributions to the study of Algebra itself were minimal when compared to other civilizations both before and after the so-called Islamic Golden Age.

Claims of historical greatness within Islam and its Golden Age often wither and wilt under closer scrutiny. This example is just one of many.

Moving Forward to the Past

So, if we take an honest look at Islam today, in what should now be a *true* Golden Age, with many Muslim nations possessing banks full of oil money, what do we see? A plethora of Nobel Prize winners? Amazing Olympic athletes? Muslim astronauts by the dozens? New innovative technologies? No. We see what we have always seen – endless wars, backward laws, violent abuse of citizenry, a lack of value for human life, terrorism, and abject poverty in those Muslim nations not lucky enough to have settled their tents over vast oil fields. When you do find a successful Muslim, there is a very high probability that he obtained his success while living in a free, non-Muslim nation, and/or after being educated in a non-Muslim university.

Getting an education solely from a religious book, won't get you very far, as we will see next...

SCIENCE AND THE QUR'AN

Islam is notorious in the 21st Century for making a claim that the Qur'an has predicted many scientific truths before science was even around to confirm those truths. This is a weak attempt to tell the world that the Qur'an must be true because the science within it is also true, and therefore all science must have come from their god, Allah. After all, how could these poor desert dwellers have known about such great scientific ideas without the aid of Allah? This, of course, is an argument from ignorance. It is possible for a book to have scientific truths and still be full of falsehoods about deities. But, that's not an option Muslims want to consider.

The second Muslim assertion that follows is this: If the Qur'an is true then Allah exists. It's a rather backwards way of looking at a deity. Shouldn't it be, Allah exists, therefore the Qur'an is true? After all, which came first, and which is more sacred and powerful? Shouldn't the believer of any deity show us the deity and then tell us what is written about him? But what do those of us who doubt their "truths" get instead? We get first some written text which tells us about a deity that never appears. This of course, is what all religions present – a written claim which they proceed to state is the evidence for that very same claim. It's so intensely and tightly circular, if it was three dimensional, it would turn itself into a black hole.

But let's get back to the Islamic claim that the Qur'an predicted scientific truths. First, we'll do a logical comparison. Do all the astronomical assumptions made by the Mayan people, most of which have been shown to be quite accurate, presuppose that the deity they also worshiped, Kukulkan, is the one true god? Somehow, without telescopes, they already knew the recently discovered fact that the Orion Nebula is not a stellar pin-point. Does the amazing astronomy of the Mayan people mean we should all now worship Kukulkan as the Creator of the Universe?

The 14th Century seer Nostradamus also made written predictions, some rather scientific in nature. With a bit of creative manipulation, much of which is not nearly as complex as the machinations of Islamic text, one can discern quite a large number of science-based "predictions" such as airplanes, cars, tanks, computers, etc. Nostradamus was a Catholic. Should we all become Catholic now and follow his teachings? And because the writings of Nostradamus came *after* those of Mohammed, wouldn't the writings of Nostradamus be the "Final Word" from God, superseding those of Muhammad?

As with any religion, the defense of never having to exit the circle – that the claim is evidence for the claim – is to take smaller claims within the larger claim, insist that those smaller claims are true, then declare that all the larger claims must be true as well. Because Mecca was mentioned a long time ago, and we know Mecca exists now, should we believe everything anyone ever said or wrote about Mecca is also true? That would be the logic of a preschool child – or one who is self-deluded by stubborn choice. But, it is this exact preschool level of logic that Islamists use to make their case for their god.

If you're a non-believer, one of the first things you will notice is how strongly Muslims defend their book, the Qur'an. If fact, you will see a hierarchy of defense which proceeds most often like this: 1. The Qur'an. 2. Mohammed. 3. Allah. Oddly, you would think Allah would get top billing, but he doesn't. It appears, at least on the surface, that the so-called creator of the Islamic universe is not as discussed or revered as much as the book about him, or the prophet that allegedly had conversations with him. The culture that surrounds Islam is so profoundly devoted to their holy book, it's as if the Qur'an itself is their god. The word Islam means to "submit." But, most new converts learn soon enough that it's not service to a god – it's slavery to a book.

As for Muslims, they have a long way to go. They have had no Reformation and no leaders to write reinterpretations of their Qur'an. It's the Qur'an or nothing. Islam is the religion to watch and the religion to worry about until they finally come to the conclusion that they must change their primitive beliefs or be destroyed – either by the hand of their own people, or by others outside their realm.

Science of the God(s)

One of the ways Muslims claim that the Qur'an was written by God or Allah is to further claim that the Qur'an holds many scientific truths within its pages, truths which, when written, could have only been known by a divine being. This ploy is obviously directed at the West, with its high-tech and its overabundance of believers in science, whether Christian, Jewish, or atheist. However, ironic as it may seem, it completely ignores the fact that the true scientist, and science itself, never points to a god of any kind, because within the study of science, a god is wholly unnecessary. Insertion of a god, or removal of one, has no effect on the scientific outcome. This does not stop the Muslim missionary from pressing this ignorance-laced maneuver to gain converts. The push is often relentless, despite the Qur'an's obvious primitive and superstitious content.

Despite this odd and unnatural claim that a non-scientifically evidenced god is somehow also a scientist, let's plow through some of the Muslim claims about the wonders of science to be found in the Qur'an.

We should start (close to) the beginning...

> **We** created the heavens and the earth and all between them in Six Days, nor did any sense of weariness touch **Us.** – (*Qur'an 50:38, Yusuf Ali*) [Emphasis Added]

The idea was lifted from the Bible, directly from Genesis 1:1. Although, it seems the Muslim committee known as "We" didn't rest on the seventh day like the Jewish and Christian group did – because all that creating led to no sense of "weariness."

Muslims will admit that much of their historical claims come from the Bible, such as stories about Moses, Abraham, Ishmael, and Jesus. But, somehow, just mentioning "heavens and earth" anywhere in the Qur'an has Muslims all aquiver with claims of "science."

Killing Demons with Star-Missiles

In another time and place, Muhammad could have been the poster boy for any nation's burgeoning literacy campaign. In the passage below, we see that Muhammad apparently thought all stars are small and that they eventually fall from the sky like comets or meteorites. Here's his primitive analysis:

211

And we have, (from of old), adorned the lowest heaven with Lamps, and We have made such (Lamps) (as) missiles to drive away the Evil Ones, and have prepared for them the Penalty of the Blazing Fire. – (*Qur'an 67:5, Yusuf Ali*)

What he calls "lamps" in the sky are stars, and when they zip through the atmosphere, they somehow torment devils as a way to prepare those demons for Hell. How could anyone *not* praise such wonderful "science"!

Building a Better Muslim

The following is a claim that Allah, who is again referred to as a "We" (he apparently splits into parts, much like the Triune god of the Christians), had a hand in the expansion of the universe.

With power and skill did We construct the Firmament: for it is We Who create the vastness of space. – (*Qur'an 51:47, Yusuf Ali*)

The key word in this passage is "construct." Constructed means exactly how you would think the word should be used – to construct a building, for example. However, the word "extend" is a little tricky. As the Big Bang Theory became more well known, translations of this passage began to appear that were obvious attempts to make the passage match the theory by using the word "expand." See below:

- ...We it is Who make the vast extent (thereof). – Pickthall (1930)
- ...We extend it wide. – Arberry (1955)
- ...We are Able to extend the vastness of space thereof. – Khan (1977)
- ...We expanded it. – Muhammad Sarwar (1981)
- ...We are [its] expander. – Sahih International Translation (1997)

This is a short list, but these (and others) can't all be accurate. Whichever translation you choose, you'll find some are in past tense, some are in present tense, some refer to a current fixed size of space, others to the on-going process of making the universe larger. So, is this an observation that the sky is big, or that the universe is expanding? Coming, as it is, from an illiterate desert nomad (Muhammad), *who also thought stars were missiles made to kill demons,* it is not very likely he is referring to the expansion of space, especially when earlier translations refer to an observation of size, not a process of making objects in the universe move away from one another.

Let's put it in proper historical context. If *expand* was the word of the day, it was most likely used in much the same way as you would expand your house by adding on another room. People built homes and expanded them in the 7th century, as needed, as humans have always done. The writer of the Qur'an supposed that the "heavens," where Allah and the other gods *resided,* were similarly built and expanded, or even "extended." There is no indication that knowledge of The Big Bang was present, not by Muhammad, nor his translators, nor Allah and his creator friends (the Holy "We.")

Us and Them

Another "We" creator quote goes like this:

> Do not the Unbelievers see that the heavens and the earth were joined together before We clove them asunder... – (*Qur'an 21:30, Yusuf Ali*)

Saying the heavens and earth were "joined" together implies they were first separate, and then joined. There is no evidence for such a gathering of matter prior to The Big Bang. Everything was together first, then The Big Bang followed thereafter. Furthermore, The Big Bang was an expansion, not a "splitting." This erroneous passage reveals nothing new or awe-inspiring.

Round and Round

This is a favorite of the Muslim proselytizer:

> It is He Who created the Night and the Day, and the sun and the moon: all (the celestial bodies) swim along, each in its rounded course. – (*Qur'an 21:33, Yusuf Ali*)

"Rounded course" is an orbit. Unfortunately for the faithful, who desperately wish for their holy book to be a science textbook, orbits were already known in the 7th century, so this is no great revelation. The only difference is that during Muhammad's lifetime everyone incorrectly thought that the sun and all the stars orbited around the earth. This primitive belief is known as *geocentric.* There is nothing to indicate that the transcriber of the Qur'an thought differently.

The Sun Takes a Break

Another sun-related quote goes like this:

> And the sun runs his course for a period determined for him: that is the decree of (Him), the Exalted in Might, the All-Knowing. – (*Qur'an 37:38, Yusuf Ali*)

This passage hints that the sun runs for a while and then stops somewhere else before returning back to where we can see it again. And in fact, other translations use the phrase "resting place." The Sahih International Translation actually uses the words "stopping place." We all know that the sun does not have a resting or stopping place. This passage is just flat out wrong. Apparently, the "Almighty" Allah doesn't actually know it all, after all.

Our Daily Taco

Remember, for the Muslim searching for scientific truth in the Qur'an, any mention of "Heaven and Earth" is a sure sign that "science" must follow:

> He created the heavens and the earth in true (proportions): He makes the Night overlap the Day, and the Day overlap the Night... – (*Qur'an 39:5, Yusuf Ali*)

Other translations use "folds up" (*Ahmed Ali*) while others use "wraps" (*Abdel Haleem*). Days and nights are not wrapped or folded up like blankets. Perhaps the writer of the Qur'an thought the earth could fold itself over like a tortilla? Just in case anyone is trying to read something more into this verse, this is not a reference to the bending of spacetime. It's about Muslims observing sunrise and sunset, then saying "Allah did it."

Muslims and The Ozone Layer

We begin here:

> And We have made the heavens as a canopy well guarded: yet do they turn away from the Signs which these things (point to)! – (*Qur'an 21:32, Yusuf Ali*)

The Qur'an is wrong again. The sky is not a protective canopy. The atmosphere is. When you look up at the sky on any clear day or night, you are seeing *past* this "canopy" – past the atmosphere, into the vastness of space. The key to knowing that the Qur'an writer was referring to things *beyond* the atmosphere is when he says "our signs" – which are objects (sun, moon, stars) *outside* of the atmosphere. There is no "canopy" beyond the atmosphere. This statement that the sky (the vastness of space) is a "canopy" no doubt comes from the Bible and its own reference to that same vastness of space being a "firmament."

The God of the Gaffs

The atmosphere is incorrectly referred to again:

> It is He Who hath created for you all things that are on earth; Moreover His design comprehended the heavens, for He gave order and perfection to the seven firmaments; and of all things He hath perfect knowledge. – (*Qur'an 2:29, Yusuf Ali*)

The Muslim apologist points to this passage as proof that the God-inspired writer of the Qur'an must have had knowledge of the "seven layers" of the atmosphere. But this suddenly implies that heaven is limited to the atmosphere alone, not the vastness of space. Which is it? Is "heaven" all of the universe beyond earth, or does it end at the *exosphere?*

This is another theft of Biblical proportions, so to speak. The idea of seven heavens (*shamayim*) comes directly from Judaism which preceded Islam by at least 1800 years.

Furthermore, this Islamic claim completely ignores the fact that there are actually *five* principle layers of the atmosphere, and at least *four* other secondary layers. Five plus four equals nine in the real world, not seven. But that doesn't stop Muslims from practicing fantasy science and fantasy math.

Wash, Rinse, Repeat

More of Mister Obvious Muslim being obvious:

> By the Firmament which returns (in its round)... – (*Qur'an 86:11, Yusuf Ali*)

Another reference to orbits. This is one more "amazing" claim which simply expresses what we already know, and knew. Yes, even the primitive Pagan Europeans at Stonehenge knew about the cycles of the objects in the sky. The Qur'an is saying nothing new.

Ya Gotta Have Faith!

Perhaps Islam noticed Jesus moving mountains with the faith of a mustard seed when this was written:

> Thou seest the mountains and thinkest them firmly fixed: but they shall pass away as the clouds pass away. – (*Qur'an 27:88, Yusuf Ali*)

This has never happened and never will. Mountains, due to the tectonic plates, move extremely slowly. It takes millions of years to form a mountain. And they don't zip past us in a few hours like clouds. Other translations use phrases such as "thou shalt see the mountains... passing by like clouds..." (*Arberry*). This verse is simply more absurdity from the Qur'an.

Iron Man

The following, although mentioned as "scientific proof" by Muslim apologists, is more of an observation about a metal than a scientific claim:

> We sent aforetime our apostles with Clear Signs and sent down with them the Book and the Balance (of Right and Wrong), that men may stand forth in justice; and We sent down Iron, in which is (material for) mighty war, as well as many benefits for mankind... – (*Qur'an 57:25, Yusuf Ali*)

At last, Muslims entered the Iron Age, apparently after everyone else had already done so! Now we all await their entry into the modern age. Note again, that because something exists, God (or Allah) gets all the credit, without ever demonstrating that God (or Allah) is real.

Two For the Price of One

A grown Muslim notices that things come in pairs:

> Glory to God, Who created in pairs all things that the earth produces, as well as their own (human) kind and (other) things of which they have no knowledge. – (*Qur'an 36:36, Yusuf Ali*)

Again, this is not something difficult for a human to observe in *any* era: man and woman, big and tall, fat and skinny, two eyes, two ears, two feet, two legs, etc. Was this reference stolen from the Chinese (Yin and Yang)? What is obvious to the rest of mankind is "amazing science" to the Muslim.

A Long Day's Journey Into Night

The Qur'an acknowledges long periods of time:

> Yet they ask thee to hasten on the Punishment! But Allah will not fail in His Promise. Verily a Day in the sight of thy Lord is like a thousand years of your reckoning. – (*Qur'an 22:47 Yusuf Ali*)

This is another direct theft from the Bible that preceded the Qur'an. See: 2 Peter 3:8 for the Christian version. See: Psalm 90:4 for the Jewish one.

Walking On a Moon Shadow

This one's kind of embarrassing (for Muslims). It states that the moon is a light. And as we all know, the moon is just a rock. It reflects sunlight, but it produces no light of its own. Here's what the Qur'an says:

> It is He Who made the sun to be a shining glory and the moon to be a **light** (of beauty), and measured out stages for her; that ye might know the number of years and the count (of time). – (*Qur'an 10:5, Yusuf Ali*) [Emphasis Added]

The above is an early translation. Now you find newer English translations that say, "the moon, a derived light," or "the luminous moon," but the original Arabic simply says "light." The Qur'an claims error-free science, but fails. And if one part fails, the whole thing is questionable. Of course, Islamists know this, therefore they *redact* accordingly.

Water Doesn't Only Kill Witches!

As one might surmise from a religion born in the desert, Islam is somewhat obsessed with water and rain:

> That sends down (from time to time) rain from the sky in due measure;- and We raise to life therewith a land that is dead; even so will ye be raised (from the dead). – (*Qur'an 43:11, Yusuf Ali*)

This is another simple observation about rain that anyone can make. It rains, then it evaporates, then it rains again. Plants are revived by it, animals have their thirst quenched by it. But the idiocy of bringing people back from the dead with rain is the glaring error here. It has not yet been observed that rain causes resurrections. Even if this is simply a metaphor, resurrection of the long dead is not possible. It is not *scientific*.

Dorothy Spots a Tornado

More "rain science" begins here as Islam predicts the weather:

> It is Allah Who sends the Winds, and they raise the Clouds: then does He spread them in the sky as He wills, and break them into fragments, until thou seest rain-drops issue from the midst thereof: then when He has made them reach such of his servants as He wills behold, they do rejoice! – (*Qur'an 30:48, Yusuf Ali*)

Somebody actually watched a rainstorm in the land of Muhammad, commented on it, then said, "Allah did it!" Not exactly pure genius.

Salt or No Salt?

This could be about natural dams or other water barriers, but Muslim apologists use it to show how their "scientific" god separated water into types:

> He has let free the two bodies of flowing water, meeting together: Between them is a Barrier which they do not transgress... – (*Qur'an 55:19-20, Yusuf Ali*)

Supposedly, Muslims finally figured out that there is salt water in some places and fresh water in others. Something the rest of humanity already knew. But, not everyone is fast in science.

A Planter's Nuts

Here it gets a little embarrassing for the Muslim believer:

217

Does man think that he will be left uncontrolled, (without purpose)? Was he not a drop of sperm emitted (in lowly form)?
– (*Qur'an 75:36-37, Yusuf Ali*)

This idea that a man comes from his father's "seed" (or sperm), and that a drop of semen is a single seed, is very old, and again, this was likely stolen from Judaism. But Judaism and Islam are both wrong. A man cannot be defined as being once "a drop of sperm emitted" due to the fact that semen is only *male* DNA – half of what makes a human being – (and not viable) without an egg from a human female. So, why did both religions miss this vital point? Because they had no idea women had ova (eggs), or that women even contributed to the process of human reproduction beyond being the "vessel" for procreation. So much for ancient "science."

The Scientific Conclusion

There's more we could address, but why should we? Even if these ridiculously forced narratives from the Qur'an could be shown to be "scientific," that itself in no way proves *any* god exists, including Allah. It would only show that someone who had a knowledge of science was also able to write a religious book. This is not the same as proving a god exists. Muslim apologists seem sorely lacking in the ability to grasp this very basic truth.

Duran Duran, not Qur'an Qur'an

Lastly, look at this Qur'anic statement about the Qur'an itself:

Do they not consider the Qur'an (with care)? Had it been from other Than Allah, they would surely have found therein Much discrepancy. – (*Qur'an 4:82, Yusuf Ali*)

Of course, we did find "much discrepancy," as demonstrated throughout this entire chapter. In any event, the above passage implies that there could be *other gods* who write books, and that questions the veracity of monotheism itself. But its main assertion is about "discrepancy." (Note that other translations use "inconsistencies" or "contradictions," all of which mean the same thing.) If we accept this passage as true, then any book or writing with no inconsistencies must be from Allah. Therefore, if a Satanic Bible has no inconsistencies, is it also from Allah? If any person's opinion about anything which has no inconsistencies, even if unethical, or immoral, is that also from Allah? Or is it simply not possible for someone other than Allah to write something without inconsistencies?

Of course, the actual intended claim here is that Allah would never write anything that contained inconsistencies. Then are we to believe that the Qur'an has Allah as its author, and no inconsistencies, simply because the Qur'an says that about itself? It seems the Qur'an's own claim regarding its inconsistencies is inconsistent with logic! The conclusion, therefore, is that the Qur'an could have been written by a human being and still have no inconsistencies. No Allah/god needed.

CHRISTIANITY VS. ISLAM

Thus far we have dissected, rather ruthlessly, both Islam and Christianity. Perhaps we should compare these two off-shoots of Judaism (and their founders) to determine which is more meritorious. Consider this passage from the Qur'an:

> O ye who believe! there are indeed many among the *priests and anchorites,* who in Falsehood devour the substance of men and hinder (them) from the way of Allah. And there are those who bury gold and silver and spend it not in the way of Allah: announce unto them a most grievous penalty. – (*Qur'an 9:34, Yusuf Ali*)

"Priests and Anchorites" is often translated as "Jews and Christians." Despite the fact that we can only guess about the specifics of what "most grievous penalty" actually means, from this, and other more blatantly violent passages, we can deduce what Islam thinks of its neighboring religious faiths – and it isn't universal love.

From the viewpoint of Islam, both Muhammad and Jesus were prophets, with Muslims declaring Muhammad to be the "final" messenger of Allah/God. But how are these two alleged prophets different, not just in what they said, but in what they did?

As far as the story goes, Jesus never killed anyone. In fact, it is alleged that Jesus even brought people back to life. By contrast, Muhammad was a tribal warrior who killed thousands of innocent human beings. In battle after battle, Muhammad attempted to convert others through the threat of a sword. Jesus, on the other hand, threatened others with a promise of a future eternal, ethereal fire. (Muhammad did this too, by the way.) However, we can see from this simple comparison, one of these prophets is merely a narcissist with delusions of grandeur, while the other is a war mongering psychopath.

And... regarding the well documented fact that Muhammad married a 6 year old girl, we must ask, why was Muhammad *not* at the forefront of what he must have *known* (if he truly was a prophet) would someday be a moral problem? Why did he not become the new great ethical leader of his time declaring that "no man shall marry a child"? Why is this declaration from Muhammad conveniently non-existent? The modern Islamic world now either denies that this ever took place, or they downplay the event, even stating that Muhammad at least waited until she was much older (at age nine!) to consummate their marriage. Why did it take many centuries after the death of Muhammad for the Islamic world to curtail such an abhorrent and immoral practice? (Again, when we compare Jesus to Muhammad, despite the heightened narcissism of Jesus, there is no indication that Jesus was interested in marrying little girls.)

219

However, Islam does have one very important and fundamental idea in common with Christianity: It prods followers to emulate Muhammad in much the same way that Christianity encourages Christians to be like Jesus. To be like Muhammad, therefore, means to deceive, rape and enslave *kafirs*. And to additionally hate, forcibly convert, or even kill those non-believers is to be the perfect Muslim.

Why does any of this matter to an atheist? Comparing religions to ascertain their relative merit to one another, from an atheist viewpoint, may seem like an exercise in futility. Naturally, we aren't making religious comparisons in an effort to join. Instead, we do it to determine which belief is more of a danger to humanity, and which belief we should avoid first and foremost. Every atheist will realize at some point that he or she is in a battle for truth. The religions of the world do not have truth. They instead insist on perpetuating falsehoods disguised as truth, blinding humanity's future. When engaged in these battles, it's imperative that an atheist knows what kind of war is being waged and which fanatical ideas do the most harm to the world.

Clearly, in this case, based on their terrorist actions, both historically and currently, and based on the rigid, archaic, war mongering content of their holy book, the one religion that is currently the greatest threat to human beings around the world is Islam.

Shia vs. Sunni Worse than Protestant vs. Catholic?

This is more of a footnote to all of this insanity, but there seems to be one thing that has at least partially slowed down the Islamic onslaught, and it resides in their own back yard. It's the schism between the two main factions of Islam – the *Sunni* and the *Shia*. The rift got started after the death of Muhammad in 632 C.E., and it was mostly wrapped up in which one of Muhammad's in-laws should be his successor. The two factions have been at odds (or at war) ever since.

The most recent subject of contention between these two groups regards the *Madhi* (a type of Islamic savior, or messiah-like figure), who is expected to come to earth (strangely, *with* Jesus) to usher in a new era for mankind. One of these groups thinks he's already among us, the other thinks he hasn't made it yet. There's much more to this, but this is not the place to discuss internal religious, ideological (and political) rifts. For atheists, it's simply more convoluted nonsense meant to keep the business (religion) in business.

CONCLUSION

How many more good people would there be in the world if there was no Qur'an, no Bible, no Talmud, and no religious books at all? To paraphrase Steven Weinberg, "Good people do good things, and bad people do bad things, but for good people to do bad things, it takes religion." Had the Qur'an never existed, how many innocent lives would have been saved?

Judaism has evolved into various branches. Christianity has evolved into various denominations. And with each reform came more civilized, peaceful, religious beliefs. Islam, however, has not evolved. It is the *coelacanth,* or "living fossil," of the religious world. In more personal terms, Islam is the current religious bully on the block. And the only way to stop a bully is to stand up to him.

Even if the non-Muslim world had taken a step back from their former glory, in this tortoise and hare race to civilization, we know the outcome. Islam lost. The centuries-long marathon was won by Europe and her descendants. While Islam was suppressing and oppressing the minds of half its population (women), and beheading or disabling those who questioned the "genius" of Muhammad, the West was building new cities with centers of learning, and inventing new ways to travel – eventually walking on the moon – a moon that Islamists revere to such a degree that it's emblazoned as a crescent on their national flags.

And now we must face the following truth... The religion of Islam is diametrically opposed to the values and beliefs of every idea put forth by liberal democracy. Where we work to abolish the death penalty, Islam works to enforce it (often brutally.) Where we work to grant equal rights for women, Islam works to deprive women even further. Where we work to give people freedom of expression (which leads to innovation), Islam works to smother such freedom even to the point of death and self-destruction. The West cannot live under Islam in the same way that Islam cannot function in any Western democracy. Oil and water. Fire and rain. We cannot ever be combined.

We live in a great time in the history of the world. Great advances in medicine, technology and science are all around us. We, at least in first world nations, have given up the notion of slavery, insisted on the establishing the rights of all humanity, and have taken great strides in lessening the cause of war. And yet, Islam is trying to take us back in time – to a dark age – to a time when slavery was sought after, when only the very wealthy had rights, and when brutal killing, war, and capital punishment were considered great achievements.

Not all religions are equal. And it is clear that Islam needs reform, and desperately so – reform that is honest, without *taqiyya,* and without violence. Perhaps the expected Islamic Madhi should appear, and as the *final* "Final Messenger," fix what is wrong with Islam – teach the Islamic masses that most of what Muhammad said is now obsolete, and that loving your neighbor applies to *everyone,* not just Muslims.

CHAPTER TEN

Evolution and The Garden of Eden

"It is not the goal to bless theories with claims of certainty or justification, but to eliminate errors in them."
– Karl Popper

"The Universe is screaming our insignificance, and we all refuse to listen."
– Edward Trillian

Before we start, we should make one thing perfectly clear: This chapter is less about science than it is about religious believers' own fanatical obsession with the Theory of Evolution. We've said it before, but it cannot be over-emphasized: A belief that the Theory of Evolution is true is not a requirement for being an atheist. Any scientific theory, the Theory of Evolution included, can be irrelevant to what an atheist thinks or believes. As we know, atheism existed long before the Theory of Evolution was ever proposed, and will continue to exist even if the theory is thoroughly debunked. Atheism is the absence of belief in gods, not the presence of belief in the origins of life on Earth.

CREATIONISM VS. INTELLIGENT DESIGN

The religious movements in the battle against science, the Theory of Evolution, and free-thought in general, are known as *creationism* and *intelligent design* (or ID). These two are virtually the same. Intelligent design originated as a revamping (and renaming) of the quickly eroding Christian fundamentalist movement of creationism, which itself was formed to offset the teaching of evolution in American public schools. Intelligent design encompasses more scientific fields of study and strives to use more science (more properly called pseudo-science) than the original creationists of the past. However, because this "science" is not rooted in *actual* science, and seeks only to disprove existing science, intelligent design has encountered even more ridicule than its creationist predecessors. In this chapter, because their goals are the same, creationism and intelligent design will be used interchangeably.

(It's interesting to note, and apropos, that intelligent design has the monogram "ID," as *the id* is the baser part of the human psyche.)

So... What the Hell Does Atheism Have to do with Evolution?

Should we really discuss evolution when atheism isn't about science? Should we even debate with the god-believers about this when the only true commonality among all atheists is that they simply don't believe in a god? Why do avid religious believers insist on talking about this with atheists? And why would they assume that atheists are somehow experts in science, especially when it comes to the Theory of Evolution? The study of evolution isn't what drives atheists to become atheists. Most often, it's religion that does that.

It seems strange, at least at first glance, why modern-day believers in a god insist on debating atheists on the subject of science, in particular the scientific studies of evolution and astrophysics. What is even more perplexing is the believer's insistence upon combining the two (astrophysics and evolution), often jumping from one to the other, or even thinking these two disciplines are one and the same. But, the wonderful thing about being an atheist is that you do not have to have any knowledge of science, or even any interest in science, to be an atheist. Because the definition of atheism requires only the rejection of the notions of theists, it does not remove our rational response to the believers' position in any way.

Other Theories

It's rather fascinating to note that religious persons do not have a quarrel with other scientific theories to the degree that they have toward the Theory of Evolution. You don't see anyone getting up in arms about Germ Theory, or The Theory of Relativity, or Atomic Theory, or Quantum Field Theory. No one is protesting outside schools because of Cell Theory, or the Kinetic Theory of Gases. Why aren't Christians and Muslims accusing scientists of getting those theories wrong, or of having "no real evidence"? These other theories have approximately the same amount of research (and sometimes even less) to test these ideas than the Theory of Evolution, yet for some reason these other theories are left conspicuously all alone.

As we will soon see, the objections to the Theory of Evolution are actually all about the believers *own* unbending narrative about how life began. Had the believers' holy books had a narrative that described how germs cause disease – one which appeared to them to contradict modern Germ Theory – creationists would be protesting Germ Theory. Likewise, because the childish Adam and Eve story hardly holds up to scientific scrutiny any better than a Dr. Seuss book, the spotlight is turned away from that primitive tale and focused instead upon the "errors" of the real scientific alternative.

The rhetoric and fanaticism against the scientific study of the origins of life on earth is so off-track, some creationist believers think evil atheist scientists deliberately created the Theory of Evolution as a way to disprove the literal existence of Adam and Eve, and they take any mention of the theory as a personal attack on their religion. It places believers in an automatic state of agitation. It's quite amazing to see. But, as we'll soon discover, this religious conspiracy theory is greatly exaggerated, and wholly unnecessary.

So, what else is going on in the theists' collective heads? Is this a new type of conversion tactic? Is it to make atheists conclude that "creation science is better than atheist science, therefore god exists"?

The Theist's Challenge

The problem theists have is incorrectly supposing that disproving this one theory on the origins of life will somehow prove God exists. It doesn't. All it could ever do is prove this one theory wrong. Then it's back to the drawing board. What true-believers should be doing is presenting a valid, evidence-rich theory of their own – that proves the Garden of Eden story is true.

We should ask, "Does that theory of the origins of life – that two humans were suddenly created from an ethereal, mystical god (the first one from dust, the other from the former's rib) – have any merit? Is it based on logic, evidence, reason, or even reality? What are the probabilities of this ever happening?"

No one will be holding their breath waiting for creationists to present such evidence. So, that leaves us no choice but to go ahead and look at The Theory of Evolution anyway. Let's let our defense be our best offense. Are the theists anywhere near debunking evolution?

What is Evolution?

First, let's state what evolution *isn't*. Evolution isn't chaotic. It isn't happenstance. And it isn't random (at least not in the pejorative sense used by creationists). There is actually something driving the stagecoach.

Evolution is about the origins of life on earth. And, at the core of that study is something called "Natural Selection." And the very fact that the word "selection" is used to describe evolution demonstrates that evolution itself is far from "random."

Of course, genetic mutations can be random, but the process of evolution itself, when those mutations occur, isn't random – we know what will happen next – an organism will either adapt to its environment with that mutation and live long enough to reproduce itself with that mutation intact, or it won't. Unfortunately, that word random is something creationists use against those atheists who happen to think evolution is the best possible explanation for the origins of life. The accusation is this: because atheists do not believe in a divine creator, they must think *everything* came about without any order – through utter chaos, by accident, with no predictability, i.e., by "random" chance, and as such, an atheist must think that everything on earth is merely a roll of the dice. This charge is leveled at atheists at every turn – not just regarding evolution or astrophysics, but in everything an atheist allegedly does. This is simply another case of believers not understanding (or not wanting to know) their opponents' belief system.

Natural Selection

Among living organisms, variation is the norm on planet earth. When mutations occur in the genome of an organism, such as in a human being, these mutations can be passed on to that organism's progeny. During the organism's lifetime, the individual's genome interacts with its environment to cause variations in traits.

Individuals with certain variations of a trait may survive and reproduce more often than individuals with other variations that are less desirable. Thus, over time, the entire population in which the individual resides *evolves.*

That shouldn't be so hard to understand, but creationists, who operate more from the realm of magic, rather than science, seem to have hard time...

Enter Abiogenesis

Abiogenesis is the idea that life may have formed when a combination of simple inorganic materials, given time, and the necessary outside pressures of their environment, came together to form single-celled organisms. The most oft-cited, "I gotcha!" moment for creationists is their contention than modern scientists have yet to replicate this process in a lab. For some reason, not being able to re-enact an event that happened billions of years ago, somehow means humans were created in a garden, fully complete, in an instant, by the magic hand of an invisible deity. Such a conclusion is, of course, light years from logic.

What theists fail to acknowledge is the clear possibility that planet Earth never had all the components necessary for life to form on its own anyway. It simply had most of them. It is therefore quite possible that some other celestial object (another planet, comet, or asteroid), *did* have that other final component, and that other object long ago collided with Earth, pollinating the planet, so to speak, (known as *panspermia*), thereby bringing us that small piece of the puzzle we didn't have. And the rest, they say, is history. This is analogous to a human egg not developing into a human until that final element – a human sperm cell – is brought from another relatively faraway place (the male testes) to give the egg the final component needed to make life. (Unfortunately, this analogy is likely one that makes deity-lovers cringe.)

Where did blue eyes come from?

Humans with blue eyes. The is one of the best examples of how evolution is fact. There is a real, verifiable genetic mutation that occurred between 6,000 and 10,000 years ago that makes people have blue eyes. Prior to this single genetic mutation, all humans had brown eyes.

This mutation affects the human OCA2 gene, which is involved in the production of melanin. Melanin gives color to our skin, hair, and eyes. A mutation of this gene can disrupt melanin production, which can lead to albinism, or it can simply lighten our eye color.

Every person on earth with blue eyes carries this same genetic mutation and every person who has blue eyes is most likely related through a distant common ancestor. Unlike gods and humans, DNA doesn't lie.

This genetic switch spread throughout ancient Europe and more recently to other parts of the world. Our planet went from having nobody with blue eyes 10,000 years ago to having over a third of all Europeans with blue eyes. How did this happen? Via the usual suspects – war, migration, and sexual reproduction. Apparently, humans have decided that blue eyes are very, very attractive!

The deeply religious would have you think that mutations either do not occur at all, or that all mutations are always destructive. Mutations must produce mutants, if you blindly follow the musings of the undereducated creationist. The fact is, you may not see it occurring up close, but evolution is happening before your very (blue?) eyes!

Original Sin and DNA

In the Garden of Eden, Adam and Eve committed a terrible sin – they acquired knowledge and passed it on to their children. But have scientists found the place in the human genome where the alleged inheritable sin of Adam is located? If it's real, we should be able to find the error (sin) somewhere in the sequence.

We know why Christians are so opposed to evolution – because it ultimately negates the need for a Christ and makes Christianity's *raison d'être* null and void. But, what if their god had simply used evolution to create mankind? Some Christians have no problem with this, although they are in a rather small minority. How they can justify this won't be discussed here, but rather we will discuss some of the claims made by the majority who have not become so enlightened.

Accusations of the Anti-evolutionists

Creationists are not just about proving their own versions of science. Much of what they say is a direct attack on atheists and the non-religious. A few examples follow...

> *"Evolutionary processes cannot provide an objective view of right and wrong, good and evil, and true and false."*

Having a concept of god won't get you there either. The truth is, you cannot have a completely 100% objective view of anything in the universe. That includes any and all revelations from any and all gods. Why? Because each one of us is a tiny human in a vast universe, and our miniscule perspectives of that universe will always be either skewed, distorted, limited, or delusional. We have no other choice but to be in the position we're in. We are not all-powerful, all-knowing, or everywhere at once. There has never been a religious person or religious text with an objective view. Religious people simply refuse to accept that fact about themselves or their religion, but that doesn't make it any less true.

"Neurons randomly transmitting information in the brain will never create truth."

Religionists are keen to use the word "random" when they do a little atheist-bashing, and especially when doing so within the context of science. How a religious person knows that the neurons in your head are random is quite a mystery! Randomness is a lack of any pattern (or predictability) of events. The fact that anyone has a coherent (patterned) thought of any kind demonstrates the fact that thoughts (and therefore truths) are not random.

"Atheism is all about the Survival of the Fittest."

From the beginning of the debate, between those who study evolution and those who attempt to discredit evolution, religionists have accused atheists of having a "survival of the fittest mentality." To them this is reinterpreted to mean "Survival of the Strong, and the Weak be damned!" The accusation is used to strip the atheist of all humanity and empathy. Creationists, by using a skewed view of evolution, can portray an atheist as a practitioner of "dog eat dog" and "eye for an eye" philosophy. This straw man argument stems from a fundamental misunderstanding of what evolution does.

Evolution itself has no goal of survival because evolution is a *process*. It is not a conscious entity with goals in mind. The survival instinct is the *result* of evolution, not the aim of it. Whether an atheist knows this or not is irrelevant. A religious believer, however, should know this before making false accusations against non-believers.

Once more, this is the theist's mistake of not knowing what "survival of the fittest" means, and of equating all atheists with evolutionary theorists. Survival of the fittest simply refers to whether or not a species is "fit" to survive in their current environment. It has nothing to do with weak vs. strong. Being small and weak and able to hide can actually make a species *more* fit, whereas, being large and terrifying in a nutrient-poor environment can make a species *less* fit. (Just ask the dinosaurs.)

And though most atheists probably do have a strong affinity for evolution, they do so because it makes sense, not because it is "anti-Christian" or "anti-Muslim." Evolution is based on science, which is neutral, or rather *silent,* in regard to the existence of a deity. As such, evolution wasn't theorized as an alternative answer to Biblical teaching. Scientists don't study evolution to do battle against religious ideas. When it comes to religion, science simply doesn't care.

"Atheists are nothing more than Darwinists!"

Creationist theologians, who think they have a (dinosaur?) bone to pick with atheists who happen to endorse evolution, will often label those rather irreligious persons, "Darwinists." It's rather odd to call anyone a "Darwinist" when anyone with an ounce of historical curiosity can quickly discover that Darwin's *Origin of Species* was published in 1859, at a time when virtually nothing was known about modern genetics. A true "Darwinist" would have to overlook more than 150 years of discovery by modern science. The reality is, no one on earth is a "Darwinist." It's akin to calling electrical engineers "Franklinists" simply because they agree with Benjamin Franklin that lightening is indeed electricity.

Discoveries in molecular genetics, in the time since Darwin's book, have advanced many causes, not the least of which is to reinforce many of Darwin's ideas regarding natural selection and adaptive evolution. But being a molecular geneticist doesn't make you a Darwinist.

"Studying evolution leads to immorality."

Creationists also like to tell us that studying the Theory of Evolution will lead people away from God, and the horrifying result will be utter chaos and a dissemination of unfettered immorality.

As it turns out, evolution created morality. Doing good things, behaving well, and altruism are all great survival strategies, all born from the evolutionary *process.* The tendency to be good comes directly from natural selection. To put it simply, if you kill your neighbor, you deprive yourself of his knowledge and skill. If you rape your neighbor's wife, you risk getting killed yourself. Bad behavior begets revenge. Those who figured this out early, and helped one another, survived, and those who didn't figure it out, *died out*. Like it or not, morality makes more sense from an evolutionary standpoint than from a Biblical one.

We've only barely scratched the surface when it comes to the odd things creationists think atheists believe. But, now it's time to look into some of the bizarre things creationist say about evolution itself...

CREATIONISTS CREATING IDEAS (FROM NOTHING)

Creationism, and its identical twin sister, intelligent design, have a history. And that history is full of debunked ideas. But, it seems, no matter how many times these ideas are proven false, they just keep popping up again like *parasola plicatilis* (mushrooms) after a hard rain.

Let's look at few examples...

The Earth is 6000 Years Old

Believers in a young earth are like the founding fathers of creationism. Almost all creationism comes from this belief. It has its roots in the Bible and its literal interpretation that space, time, earth, and humans were are created in less than a single earth-delineated week.

Of course, a young-earth has been debunked numerous times through *radiometric dating* (see further down), making any number less than 4.5 million years ago seem rather archaic and primitive.

So, what does this have to do with evolution? It's important because the Great Deluge of Noah is the reason given by creationists for the fossil record. For the creationist, the Great Flood produced the fossil record, not the gradual dying off of species over a long period of time. To them, the Biblical timeline is literal history, and Noah's Flood is the "evidence" that debunks the fossil record, and by extension, the ideas of evolution.

One of the examples creationists give for the speed at which things supposedly happen on earth is the Grand Canyon. It's a way to cram 4.5 million years into a tiny drop of just 6000. (But for some reason they think all matter being clumped together prior to the Big Bang was impossible?)

Try not to laugh.

The Grand Canyon Was Made in a Jiffy!

The Grand Canyon in northern Arizona is quite beautiful. Although it looks old, creationists claim it was made *stat* – fast and furious, quick and easy, by God of course, with a little help from some receding flood waters (at the time of Noah, of course). Some creationists have even claimed that the 300 mile long canyon could have been formed in five minutes! That means the water rushing through would have to travel at a speed of over 4000 miles per hour! Yep, that's pretty fast!

There are a lot of ways to debunk this one, but here a just a few obvious ways... First, the tributaries of the Grand Canyon are as deep as the canyon itself and almost perpendicular! A flood on a massive scale, that was sudden and torrential could never create a configuration of tributaries like the ones we see in the Grand Canyon. Second, if the Noachide deluge formed the Grand Canyon, and the flood was really worldwide, we would see Grand Canyons worldwide. And although canyons exist in other places, few even come close to the unique formation of this one. Thirdly, the flood somehow had to carve the Grand Canyon while at the same time deposit miles of sediment and lava flows. This simply isn't possible. (Unless you use sky magic.) There are other ways to prove that the creationists really need to leave this argument alone, but they are too numerous to list.

Dinosaurs Lived With Humans

Modern creationists have had to reluctantly acknowledge the existence of the fossil record, but have still insisted on holding on dearly to their young-earth hypothesis. This decision has had them reach the rather frightening conclusion that dinosaurs and humans lived on earth at the same time. Were that so, Adam and Eve would have been trampled to death or eaten within the first few minutes of being tossed out of their garden.

The fossil record does not show any sort of die-off within the last 6000 years that would have destroyed all the dinosaurs, and that includes any kind of world-wide flood that the disconcerting Noah account could ever possibly explain. Something had to kill off the dinosaurs and the surfeit of evidence points to a very large comet or asteroid hitting the earth approximately 66 million years ago – at a time the fossil record indicates that dinosaurs actually lived – without a human in sight. What other more recent scenario could possibly give the extinction any credence? Perhaps, when it comes to dinosaurs, creationists believe humans ate them?

Macroevolution Doesn't Exist

Microevolution, as you might guess, is the kind of genetic change in organisms that occurs on a small scale and in a short period time. A good example can be seen in viruses that develop resistance to anti-viral drugs. Macroevolution, which happens over a long period of time and can lead to speciation (creation of new species), is the kind of evolution that creationists claim has never been proved or observed, and for them it's "impossible." Apparently, if they can't see it, it doesn't exist. (One wonders why they don't apply the same standard to their gods.)

Of course, creationists, without any supporting evidence, are self-confined to only a short time span of 6000 years for any sort of evolutionary events to take place. Under those parameters, speciation would be more difficult to detect or prove. But, the process of macroevolution and microevolution is exactly the same! The only difference is *time*. And as many scientists have shown again and again, the universe has time aplenty.

God or Satan Created a False Fossil Record

For a rather long time, creationists would argue, as more and more fossils were unearthed, that the fossil record was simply the work of Satan. Forget Noah and his flood, it was Satan who apparently placed those fossils there, in advance, to fool humans and lead them away from a belief in God. That would be quite laughable on its own, but now some are claiming that God, not Satan, placed them there to test the faith of the religious! Perhaps God and Satan are working together on this one? Obviously, a person's frail grasp of reality is proportionate to the lack of soundness in their religious beliefs

No Transitional Fossils Exist (The Links Are Still Missing!)

Creationists like to point out that there are "no transitional fossils." The only way they could make this statement convincingly, however, would be to simply refuse to read the evidence. Or cry that there isn't *enough* evidence.

The fossil record covers a rather long time span. To assume that every single type of animal that lived in the past left us at least one fossil (how kind and convenient of them!), or that scientists have already found every example of every living thing in the fossil record, is simply absurd. When examples are given, they are ignored by creationists – even ones that are hard to ignore – such as:

- Archaeopteryx (transitional from dinosaur to bird)
- Pappochelys (transitional turtle)
- Proteroctopus (early version of the modern octopus)
- Sphecomyrma (earliest known ant ancestor)
- Cladoselache (earliest type of shark)
- Acanthostega (a fish with feet instead of fins)
- Ichthyornis (another transitional dinosaur to bird, one of *many*)
- Archaeothyris (undeniable mammal-like reptile)
- Protylopus (earliest camel, which was quite small)
- Purgatorius (the first proto-primate), etc. and etc., *and* etc...

This is just a tiny sampling. The actual list is amazingly long – going all the way up to humans. It's as if creationists haven't opened a book on paleontology since 1800.

With creationist reasoning, you could dig up a 10,000 year old man and his grandson, check their DNA to verify that they are indeed related, and the creationist would probably say that the two *aren't* related because you haven't found the grave of the boy's father. Yikes!

All Mutations Are Bad, Very, Very Bad!

Creationists shouldn't be basing their ideas on cheap horror movies about radiation-exposed mutants. Mutations are not always bad. Genetic mutations can be harmful, neutral, or beneficial. Mutations are random, the changes are often small, and may appear as seemingly insignificant. It's the organism's environment and the organism's adaptability to that environment that decides whether or not a mutation is beneficial (or neutral or harmful). Ultimately, then, it is the process of natural selection that will have a say as to whether those mutations are passed on to the next generation. It's important to note that the vast majority of mutations have no effect on an organism at all. The fact that creationists think otherwise is most likely because they simply haven't read the massive amount of evidence on this subject. But no one is hiding it from them.

No Monkey's Uncles Allowed!

The more fundamentalist the believer, the more often you'll hear absurd logic like, "If we came from monkeys, why are there still monkeys?" That's sort of like saying, "If we emigrated from England, why are there still Englishmen?" For the creationist believer, hominids are always apes or humans, never anything in between, and apes could not ever "turn into humans."

The reality is, humans and apes share a massive amount of similar DNA. When looking at human chromosomes, we can see that our chromosome number 2 is clearly a fusion of two great ape chromosomes. That in itself is the smoking gun for apes and humans having a common ancestor. Obviously, we *are* descended from great apes. There is no way around this scientific fact.

Furthermore...

The human genome shows evidence of endogenous retroviral fragments – which were inserted in the *exact same place* in apes as they are in humans. If chromosome 2 is the proverbial "smoking gun," these retroviral fragments are the body with the bullet holes.

Additionally, and in laymen's terms, because these retroviruses can affect and often *enhance* the gene structure, it is quite obvious that this did occur in some early apes, and over time, this helped them evolve into human beings. Of course, this didn't happen to every ape species, which is why we still have apes that are not humans. (In the same way we still have Englishmen!)

Radiometric Dating is Inaccurate

Creationists hate radiometric dating. They always have and probably always will. But radiometric dating is *extremely* reliable. (NOTE: *Radiocarbon* dating is similar, but is concerned mainly with things that were once alive, such as those carbon units known as humans. And creationists hate radiocarbon dating as well.)

Science has shown again and again that consistent results can been obtained for both radiocarbon and radiometric dating using various independent techniques, such as the thermoluminescence dating method and Milankovitch cycles. This consistency is due to the fact that radioactive decay is known to occur at a constant rate. All known methods also have internal checks to verify and re-verify the data (e.g. isochron methods, stepwise degassing, etc.). Scientists don't just grab a random rock, zap it, and then say, "Voila! This is 4 million years old!" Science doesn't operate on the simple idea that "something is true because I say it is," like religion does. A lot of work goes into this process.

Think of all the things religionists could discover if they actually did some real work, and read more than one book.

Evolution Is An Atheistic Religion

Strangely, creationists, and believers of all sorts, think that if you spend your time studying anything through the use of science, and you haven't gotten all the answers from your endeavors, you have created a "religion" – your conclusions are based on faith – and it really doesn't matter if you have mountains of evidence for what you've studied. With that line of reasoning, a cancer researcher, attempting to find the perfect anti-cancer remedy is really practicing religion because he has "faith" that his discoveries will someday achieve their goal. (No one said creationist logic could ever be used in the real world.)

The truth is, evolution is based on science and that science is based on fact. Science is not religious, nor is it anti-religious. It is secular. It doesn't look for God or gods. When it comes to religious ideas, it's neutral. Science simply looks for real facts in a real world. If a scientist flips over a rock and a god pops out, then the scientist will simply study that god and record the facts.

It's All "Just a Theory"

Here, creationists are using the colloquial form of the word "theory" – as in "an educated guess," or as a substitute for the word hypothesis. Or they are using it in a pejorative sense, in much the same as some do toward *conspiracy theorists*. This is a fallacy of equivocation and thus side-steps the actual definition of a *scientific* theory. In science, a theory is the pinnacle of scientific thought and is achieved via the *scientific method*. This repeatable method requires one to go through several specific stages to get to an actual theory. Those stages are: the formulation of a question; an hypothesis; a prediction; testing; and finally, analysis – an often painstaking process that is not exactly somebody's wild ass guess.

In summary, a scientific theory is based on facts and must be falsifiable (testable). Because it is based on facts, there is no better outcome than the establishment of a theory. Portraying the accumulation of *facts* and their conclusions derived via the scientific method as "just a theory" – is just absurd.

CONCLUSION

The Garden of Eve-olution

Christians *need* evolution to be wrong. In some strange convoluted way, God-believers in the western world think that disproving evolution will automatically make their Adam and Eve story true. But, logic doesn't work that way. That little myth in the Garden of Eden needs its *own* substantiating evidence. And it doesn't attain that through the debunking of evolution. Instead of haranguing against evolution, religionists should prove that the Biblical creation story is true.

Religious believers in a literal Bible and Qur'an are worried, because without original sin, there is no need for a Jesus or Allah to save them from it, (physically or otherwise) and, ergo, no need for their religion(s).

What We Really Know

DNA research has strengthened the Theory of Evolution to the point no one questions its validity, except for the barely educated, and the religious sector, which has an agenda that requires them to embrace a dubious alternative view, disingenuously designed to prop up ancient myths.

Unfortunately, Christians (and Muslim apologists as well) are now so attached to their talking points, and have them so imprinted in their minds, that they spew them out by rote, and they are not even aware of the numerous times they are being contradictory, fallacious, or hypocritical.

Religious folk used to have a center, a core, based almost entirely on "testimonies," where real people would tell everyone they encountered, how their life changed with the awareness of their God. The current *modus operandi* of the modern maddening crowd of believers is to try to disprove science. They have turned their own religions upside down, into an argument about evolution, philosophy and astrophysics. The jury is still out as to whether or not Jesus or Muhammad would be proud of their believers' *evolution* from faithful followers to rabid debaters.

The War on Evolution

Every year, here in the Western world we hear the media talk about the "War on Christmas" or the "War on Religion." But, what we don't hear much about is the "War on Science." This is a war started by the absurdly religious and it's completely due to the vast amounts of scientific knowledge pouring into our culture at a rate that makes the Great Flood look like a drop of spilled coffee. And this scientific knowledge sits squarely in opposition to the traditional beliefs of how the world came to be, or ought to be, if you follow the holy writ. It is the heart of the radically religious follower's hatred of science.

However, scientific truths do not deliberately attempt to contradict religious thought, nor do they seek out religious ideas to destroy. Scientific inquiry doesn't have that goal in mind. Scientific facts are just a part of reality and religious ideas aren't. It really is that simple.

The true believers in the fundamental religions are losing the scientific battle. Their world and beliefs grow smaller as the scientific realities grow larger. The inevitable end is the extinction of religion. And there is no need for a war to make that happen. Religion will either evolve and adapt to the new environment, or die off. When the last religious person on earth finally sees what has happened, perhaps then, he or she will understand what evolution really is.

CHAPTER ELEVEN

In a World of Perfection and Chaos

"Every unfalsifiable hypothesis is equal.
There is no difference between time traveling space-kittens and God."
– Edward Trillian

"The Bible shows the way to go to heaven, not the way the heavens go." –
Galileo Galilei

"God is an ever receding pocket of scientific ignorance."
– Neil DeGrasse Tyson

When introducing science, it should go something like this: "Human, Meet Science. Science Meet Human." It should be the beginning of a beautiful friendship.

However, when the purveyors of intelligent design (Creationists 2.0) discuss creationist theory, they are not simply talking about the first man or the first woman, they are also talking about the first of anything that ever existed, back to the Big Bang, and even back before time and space began. This is important to note because it often seems that the novice follower of creationism is bouncing back and forth between cosmology (the study of the stars and the universe) and evolution (the study of the origins of life on earth). To the creationist, it's all the same thing. It's all "Intelligent Design." It's all "Creationism." This is because, according to creationist (religious) theory, the beginning of our universe and the beginning of life are both outlined in the Book of Genesis. Unfortunately, despite the fact that these are rather complex questions, in the Bible, they are explained rather quick. From the Big Bang to the creation of man only takes a few pages.

But the Genesis story in the Bible is not the only one. Most religions have their creation stories. This is no surprise, as mankind, once achieving sentience, wondered often about where it all began. And the devout followers of all those other religions will basically have the same argument for their creation stories – *their* god did it.

Despite the habit creationists have of lumping all scientific study into one pile, for our purposes, we have attempted to divide evolution and cosmology (with its subsets of astronomy and astrophysics) into two separate parts. This chapter will cover cosmology only. (We approached evolution in the previous chapter.) There won't be an excess of scientific detail in this section – just enough to make the necessary stated positions clear. Our approach is from reason and logic and our perspective is that which is essential for atheists.

What is Science?

Science is about knowing what we *can* know. Science is not atheistic, but neither is it religious. When it comes to a god or gods, science is neutral. Science is about observation, and making conclusions that are based on the observed evidence only. It doesn't go any further than the conclusions reached, and maintains those conclusions until new or better evidence is presented. Science is factual. It is not philosophical, not ontological, not religious, not political, and not theological. It has only one goal: discovery.

Science vs. Atheism

Let's clarify our position as atheists before we begin any discussion involving the very *separate* ideas contained in science: There is no entry exam to become an atheist. You do not need to have a degree in science, know anything about science, or care one bit about science to be an atheist. An atheist is simply someone that rejects some other person's idea that a god exists. If the theist hasn't met the burden of proof that there is such a god, the atheist has no reason to believe the claim. We are once again stating something that *should* be obvious, but obviously isn't.

When discussing things outside the realm of the singular atheist position, it is necessary to repeat again and again the qualifiers needed for an atheist to be an atheist. For some reason, this very clear definition eludes the god-believer in every discussion, and frequently within the *same* discussion, even after adequate explanation has been given.

So, why do atheists discuss science? It's often the theist who brings up science, not the other way around. The god-believer is aware that in the modern world, science is real and it works. He therefore desperately wants to reconcile his god belief, for which he has doubts, with the science he knows is true.

Although there are many atheists that came to unbelief simply because they couldn't swallow the jagged little pills of religion, most educated atheists came to their atheism through well-considered contemplation and study. And these atheists do embrace science because it provides utilitarian answers for the real world we live in. These non-believers also likely arrived at their atheism through a kind of scientific process, even if they were unaware they were doing so. And now the unavoidable trend is that the entire world's population is increasingly using science to run their lives and their thought processes are starting to reflect this model. Technology, and the science from which it came, is what gives atheism the edge.

Now, before we start ripping the seams of time and space, there are at least two very important concepts everyone should be aware of before discussing our place in the universe, and they are: *The Primacy of Existence* and the definition of *The Laws of the Universe.*

Primacy of Existence

The universe exists.... Period. We know that it does, and whatever it is, an objective view of that universe also exists, but we as humans, taking up a tiny dot in that universe, can never have that objective view. We cannot be in two places at once, and even standing side by side with another human being, our view will still be slightly different than the other person's. Because of this, our viewpoint will always be somewhat subjective. This applies to all human beings, no matter how many "revelations" they think they are receiving from any sort of deity. And it's true for every scientist who studies the universe.

The Primacy of Existence is consistent because it acknowledges the imperfection of the subjective view of the universe that each human has, while also acknowledging the perfection of the objective view of the universe we know we cannot observe. The universe is perfect in its own way, and we view it through a limited lens. Through this lens (our minds and bodies) we see consistency in the universe, but we can't see all of the universe. This is why we are often only partially right about things – because we have a partial view. Again, this reality applies to every sentient being on earth.

Laws of the Universe

Physical or scientific laws, whether mathematical or empirical, are fact-derived principles, applied to phenomena, that always occur if certain conditions are present in our universe.

These "laws of the universe" are not laws in the sense that they have anything to do with legal terminology. The laws of the universe are descriptive only – they describe what is happening in the universe. They are not prohibitions – they do not proscribe anything, nor do they limit anything. The universe does what it does, and we observe and learn. When events are true, universal, simple, and absolute, we can use a "law" to describe those events – and describe them is all we can do. The universe *is what it is* and *does what it does* with (and without) our observation or existence.

IN A PERFECT WORLD

In our "perfect" world, there are sometimes imperfect people with some very imperfect ideas. Intelligent design and creationism are in the category of extraordinarily imperfect ideas. Intelligent design, also known as I.D., and creationism, can be used interchangeably – they both argue that everything in the universe was brought about by a divine intelligent creator. Their argument is that life and the universe could not have arisen randomly, or by chance, and that the

239

cause of such creation was purposeful. Unfortunately, none of this is backed up by any real science.

Beyond the ID

Not only do creationists staunchly believe that everything that *matters* was designed by an intelligent designer, these dauntless defenders of deities also say that the Universe is *perfectly* designed for life, fine-tuned specifically for us lowly and lonely humans to live out our short lives on this Earth (our one and only tiny planet), on the edge of one of billions of galaxies in our universe. And they even have a few scientists who back up this idea. But, before we get into the idea of fine-tuning, at what that really implies, let's take a look at how "perfect" our universe really is.

Orbiting Perfection

Everything about the earth, its position, the size of its moon, its distance from the sun, its speed of rotation – it all appears to be perfect. It appears to be designed especially for us in mind. But looks are deceiving. "Perfection" is a coincidence because perfection is simply a *perception by way of a particular perspective.* (Alliteration unintended.)

Humans can perceive the possibility that things *could* have perfection. Perfection is a possibility – as in the orbit of one celestial body around another could be consistent at all times – never wavering an inch from its distance from the other object. But, that doesn't actually happen in the real universe. Orbits are not perfect because perfection is stagnation. Perfect orbits everywhere would not produce change, and the order of the universe is dependent upon change. In fact, the only real perfect (and constant) thing about the universe is that it *changes.*

In a World...

Anyone visiting California will realize instantly what a beautiful place it is. California is not just famous for its beauty, it's also famous for its fierce winds, landslides, wildfires, earthquakes and even the occasional hurricane. And that's the reason why California is so beautiful – because it gets those fierce winds, landslides, wildfires, earthquakes and occasional hurricanes. Nature, in a violent way, made California beautiful. And the "violence" of nature, from the perspective of the earth itself, isn't violent at all. It's only violent from the perspective of the tiny creatures that live on it. When you get pimple on your face, that's not exactly violent or life-threatening, but it would seem that way if you were a tiny sentient cell living adjacent to that pimple!

Back to the Universe... The Universe does what it does, with huge objects flying at high rates of speed in all directions, exploding and collapsing, escaping and colliding, deforming and reforming, creating and destroying whatever gets in the way. From the perspective of the Universe itself, life anywhere arising or failing is irrelevant. To put it bluntly and simply: *The universe doesn't care.* If life extinguishes in one place, it will likely be created somewhere else. (Or, not.)

The old phrase "walk a mile in my shoes" can apply figuratively or allegorically, if you look at things from the perspective of inanimate systems or objects, or ideas that aren't your own, or that aren't even human. The lottery for instance, from the perspective of the lottery itself, just throws out numbers. It doesn't target anyone specifically to win. *It doesn't care.* Someone does win, eventually, and that person may think they're special because of that win, but the reality is, their winning was just a random occurrence. They got "lucky." And luck is always a coincidence.

If the Universe doesn't care, that would mean whatever created the Universe probably doesn't care either. Saying "God loves you" begins to sound rather silly when viewed from that perspective.

The Perfect Imperfection

Our next question should be: Which suggests a designer, perfection or imperfection? The fact is, it could go either way. Everything a human makes is imperfect. Likewise, everything a human can see, or sense, or know about in the Universe is imperfect. When we are observing the degree of perfection of anything, what happens on earth can be seen to happen everywhere else. This could suggest a designer, perhaps even an imperfect one. Or, that same imperfection could suggest a lucky coincidence. Yet, this imperfection is what is perfect – for us, anyway. No life would exist within a perfect Universe. Imperfection breeds variety and change. Variety and change creates life. What makes us perfect, ironically, is our imperfection. Poetically and paradoxically, the imperfection of the Universe *is* its perfection. Without the imperfection of the Universe, we would not exist, and to us, that's absolutely perfect.

Let there be luminosity!

Let's keep this simple to make our argument clear. From our human subjective position, the universe is complex. That may be so, but what we also observe is that the universe is unstable. The universe is in constant flux, constant change. After the Big Bang occurred, those fragments of our new expanding universe were not thrown about with absolute symmetry. There is no symmetry in space. Everything is a little askew, even if by just a tiny fraction. There are too many forces in space exerting their influence upon various *other* forces that no celestial orb can remain fixed or symmetrical.

Therefore it is *asymmetry* that produces change, and change is what forms galaxies, stars, planets and ultimately life. Change is why you are born and why you die. Whatever was before the Big Bang had to also be unstable to initiate the change that made everything go from small condensed matter to expanding universe. To be sure, the creators of the universe (and of all life) are Asymmetry, Instability, and Change. That is the real Trinity. Not something to be worshiped, yet still something we should view with utter amazement and contemplation.

* * *

241

Other Imperfect Universes (The Universes that didn't make it past the first few trial runs.)

Stephen Hawking has postulated that perhaps there are other universes that could have formed very different from our own, and maybe not so "perfectly" as our own. He surmises that if our universe had not formed the way it did, life like us might not exist. But, that's the operative phrase – life "like us." In other universes, if they do exist, life *not* like us might exist. Life in those universes could be so different and odd, that when we examined such, we would not even be able to recognize it as life. Life in those universes could be all around us and we wouldn't be aware of any of it.

WHAT IS FINE-TUNING?

All "fine tuning," like anything from our perspective that already exists, appears "perfect" even when it isn't. For example, the human body is a perfect host for viruses and bacteria (and from the perspective of the virus, it's a "fine tuned universe"), but the body is not a perfect host for other substances such as arsenic, boiling water, or fire. It really *is* all about perspective.

A billionaire sipping champagne inside his own luxurious private jet, ordering all he needs by phone at his own leisure will think the world is perfect, and designed with him in mind. A poor farmer in India, with cholera, whose crops have failed, barely able to eat a tiny meal each day, will think the world is a horrible unfriendly place and life is not worth living. Have the farmer and the billionaire trade places and see how their opinions about the world change. Life, both literally and figuratively, is about perspective. And your perspective doesn't get precedence over others. A fine tuning from your view doesn't prove a "fine tuner."

Life only appears fine tuned to us because we are the life forms looking back at the universe. If the expansion that caused the universe to form had occurred differently, at a lesser speed, or in some other way, you might be a completely different life form, also looking back at the universe, thinking how perfect it is, but it would be a completely different universe, and you might be an insect. Fine tuning is in the eye of the beholder.

Tune In to Fine Tuning

Let's be clear... the wonderful positioning of the Earth, or the "perfect" construction of our physical selves, is not precisely what intelligent design proponents are referring to when they declare that the universe was "fine-tuned" just for us humans. The creationist/intelligent design argument goes much deeper, and quite surprisingly, much more scientific than that. They refer to the cosmological constants within the observable universe, such as the speed of light, the gravitational force, the rate of expansion of the universe, the electromagnetic and nuclear forces, etc., all of which are *constant* (in that they follow certain physical laws), and must be so for our universe to even exist.

242

Even a tiny percent deviation from the parameters of these forces would mean our universe would be something very, very different, if it existed at all.

But, do these constants suggest a sentient god, or the lack of one? Creationists cite the idea that the need for all of these ingredients being so precise, suggests an intelligence was behind the universe's construction. This ignores two very important points of reference. First, it ignores the fact that, despite its awe-inspiring beauty from the perspective of sitting on a mountain looking out into outer space, the universe is a terrifying, vast, and extremely dangerous place for life. If a creative force such as an all-knowing, all-powerful god existed, and his ultimate goal was to produce life, there would be no need for all the things in the universe that destroy life (gamma rays, black holes, the vacuum of space, and almost everything that isn't situated in the sweet spots between the north and south poles of planet Earth. The earth itself has only a small portion which can sustain human life.) The fact that life *isn't* everywhere, that the majority of what makes up the universe is lifeless, and even detrimental to life, suggests no creator at all. Or, it suggests a creator who wasn't really interested in making life his number one priority. Perhaps the purpose of the universe was not to produce life, but instead, beautiful orbs, and life is the mold and rust that forms on those lovely stones. Knowing what we know about the anti-life environment of the universe, the idea of an all-knowing, all-loving god goes out the window when you consider the hostile universe in which we currently reside.

The other idea that creationists conveniently ignore with their god hypothesis is *coincidence* – the idea that given enough chances for something to occur it will likely occur. In a place of infinite time and infinite space, the right universe could be formed – one with constants that are just right for making such a universe. Coincidence or happenstance is all around us. Most of the time we hardly notice. And sometimes we do...

Coincidence and Life

On September 6, 2009, the Bulgarian Lottery randomly chose the following numbers for the winning jackpot: 4, 15, 23, 24, 35, and 42. In the next drawing, those exact same numbers appeared again. What happened? Simple coincidence, or fraud?

Although it appeared at first glance that the lottery was rigged, it was a simple act of coincidence when you consider how many times numbers can be drawn, and how many number combinations there are in a six number lottery – numbers that are quite vast. This means there are lots of chances to make it happen. Given the number of chances it *could* occur, such a "perfect" set of consecutive identical draws was bound to happen someday. In the case of the Bulgarian lottery, the chance of any particular set of six numbers appearing is 1 in almost 14 million. That also means that the chance those same numbers will appear again, either in the next draw, or in any other draw, is still 1 in 14 million. The way coincidence works is this: if it *can* happen, it probably will... eventually. (And, sometimes, even suddenly.)

As for universes being formed – our kind, or other varieties, multi-verses, or universes in other dimensions, if it can happen, given enough time, it probably will. The fact that we happen to live in the "ideal" universe with the ideal constants, means we sort of won the universe lottery.

The Evidence

If the universe appears to be fine-tuned, it is circumstantial evidence, no matter how complex our universe is. It is not direct evidence. And what most theists fail to see is that anyone can suggest anything, and all suggestions without direct evidence are equal. A person could suggest a celestial unicorn designed the universe, or that the universe was created by a malevolent being, or that whatever created the universe ceased to exist moments after the creation. There are many other possible explanations for the same data.

For all we know, the Big Bang, if it occurred at all, was simply the creator God, the powerful essence of pure energy and matter, killing himself in one giant self-extirpating explosion, and we are like the bacteria that grows on the bits and pieces of the remaining and scattered human flesh after a suicide bomber has annihilated himself in a crowded mall. Perhaps God has been dead from the beginning.

Or, the function of the Universe is to make rocks – shiny different colored rocks, some fiery ones, some extremely dark ones, mostly spherical in shape, and having the ability to twirl around one another in a celestial almost never-ending dance. The fact that some life forms have gathered like moss onto some of these spheroid rocks may just be a minor nuisance to the rock-builder. And gamma-rays are the disinfectant.

Here, theists will point out that rarity of life makes it more precious and therefore more valuable. That's a rather disingenuous statement coming from a crowd that thinks you not only get an extra life (an afterlife), but you get it forever. Yes, rarity is important, but its value is subjective. When you look at the universe and you see the rarity of human life, it only has a value to you because you are a part of human life. A precious diamond to one life form is just a plain rock to another. Radioactive promethium is also very rare, but is toxic to humans. What we must do is look at the overall system. What is this system (the Universe) trying to do? Make diamonds? Or life? Or something else entirely?

When a scientist says the universe is fine tuned for life, it means something very different from what a follower of the intelligent design hypothesis (seeking to confirm their bias) means. What most astrophysicists will say, is that this environment *appears* to be the perfect set up for life to have formed somewhere in the universe. How do we know this? Well, we do know life exists – on Earth anyway. And we know that changes in our universe's structure would likely mean that life could not exist at all. That does not mean however, that it was some sort of "plan." It could just as easily mean that the universe formed and life was a coincidental by-product of that formation. The argument for life cannot go much further than that without more information about the what occurred *before* the formation of the universe.

The Big Bang Theory Expanded

What if... The Universe is constantly expanding and imploding?

What if... This is the billionth time it's done that?

What if... There are lots of Big Bangs and lots of universes? Maybe we live in a neighborhood of billions of adjacent universes?

What if... Our universe is on a collision course with another universe? Maybe even a bigger one!

What if... Our universe is just a tiny dot inside another larger universe that we aren't even aware of, and that universe is inside another, and so on, like a set of Russian matryoshka dolls?

The "What if's" can be endless. The notion that whatever it is we are a part of must somehow be constructed by an earthling-delineated god is just another "what if" with zero evidence.

To Tune or Not to Tune?

It's perfectly acceptable to say that our universe is "fine-tuned" to be what it is. The universe exists objectively, and we know it works, but that's a bit too obvious for most anyone. Yes, the universe "is what it is." (The first law of logic.) But the concept of fine-tuning itself does not imply a god. The universe may look designed, but that doesn't mean it is. The *appearance* of a fine tuned universe itself isn't the problem. Saying that you *know* an intelligence was behind it – that's the problem. Then, saying that a very specific god is that intelligence becomes an even bigger problem.

Children of a Convenient God

The really sad thing is that religionists postulate that our universe (with its billions of galaxies and trillions upon trillions of stars) has a *specific* creator. They think that whatever that creator being/entity/god is, it's also the same one they pray to when they go to a church, or a mosque, or a temple. The chance that whatever brought the universe into existence is also the fatuous father/son pair of the Christian Bible, or the carbon copy god of the Islamic Qur'an, reaches a number that is so small, it's almost infinitely small. That's just a solid *guess*, but it's being very generous to the god hypothesis. Logic demands that any entity who could put together even a single planet, much less the entire universe, would not be anything similar to the human-like gods of any earthly-scribed holy book. Therefore, anyone could be right about a creator, and be completely wrong about their god having been the one who did all the creating.

Fine Tuning Possibilities

It's clear that the theist has a problem interpreting the data. Because the believer wants so desperately to have a creator of the universe, he takes the data of cosmological constants, expansion, gravity, etc., and decides that the possibility that the universe could have come together by accident must be impossible. The exact same data, to which the atheist and the theist both have equal access, could also be an argument for everything being a natural occurrence without the need for a god. We could even argue that if a designer was really trying to promote life, and was all-knowing and all-powerful, there would be no need for anything but a single planet and one star like the sun. But the evidence shows much more than that. It even shows a universe that is mostly hostile to life. The exact same data both have is an argument for *no* designer.

Accidents do happen. Everything does not have to be planned by a designer. And the universe appears to have been put here without life as its top priority. And this is true no matter how many times you measure gravity, or cosmological constants, or the acceleration of the expansion of the universe.

More Arguments Against Design

John Polkinghorne, a former theoretical particle physicist at Cambridge University and ordained Anglican priest said, "If a theory allows anything to be possible, it explains nothing; a theory of anything is not the same as a theory of everything." This exact statement, which was a condemnation of the multi-verse hypothesis, can also be a condemnation of a god-as-designer hypothesis. A god or designer would, of course, allow "anything to be possible," therefore a designer explains nothing. It means all physics could be changed on the whim of the designer from one day to the next, and could even make us think it hadn't changed at all!

The argument for a designer states that the universe is adapted for life rather than life being adapted to the universe. But this could be because we are in the "sweet spot." It simply *appears* as though the universe was made for life because it just happened to work out like that for *us*. Similarly, the earth is in a "sweet spot" in its distance around the sun, and has a moon the perfect size to help maintain life on our planet. Everything appears to be perfect – for us, from our perspective. Go further away from the sun – just one planet further – to Mars, and your perspective will change. Not such a good place for life, is it? Our sister planet Mars and a large portion of the rest of the galaxy *lost* the celestial lottery. If you're a life form on another planet, life might not seem as nice as it is here (or it could be even better). Expand the idea of the earth's "sweet spot" to that of the entire universe. Perhaps our universe is the only one out of millions of universes that managed to "get it right" and life managed grow in a few remote places. This supports the idea of multi-verses, of course, but like all these hypotheses, it is all speculation. Looks are deceiving. And what looks like it makes sense in the world of physics and astrophysics could be completely destroyed and irrelevant 100 years from now.

A Universe from Nothing

To counter the idea that a perfectly fine-tuned universe could easily exist without the need for a god, the religionists will defiantly declare that "Something cannot come from nothing!"

Perhaps. But, what is "nothing"? Is it the absence of something, or the absence of everything? What does that nothing look like, feel like, taste like? When defining nothing as whatever there was prior to the Big Bang (the oft-quoted "beyond Space and Time,") we have some serious conceptual conundrums. The fact is, no one knows what *nothing* really is, and no one has ever found *nothing,* therefore no one can really say what *nothing* is. This means no one can accurately say, "something cannot come from nothing." Everything a human knows about is a *something.* Everything we know about comes from matter, which is something. Therefore, everything comes from matter. And we know of no exceptions.

So, if we can't say what nothing is, can we say what nothing isn't?

Obviously, there is more than one way to look at the word "nothing," but the only real definition that is useful to humans is "the absence of something." When you open an empty box, expecting to see something, and that something isn't there, you are still referencing a *something* in order to make the assessment that "nothing" is in the box. And this even excludes the obvious fact that the box still has air, dust, photons, electrons, and other invisible particles within that box. Therefore, creationists are referring to the *absence of a god* when they say the word "nothing," even though there could have been a something, or a nothing, and neither of those things were God.

Nothing, in an absolute sense, is a condition devoid of all matter, energy, volume, or space. For humans, who have no actual experience with this type of reality, this is a very alien concept. We cannot reference nothing to describe nothing because we've never really experienced nothing in its truest absolute sense – and this is true because, as stated before, everything we know about is something. So we're back to square one. Even the word nothing is something. And the "absence of something," the only useful definition of nothing that we stated above, is still something because we can perceive it. *True* nothing would be imperceptible and indescribable. And none of us know what that is.

So, what does this leave us with? Nothing perhaps?

No. It simply means we cannot argue either way about something (in this case, *nothing*) if we don't really know what it is. Remember this the next time someone says, "...created something from nothing...," whether it's a universe creating itself from nothing, a god creating itself from nothing, a god creating a universe from nothing, or a god's creator creating a god from nothing, then allowing that god to create a universe, etcetera, ad nauseam, and in regression to infinity.

Was there nothing before the Big Bang, or was there something? Not knowing either way does not produce a god.

If all of this is making everyone feel a little dizzy, don't worry. It's nothing, really.

The Burden of Probability

Is it possible that invisible pink kittens the size of pinto beans created the universe? You can say it's possible, but the probability of such a thing is almost zero. Is it possible to deal 160 cards out of a deck of only 52? We know this is not possible. It has a probability of zero. Although the idea of the pink kittens is not testable and therefore has a probability only slightly higher than the testable hypothesis of drawing 160 cards from a deck of 52, anything approaching zero, and anything *at* zero, carry virtually the same weight in regard to being a part of human reality, and as such, both should be scuttled from any framework of discussion.

Even the *possibility* for something has, if someone should bother to pursue it, a burden of proof, or in more specific and preemptive terms, a *burden of probability*. The person making a claim of something being possible should present a sound hypothesis as to why the possibility has a reasonable *probability* for its occurrence. A poor hypothesis for an idea negates any need to pursue that idea. For example, does it make more sense to pursue the possibility of life on other planets due to its high probability, or should we rather try to show that frogs could live on the sun? Absurdity is a low probability venture. Most religious claims lie in this same realm of absurdity.

CREATION vs. DESIGN

Designing is not the same thing as creating. Human beings don't actually create anything. They move or reshape already existing matter, but the matter itself they did not create. And no one can claim to know how the matter got here.

When a person builds a birdhouse, he or she is simply taking already existing matter in the shape of wood, nails, and paint and re-arranging those things into a three-dimensional pattern that the human can recognize as a birdhouse. It's not creation, at least not in the sense of *producing matter from nothing,* which is the definition creationists use when declaring their god to also be their "creator."

The fact that humans do not create anything, and cannot create anything, destroys the common analogy creationists use for a "designer" of the universe. Their analogy goes something like this: "A painting doesn't paint itself, a building doesn't build itself. These are obviously designed by some kind of intelligence. Therefore, when we look at the universe, it too, appears to be designed because it is so perfectly made."

Ignoring the fact that the universe isn't exactly perfect for a moment, we can immediately see that the flaw in the analogy: the matter from which the painting and the building were derived was already here. That matter was simply rearranged into paintings and buildings. In other words, human beings already had something to work with – matter. If all matter was designed, what did "god" (or the "creator") have to work with to intelligently design matter? Did matter come from "nothing," or from something else? Did God simply do what we do with matter – rearrange all existing matter into a universe? If so, what was this god made of himself when he did all his rearranging?

As you can see, it's easy to ask all sorts of unanswerable questions and you get into such ideas as "who created the god that created the universe?" and so on into infinity. It becomes a sad example of ignorance when a theist claims to know the answers to such things.

A Complex Design of Infinite Regression

The premise posited by many theologians is that "complex things require a designer." Yet, isn't God a complex thing? If complex things, like the universe, require a designer, then the most complex thing that exists, more complex than even the universe, is God. Therefore, based on this line of reasoning, God must also have had a complex designer. And his complex designer must have been even more complex and would, prior to its existence, have also had an even more complex designer, and so on, *ad infinitum.* From this we can conclude that, if true, God-believers are just praying to the middle man – or just upper management, but certainly not the CEO!

One More Big Bang Allegory

It's rather fascinating how creationists can see and know how a small seed can grow into a giant oak tree, or the tiny cells of a human zygote can grow into a 6 foot, 4 inch, 225 pound man, but for some odd reason, the idea of matter expanding and "growing" to create a Universe is somehow not comprehensible, or even possible. This, despite the fact that objects within the Universe, expand, contract, explode, and implode constantly and continuously.

The creationist position would be tenable if approached from a truly scientific angle. If creationists had a valid alternate scientific response that proved a different origin to the universe, science would consider it and possibly accept it as truth. But, creationists do not use science to object to the Big Bang as much as they use their argument for an *exo-natural* god. The constant creationist logic-gap assumes, if this one origin-theory of the universe (The Big Bang) is found to be wrong, that will somehow miraculously make the idea of a creator god valid. This tactic never seems to be far away from the creationist's motive – and rabid desire to debunk The Big Bang.

So, what if the Big Bang Theory was found to be false? And what if it and the Theory of Evolution were both found to be so full of flaws that every scientist who had previously claimed they were true was suddenly shunned for life? Then what?

Today there is real, testable science to back up the Big Bang Theory and the Theory of Evolution. But, unfortunately for Biblical theorists, there is no science to back up talking snakes, giant pillars of fire, talking donkeys, a spirit killing all the first born of a nation, prophets ascending into heaven on chariots (or winged horses), virgin births, making blind people see with mud, bringing dead humans back to life with mere words, and anything else that is supernatural. Unfortunately, theists try to debate by comparing oranges to mangoes. As stated elsewhere, destroying a scientific theory, even if it could be done without a shadow of doubt, will not magically, nor automatically, make the fanciful stories in the Bible and other holy books true.

The Cosmological Argument for God

Theists are not only wrong when it comes to what science has shown them, they are just as wrong when it comes to their own theories about their own beliefs. A favorite argument for the existence of God is officially known as the *Cosmological Argument.*

Its main assertion is that everything that exists has a cause for its existence. The universe exists, therefore the universe also has a cause for its existence. Since there is no scientific explanation for this cause, the cause must be personal – via a "personal agent" – defined (claimed) as "God" or "Allah," or whichever deity you choose. Put simply: Everything has a beginning and an end. If things did not have a beginning, they would be infinite and could not actually exist. Therefore, God exists as the consciousness who authored all the beginnings and endings of everything.

Even when putting aside the question of why the idea that "everything must have a beginning" miraculously doesn't apply to God, we can see that we have very little reason to get into this too deeply. And the reason for this is obvious. The entire argument is an argument from ignorance.

God is not logically necessary for the universe to exist. For something to be logically necessary, its opposite would have to be impossible or inconceivable. For example, it is logically necessary for a triangle to have three sides because we cannot conceive of one having any other number of sides.

Therefore, if we *can* logically conceive of this idea of *no* god, then no god existing is clearly a possibility. The concept that a god *must* be the cause of the existence of the universe is not a given, and is not logically necessary. What should be obvious is that if a god is simply a possibility in all possible worlds, then that god *not* existing is a possibility in all possible worlds. If one can supply the idea that a god is the cause of the existence of the universe, but is not necessary, we can also postulate other contingencies for that same cause: the Big Bang, the universe itself, a consciousness, an unknown force beyond our access, etc.

The Cosmological Argument has many forms, and has been discussed by many great philosophers (Kant, Aquinas, Russell, Hume, etc.), but it has many more objections than supports. Some have studied this to an extreme, even at the atomic level, using quantum physics to demonstrate the absence of causality. Suffice to say here, that the Cosmological Argument for God does not go very far without the presumptive belief in a supernatural non-falsifiable god at its own beginning – a beginning for which the causality is superstition.

(For another, more logic-based version of the Cosmological Argument, see the chapter, **Religious Arguments and Fallacies.**)

Let's take a look at a few more godly theories...

Psalms and the Earthly God

> When I consider thy heavens, the work of thy fingers, the moon
> and the stars, which thou hast ordained... – (*Psalms 8:3 KJV*)

Religious folk use this, and other scriptures, to claim their god as "creator of the universe." But this is taken out of context by the religionists themselves. When reading the entire Bible, we find that Psalms is clearly referencing a particular earthly god, Yahweh – a god that is very much humanoid in "his" behavior, with human emotions and actions (anger, jealousy, he makes mistakes, etc.). Nothing in the Bible has ever described whatever it is, or was, that *could* have created all the billions of galaxies and trillions of stars in our universe. The Bible references, in all passages, a god who created a big earth, with a small sun revolving around it, and a sprinkling of tiny stars. The god-concept is as small as the people who invented it. Within a universe so vast, there is no reason to take it seriously.

The Supernatural

Because the "supernatural" is beyond nature, that is, beyond matter, and does not behave as matter does in the natural world, how is it able to pass in and out of the natural world and have any effect on it at all? Or, how can this interaction not have any effect on itself? And how is it detectable by beings that are *not* also supernatural or outside of nature? Ideas about "supernatural" things, or entities, can never be demonstrated to be anything more than one's own imagination. By definition, the supernatural is not a part of our reality and for all intents and purposes, does not exist in our reality. Therefore, we have no other choice but to assume that it does not exist at all until the above questions are adequately addressed with evidence.

CONCLUSIONS

Those who declare the universe is fine-tuned, specifically for making life, ignore the fact that there is really very little life in the universe relative to everything else. To assume a creator made everything for the sole purpose of producing life forms is absurd when we look through a telescope and see everything *except* life. If life does exist elsewhere, its presence is a tiny minority, a miniscule fraction of what the universe has to offer.

Any statement that the universe is fine tuned for life is an argument from ignorance. It is simply a rehashing of the God of the Gaps fallacy. "Fine-tuned for life" is on par with someone stating that iron and oxygen are fine-tuned for making rust. It has its equivalence in a virus thinking that the human body was made specifically for viruses. All are equally fallacious assumptions.

Unnecessary Complexity

Because not all atheists are scientists or philosophers, we operate in the realm of "what is the best possible explanation for what we know in the present." And so, we ask: Could there be an "intelligent creator"? Yes. Have we seen one? No. And we haven't observed anything else outside of space and time because we ourselves are not outside of space and time. The truth is, all conjecture is equal. Because none of us actually know how the universe began, we can only process what we can observe. Creationists will argue that science is attempting to "remove the belief in a creator" from the equation. This is hardly the case. God hasn't been included in any hypothesis because God hasn't been observed. When evidence for a god shows up, it will be included. Until then, there is no reason to include such a thing because any other odd conjecture is just as valid as the idea that "God did it!" In our universe, we know $2 + 2 = 4$, it is not $2 + 2 = 4 +$ my creator god. We may never know how the universe began, but throwing gods into the mix is an unnecessary exercise in futility.

Big Bang! You're Dead!

The Big Bang being the "right" or "wrong" theory about how the world began is really irrelevant to most atheists. We don't mold or adjust our lives around this theory being true. However, religionists *need* to be right about their ideas of how the world began. For Christians, specifically, the whole view of the world hinges on whether or not Jesus was real and whether or not he was able to come back to life. But their Theory of Resurrections has less validity and scientific proof than the Big Bang Theory. And their Theory of the Garden of Eden has a whole lot less evidence than the Theory of Evolution. Instead of trying to knock down theories they think all atheists believe in, Christians should be attempting to make *their* theories stand on their own two feet. If the only weapon they have to support their theories lies with destroying other theories, they've lost the debate before it begins. Perhaps true-believers should start all over with some new myths that are more in line with what 21st century man knows, rather than what Bronze Age man doesn't.

The Significance of Earth

Knowing what we know about the Universe, it's quite striking to realize that the Universe doesn't care about the Earth or what happens to the people on it. And it's very disconcerting to know that you care and the Universe doesn't. You care and you care a lot – about your family, your health, your earth. But the Universe, of which you are a part, and from which you were made, can barely acknowledge your existence. The earth could be hit by a huge burst of gamma rays and kill all life on the planet, and the Universe would barely elicit a shrug. It would simply go about its business of making light and rocks – and that stuff they call *dark matter*.

"The Truth Is Out There"

The difference between supposing a god exists, and supposing a *specific* god exists is immeasurably vast, due to the almost infinite possibilities of what a god could be. Therefore, real science doesn't look for God. If it stumbles upon a creator, so be it. After all, facts are facts. But so far, science, whether in the field of astrophysics, biology, or chemistry, has yet to discover a deity. When looking out at the universe from the vantage point of our planet, beyond us in every direction we see mostly vast unfathomable areas of darkness and void, and the tiny areas where we do find light and substance are dangerous places, wholly hostile to life.

To date, science can conclude that there is no Super-Someone, or groups of eternal creator beings watching over us. We are here and the universe is not the least bit concerned. You may ask, beg, and pray to whatever you wish, but no one is listening, because no one is there in the darkness, and nothing speaks from the light.

Reality and Acceptance

At the dawn on mankind, when homo sapiens began to reflect upon death, the world became simultaneously wonderful and a place to be feared. The knowledge that we die is as frightening to us now as it was to the first human being who came to that realization. And now we understand even more about death. We know now that earths die, suns die, galaxies die, and even our own universe will eventually die. The view that life is pointless is now *more* pervasive with this new knowledge. We desperately want to ignore these facts, curl up into the fetal position, and have someone tell us it just isn't so, that we don't have to die, that there is something after death. But, truth is truth, even if we don't like that truth.

To enjoy the life we do have, we must accept these facts as real, without any sort of fantasy or delusion telling us that things aren't what they really are. Nothing has changed in our world since we gained sentience. Death was always real then, just as it is now. For us, and for the stars. Religion doesn't deal with these facts very well, if at all. It offers the delusion of an afterlife in the same way a maniacal person is offered a sedative. "Take this and all your bad thoughts will go away." But when the medicine is gone, the reality comes back into view. The real world hasn't changed, your perception has. The most important place on the road to healing is *acceptance.* We have to toss out the religious sedative and accept our reality. We die. And this life is all there is. Let's all make the most of what we have.

CHAPTER TWELVE

Trillian's Hypothesis

"Dark Matter has not been detected, but we know it exists. The sum of the parts of the universe require it. Dark Matter may be made up of tachyons – particles which move faster than the speed of light. Moving faster than the speed of light is why they cannot be seen, why they cannot be detected, and why they may be the very thing that ultimately controls our universe."*

(Disclaimer: See the first line of the first quote on page 237.)

CHAPTER THIRTEEN

Religion Shopping – Never Pay Retail!

*"The hardest thing of all is to find a black cat in a dark room,
especially if there is no cat."* – Confucius

"Keep peeling the onion and you get no onion." – Vera Nazarian

*"I oppose religion because I believe no one
should have to live an irrational life."* - Edward Trillian

This religion store is huge! And that's because there are only about 11% of us living on this planet who admit to being atheists. Being in this kind of minority will get you into trouble in just about any place you choose, therefore, until we gain our eventual future majority, it pays for us to be externally vigilant, yet internally proud. In the meantime, it won't hurt for us to check out some of the other kinds of beliefs that are keeping our numbers down.

This chapter is mostly about the smaller religions of the world, or ones that are represented nominally in the West. It certainly cannot cover them all. There is such a vast array of sects, denominations, and off-shoots, it would take volumes upon volumes to cover them all. We will just include the more interesting ones here. Christianity and Islam are addressed in other chapters because of their greater size and scope.

Choosing Wisely

When you hear media pundit say, "All religions are the same," in a vain attempt at being "fair," you can be quite certain they haven't looked at other religions very closely. The members of the religions themselves don't think all religions are equal, so why should the secular world embrace such an simple-minded idea? Religions are *not* the same. And some are worse than others. To an atheist, none of them are useful at all due to the inherent flaw that sits in the reactor core of their the belief system – the idea that a deity exists. Regardless, let's take a good (but brief) look at some other religions and let's assess them on their pros and cons, alphabetically, of course:

Bahá'íism

The Bahá'í faith could easily be called the Unity faith. Bahá'ís believe in one god, but also believe that all the other religions that worship one god are worshiping the same one they are. They also believe in the unity of humanity (all are equal), and the unity of diversity through the acceptance of all races and cultures. However, the Bahá'í faith does not recognize homosexual unions (giving credence to the idea that there are no perfect religions).

Bahá'í is a relative newcomer to the world of religion, having only been founded in Iran in the 19th century by Bahá'u'lláh, a man considered to by his followers to be a "Messenger of God." Bahá'u'lláh was born a Shiite Muslim and Bahá'ís are considered apostates by the vast majority of other Muslims. Despite their lofty goals to unite all humanity, (or perhaps because of it), Bahá'ís are routinely persecuted in their country of origin, Iran, and in other predominately Islamic nations, most often, Egypt.

Buddhism

Is this really a religion? Yeah, sorta, kinda. And not. People refer to it as a "non-theistic" religion, or a philosophy. The rituals, beliefs and traditions are based on the teachings of a fellow referred to as Siddhārtha Gautama Buddha who lived about 2500 years ago in Eastern India. Buddha means "Enlightened One," so Buddha wasn't just some mundane guy off the street.

Buddha taught the "Middle Way" as the right way to live your life – somewhere between extreme sensuality and extreme self-denial. Pretty good advice in any era.

Buddha, however, is not considered a god. But, because he is so deeply venerated by those who follow his teachings, one looking on might think otherwise. After all, he is called a "teacher of gods..."

And even if Buddhists themselves don't consider Buddha a god, other religions do. Some Hindus regard Buddha as the 9th avatar of Vishnu. Ahmadiyya Muslims consider him at least a prophet. The Bahá'ís call Buddha a "Manifestation of God." The Vietnamese Cao Đài religion revere Buddha as a "Son of God." Even Christianity has a link to Buddha: Barlaam and Josaphat, early Christian martyrs, have stories that are most likely based on the life of Buddha.

With all this venerating, and all those giant statues of Buddha sitting in the lotus position at the center of every Buddhist temple around the world, Buddhism finds itself in the "Middle Way" – between a non-theistic and a theistic religion. It would probably be better for everyone if they would just make up their minds.

(A side note: Just because you see statues of a fat Buddha everywhere doesn't mean the real Buddha was actually chubby. In fact, some of those statues aren't even Buddha! No one really knows for sure how big Buddha was. Most likely, he took the *middle way* between fat and skinny.)

Hinduism

(Okay, so maybe we lied a little when we said we would only cover the "smaller religions.") Hinduism is a rather large group of believers in terms of numbers, consisting of about 1 billion people. Although you will find adherents all over the globe, the great bulk of Hindus are concentrated in one region of the earth – the sub-continent of India, and is included here for that reason.

As you might expect with a religion so large, Hinduism has a lot of different denominations with varying beliefs. But it also has various gods. This even includes a Supreme Being, a creator god called *Brahma,* who is the father of *Manu,* who in turn is the father of all mankind. (Hindu *Brahma* is not the same as the Hindu *Brahman,* which is the ultimate, genderless, all-encompassing soul, the final cause, the unchanging cause that causes all change in the universe, the infinite eternal Truth. Or something like that.)

Confused yet? There's more...

Unlike the gods in most western religions, a Hindu god can be depicted as male, female, a combination, or having no gender at all. Hinduism does have elements of monotheism, but most often in the form of *henotheism* (belief in one god, but acknowledging the possible existence of other gods). *Pantheism* and *panentheism* are also elements included in Hindu belief. With so many diverse views on a god or gods, Hinduism can be a rather daunting road to travel for anyone trying to decide which way to believe. A newbie can get lost in a vortex of belief. It's the concept of *overchoice* all over again. Which god should you worship and in what form?

The best choice, of course, is none of them.

Jainism

This religion is so peaceful, practically no one has ever heard of it. Jain, comes from a Sanskrit word meaning victory. Victory for Jains is victory over personal passions, such as desire (including sexual desire), greed, anger, pride, etc. Jains believe in the concept of *ahimsa* – non-injury to all living beings. Anyone who succeeds in conquering all their inner desires is said to possess pure infinite knowledge. Some of their other goals are "open-mindedness" and being non-possessive of material things.

Jains do not believe in a creator or destroyer god. However, they do believe that a person who overcomes their passion can become a god. This is sometimes referred to as *transtheistic* – meaning it is neither theistic or atheistic. It claims to be above both. Of course, becoming your own god is still rather theistic, if not a bit narcissistic. We can presume that if you're suddenly a narcissistic god, then you have to go back to square one and get rid of this obvious passion of the Self.

Jainism – some good ideas, but still a religion with a god hiding inside.

Judaism

Judaism may be the most evolved active religion in the world, at least when you're talking about the major religions.

Judaism isn't just about the Torah, (the first five books of the Bible). Judaism also has a massive amount of Oral Law, (which is now written down), containing stories, and events about characters already in the Bible. These serve as a parallel to the Torah, often adding to, clarifying, or reinterpreting the events in the Torah itself. This is a rather expedient way of making some of the strange primitive morals, dastardly events, and physics-defying myths in the Bible seem not so bad after all. Of course, the Oral Law itself is also quite old, and as you might expect, is also full of some rather odd rationalizations and impossible occurrences.

It's all a way of keeping your holy books while at the same time adhering to the more enlightened morality and practices of modern times. Evolving the meaning is a grand way to gloss over old texts – a way to keep followers from ever having to contemplate the concept that there may be no god at all.

From Boiled Goats to a Ban on Mixing Foods

But, wait! That's not the whole megillah! There's so much more. There's not just the Torah, but also the Talmud – which includes all that Oral stuff, plus the Mishnah, the Gemara and other writings (more interpretations of interpretations) and in standard print, this whole thing comes to about 6200 pages! So, now you know why Jews make such good lawyers!

The core purpose of the Talmud is to study every conceivable angle of a problem or situation, ask every possible question, and formulate every possible solution. And solutions are often juxtaposed, combined, and deconstructed innumerable times. Is it any wonder that, in the end, the conclusion appears to have no relation at all to the original question?

"Do not boil a kid (goat) in its mother's milk" has evolved into don't eat meat products with dairy products. This is loaded with other extra-Biblical addendums, including specified times to wait between eating one type of food versus another type. This is all about keeping Kosher *(kashrus)* – following the rules of *halacha,* or Jewish Law, within the Jewish household. Each of these bizarre rules have an explanation, or rationalization, but it doesn't make any of it less bizarre or difficult to do.

This kind of transformation of original godly commands into something completely different is a (sort of) practical way of obfuscating the outdated or the ridiculous. Obviously, creativity is essential in this process.

Not Enough Rules?

Besides the 613 Commandments in the Torah, here are a few general things you are told *not* to do if you are an Orthodox Jew:

- You must never speak God's name

- When a close relative dies, you must not forget to say a prayer for the soul of the deceased every day for eleven months
- If you are a woman, in public, you must not allow your natural hair to be seen by men
- Do not work on the Sabbath (a.k.a. Shabbat)
- Do not drive on the Sabbath
- Do not write on the Sabbath
- Do not turn on lights on the Sabbath
- Do not carry things on the Sabbath

There are actually 39 very specific and detailed things you should not do on the Sabbath alone. Of course, *not* doing things is really not so terrible. But, from our atheist perspective – these are rules that are wholly unnecessary – for anyone.

Conversion

The fact that Judaism does *not* proselytize is a huge difference between itself and most other religions. Even if you are the most rampant anti-theistic atheist on earth, you probably have at least some respect for any religion that has no desire to get you to join. It is here that you are on equal ground. A religion that seeks *no* converts can be a partner in a democracy of discourse. And this is manifestly important to an atheist seeking independence from religious thought.

Mormonism
(Organized, Re-organized, and Disorganized)

Mormons are Christians ... sort of. With an extra Bible or two. The actual name of the Mormon religion is "The Church of Jesus Christ of Latter Day Saints." And, there is an off-shoot, which is very much at odds with the former, which used to be called "The *Re-organized* Church of Jesus Christ of Latter Day Saints." (It's now "The Community of Christ.") And there are other off-shoots, just as antagonistic toward the original "mainstream" church, which have formed solely because they still adhere to the idea of polygamy.

Yes, polygamy. (Islam is another religion that supports the idea of more than one wife for the "oh, so lucky" man, but limits it to a maximum of four ladies.) The original Mormon concept practiced in the 19th Century was for a man to have as many wives as he could handle! This, of course, follows *exactly* how the Bible views marriage – one man, and lots of wives. The modern concept of "one man, one woman, equals marriage" is completely *non*-Biblical.

Jesus Goes Looking for Some Panama Red

A lot of people view Mormonism as strange, weird, and not even Christian. Well, the weirdness part gets even weirder than just plain old boring polygamy. Mormons have other books they refer to besides the Bible. These are *The Book of Mormon, Doctrine and Covenants,* and *The Pearl of Great Price.* Nothing wrong with having books, however, the first of these claims that Jesus Christ appeared to the people of Central America at the same time he appeared to the Jews in the Middle East. Jesus had to go there, apparently, because of the vast migration of Jews to that region prior to his appearance.

This amazing story was revealed by an "angel of light," in 1823, to Joseph Smith, an American religious zealot living in New York. Smith was somewhat of a raconteur and got himself into trouble with the law on more than one occasion for hiring himself out to others for the purpose of treasure hunting. Smith used a "seer stone" for this and was notoriously unsuccessful.

Smith claimed he got the information about the Central American Jews from "golden plates" buried on a hill near his home. The translation of these golden plates became the *Book of Mormon.* Of course, despite the fact that today, DNA samples show *zero* evidence of any large migration of Jews to Central America – ever, Mormons continue to believe this story. Mormons also await the re-excavation of the alleged golden plates, now hidden, that will someday corroborate Joseph Smith's elaborate tale.

As for the Christian accusation that Mormons are not really Christians, that perfidy is based on... Mormons stating that Jesus is the "literal" son of God, and that Jesus was simply a procreated "spirit child" – God's first one, just waiting to be placed into the body of baby Jesus, in the same way everyone else is... supposedly. To non-Mormon Christians, this makes Jesus not-so-special, and this is very close to blasphemy. Stating this sort of thing is the kind of stuff that could get you tortured or killed, back when torturing and killing were part of the daily Christian routine. In the 19th Century, it got you (self) exiled to Utah.

All of this "spirit child" vs. "Son of God, equal to God" stuff is simply splitting imaginary short hairs to an atheist. It's all quite silly. And we don't even have to discuss the fact that Mormon priests wear special holy underwear during special ceremonies. And, yes, they really do that.

Scientology
(Not to be confused with Christian Science)

When a religion is sort of a cross between science fiction, the philosophy of a motivational speaker, and a cult, you get Scientology. Born from mid-twentieth century pop culture and its co-opting of New Age insanity, Scientology evolved into the religion of slightly eccentric entertainers and actors, with Tom Cruise and John Travolta as the most famous Scientologists of all time.

But, Scientology is so weird. It's the only religion invented by a science fiction writer (L. Ron Hubbard). And it didn't even start out as a religion. It was supposed to be a counseling technique and a new form of psychotherapy. The idea, dubbed *Dianetics,* was supposed to make people "more rational" by tapping into an individual's past traumas, and then learning to suppress the emotions caused by those traumas. The biggest problem (or greatest aspect, if you're building a religion from psychotherapy) is that these past traumas could have come from a "previous life" – in other words, through reincarnation. This is where and when (1951) the sci-fi writer/founder introduced the *thetan.* (No, that's not someone with a lisp trying to say "Satan.") The *thetan* is similar to a "soul" and this is where Scientology goes off the rails and into the spooky woods. As the story goes, these *thetan* souls, which are in the billions, originate from earth's past, when an intergalactic dictator named *Xenu* brought humans here and had them executed. (We can assume Hubbard knew of this story from accessing one of his own past lives?)

In any event, Hubbard soon published a new set of teachings called, *"Scientology, a religious philosophy,"* as he began to build the evidence he needed to declare the whole thing a religion. Eventually, the Church of Scientology was born. Where it failed as some rather oddball counseling, it worked as a new religion. Finally, you could have your quirky science and your religious delusions all rolled into one! Even the symbol for Scientology looks like a glistening gold cross. It turned out that the psych-counseling, trauma-suppressing, re-incarno therapy-religion was a big hit.

Is Scientology a religion? Yes, it is. From an atheist's perspective, *thetan* alien souls from planet *Teegeeack* are no more nutty than talking snakes and flying chariots.

Some people say Scientology has millions of members. Others say that number have already quit. (Ahem.)

Oops! Meant to say, Amen!

Shintoism

What's good about Shintoism? Well, if you like gods, it's got a lot of them, each of which have their own special role in your life. However, it's the native religion of Japan and venerates Japan and Japan only. It has very little purpose outside of Japan and therefore cannot spread itself very far. If you aren't Japanese, you can forget this one immediately. And you thought Judaism was exclusive?

Zoroastrianism
("Thus Spoke Zarathustra!")

Yes, the followers of the ancient creator god, Ahura-Mazda, do still exist. There are approximately 2.6 million followers today, mostly living in Iran and India. Zoroastrianism predates Islam and has its origins in ancient Persia (modern-day Iran). The religion gets its name from its founder and prophet, Zoroaster (a.k.a. Zarathustra), who lived sometime between the rather large time window of 1700 BCE to 500 BCE.

Though relatively peaceful, it is from here that many of the primitive and destructive ideas contained in the Abrahamic religions began. The idea of a fiery hell comes from here. (Jesus Christ most likely borrowed this concept from the Greeks, who had already borrowed it from the Persians, and subsequently inserted it into his own offshoot of Judaism.) Zoroastrianism also gave us the concept of an immortal afterlife and heavily influenced Judaism, which in turn shaped the beliefs of Christianity and Islam. It also contributed the concepts of divine judgment, a war between good and evil, and the resurrection of the dead.

(Thanks, Persia.)

THE PURPOSE AND ARROGANCE OF RELIGION

All religions are *cults of superiority*. Religions, by design, build a wall of separation between themselves as a group and everyone else outside the group. It's a way of saying, "Our group is better than your group. We are the superior group. You are nothing without us." Many clubs, organizations, and political parties do this, of course, but religions unapologetically claim to be above and way beyond such attitude and behavior. They realize, instinctively, that exclusivity often implies hatred toward outsiders, and no religion, no matter how segregated, wants any outsider to think they are an organization of hate. A façade of tolerance must be maintained in order to gain more converts. You only get schooled on who and what to hate after you've joined and are comfortable with your decision.

Religions are the most egregiously guilty of this sort of arrogant behavior. Of course, this fact has to be constantly denied by the adherents, otherwise the wall of separation comes tumbling down. Every arrogant act, arrogant comment, or arrogant edict springing forth from the religion is consistently relabeled as "righteous" or "godly" and even "humble." The excuse for the arrogance is always passed on to a higher authority, "But God said..." or "And Allah said..."

Yet, those of us on the outside looking in can clearly see that their humility is feigned. Even the slightest hint of a humble act is backed by arrogance. It is the arrogance that believers *know* their "humility" comes from their own powerful god, and everyone outside the group has a false god. It turns genuine humility on its head, and as you might expect, makes no apology for doing so. The individual religious cultist is too happy knowing he's superior to ever bother with the nuances of his hypocrisy.

And once you strip away the unnecessary rituals, the outdated laws, and the impossible myths, we see that religion has very little reason to exist other than to separate people from other people. Superiority and separation is what lies beneath the emperor's new clothes, and it has been this way from the very beginning.

Those rituals, celebrations, holidays, dogmas, scriptures and liturgy, are there to create the illusion that as a member you are somehow different, when in the real world, we are all basically the same.

CONCLUSION

The religion you choose, or the religion you are born into, will have a long-lasting, and possibly dramatic effect on how you live your life. And so will choosing *no* religion. Choosing no religion, however, means that you will have total control over what you think, do, and say. Having that independence will give you insights into reality that you could never acquire with any religion of any color. Religion attempts to reshape, control and eclipse your reality. And as any atheist knows, experiencing reality means stepping into the light. Belief in the unknown (or unknowable) means remaining in the darkness... forever.

CHAPTER FOURTEEN

Excerpts from Hell: On-Line Arguments with Believers

"Time spent arguing is, oddly enough, almost never wasted."
– Christopher Hitchens, from Letters to a Young Contrarian

"You don't have to believe in a god to get good advice."
– Edward Trillian

The Internet is a terrible thing to waste. So is time. But you have to keep busy doing *something*.

This chapter is devoted to actual argument, discussion, and debate between The Author and other persons on various on-line forums, blogs, social media, and video sharing websites. These are snippets and excerpts only. Entire discussions are not shown.

The *first* section of the chapter is devoted to individual comments made by The Author regarding specific ideas mentioned in a specific video or first brought up via an original comment. Any previous comment from another person has been omitted, but can be implied or inferred from the response. (Note: Some of The Author's comments have been used as the basis for discussions in this book.)

The *second* section is devoted to actual exchanges between The Author and others, with the names of the other person withheld to protect their identities. Incorrect spelling, bad punctuation, and poor grammar have not been edited out in any of the comments. They are published as originally posted.

The *third* group comes from emails and personal messages received from individuals that wanted to take the discussion out of the public forum, and debate ideas one-on-one.

The *final* section contains comments from other like-minded atheists that The Author considered to be worthy of publication. Again, as always, names have been withheld to protect their identities.

INDIVIDUAL COMMENTS ON LINE

The Author's individual comment on myths:

Which is most likely to have occurred? A talking snake, or a flying reindeer? A burning bush that talks, or a man shrinking himself down in size so he can fit inside a chimney? The sun standing still in the sky for a day, or a man delivering toys to billions of children in one night? A woman turning into salt, or elves living at the north pole? A virgin magically getting pregnant without sex, or a giant rabbit hiding eggs in the grass? Do you see any difference because I don't.

The Author's individual comment on the maturity of belief:

So many people are emotionally stuck at approximately the equivalent of age of 5 or 6, when reality is just beginning to bud and a person just beginning to be consciously self-aware. That's where you are: When believing in imaginary things is easy (Santa Claus, Easter Bunny, Talking Snakes, God, The Devil, etc.), and denying their existence is hard. It's sad to see so many people take so long to grow up!

The Author's individual comment on a creator:

Believing in a god is silly. Try the following: Get a telescope and look at the stars. Do some math regarding the size and distance of those stars relative to the earth. If you can comprehend the magnitude of what you discover, you'll also see that whatever made the trillions of stars and the billions of galaxies could not possibly be Yahweh / Jesus / Allah. A creator that can do that doesn't get jealous, it doesn't command tribes to carry out genocide, and it needs no resurrection or hell to cure the mistakes of his creation.

The Author's individual comment on *argumentum ad populum:*

Just because millions believe in something doesn't make it real. Millions have believed the world was flat and they were wrong. Millions believed the sun revolved around the earth and they were wrong. Millions still believe an invisible being has "a personal relationship" with earthlings, and they are wrong also. In the end you have no proof of your deity. The default position is: no god until such is proven to exist. Parents have been lying to their children for generations about this. It's time to stop.

The Author's individual comment to Christians:

Dear Christians,... It is not an atheist's job to explain the Universe to you, how it came to be, or why. I know you hate us and hope that we burn in your mythical hell forever, but please understand, we simply do not believe in any gods, and most especially we don't believe in your god, okay? Quit asking us to explain evolution also. It's not our job. We just want to live our own lives without your silly ideas or angry "god" in our heads. If you stop bothering us, we'll stop calling you stupid.

The Author's individual comment on Biblical truth:

Regarding the words in the Bible: Saying the words louder, doesn't make them true. Having been written long ago, doesn't make them true. Translating them into another language, doesn't make them true. Telling others about them, doesn't make them true. Believing in them with all your might, doesn't make them true. Knowing that billions of other people believe the same thing, doesn't make them true. There is only one thing that can ever make them true: Evidence.

The Author's individual comment on God's presence:

Apparently, god is dead. He no longer produces pillars of fire, he doesn't set bushes on fire and talk through them, he doesn't part seas anymore, he doesn't magically wilt fig trees anymore, he no longer commands bears to kill children (thankfully), he doesn't write words on stones with his fiery finger, he stopped showing his backside to prophets (again, thankfully), he stopped ordering prophets to cook their food in their own shit (yes, it's in the Bible), etc. So, yeah, he's dead, or he's senile.

The Author's individual comment on the supernatural:

So, you assume the story is true, and then proceed to call the explanation for the obvious absurdity of the story "supernatural" because that's the convenient cop-out for things you can't ever prove. "Supernatural" is your go-to explanation for absurd events. Of course, you're not alone in that regard. It's the same weak logic many believers in many other religions use to keep themselves convinced. The problem is, it also keeps you less self-aware, and less a part of the real world. And that's not what life is supposed to be about. To really embrace the world, and really see the world, and really appreciate the world, you can't think like you think. Your world view cripples you and that's why I feel sorry for all religious people. Their world, your world, is a nebulous fog of sin, hell, damnation, empty promises, worthless prayers and failed hope. Life is rare and precious and you choose to waste it on a very questionable event that was never necessary to begin with.

The Author's individual comment on the resurrection of Jesus

It's funny how Christians think because Jesus actually lived, and was actually executed, (both debatable), that automatically means he was also resurrected. It doesn't. If an itinerant preacher named Jesus did live and then died, he is still dead. People don't come back to life. Sorry, it just doesn't happen.

And if you respond in reference to Near Death Experiences, they are called *near death* for a reason. *They aren't actually death experiences.*

The Author's individual comment on God's omnipotence:

God and Satan are the same god. He plays all the sides. He has no other choice. If he alone created everything, the only person he can play with fairly is himself. Human beings and angels (good or bad) are just game pieces on a giant game board.

The Author's individual comment on The Big Bang:

The difference between speculating about the Big Bang for the creation of the universe, versus believing in an invisible god for the creation of the universe, is this: No one has ever sacrificed another person for the Big Bang, no one has started a war for the Big Bang, no one radically changes their behavior for the Big Bang, no one mutilates anyone's genitals for the Big Bang, no one tortures another human being for the Big Bang, no one has ever enslaved anyone for the Big Bang, etc. But, all these wonderful things have been done for the sake of religion. See the difference?

The Author's individual comment on Bible-worshipers:

You said: "What was acceptable back then is obviously not acceptable to us. You will need to understand the people of that time period to understand lots reasons for what he did." I agree that people thought differently back then. No doubt about it. But that still doesn't make it moral or justifiable. Rape is still rape and it is still wrong no matter when it happened. And when you read passages like Deuteronomy 22:28-29 and try to say this commandment (instructing a rapist to marry his victim) is from God, you insult your own God. You obviously worship the Bible and not God. Your view, whether you are conscious of it or not, is that the Bible cannot be wrong even if it demonstrates that God is wrong. In other words, your practicing belief is that the Bible takes precedence over God. If you really did believe in an all-powerful God, you would believe in him without any need for a Bible.

The Author's individual comment on Biblical absurdities:

Not only did God kill his own son, he was his own son, so he actually killed himself! Plus, he impregnated his own mother, and he was his own father! Wow! Christians really love their godly incest!

The Author's individual comment on Christian humility:

Excuse me for jumping in here, but humble you're not. Your humility is fake. You come into every conversation with a kind of smug arrogance that you know exactly what your... (wait for it!) ... *invisible* god knows, does, and wants.

268

And you get all that from nothing. You either make presuppositions (with a false air of authority) as you go, or you refer to the thousands of re-hashed and re-twisted interpretations of interpretations of a "book" that was written by primitive man. Humble? Not a chance.

The Author's individual comment on prayer:

You said: "God is not here to prove his existence." Okay, then he is not here to have a conversation with you either. When you pray, you are just talking to yourself to alleviate your fears. That's fine if it makes you feel better, but it's still not real.

EXCHANGES BETWEEN THE AUTHOR AND OTHERS

The following are excerpts of exchanges between The Author and others on various forums. Names have been withheld to protect each individual's privacy.

Comment from (*Name Withheld*):

I know my mind is gushing with ignorance and I'm not gonna lie it sucks. So please sir will you humble yourself and share some of your vast knowledge and wisdom because I would like to feel what its like to have at least a fraction of your vast understanding. Seriously im not pullin your leg share with me or am i not worthy of such an honor? Im just messing with you but yea im pretty ignorant. so tell me why you think i am please

Author's Reply:

Certainly. I watched your suggested video: "The Case for a Creator," and as always, Christians, and people of other religions, fail to even consider the following: *If* there is a creator, that creator is probably *not* the one you've been praying to. It's very likely no human being has ever been able to touch, describe, view, know, or contact an entity that can create *billions* of galaxies. Humans aren't that bright. And their holy books and gods clearly miss the mark for such a creative force.

Comment from (*Name Withheld*):

…it is surprising that some people turn their backs on scientific principles, primary deductions and propositions based on reflection, and deny the existence of the Creator….a considerable number of scientists have a religious outlook as part of the intellectual system; they have come to believe in the existence of a creator, a source for all beings, not only by means of the heart and the conscience, but also through deduction and logic.

Author's Reply:

I'm getting tired of seeing this phrase: 'deny the existence of the Creator' when referring to atheists. Most atheists don't actually do that. 'Deny' implies not accepting an obvious fact. What atheists really do is this: we do not accept your supposed *evidence* for a creator, not a creator itself. That's a huge difference that you (and others) fail to understand. And you, as a believer, cannot use the terms deduction and logic, and remain credible, when you haven't met the burden of proof for your god.

Comment from (*Name Withheld*):

John 19:30: When he had received the drink, Jesus said, 'It is finished.' The 'it' Jesus referred to was the fulfillment of the Law. It is impossible for anyone to live by God's standards. That is why God sent Jesus. He is the Ultimate Sacrifice for all of our sins.

Author's Reply:

Any being, entity, god, creature, thing, or person that would require a sacrifice of any kind (involving the death of someone) is not worthy of worship. That's just horribly sadistic and ridiculously stupid. It's unnecessary. If I want to forgive my children, I don't slash my wrists, try to hang myself, shoot myself, or set myself on fire, and I don't set myself up for execution either.
I just forgive them.

Comment from (*Name Withheld*):

Would you consider yourself to be ungodly?

Author's Reply:

No, I consider myself to be un-Batman-like. Look, I don't compare myself to imaginary beings or fictional characters. I'm just a human. Now, you? *You* are ungodly.

Comment from (*Name Withheld*):

ultimately the outcome of life in a galaxy is clearly the purpose of a galaxy we are are not going to come up with anything that will suffice a description of God. If you have ever in your right mind red Psalms you would understand that the Bible is a book that is filled with poetry dedicated to the works of the force that binds everything. His mercy is displayed throughout the cosmos we are within a thin marginal window that keeps us alive light years beyond earth are nothing but death dude.

Author's Reply:

No, Psalms is clearly in reference to a particular earthly god, Yahweh, a god that is very much humanoid in 'his' behavior with human emotions (anger, jealousy, makes mistakes, etc.). Sorry, but it's not a match. Nothing in the Bible has ever described whatever it is, was, or could create all the billions of galaxies and trillions of stars in our universe. The Bible references, in all passages, a being that created a big earth, with a small sun revolving around it and a sprinkling of tiny stars.

Comment from (*Name Withheld*):

...everytime the word 'god' is brought up u have to jump their shit throwing around false information, even most ppl that believe in a god dont attack athiests, ur the bullies not us

Author's Reply:

You think atheists are the bullies? That's hilarious! Look where you are posting. You're on an atheist site. You came here. No one invited you here. You start talking *your* shit and you expect no one's going to give you hell for it? Are you really that naïve? At least no one is pouring hot boiling oil into your orifices like the Christians did to non-believers during the Inquisition. Feel a little bullied? Too fucking bad. You've had it coming to you for hundreds of years!

Comment: (*Name Withheld*)

We could discover the reasoning behind every single natural occurrence in the next 1000 years, and it wouldn't contradict God's reality. If you discover a painting is made out of bonding agent, pigments, water, and other chemicals, it doesn't make it less of a painting, it simply explains its existence. You can discover the painting process, the brushes, the canvas, but that doesn't negate the art's deliberate nature.

Author's Reply:

You said: '....and it wouldn't contradict God's reality.' Well, it certainly doesn't prove God's reality either. You presume God, and you presume too early. What is frighteningly illogical is how god-believers presuppose a god, with no evidence, (that's bad enough), but then they arrogantly follow it up with, 'Oh, and, by the way, it's this god over here! The one I believe in!' It's adding something inanely preposterous to something already preposterous.

271

Comment from (*Name Withheld*):

Without the existence of such an unconditional being, the source of all causes and the foundation of all existence, the order of creation cannot EXIST. Simple common sense!

Author's Reply:

That's a huge assumption, but let's just say, (for argument's sake only), that you're right... Guess what? That 'unconditional being' is not your Allah or your Jesus. Those 'gods' are man-like. And the petty crap that happens between humans on this tiny, tiny, tiny planet is incomprehensibly trite compared to the rest of the Universe. You're shining a light up the wrong asshole, and looking in the wrong galaxy if you want to find this 'creator' being you so desperately need.

Comment from (*Name Withheld*):

What do you mean burden of proof? lol Ha ha please... How is proof a burden?

Author's Reply:

A burden is something you, and only you, have to carry. Like a cross, I suppose. Proof isn't easy to obtain, therefore it is sort of a burden. This is getting away from the legal definition of the 'burden of proof,' but it's being simplified here so you can understand it. If you make a claim that a specific god exists, it is your *burden of proof* to provide evidence for it. It's not for someone else to disprove. Pick up your cross (your burden of proof) and carry it. Prove your god exists. With real evidence.

Comment from (*Name Withheld*):

The atheist Delusion! Do scientific discoveries and knowledge cause such a scientist to conclude that matter, *unknowing and unperceiving *, is his creator and that of all beings? No? Then how can the duped atheists and some of the scientists delude themselve and *believe* that hydrogen and oxygen, electrons and protons, should first produce themselves, then be the source for all other beings, and finally decree the laws that regulate themselves and the rest of the material world?

Author's Reply:

I don't know of any scientist who thinks 'matter produced itself' as you imply. As for what could have made matter,... you are a human, therefore you will never know the answer to that question, and even if you do find out, you will not be capable of comprehending it. That's how small and insignificant you are relative to the Universe.

Comment from (*Name Withheld*):

better to die believing christ is real and finding out he isent then to believe he isent real and finding out he is ,

Author's Reply:

You're an idiot. If all it takes is believing Jesus is 'real,' then wouldn't the *other* god in your pantheon, Satan, also get a free ride to heaven? Doesn't your Satan character know Jesus is real? Have you considered that you are referencing the mind of a guy (Blaise Pascal) from the 17th Century? And have you figured out yet that old ideas aren't always the best ideas? And really old ideas (the Bible) are often deeply flawed because they are based on ancient (i.e. limited) knowledge?

Comment from (*Name Withheld*):

According to countless sources atheists are ungodly people which turns out to be wicked,corrupt,immoral,sinful.vile,evil,dredful so on and so on. How do you feel about that? Being an atheist is nothing to bragg about, as a matter of fact its quite shamefull.

Author's Reply:

No, it's only shameful to you. And you should be ashamed of your religion. It has killed millions in the name of your god over many hundreds of years, making your religion wicked, corrupt, immoral, sinful, vile, evil, and dreadful. And if that's considered 'godly' by you, why would any sane or good person want to be a part of it? Most people are more moral than your god anyway. Therefore, we may be ungodly by your standards, but you are inhuman by ours.

Comment from (*Name Withheld*):

Atheist are so concerned about the existance of Jesus, they don't even get his message.

Author's Reply:

Nope. We got Jesus message loud and clear. It's convoluted, ignorant, primitive, narcissistic, cruel, threatening, dictatorial, and ridiculous. He says only about two lines that are worthy of repeating, but none of them are even original. You are so convinced that Jesus must be real, that you have not bothered to actually analyze what he said (or did) beyond what your preacher has already told you.

Comment from (*Name Withheld*):

I'd like to see things from your point of view but I can't seem to get my head that far up my ass.

Author's Reply:

That's not actually my head up your ass, that's my boot! I'll take off my boot so you can get your head in further! Good luck!

Comment from (*Name Withheld*):

so Francis Collins a physician-geneticist also director of the human genome project has the logic of a four year old too? he's the author of the book the language of god do you know what the HGP is? its a pretty big deal bro this is a huge step toward the advancement of genetic mapping and origins of physiological functionality. Im telling you bro you cant deny the things of the spirit man its like vital for you bro you need it for your daily life I was in your shoes once i didnt give a rip dude

Author's Reply:

Mr. Collins is obviously a very intelligent man, however, he has the same amount of evidence for a deity that you and everyone else on earth has: NONE. His theistic evolution ideas are more sound than most creationists, but he's still using the God of the Gaps fallacy to support his ideas. Of course, the biggest problem you have is, for some bizarre reason, you think there are some dire, horrible consequences for a human being not accepting ideas about the supernatural.

Comment from (*Name Withheld*):

If you have any verses which promotes torture, injustice, abuse to slave, Please write. Other wise don't accuse GOD of the Bible. Because He is Just GOD. If I take money from you, automatically I becomes a slave Till I paid all your debts. If I Not pay or can not pay by any mean. Do you not think, it would be injustice with you ? Then Who will pay your money and give you right justice ? Pay your debts or be ready to be a slave. Its equally justify. Problem was EVIL master Not kind of Slave money

Author's Reply:

You are in no way worth the time it takes to tell you anything. You have posted numerous times trying to justify the obvious slavery in the Bible, trying to reinterpret it, gloss it over, rename it, but it just won't work. Slavery is slavery. You cannot get past that by calling it something else. Again, if god was just, OR merciful, he would have added this to his commandments: 'Make no man, woman, or child your slave.' How many lives would have been different if he'd added those 8 little words?

Comment from (*Name Withheld*):

If you are not able to pay back my money, then it is justify to be my slave. You can pay back by giving service to me till your debts are fully paid. But if I torture you, oppress you, abuse you and kill you, then GOD will Judge proportionally too. Look what GOD commands to Masters in – Colossians 4:1 Masters, treat your slaves justly and fairly, knowing that you also have a Master in heaven. If you want to see Evil, every good thing will also seem to you evil only. Dear, Try to be humble

Author's Reply:

Stop. Seriously, just stop. No one agrees with you. Humanity despises slavery *in all forms*. Understand? Most of us, (except for you and few other morons) have moved past this abomination. And the only *real* reason you try to support it is because you are afraid that your stupid Bible (or Qur'an?) might be wrong! If it is wrong on this matter, what else is it wrong about? Just face your greatest fear: that your holy book is all fables and fiction, and move on to something more enlightening.

Comment from (*Name Withheld*):

there is more manuscript evidence for Jesus christ than any other person , your universities have them , but you blindly follow your text books and dont even question there integerity but are ready to shut down a possibility of a god. As the Bible says in the end times there will be eyes that do not see and ears that do not hear, Fear , love , hope, and courage cannott be seen either nor the air you breath , God is Real

Author's Reply:

No, you can't count manuscripts written after the life of Jesus. Most of what you Christians reference, other than the Bible itself, are manuscripts written hundreds of years after the fact, and you call that 'testimony.' You're cheating the truth when you do that. You refuse to live in the real world out of fear, so everything's skewed to fit your fantasy. What a waste!

Comment from:

[Original Comment Removed]

Author's Reply:

You are a human, a sentient being, living on a very tiny planet on the edge of a remote solar system which is part of the Milky Way Galaxy, just one of literally billions of other galaxies. Your God(s) Allah, Yahweh, Jesus, Vishnu, etc., are all too petty, too small, too ignorant, too angry, too evil, too psychotic, and too worthless to be the energy or mind that created all those trillions of stars. Those are the facts. Buy a telescope and open your mind.

Comment from (*Name Withheld*):

You sound like a very nice person, however, we are here on this earth for only a short time. We all have free will to choose as we please. Jesus promises eternal life if we believe in Him and follow the Commandments given to us. My mission in life is to be a good person, like yourself, and do good deeds for my fellow man, and follow the Commandments and help my children get to Heaven, when I have kids.

Author's Reply:

Please don't have kids until you have cleared up your delusional tendencies. It's wrong to bring up kids with fantasies about invisible Boogy-Man gods that will do bad things to them if they don't obey.

Comment from (*Name Withheld*):

Greeting of peace, On December 21, 2006, God revealed the truth that image or statue liken Jesus is idol! This truth is the key to open the prophecy of Act 17:29-31, now God commandeth all men everywhere to repent.

Author's Reply:

Acts 17:29-31 is not a prophecy. Prophecies are guesses, and the more ambiguous the 'prophecy,' the more you can say it's hogwash. In this particular verse it says a day (someday) has been set aside for your god to judge everyone. This 'prophecy' may be the most ambiguous of all time. You could just as easily say, with certainty, 'Someday an earthquake will happen!' Or, you could say the

276

following with no certainty, because of its absurdity, 'Someday we will be ruled by pixies!' Neither are prophecies. Sorry, but Acts 17:29-31 is in the same category.

Comment from (*Name Withheld*):

Any one who loves God feels sorrow for athiest because they are but fools not knowing it. Psalm 14:1 The fool has said in his heart, there is no God, They are corrupt, they have done abominable works, there is none that do good

Author's Reply:

Only a fool quotes the words of a people who thought the world was flat.

Comment from (*Name Withheld*):

The Bible isn't a lie per sé. It's a collection of myths. If someone calls it a lie, then they should also call Homer's Iliad a lie, and Hans and Gretl. That having been said: people who claim, against better knowledge, that the Bible is completely historically accurate in all details, they *are* lying. Bible scholars, historians and archaeologists all (well, except the handful of fundamentalists, of course) agree that large parts of the Bible are not *literally* true.

Author's Reply:

I think you can say that much of the Bible is a lie because of the motivation of the authors that wrote it. It wasn't written as a story of fiction to be told for entertainment. It was written as a means of controlling people. It was humanity's first attempt at government. It was useful once, but today it fails. We have governments in place that do a better job (though flawed as well.) But religion, (like our tonsils, wisdom teeth, and appendix), should be removed and thrown away.

Comment from (*Name Withheld*):

If God did every little thing for us, people would become too dependent. That's why miracles are miracles, not every individual's wishes come true.

Author's Reply:

I guess the wish to eat a good meal and not starve to death would just make a poor hungry child "dependent," right? But you, miraculously finding a $20 bill in the yard is simply God doing his job of letting you know he's there? The more I talk to Christians and Muslims, and really get into what they actually believe, the more I realize how immoral and cruel they are – and all the while, they think they are "good"! You know, you really can't have a clue about who you are when you believe your own bullshit.

Comment from (*Name Withheld*):

Jesus made a pretty good case, if he did, in fact, rise from the dead. I believe in the advancement of intelligence to a level that we are unable to comprehend. There are experiments being done in quantum mechanics and genetics that foreshadow an 'event horizon' where humans become gods. Why choose to close your mind because some jackass told you to only believe a book. I came to what i believe after many years of analysis and study of odds and probability-My answer is simple -we are NOT alone!

Author's Reply:

Sure, we are probably not alone in the universe. I've never stated otherwise. I'm not sure why you think I'm closing my mind to such things. Maybe you have me confused with some other person you've been conversing with. But, again, being not alone, doesn't mean Jesus rose from the dead. It doesn't make him a creator of stars and galaxies. It might make him an alien from another planet, but do you want to worship aliens? If you want to find these intelligences, first, set your Bible aside.

Comment from (*Name Withheld*):

Quibbling in vain! Let alone you! How could some of the scientists permit themselves to make a claim that would necessitate knowledge as extensive as the scheme of the universe, when their knowledge of the total scheme of being is *close* to zero, when confronted with a whole mass of unknowns concerning this very earth and tangible, lifeless matter, let alone the whole universe? The atheist Delusion! ... Praise Allah

Author's Reply:

I see. So, you think because humans haven't yet learned all there is to know about their universe, they should just give up and start believing your unproven nonsense about a magical sky god? Really? I think you just went "full retard!"

Comment from (*Name Withheld*):

Proverbs 3:5 Trust in the LORD with all thine heart; and lean not unto thine own understanding.

Author's Reply:

How convenient. Sure. "Don't use the brain I gave you, use magical dreams and random coincidences in your life to understand what I want from you." – (Yahweh the Insane, 1:22)

Comment from (*Name Withheld*):

if i say to you, the evidence you seek requires opening your mind to the possibility of higher intelligence, and you, in rebellion mock me, you choose ignorance over enlightenment. You are like the fools who were first told that there is bacteria on meat, you scoff and say "PROVE IT!" and I say "LOOK INTO MY MICROSCOPE" and you say "That wicked glass from the devil! No way!" – same fucking troll as always, never submitting to truth, covering his ears and humming really loud. Smh

Author's Reply:

I never said there is zero chance of their being a creator of the universe, or some higher intelligence. What I have said to you and many others is that the higher intelligence or creator you seek is clearly NOT the one you worship. No human has, or could thus far, know or describe such a creative intelligence – not one that could put together the billions of galaxies in this universe. Not a single person has ever done so. And none of you have put forth any evidence for anything even remotely resembling such a being. It's not about 'rebellion.' It's about truth.

PRIVATE MESSAGES AND EMAILS

The following are responses to Private Messages (PMs) the author received from people on the web. These are excerpts only. The entire transcript of all of the emails and personal messages received by questioning Christians would probably fill several books of this size. These are replies only. Included here are some of the most interesting responses, without including the actual questions or comments they made prior. This is done to protect their privacy.

Reply to a Christian after stating why he got married:

You said you married your wife to end fornication?! I married mine for love. I think your reasons for doing things are skewed a little, and again, this is because of your enmeshment with primitive Biblical ideas. But you don't see how the Bible promotes those primitive ideas because your mind is so deeply embedded in Christian dogma and tradition, it makes you blind.

Reply to a Christian that wanted to re-interpret a Bible passage:

Regarding Isaiah 45:7 – What part of "I create evil" do you not understand? The biggest problem I have with Christians and scripture is that when something is crystal clear and can have no other meaning than what is stated, you will still assign a new meaning to it anyway. And when things are vague and ambiguous, you fill in the blanks and assign events and "facts" that never existed. You would much rather defend the Bible than your god. If you think defending the Bible is defending your god, then the Bible is really your god.

Reply to a Christian regarding Satan and free will:

You told me, "God created things perfect and a free will agent (Satan) ruined it." No, God ruined it by creating the free will agent to begin with, or ruined it by not destroying or caging the free will agent that did all the ruining. But, God must have wanted things to get "ruined" or he wouldn't have created that free will agent in the first place. Or, God had no clue how his experiment would turn out, and even now, he's still just guessing at the outcome.

Look, if your god is the creator of everything, he's the creator of everything from the tiniest molecular particle to every idea every sentient being has ever had. He's the author of all the good, bad, ugly, pretty, strange, knowable, unfathomable, bizarre, living, dead, large, small, invisible, tangible things, and every other thing in between. You don't get to have an all-powerful god only when it suits you – only when it fits your Biblical doctrine, and the rest of the time he's just "sort of" all-powerful. It destroys the entire idea of "all-powerful."

Reply to a Christian admitting he could not prove the existence of his supernatural god:

Not only is there no way to prove the existence of a supernatural god, there is no way for you to prove *anything* supernatural. Why? Because you don't live there (in the supernatural world) and you've never been there. And you can't point to it, and no one can either. That's rather suspect, don't you think? Doesn't this supernatural world sound imaginary?

Reply to a Christian that stated Old Testament Laws No Longer Apply:

If you want to think you are not under the Law of the Old Testament, why do you people always quote the Ten Commandments? It's in the Old Testament, remember? If you're not under those laws, don't quote them. And don't argue that they must be obeyed, or displayed in court rooms, if they are not a part of your Christian doctrine. If you want to quote and obey those laws, you need to quote and obey the other 603. It's disingenuous, hypocritical, and confusing if you just pick a few you like and disregard the rest. Under the Law, or not under the Law, pick one. The rest of the world is tired of your self-convenient selectivity on this issue.

A closing comment to a Christian that wanted to argue a combination of evolution and astrophysics, instead of his original assertion, that he could prove his god exists:

All in all, you gave me some interesting replies, but nothing too exciting. And I am greatly disappointed in the fact that, after several requests, you have not presented your case for a creator god and its existence. When are you going to do this? I can sit here and discuss the order (or chaos) of the universe all night, and even if you proved every point I made to be false, that in no way proves a god exists.

So, now I await your response regarding what I asked for in the first place. (I would think this would be an easy task for you, if you are so certain of its validity.)

Response to a devout Christian who stated she had watched some of "The Universe" programs on television:

Happy to see you are watching science shows. Just think about this: If you can wrap your head around the fact that there are billions of galaxies like our own Milky Way, with trillions of stars like our sun in each, then you may be able to comprehend the fact that a little Jewish man in a remote desert, on this tiny remote planet, in only one of the smaller galaxies of those billions of galaxies, didn't create anything. He didn't even create the religion surrounding him. He's not a god. He was just a man that someone decided should have superpowers in their obviously fictional stories.

Try to put things in perspective.

Response to a Christian that stated there was no proof of evolution ever happening:

I'll bet that's not the stupidest thing you've ever said, but it's probably close. We have evidence, solid, verifiable evidence, the kind you can touch, the kind you can observe, the kind you can study. You have none of that. You don't have *any* witnesses at all. You have stories written many decades after the event where claims are made, but no real eye-witness accounts. None. And we don't reject your god because we *like* doing so, we do it because it's logical and reasonable. If you were to present some real evidence for your god, plenty of people that are now atheists, me included, would accept it as truth. Why? Because we aren't trying to be stubbornly resistant to your claims, or those of anyone else, we only want the truth and nothing but the truth. And you obviously can't provide it.

Response to a Christian that insisted that the Theory of Evolution must be false:

The atheist position on evolution is irrelevant to whether or not a God exists because atheism is not born from evolution. It is born from the fact that your side, the religious side, has presented *zero* valid evidence for the existence of, not just your god, but any god. Let evolution be wrong, I don't care. It's a mind-bogglingly painful and boring discussion for most people anyway. I personally think evolution makes sense, but not because I'm trying to make a statement such as, "See? Evolution proves there is no god!" I can't make that statement because evolution, even if true, doesn't do that. Evolution only shows how things changed, not how they got here.

Response to a Christian that stated evolution removes humanity's purpose for existence:

I find it interesting that you attack Evolution on the basis that it destroys a "purpose" for life. In doing so, you make the erroneous assumption that *you*, of all the people on the planet, know beyond a shadow of doubt, either that there is a purpose, or should be a purpose, or that if there is a purpose, you could even comprehend that purpose. Your arrogant position comes from the bias of your other assumption that a creator god exists, and not just some creator god, *your* creator god, the one you've been taught to believe in. And you refuse to waver.

You are missing the idea that a purpose could exist that you don't know about, or that a purpose could exist that you could never comprehend, or that a purpose could exist that was *not* benevolent, or that a purpose could exist that does not come from your creator god, or finally, that no purpose exists at all. None of these is knowable by you because you are not all-knowing. Simple logic, standard or no standard, says that you cannot fill in all the gaps of what you don't know with whatever you want to exist. That's called the "God of the Gaps" fallacy and you just stepped into a big stinking shit pile of it.

Response to true believer who insisted he had "proof" his god created everything:

You said: "You have proof but it does not satisfy you." Really? What proof have you shown me? I'm still waiting. You've given me a lot of opinions, but anyone can do that. You have to give me something mind-boggling and amazing as proof. After all, we are talking about a being that can create galaxies, so whatever proof you give has to be really spectacular. The galaxy itself could stand as a sort of proof, if you can show that it was your God that made it. The burden of proof is yours. It's like a murder mystery… Who killed the victim and what proof do you have that the *specific* person you've chosen actually did it? I'm not opposed to there being a god at all. I am opposed to it being *your* god. Your *evidence-poor* god. See the difference?

Response to a person determined to convince the world that Jesus absolutely positively had to exist:

As for the actual crucifixion itself: Being crucified and being resurrected are two different things. I don't care that he was executed in this way. Lots of people were at that time. (And Muslims still do this to Christians.)

You also said, "The claims that Christians made were massive." Have you ever heard the phrase "the bigger the lie, the more likely someone will believe it?" It's generally true. The lies about Jews, that the Nazis used to justify the Holocaust, are one very big example.

You also said, "If he was never crucified then that would have been documented." No, that's not true at all. There weren't many people saying much of anything about Jesus during his lifetime anyway, so why would they document, even as a footnote, "Oh, by the way, he was never crucified." That's just laughable. Lots of celebrities *don't* have things happen to them and no one writes about it. No one says, "Celebrity X died of cancer today. Oh, and just in case anyone ever asks, he definitely *didn't* get hit by a bus."

You said, "To think that a non-existent figure could have such an impact and not have a single document at the time refuting his existence is just downright silly." Wrong again. If, during Jesus' lifetime, there exists only a few lines describing him, then why would anyone bother writing even a single additional sentence that this relatively unknown fellow *didn't* actually exist? Why waste the paper?

A long response to a Christian who wanted to ask a question that he thought would create a discussion about Biblical morality:

You asked the following question: 'Just suppose that God does exist, and the rules in the Bible do exist. Just for a moment suppose, hypothetically if you will, would that change anything in your daily behavior? Would you have to stop or start doing anything personally, according to those rules?'

Okay, let me try to answer that. Having read the Bible, both Old and New Testaments, I would have to say that, yes, I would have to change some behaviors if I made the decision to live by those rules. The problem is, I'd be going back and forth doing contradictory things all the time, and doing things that go against any decent human being's morals.

If we take Jesus' stand in Matthew that the Law of God (which includes the Old Testament) is *never* to be changed until "all is fulfilled" – meaning until Jesus comes back, then I'd probably want to get some slaves. I'd also be worried about someone raping the women in my family, as the women would have to marry their rapists. If God told me to slaughter innocent people, I guess I'd have to do it, just like god commanded people to do in the Bible. (As you probably know, the commandment against murder doesn't really count if God tells you to do it.)

In any event, I'd be constantly worried about whether or not today was the day I had to pluck out my eye for lusting after some woman, or perhaps cutting off my hand for doing something bad with it. I'd ponder whether or not to go to the doctor and get surgically castrated as Jesus suggested some should do. And, since Jesus felt it was best not to be married or have kids, I'd probably regret having already done so. I'd be doing my best to keep all 613 Commandments, not just everyone's favorite Ten. That would take up all my time and I doubt I'd have much time for work. I wouldn't own anything because it would be better to give all that stuff to charity. I guess I'd have to walk the 30 miles to work instead of owning a car (that is, if I still had a job). And, I'd never get into fights or defend myself against an attacker because it's best to turn the other cheek, so I'd probably get beaten up a lot. I'd probably smell pretty bad because not owning a house or having a job would mean I'd rarely take showers. Although I'd likely be living in a cardboard box like a homeless man, I'd be obligated to stand on the street corner and tell everyone about Jesus, even on days when I really didn't want to. I might be in a lot of pain with only one eye, one hand, and no balls, but hey, it's all for the glory of god, right? So, yes, to answer your question, and to be a "real true Christian," I guess my life would change quite a bit. How about you? When are you going actually do what your Bible says? (Hypothetically, that is.)

COMMENTS FROM ATHEISTS AND SKEPTICS

Some people *do* pay attention to the world around them! Yes, some people do use their brains! Many of these are brilliant, well thought-out responses from fellow atheists. Enjoy!
(Names have been withheld to protect their privacy):

Comment:

There is no 'cause of the universe' for to do that requires a *time* when there was no universe. Which, of course, cannot have happened given there is no time in a singularity.

Comment:

Just some friendly advice. Merely point out to anyone debating evolution that their willingness to admit god into science says god is something that can be measured, ought to be tested, and can be understood by humans. All of these things contradict their definition of god.

Comment:

...the argument from design is moronic. it fails on basic logic. if nature needs a designer, then why not god? and if god doesn't need one, why does nature? the above inconsistency is why it is moronic. anyone should be able to see the problem it throws up; even small children can often see it. the only conclusion is that theists are THICK AS SHIT

Comment:

You know, you can't prove a negative. If something doesn't exist, it leaves no evidence of it not existing.

Comment:

From parents and from society. That's where everyone gets their morals from. It comes from a recognition (that) my actions have consequences to others and caring whether or not I'm causing harm or doing good in the world. If your question is why not be selfish and the hell with everyone else? Then I would say you're not really a moral person if you only do the right thing because you think a God will reward or punish you in an afterlife. Doing the right thing should be its own reward.

Comment:

Christian logic: 'Wow, my life is great! God must be rewarding me because I have so much faith!'

'Wow, my life is horrible! Satan must be throwing obstacles at me because I have so much faith! (Or, God must be testing me!')

'Hey, that atheist's life is great! God is going easy on him because he knows that he'll suffer in the afterlife. (Or, he must have made a deal with the Devil!')

'Hey, that atheist's life is horrible! God must be punishing him for his lack of faith!'

Comment:

History isn't the same as the past – i.e., the true course of events. Sometimes historical accounts are accurate, occasionally amazingly so…but there are many examples where the accuracy of history leaves much to be desired. The Bible is an example where we don't need science to know it's very unreliable, because the Bible contains numerous accounts which are often contradictory.

Comment:

So atheists have to produce scientific proof of everything, but the religious just have to point to an incoherent bronze age book? Do you not see that your objection applies equally to the religious?

The difference is that scientists actually do have evidence backing up their claims (that's what science is). Whereas, religion is about not only having zero evidence, but claiming having no evidence is a good thing.

Comment:

It's easy enough to prove or disprove the existence of a god IF a full description is given. For instance, if, in the description, you use words like all-knowing, all-loving, or all-powerful, and refer to the god of the Bible, Torah or Qur'an,... this god does not exist. An all knowing god would not make so many mistakes, an all powerful god could correct them instantly, and an all loving god would not murder all but two of every species on the planet. See how simple that is?

Comment:

Let's define the Universe as everything. There is nothing else but the Universe by this definition. There was no 'cause', since the Universe itself includes everything that exists (and has ever existed). There can't be something 'else' from everything that caused it to exist.

Comment:

There is no faith in science. You accept it or you don't. Science still exists regardless of anyone's beliefs about it. It's not based on assumptions. It's based on verifiable evidence, and testable hypotheses. Religion rests on the assumption that the ideology is correct to start with.

Comment:

Dear God, Please temporarily modify the laws of the universe for my convenience. Thanks in advance, Your faithful servant.

P.S. Jesus, make sure that God does what I want.

[sarcasm]

DISCLAIMER

All comments and statements above are part of the public domain. The names have been withheld to protect the writers' identities.

CHAPTER FIFTEEN

How to Talk to Parents, Friends, and Family About Atheism

"The men the American people admire most extravagantly are the most daring liars; the men they detest most violently are those who try to tell them the truth."
– Henry Louis Mencken

"Nothing destroys self-esteem like religion.
But, perhaps that's been the plan all along."
– Edward Trillian

"Friends show their love in times of trouble, not in happiness."
Euripides

Atheism is growing. And there is a strong correlation between a nation's rising prosperity and the rise of atheism. Biopsychologist Nigel Barber estimates that by as early as 2038, the world's atheists will outnumber the world's religious. That's seems rather quick, but it's really anybody's guess, especially when you consider this estimation is based on economic growth rates which are often unpredictable.

And there are other statistical problems. A 2010 Ipsos-Reid poll taken in Canada revealed that more than half of that nation's people believe in a god, but anywhere from one-fourth to one-third of Canadians who declared themselves to be either Protestant or Catholic do *not* believe in a deity. And we have to assume that at least some of those non-believers are actually attending religious services! And there must be plenty of people sitting at home every weekend, watching football or hockey, who are quite certain a god exists.

It makes you wonder, who really is an atheist and who isn't? But, as far as the numbers of people who openly declare themselves to be non-believers, that number is rising. The shift is coming. And the number one thing that's fueling this rise was not suggested by talking snakes, influenced by flying demons, or coerced into existence by jinn from a smokeless fire. It turns out it's something rather new, and deemed quite essential...

NON, UN, AND DIS-BELIEF

The following statement, in various forms, has been around for a few years:

"The Internet... where religions go to die."

Some anonymous person (from the Internet, of course) came up with that now semi-famous line. And it's starting to ring true.

But atheists aren't alone on the internet. For many religious people, blogging has become their ministry. People can now preach in their underwear. Some religious folk try to gain converts via YouTube, Facebook, and Twitter. If there's a way to get out the "Good News" of Jesus, or the Message of Muhammad, the religious will find it and use it.

By the same token, atheists and anti-theists have the same equipment and they're fighting back – and winning. Where Christians have their Bible and Muslims have their Qur'an, non-religious people have every other book on the planet, many of which are polar opposites of the religious message. To win an argument on an Internet forum, it only takes a few clicks onto any secular wiki to cause any naively religious person to wonder why they haven't correctly memorized their holy scriptures.

Gone is the era of a preacher quoting a line from his holy book and everyone just accepting it as truth. Now, those theists are often caught with their pants down and toilet paper stuck to their shoes when an atheist has to correct a believer's misquoted line of scripture. And the shakedown is done in an instant.

Atheism and Religious Services

Despite the growing trend, many atheists continue to attend religious services and do so for a variety of reasons. And there's really nothing wrong with doing so. For some it's cultural. It's more comfortable to be around people you know, especially if you have family members attending frequently. For others, it's economics. It makes sense, if you have business partners that attend, or your particular business caters to those same people within that congregation. That's the positive side.

On the negative side, you find atheists still attending services due to the supposed backlash they could receive for "suddenly" not believing in a particular god. For Jews, other congregants' reactions might be a shake of the head, sadness, disgust, or avoidance on the part of those who know. For the ex-Christian, reactions might be fear, shunning, incessant preaching, or even outward threats of hell. For the ex-Muslim, (depending on what part of the world you're in), it could be death. Although these reactions are sometimes real possibilities, they are often exaggerated in the mind of an atheist. Individual reactions to your new found belief are most often unpredictable.

But it's not just the people in the congregations who are turning to atheism... Members of the clergy are too – ministers, preachers, rabbis, imams, and priests. It's happening enough now that a new non-profit (The Clergy Project) has emerged to help the clergy transition from their former belief (and responsibility to their followers) to a new one where they can find new employment and re-integrate into society as atheists. If they can do it, the rest of us can find help too. (See the list of atheist organizations at the end of the book.)

THE STUFF YOU HAVE TO DEAL WITH

Your own little secret...

It's not easy being an atheist, out in the open. In the minds of true believers, you're not only doomed, you have no morals. You could go crazy any minute and do something horrible!

So, don't run out and tell everyone right away. There's no rush. Certain people, such as older, more devout relatives, are those you may want to *never* tell. Your 80-year old grandma can be spared the news that her favorite grandson thinks Jesus never existed.

Be careful who you pour your heart out to. They may turn on you, even if you think they are "open-minded" about most things. Religion may be the one thing that is "non-negotiable."

Be ready for the backlash. You know you will lose friends, but you probably won't know which ones. But it will happen somewhere along the way.

Don't back away from what you believe and don't apologize for it. It is what it is. And your thoughts are your own. Defend them as needed. And do so with logic, reason, and without anger.

Join with other atheists or skeptics. Find a local atheist group that meets often. Intermingle with other atheists in person and on-line. Having a person around who is also an atheist, even if it's just one, is a wonderful relief from all the religious redundancy you already have to encounter day to day.

Disbelief About Your Non-Belief

If you do come out and tell everyone you're an atheist, believers will have a lot of questions for you. Here are some of the more common ones:

"Did some religious person in your past do something bad to you?"

"Do you hate your family?"

"Why do you hate God?"

"Are you a Satanist?"

"Why would you want to go to Hell?"

"Are you insane?!"

To an atheist, these questions are almost funny. And they would be, if it were not for the fact that the person asking you these questions is in a state of sincere and sudden shock. Some of these people are angry. Some are even worried that you (or your soul) really will roast in some unknown fiery hell – after you die, of course.

This sort of jaw-dropping bewilderment from god-believers about your own personal revelation is to be expected. What isn't always expected is what follows. Some will get you in a corner and tell you that "you don't really believe that?" They will try to convince you that you're just "doing it for attention," or that "deep down" you really do still believe. But, hey, at least they're still talking to you. Some friends and even family members will give you the silent treatment, or disassociate themselves from you completely. Perhaps they're worried that atheism will rub off of you and on to them? Or, they will get infected with the "atheism virus" if they get too close? In any event, it's rare to find someone who will just shrug their shoulders and say, "So, what?" when you tell them you're an atheist.

Therefore, the process of telling anyone should be well thought-out. The who, when, where, and how should be considered very carefully. A personal decision shouldn't be the kind of thing that separates people, but it often does.

Last Minute Attempts to Pull You Back

When you tell a believer the truth, that there really isn't a lot of evidence that a god exists, you'll often get the following...

"What kind of evidence would make you believe?"

This question is asked by those concerned friends or family members who are desperately trying to bring you back to the plantation. It's a question often asked by deity-believers at the end of a debate they have clearly lost. Out of desperation, they feel they absolutely *must* convert you back to their delusion. The idea is, if you would simply tell someone the *kind* of evidence you needed, they would immediately go out and get it for you. But, we know that's not really how it works.

The problem with this question is three-fold. First, it isn't the job of the non-believer to do this for the believer. The burden of proof is on the one making the claim – the believer in a deity. Second, wouldn't a believer already know the kind of evidence needed? Wouldn't he or she have a bullet-proof, ready, believable, evidence-laden response for all non-believers that couldn't be questioned or refuted? And wouldn't they know exactly what that is, having already seen it themselves? Thirdly, the believer in a god or gods is most likely going to be looking for this evidence in the non-existent supernatural world. When you're looking for something in place that doesn't exist, (or can't be shown to exist) all you'll ever find is nothing.

So, this is a question that cannot be answered by atheists. It is a question that believers should ask themselves: "What kind of evidence do I need to prove my god exists?" This is a question that might be frightening to a devout believer.

Once honest research on this is done, and the believer discovers that there is no real or direct evidence for his god, he may have to re-think much of what he believes. If there is no evidence for something, there is no reason to believe it exists. This epiphany will inevitably change the god-follower's view of life, and suddenly quantify his place in the universe.

Unfriending You

Be prepared for possible mean tweets on Twitter, or public interrogations on Facebook and other social media. You can get yourself "unfriended" in a hurry just because you have some serious doubts about imaginary things. Crazy, huh?

Remember, if a person turns against you because you became an atheist, that act in itself is evidence for the destructiveness of their religious belief. Atheism is simply a rejection of a claim about a god. It's not a declaration of war. Atheists aren't attacking anyone by deciding *not* to believe in something.

The "War on Religion" is a phantom conjured up by the paranoia of a slowly dying belief system. The "war" is no more real than the demons any self-enriching televangelist assigns to those he "heals." Walk away from those who would shun you, and let the angry be angry only with themselves.

The Sad Part

What is most disheartening, is that atheists are often rejected at the very moment they are most honest. An atheist tells someone (a person he trusts will listen), how he really feels about the world and is swiftly met with fear, anger, and rejection. It would be acceptable if the person encountering the atheist could simply reject the notion of atheism but still accept the person, in much the same way most atheists simply reject god claims but still accept the believer as a fellow human being. However, that sort of treatment is, unfortunately, not the most common.

We can conclude from this kind of reaction that some people truly fear honesty. And a part of honesty is fearlessness. As atheists, we must try to see where these people are coming from before pouring our heart out to them. It stands to reason that if a person is deeply immersed in a delusion about gods, demons, blood sacrifices, and afterlives, the likelihood they will suddenly be open, honest, loving and caring toward a non-believer's non-delusional state is very, very low.

Your World Starts to Change

It's quite an amazing experiment in human behavior. Soon after you have told others about your atheist beliefs, you begin to lose friends and sometimes familial relationships. Even acquaintances react to you differently. People that would always wave to you from their car, or say hello to you in the grocery store, suddenly ignore you completely.

All this behavior change isn't really from any wrong thing you've done, at least not something that any sane mind would consider "bad." It actually comes from something others *haven't* done. They haven't provided you with the evidence necessary for their belief in a god. They either haven't tried, or they tried and failed. And rather than admit defeat, or admit that they *could* be wrong, it's so much easier to shun you, as if their own lack of evidence, or inability to confess the truth of their failure, is somehow *your* fault.

Of course, there's one more thing they haven't done. They haven't given you any credit for being able to think your own thoughts and make your own decisions. They would much rather do that for you. To them, you and your brain are *out of control!* And, while we're discussing things out of control, there's...

The Curious Case of Madalyn Murray O'Hair...

She was known as "The Most Hated Woman In America." She was an atheist and an activist, and founder of the organization known as American Atheists. But, much to the dismay of American Christians, in 1963, she won a landmark lawsuit, *Murray v. Curlett,* which put a stop to Bible-reading in public schools. One year earlier, the Supreme Court had made a similar ruling in another case, *Engel v. Vitale,* which prohibited officially sponsored prayer in public schools. The Murray case was the second big blow to Christianity in a short span of time, and the religious community felt it was time to strike back, directly at the most visible atheist they could find – Madalyn Murray O'Hair. The fact that she wasn't exactly Marilyn Monroe, and had a rough demeanor, made her the perfect target. Ms. O'Hair would become *the face* of atheism for decades to come.

It also took decades for Americans to figure out that Madalyn Murray O'Hair was simply doing exactly what the Founding Fathers were expressing in the U.S. Constitution. Religion and government cannot co-mingle. The Supreme Court knew this and ruled accordingly. But, the average Christian American felt like the world was coming to an end. Atheism, atheists, and Ms. O'Hair were ridiculed and reviled at every opportunity. Nothing was stopping Christians from being Christians, but that didn't alter their perception that atheists were destroying civilization as they knew it. It has been more than fifty years since that decision, and many Americans still carry the same vile hatred for atheists they once held for Ms. O'Hair.

Luckily, things are changing... gradually.

On a monument in Bradford County, Florida, (the first of its kind, because it is an atheist monument on public land), the following words are engraved:

> An Atheist believes that a hospital should be built instead of a church. An atheist believes that a deed must be done instead of a prayer said. An atheist strives for involvement in life and not escape into death. He wants disease conquered, poverty vanished, war eliminated. – Madalyn Murray O'Hair

Those words are there because, in 2013, the American Atheists organization won a lawsuit that allowed them to place such a monument in close proximity to another nearby monument of The Ten Commandments. And it's about damn time!

Behind Your Back

Like Madalyn, once you've gone over to "the other side," and others know you're not coming back, you may get a lot of backlash for your own personal well thought-out decision to become an atheist, and it could happen years down the road. Be ready. It won't be pretty. You'll be lumped together will all kinds of vermin, and the lies and generalized false assumptions about atheists will come calling. Here are just a few of the lies believers tell about atheists:

- *Lie Number One:* Atheists are "self-seeking," or lack empathy.

The stereotypical assumption that a person can't be altruistic or have empathy unless they believe in a god, is horrendously arrogant. Whatever feelings atheists have for their neighbor doesn't suddenly change the moment the epiphany that "no god exists" enters their minds. In fact, some atheists will gain sympathy for their neighbors, seeing that those neighbors are still trapped in the same blinding delusion they were once in.

- *Lie Number Two:* Atheists believe in nothing.

This is a biggie. Atheists do not believe in "nothing." We believe that other people's claims about "something" is actually nothing. And how does *not* believing in your particular god equate to nothing? And what is nothing? Can the religious person define it adequately? Theists really should answer these questions before making their accusations.

- *Lie Number Three:* Atheists are going to Hell.

This one is kind of creepy. To tell a person they are going to a horrific place that they themselves cannot define properly, or locate, or even agree upon with fellow believers, is rather bizarre, if not suspiciously frightening. And what believer can be certain they aren't headed to that exact same place themselves? Jesus said, "...narrow (is) the road that leads to life, and only a few find it." So, with almost one-and-a-half billion Muslims and over two billion Christians on the planet now, what makes any of them so certain they are part of that lucky few traveling down that narrow path?

- *Lie Number Four:* Atheists are really Satanists.

This one probably makes the least sense of all. If atheists do not believe in any gods, how could they possibly believe in the lesser god, Satan? Atheists aren't exchanging one supernatural fantasy for another. Atheists reject *all* the gods, and that includes their imaginary cohorts, demons, angels, and all the supernatural mumbo-jumbo that accompanies each and every one them. And that rejection list naturally includes Satan.

WHAT ATHEISTS MUST DO

As an atheist, you should daily reconnect with your own natural feelings of empathy. What is empathy? It's the one thing psychopaths and sociopaths don't have. It's the most valuable and beautiful thing a human being can possess. Whatever amount you possess now, you should cultivate it, grow it, and harvest it in ever larger quantities. Empathy is being kind to your fellow man or woman. Try it. You never know where it will take you. Maybe it will take you to a poor neighborhood and have you volunteer to work in a soup kitchen, or it will take you to the animal shelter and have you rescue an abandoned puppy. Maybe it will make you be sweeter to your sweetheart, hug your kids more often, or remember the good times in your life you've had with your friends. Maybe it will make you smile more at the people that pass you by. All of this, no matter how tiny the effort, will make the world a better place. If there are any absolutes in life, this one is it: Empathy is a priceless gem. Keep it with you at all times.

* * *

Words for atheists to live by:

- Exceed others expectations.

- Be not what others would want you to be.

- Love yourself, but not to the exclusion of all others.

- Love your family, love your neighbors, love your world. (Mostly in that order, but not always in that order.)

- Love beyond your own expectations.

- Being different is your greatest asset. Use it wisely.

- Leave things better than when you found them.

- Appreciate life. It's the only one you'll ever have.

CHAPTER SIXTEEN

The Final Word

"You may ask, beg, and pray to whatever you wish, but no one is listening, because no one is there in the darkness, and nothing speaks from the light."
– Edward Trillian

At last, a chapter full of the rambling thoughts of a happy atheist!

EAT YOUR ENEMIES!

Often when debating religious people, when the theist has backed himself into a corner and can no longer justify or rationalize his belief system, he will exit with final comments such as this, "I love you anyway. God bless you. I will pray for you."

From the atheist viewpoint, praying is a waste time for true believers because the god to whom they are praying has never been demonstrated to actually exist. But it's the part about love that is most damning to the believer's position. When the theist is challenged with the idea that he cannot possibly truly love someone he just met in a debate, the theist will almost always accuse the atheist of not knowing what love is, stating that "for an atheist, love is just a chemical reaction and nothing more." Unfortunately, for the god-worshiper, they have it all backwards.

"Loving" everyone is just another religious delusion stacked upon a whole heap of other religious delusions. Bible believers are confusing love with *generalized empathy*. (This sort of empathy is something one can have for lots of people, for example, the people seen on TV in a distant country dying in a tsunami, earthquake, or some other disaster.) But a general feeling of empathy is not the same as having love for a spouse, or love for one's own children. And the difference is quite astounding. However, theists want to give generalized empathy and the love for a spouse the same name and same value, and it's dangerously inaccurate and completely disingenuous. The theist's approach is horribly wrong because it's falsely overvaluing one (generalized empathy), while devaluing the other (real love).

Science (See: **Dunbar's Number**) has already shown that the average adult human being can only handle stable social relationships with about 150 people at any given time. These relationships are the group from which humans choose to develop very specific and strong feelings of empathy. And because love is greater and more rare than empathy, the number of people you can truly love within this group is even less, and even this is sometimes fleeting. Theists tell themselves that they love everyone, but they are just lying to themselves to please an imaginary god with impossible expectations.

Whatever a human being experiences, the fact that it's a chemical process doesn't make it any less real. Eating is a chemical process too, but everyone knows when they're eating and can experience eating to its fullest. An atheist knows when they feel love, and like the rest of humanity, they know what it means to love and be loved. It is a very specific experience. And it is different than just casually saying you love someone you've only just met, or whom you have only conversed with over the Internet. Using it haphazardly in this way dilutes and devalues the true meaning of love.

The believer will often try to rationalize this random "I love you" statement by attempting to elevate it artificially, using the adjunct phrase, "God is Love." The statement is vacuously absurd in light of the fact that the theist has no evidence for god – making the statement tantamount to saying they have no evidence for love. In reality, the theist has much more evidence for love than for God. Trying to connect the two is like saying "Unicorns are Evil." It makes no sense because no one has any evidence for unicorns either. If the religious person states they have the same kind of love for a random human being that they have for their mother or father, or children, or spouse, they are lying – essentially *lying for God.*

What (or Who) is a religious person?

As atheists, whenever we hear someone state "I am a Christian," or "I am a Muslim," we have no other choice but to believe it. This is true for any sort of self-labeling, and this is especially true with such nebulous terms as religious identities. We have to assume the person claiming to be a member of a group is actually telling the truth, at least to the point that he or she believes what they are saying. We have no idea what is going on in their heads, no universal definition of the label, and no viable or objective way to assess what a "true" Christian or "true" Muslim (or other such identifier) really is.

The in-fighting within sects, denominations, and congregations of believers is most often about who is and who isn't a "true" member of the group. They almost never work it out, instead branching off into separate groups with new names and even stronger beliefs. To an outsider, arguing about who knows more about a non-falsifiable imaginary friend is patently absurd. But that doesn't stop people from doing it anyway. And logic, the brick wall that should get in their way to put an end to it all, was never there from the beginning.

An atheist, therefore, should never get into the middle of these types of verbal immolations between religious groups. If a religious person says they believe something, we should believe that they believe it, no matter how bizarre or absurd. We can question their beliefs, but we can't change their minds. We can plant seeds of doubt, but we can't make them grow. That's something for believers to do on their own.

Talking With a True Believer

When discussing the concept of a god with a true believer of such things, it is important to know the exact place they're coming from. The theist does not begin at zero. The theist does not come from a point that is neutral or unbiased. Here we can assign some numerical meaning to where the theist is standing, as a sort of credibility rating:

> 1. The deity-dabbler believes something spiritual exists – an ethereal entity that created all things. Count: -1 (Minus One)
> 2. The god-worshiper has no evidence for the existence of this entity, or even for any other thing which can be defined as "spiritual." Add another -1 (Minus One)
> 3. The theist brings only anecdotal and hearsay evidence to the table, again and again, all of which is inadmissible as truth. Add another -1 (Minus One)

Therefore, by believing in some *other-dimensional* creator, having no evidence for such things, and for additionally attempting to present only hearsay as evidence, the theist begins any discussion about his own belief system at a count of negative three (-3). This sort of accounting can be addressed as *negative credibility,* (a concept first made popular by journalist Dan Gillmor). What this means is that in any discussion with a theist, he or she must fix these three problems prior to any real discussion with an atheist.

If you give the theist ground, that is, if you allow the theist to debate with the assumption that his negative credibility rating does not exist, the discussion will begin with his or her presuppositions that his god *does* exist. This then turns the argument into a debate about what his god allegedly "said" or "did" or "wants," without ever addressing if the god is actually real. It becomes a bit of a farce. In many instances, anyone could replace the name of the theist's hero-god with Hercules, or some comic book action figure and get the same discussion and result. To be sure, the theist's *negative credibility* means the theist has lost the debate before it begins, which makes arguing with such zealots nothing more than entertainment for the atheist.

Because all arguments referencing a god of any kind, in any context, and for any reason, are *arguments from ignorance,* we have no obligation to listen to such arguments. There are no exceptions to this reality thus far. An argument from ignorance has zero merit. The most it should elicit from us is a shrug, and some strong advice to "return when you have some actual evidence."

* * *

Religious Views On Life

Religious persons like to claim that non-religious persons do not value life to the degree that religious persons do. Of course, quite the opposite is true. The reason platinum has such a high value (at this writing it's close to $1,000.00 per ounce), is because it's rare. Humans know, that in almost every instance, rarity gives value. Each individual human is unique, and being much more rare than platinum, is almost priceless. Certainly, everyone would agree on that, especially when talking about their own individual selves.

Yet, even knowing that, the deeply religious downgrades the value of human life in two distinct ways: One is the idea of original sin, and the other is by believing this life is just a prequel to some other mysterious eternal life to come. The religious person thinks this life doesn't matter much because they're getting another (better) one later on.

Let's use your one and only colon as an example. Let's also say your entire family has a history of colon cancer, resulting in numerous early deaths from this horrible scourge. With you having this information, how are you likely to treat *your* colon? You'll probably be very careful what you eat and see a doctor every year.

Now, let's imagine you are living in the year 2165. In that year, there is no such thing as colon cancer, and if anything goes wrong with your colon, or any other organ, you can get it easily replaced by the instant cloning of that organ, and have it put back in your body in one thirty minute out-patient procedure which leaves no scars. Knowing human nature, how are you going to treat your colon now?

We cannot be raised from the dead. This is our one and only life. It's rare, it's precious, and it's wonderful. Downgrading its value, either by saying we have inherited "sin" and deserve condemnation for something we did not do, or to say that we should not care so much about this life because we're getting another eternal one later on, is probably the worst and most unforgivable sin of all. If there was an existent god, he would be appalled to find his creation had this kind of careless attitude about the life he gave them.

Respect for Religion

There are many who will say that all religions are equal, or that all religions should be treated equally. The former is not the case at all. If all religions were truly equal, they would all agree and religious wars would be non-existent. Religions are *very* different from one another, even between similar sects and denominations. A single variation in the interpretation of one line of holy text can make them quite distinguishable, in tone, rhetoric and action. Part of a good secular education would be to recognize those differences when they appear.

So, should everyone respect all religions equally? Is that what was meant when the founding fathers of the United States of America granted individuals Freedom of Religion? Well, not exactly. People are free to worship as they please as long as they do no harm to others and don't break any laws, but that does not mean people who worship differently, or not at all, must show respect toward a particular religion. Religion is an idea, a concept, an organization of beliefs; it is not a person. People can be granted respect, but ideas *must* be criticized. Criticism is the fire that shapes ideas into actions. It may be true that all people are "created equal" in sight of the law, but it's not true that all *ideas* are created equal. Atheists know this, and most have chosen to respect the *person,* because he or she is a fellow human being, and will give further respect to that person to the degree that they have earned it. However, respect for ideas, religious ones included, are not due any special respect simply because they exist. Ideas must earn respect as well.

To believe in a god to the point of religiosity, is to live your life in a constant state of emotion. Decisions are made based on feelings instead of logic and reason. Emotional belief and emotional decision-making are not the ways to obtain the respect we referred to above, not for oneself or for one's ideas.

Christopher Hitchens said, "Religion Poisons Everything." Perhaps we should expand that to say, religion poisons, alters, destroys, castrates, infects, kills, steals, covets, rapes and enslaves everything. It does all this while demanding respect, glory, praise, and money. And it often does so with impunity. It is a dictatorship of the lowest kind. It should be disrespected, reviled, rejected and removed. If not removed from society, it should be removed from your own sentient intellect, permanently, and for all time. There is no reason for any human being to not live this short earth-bound life with a clear, free, and happy mind.

The Abolition of Belief

As others have pointed out over the years, moderate theists still empower and maintain the foundation of the radical theist's belief system. It's quite simple: If the Qur'an didn't exist, the Qur'an would not be able to inspire the radical believer in the Qur'an to blow up buildings. There are better, more uplifting books to read other than "holy" ones – books that inspire radical goodness and compassion – something holy books can only have in a minority of words, interspersed with the language of evil deeds and commands. The moderate theist would do well for the world to simply not pass on their religion with its myriad of flaws to the next generation, and should instead find another source to inspire their children to do good.

Fear and Loathing on Planet Earth

The religious have become desperate. People are not buying what religion is selling quite so easily anymore. But to those seeking converts, there *must* absolutely, positively, be a deity, and it absolutely, positively, *must* be the one they are praying to. If there isn't one, they think they will have lost all morals, all purpose in life, and all chance at an afterlife.

What they will have actually lost is a sense of mental security. No longer will they be able to plug in their fantasy and let it solve all their problems, or the world's problems for them. Now they will have to think for themselves. No more lazy mental attitudes declaring, "God did it!" No more haphazardly hidden arrogance of knowing how it will all end. Now, the world will be a puzzling place of wonderment that they will have to travel alone, discover alone, and actually *live*. It is the fear of the unknown reality vs. the security of the known fantasy.

To paraphrase a scripture (Isaiah 55:6): Seek yourself, and your world, and your life, while it may be found.

What Has Religion Ever Done For Us?

We can give credit to religion in this way: Those of us who know the truth, about reality, about the universe, and about ourselves, would likely have not arrived at those wondrous conclusions so swiftly without the lies of religion which preceded them. We found the bad, recognized it as such, and discovered the reasons why the bad was not good. Picking through, we found a little bit of good that we could use to build something great. As humans, we now know what *not* to do, and from that we can discover what we *should* do.

LIFE, PURPOSE, AND THE FUTURE OF MANKIND

A New Bible For Human Beings

The Bible is a conglomeration of different narratives, by different authors over a relatively long time span. We would naturally expect those writers' viewpoints to be different based on that alone. But, to also assert that they were directly inspired by some supernatural being is highly questionable. (This applies to all holy books, including the ones used by Muslims, Jews, Hindus, et al). The moment you say, "My god did this, or my god did that..." you open yourself up to ridicule because you have a burden of proof – a requirement to back up that assertion with factual evidence. And no one has ever done that for any of the stories and "miracles" in any holy book, anywhere, at any time.

But human beings are desperate for guidance. And they want it from the highest, most powerful being, thing, book, machine, or pill they can find. Perhaps it's time for a New Bible for everyone.

The following is what the holy books of all religions should look like. You should be able to open your holy book and see these words on Page 1:

Do harm to no one.

Page 2 should have this line:

Care for your fellow human beings.

Page 3:

Live a good life and help others live theirs.

Page 4:

Do all this and nothing else.

Page 5:

Now fill in the following pages with your life...

That last line should be followed by 200 or more bright, white, blank pages. This should be the only holy book you need. You should go to your church, or synagogue, or mosque, or temple with this holy book in hand. Everyone should open that book up and say each line together – all five pages. Then everyone should immediately close their books and go home.

Think of how much better the world would be if everyone took those five pages as the only five pages that were holy and knew that nothing else was needed.

The Meaning or Purpose of Life:

So, what is life about? You won't find it by asking someone else, or by reading it in a book. You can only find life by living it.

Remember when you were eight years old? Did you think much about an afterlife? Most people, unless indoctrinated by a fundamentalist religion, did not give it much thought. What you did do was just live life, and live it in the moment. Life was about living, and nothing more. That's how the avowed non-believer lives life – in the present moment – because that's all anyone can do. You live those precious moments one at a time, purposefully, because life's purpose is to live it!

Living your life in the past (dwelling on your "sins" or mistakes), or living your life in the future (hoping to go to "heaven," and not hell) is *not* actually living with purpose. It's living with delusion. It's missing out on reality – because reality can only be experienced in a present moment.

Each individual has to decide and determine what the meaning of life is. They must render it for themselves. It cannot come from someone else, society, religion, or some god. The journey to find meaning in your own life is the greatest gift the universe could ever give. But, to find that purpose or meaning, it must come from within the self – from exploration, from discovery, from living.

More on Living In the Present Moment

There is one thing Jesus got right, even if his motivation was quite different from what we use it for in modern times: "Don't worry about tomorrow." That's paraphrased, but it's accurate.

If you are harboring any supernatural beliefs beyond a faint curiosity or wonderment that something beyond the material world could be true, you are diminishing your own potential to live a full life. If you are letting religious dogmas and requirements run your life; you are *dumbing-down* your life experience in exchange for what is literally nothing. You are refusing to see the Big Picture of Life because your head is stuck inside a questionable book of fables. Look up and see the stars for what they really are.

The Rebirth of an Atheist

Evangelicals think they have the patent on being "reborn" or "born-again," but, alas, they do not. A new atheist also has that feeling.

As atheists, we now do what we can to live our *one-and-only* individual lives to the fullest, aware that this life is the only one we will ever have. We acknowledge that we can live only in the moment, and try our best to cherish each and every one of those moments.

Perhaps, as newly formed atheists, we should create the ultimate metaphor and give thanks to the universe for allowing us to get rid of the "demons" of Allah, Jesus Christ, Yahweh, Brahma, or any other invisible, magical, and harmful deity that sought to destroy us under the guise of their own "glory," designed as such by those who stood behind these fake phantoms for their own personal gain. We understand now that these demons were only as real as we allowed them to be. The human beings that came before us invented these evil entities to control the generations that followed them. But, those previous generations are long gone, and it's time to make our own way, with our own ideas about the universe, and do so, *for the first time,* armed with the tools of logic, reason, and sanity.

Let everyone who has ears listen: It's time to move forward.

The Last Tiny Possibility of an Existing God

Perhaps the ancient peoples of the world were on to something. There is always a remote chance that everything was put together by something... That may be the one and only thing our primitive ancestors got right. But, all that other stuff about what that "something" does, is, or desires, was all just as made up as the ridiculous fantasies they also had about the sun, moon, and stars.

Earlier in this chapter, we gave an example of what a proper holy book should look like and what it should contain, and in it there is no mention of a creator. But, if a creator and a holy book mixed together is what human beings truly need, there is one that would stand the test of time, and hurt no one. It would simply be a single white laminated card about the size of your hand. On the front it would say:

Something made everything.*

On the back, it would say:

*Disclaimer: No one knows what the Something is. No one has ever seen it, contacted it, or imagined it correctly, and probably never will. Any attempts at describing that Something, giving it attributes, discussing the origins and history of said Something,

302

or making any other extraordinary claims thereof, will be considered spurious and invalid, and will immediately be dismissed as hearsay. Now, get on with your life.

In 95 Words: How to Live a Good Life

If you want to live a good and moral life, you must combine Rational Thought with Empathy. You must toss aside superstition, purge yourself of magical thinking, cast away religion and faith, and replace each of them with Logic and Reason. Reason guided towards Empathy, and Empathy tempered by Reason, is the balance that will guarantee a good and moral life will be lived. Regrets will be few and Joys will outnumber them as the stars outnumber the galaxies. There is only one life to be lived and this is the one. Live it now.

History and Future of Western Morality

We in western society are lucky we managed to evolve a Republic, with a culture that was religious, but a government that was not – a system where one supported, or at least tolerated, the other. That's what civilization has to build on – that lucky bit of societal evolution that brought us to this place. This is the foundation that Western atheists have built their beliefs upon.

Atheists in *this* culture are not trying to destroy religion through laws, or wars, or political parties. Atheists simply want religion to lose much of its grip on society and do so through logic and reason, because it's time for human beings to grow up. Humanity no longer needs those ancient books to tell them what to do. They *know* what to do. They know actions have consequences. Humans instinctively know right from wrong – this instinct is only contravened with brainwashing from various sources – religion being one of them – with others being the media, politics, government, parents, schools, etc. It is time to set yourself free, one lie at a time.

Religious Humor and Truth

Now, some final humor for the non-believer, before we say good-bye... The following are the *simple* differences between the "Abrahamic" religions. Here, in a nut-shell, is what they are saying to us:

Islam: "If you don't follow the prophet Mohammad, and if you don't believe in the god, Allah, you must die!"

Christianity: "If you don't believe in the god-man, Jesus, your soul will go to a spiritual hell to be tortured forever!"

Judaism: "If you don't believe in our ancient primitive war-god, Yahweh, well, that's good! This stuff is not for you!"

Is this offensive? Yeah, probably. To some. But perspective is everything. Wouldn't a creator-god who invented laughter also have a sense of humor?

(Okay, maybe not.)

CONCLUSION

The Rock, Paper, Scissors Analogy

Almost every kid knows how the game *Rock, Paper, Scissors* works: The first thing is superior to the second thing, the second thing is superior to the third, and the third thing is superior to the first, and so on – round and round you go. This same idea can be applied to religion using God, Humans, and Reality:

Belief in God Destroys Humans
Humans Destroy Reality
Reality Destroys Belief in God

Religion is often like a game where nobody actually wins. People just keep going around in circles trying to best someone else, or control other people's actions. No one should look at life as a game to be played. In the real world, you don't get your life back once you lose it. There is no re-booting, re-starting, or cheats. You get what you get, and whatever that is, needs to be cherished.

Human beings like to pretend a god exists because their lives are misdirected and drifting. Believing in a god makes them feel like they have a purpose. But the true pinnacle of their direction is their hope that when they die, they can live again – supposedly forever – even if it's only on some mysterious ethereal plane. They hope this because they fear death. And they fear it more than most. It is what all religious people have in common – a heightened sense of mortality. And the most fundamental thing they forget is this – living a life for eternity would actually destroy a person's purpose. Most humans would get bored with eternity after the first 500 years. How could they possibly find joy and purpose after 500 trillion years? And what about the 500 trillion years after that? And so on...

Truth, Imagination, and Science

We live in the era of science. Science has made our lives much better in ways that religion couldn't, or wouldn't, ever imagine. The truth is, if anyone ever "finds" god, it will be the scientist, making the discovery by accident.

And, if there is creator of the universe, an entity that some may want to call "god," it's highly unlikely any human being has ever been able to describe what that is accurately and without bias. Perhaps no human being is capable of doing so. We simply don't have the mental capacity to comprehend such a vast concept. Not yet, anyway.

Imagination is a good thing. We should be open to the possibilities. And, being open to Truth with a capital "T" means accepting that truth for whatever it is, even if we don't want the truth, don't like the truth, or think we can't handle the truth.

Truth: *It is what it is.*

Religion and the Red Pill

Religion has done enough harm over the various millennia. And religious texts, although they do hold the occasional good proverb or two, are so full of admonishments, threats, horrors, and backward beliefs, it hardly makes looking for the good stuff worth all that effort. Today, religion is almost like an advertisement for a questionable medicine. When the side-effects are listed, they are often horrendously worse than the dysfunction they claim to relieve. Sure, you'll get rid of your chronic headaches, but you'll be missing a limb, having a heart attack, or die in the process. Again – hardly worth the risk.

In the science fiction movie, *The Matrix,* the protagonist, Neo, is given the choice of taking either of two pills – a red pill, or a blue pill. The blue pill guarantees total bliss, but withholds the truth about the world, and it lasts a lifetime. But, the red pill gives anyone who takes it total clarity and the view and knowledge of the real world – in other words, *true* revelation. Atheists have taken the red pill. We live in the real world, at least when it comes to the subject of deities. We have no need to delude ourselves about un-shown afterlives, or immaterial demons, or anything that defies the laws of science and physics for no *real* reason.

Epilogue:

A good friend's mother died recently at the age of 90. On her death bed she expressed to her son many regrets. She had never gone on a cruise, never traveled to a foreign land, never got to take the dance lessons she dreamed about. Her husband had died young and she never remarried. She remained a lonely widow for more than half her life. Her son asked her why she had not done all the things she had wanted. Her reply was, "There was always this voice in my head telling me not to. When a chance to do something came to me, I'd think, 'It could be dangerous and I might be tempted to sin.' God told me, 'Don't do it! Forget about this life! There's a better one coming!' But now I'm not so sure. What if I wasted my life waiting for something that might not be there?"

The best advice I can give anyone is to do all the things you always wanted to do. And do it now. Don't wait! Go on that vacation to Europe and travel the whole continent by train. Learn those dance moves you've always wanted to know. Take that cruise, and dance on the deck with strangers! Live now! The afterlife, if there is such a thing, will take care of itself.

Revisions To This Book

At any time after this book is published, if hard, extraordinary, irrefutable evidence is found for the existence of any living god, I will gladly change the content in this book accordingly.

Atheists seek truth, and skepticism is our guide. Whatever truth there is, we will accept that truth without scorn or ridicule. The universe is what it is – vast and almost inaccessible, and we are nothing but its tiniest magnifying glass. And what we experience is all we know.

– The Author

GLOSSARY

The following are some of the most important words used in this book. Some are followed by the author's commentary. This is for clarity and communication (and even humor). It's important to note that sometimes the religious definition of a word is quite different than the secular definition, often making reasoned discussion of ideas between non-believers and believers quite difficult.

Abiogenesis, also known as spontaneous generation. The idea that life formed from non-living matter.

Abortion, the termination of a pregnancy before a fetus reaches full term.
Comment: There is no mention of such a term or practice in the Bible or the Qur'an.

Abstract, existing as a thought or idea, without being physical or concrete.

Afterlife, life after death; a being's existence in another living form after physical death.

Agnostic-atheist, one who does not believe in gods, but makes no claims of knowledge that a god does not exist. This belief is also referred to as weak atheism, or *negative* atheism.

Agnostic-theist, one who does not believe in gods, but does make claims of knowledge that a god does not exist. This belief is also referred to as strong atheism, or *positive* atheism.

Anecdotal evidence, evidence from anecdotes and stories which may or may not be true, or even partially true. Reliance upon anecdotal evidence is ill-advised, as this type of evidence often loses its validity as more anecdotes are added as support for a position.

Anti-Theist, one opposed to belief in the existence of a god, or one in opposition to an existing god, or one opposed to all gods, or opposed to religion in general.
Comment: In modern usage, this word is so poorly used and ill-defined, it means an anti-theist could also be a theist. A person could believe in a god or gods, but be in total opposition to the gods he or she believes in, making that person a believer and an anti-theist. (See: **Misotheism**)

Apocalypse, a prophetic revelation. Also used as a synonym for the "end of the world."

Apocryphal, a story or statement generally regarded as untrue, spurious, or fictitious.

Apollonius of Tyana, (circa 15 CE - circa 100 CE) a Greek philosopher from the town of Tyana in the Roman province Cappadocia in Asia Minor (modern-day Turkey). It has been often claimed that his life paralleled that of Jesus, or that his life was in part the basis for the mythos of Jesus.

Apologetics, reasoned discourse in the defense of an idea (as in defense of a religious doctrine or dogma).

Apriorism, belief in *a priori* principles or reasoning; the idea that knowledge is dependent upon principles that are self-evident, or that are presupposed, without prior experiential data.

Argument from Ignorance (*argumentum ad ignorantiam* in Latin), the fallacy that the truth of a premise is based on the fact that it has not been proven false, or that a premise is false because it has not been proven true.

Argumentum ad Populum, the fallacy that because a large number of people believe in something, it must therefore be true.

Aristotle (384 - 322 BCE), Greek philosopher and the author of works on logic, metaphysics, ethics, natural sciences, politics, and poetics; established the idea that theory follows empirical observation and logic, based on the syllogism, and is the essential method of rational inquiry.

Astrophysics, the branch of astronomy that deals with the physics of the universe and the application of the laws and theories of physics to the interpretation of astronomical observations.
Comment: Creationists often mix astrophysics and evolution when discussing their opinions regarding the origins of life. This habit of conflating the origins of the universe with the origins of life on earth is so common among creationists, it's expected. Creationists cannot imagine that their god could have created the universe and not created mankind, or that their god could have created mankind, but not the universe. For them, all phenomenon, whether occurring on earth or the rest of the universe, has only one possible answer – "God did it!" This is the sum total of their a priori *argument for God.*

Atheism, the belief that a god does not exist. In practical terms, it is the rejection of theistic claims about a god derived from the theist's inability to provide sufficient evidence that would demonstrate a specific god exists.

Atheist, one that does not believe in gods.
Comment: Many get the erroneous idea that atheism is a world view because atheists are not a tiny group of loonies huddled in a corner somewhere in a remote part of the world. Atheists are diverse, and in great numbers, and easier to point out than, for example, a non-believer in the chupacabra. A name had to be given to these numerous rejecters of the theistic notion, and the name "atheist" was born. We can suppose if a large number of chupacabra-believers

310

rises up, a new name for doubters will appear in response, perhaps *"achupacabrists?"* Not easy to say, is it?

Atheist-Agnostic, (See **Agnostic-Atheist**)

Atheist-Gnostic, (See **Gnostic-Atheist**)

Axiom, a premise or starting point of reasoning which is regarded as being established, accepted, or self-evidently true.

Bayes' Theorem, a mathematical and statistical theorem about conditional probabilities: it describes the probability of an event, based on conditions that might be related to the event.
Comment: Atheists come to their conclusions about gods based on the likelihood (probability) that such a thing is real, not the fantasy (possibility) that it could be real.

Big Bang Theory, the prevailing cosmological model for the early development of the universe that states the universe originated approximately 14 billion years ago from the cataclysmic explosion of a relatively small volume of matter at an extremely high density and temperature.
Comment: For creationists reading this: the above has nothing to do with the Theory of Evolution.

Biogenesis, the production of living organisms from other living organisms.

Blasphemy of the Holy Spirit, speaking sacrilegiously or profanely about the Holy Spirit.
Comment: How odd! A loving god has a rule that even he is powerless to forgive, and it's simply a restriction on Freedom of Speech!

Burden of Proof, the obligation to prove one's assertion.
Comment: Shifting the burden of proof in any discussion about any topic is a big no-no. It is not another person's responsibility to prove that pixies live on the moon, for example. That burden, i.e., responsibility, belongs to the person actually asserting that pixies live on the moon.

Causality, the relationship between one event (cause) and a second event (effect), in which the first event is understood to be responsible for the second.

Certainty, in its absolute sense: pure perfect knowledge.
Comment: There can be degrees of certainty, which are immeasurable, but considered reasonable by most human beings. No human has yet been shown to have in their possession, absolute certainty.

Christian, one who is an adherent of Christian beliefs; a follower of Jesus Christ and his teachings.

Comment: It is quite interesting to note that whenever a person by the above definition sins badly, and publicly, the outcry of other Christians is an immediate declaration that the poor soul was "never really a Christian." It raises the question as to whether or not one's fellow believers have committed an even greater sin by abandoning them in their time of crisis.

Chupacabra, a mysterious and legendary cryptid, said to exist in parts of Latin America, where it supposedly attacks other animals, especially goats.
Comment: No one has actually captured a real chupacabra, which is exactly what is needed to verify its existence. The people who believe it exists do so on faith alone. Yet, the chupacabra has as much or more evidence for its existence than any god has.

Circular Reasoning, also called *Circulus in Probando,* the fallacy of supporting a premise by simply repeating the premise in another form; having the conclusion of an argument simply be a restatement of the original premise.

Cognitive Dissonance, the excessive mental stress and discomfort experienced by an individual who holds two or more contradictory beliefs.

Cognitive Inertia, tendency for beliefs or sets of beliefs to endure once formed; the inability to change a set of beliefs despite new information that could challenge those beliefs.

Complex Question (known in Latin as *plurium interrogationum*), the fallacy of phrasing a question in a way that presupposes a specific answer, assumes something not true, or assumes a false dichotomy; treating a series of questions as if it were only one question. Also known as a "leading question."

Confirmation Bias, the idea that people tend to favor information that confirms their already held beliefs.

Convert (verb), to change in form, character, or function; to change one's religious views; to significantly alter one's beliefs.

Cosmological Argument, the argument for the existence of a First Cause for the existence of the universe. Often restated as an Uncaused Cause. This argument is often extended to reference a specific deity as the Uncaused Cause.
Comment: Of course, one doesn't have to contemplate the cosmological argument for very long before it is easily revealed to be an argument from ignorance. Possibilities are not necessarily probabilities, and the idea that a First Cause is somehow magically exempt from a first cause itself is nothing more than the fallacy of special pleading.

Creationism, the religiously based idea that all life arose on earth, in an instant, fully formed, and was designed by an intelligent, supernatural being. This

concept also applies to all things beyond earth, inclusive of the entire universe, and anything beyond. Also known as **Intelligent Design.**
Comment: Many advocates of this model now object to the term "creationism" and stick solely with the moniker "Intelligent Design." I.D. is more all-encompassing, that is, it includes the origins of the universe as well as the origins of life on earth. However, a U.S. District Court case, in 2005, (Fitzmiller v. Dover Area School District) *essentially concluded that Intelligent Design and creationism were one and the same.*

Deductive Reasoning, (Top-Down Logic), is the process of reasoning from one or more general premises, narrowing down from the general to the more specific to reach a logical conclusion. In deductive reasoning, if all the premises are true, and the rules of deductive logic are followed, then the conclusion is necessarily true. (See **Inductive Reasoning**).

Delusionist, an individual that actively and deliberately seeks out self-delusion; a person that desires to live in a fantasy world; a religious person.
Comment: This is a new word coined by the author.

Determinism, philosophical concept that every event in the Cosmos, including all human action, has pre-existing conditions that cause that event to happen with only one possible outcome.

Deus ex Machina, "God from the Machine"; in stories, it is a contrived plot device that is used to solve a seemingly insurmountable problem through the intervention of some unexpected and unbelievable entity, character, ability, or object.

Dogma, in religious terms, the set of principles established by a religious authority that are deemed undeniably true.

Docetism, the early Christian belief that Jesus Christ only seemed human, that his human form was just an illusion.

Dunbar's Number, the cognitive limit of the number of stable social relationships the average adult human being can handle at any given time, equal to about 150. First postulated by British anthropologist Robin Dunbar in the 1990's.

Eisegesis, the process of interpreting text in an effort to arrive at a preset conclusion – one which supports one's own presuppositions, agendas, or biases. Also known as "reading into the text." A path to *confirmation bias.*

Epiphany, a sudden and striking realization.

Epistemology, the study of knowledge and (well-) justified true belief; the study of the necessary conditions and sources for knowledge.

Equivocation, the use of unclear language, especially to deceive or mislead someone.

Evidence, data on which to base proof or to establish truth or falsehood.

Evil, deliberate or pre-meditated heinous, horrific, and inhumane deeds or actions. As an adjective: irreparably malevolent and destructive.
Comment: For an atheist, evil actions are human-sourced. For believers in deities, all evil is other-worldly, or supernaturally sourced.

Evolution, the theory that the various types of animals and plants on earth have their origins in other preexisting types and that the distinguishable differences are due to modifications in successive generations.

Fact, something that actually exists; reality; truth; something known to exist or to have happened; a truth known by actual experience or observation.

Faith, belief in something without any supporting evidence.
Comment: By this definition, faith is not a virtue.

Fallibilism, the philosophical idea that human beings can be justified in holding beliefs, even if, or when, their beliefs are wrong.

False Dilemma, (also known as **False Dichotomy**), the fallacy that asserts there are only two possible conclusions to a premise, or only two possible solutions to a problem, or only two allowable options in a situation. (See **Trilemma**)

Falsifiable, in scientific theory, the ability to test an hypothesis. An hypothesis that cannot be tested, or falsified, is unfalsifiable, and can be discarded. (See also: **Unfalsifiable**)

Free Will, the power to choose, think, and act voluntarily without the constraint of necessity, fate, or external force.

Genocide, the deliberate mass extermination of people who belong to a particular racial, political or cultural group.
Comment: This is considered the worst possible criminal and immoral act any human could commit, however, it is viewed with hardly a shrug when the genocidal criminal is also an alleged all-knowing, all-merciful, unchanging, "moral" lawgiver type god.

Gnosticism, an heretical movement of the 2nd-century Christian Church, mostly of proto-Christian origin.

God of the Gaps, the theological reasoning that presumes that anything unknown can be filled in with the presence of god as the creator of that unknown. Based on its obvious and copious use of the **Argument From Ignorance** fallacy, it has almost been elevated to a fallacy in its own right.

Hell, in the Torah and the Old Testament, it is the grave, destruction, and death; in the New Testament and Qur'an, it is a place of eternal fiery torment for condemned souls.
Comment: Perhaps Hell is just a place to roast humans before Yahweh eats them? (See: **Savour***)*

Henotheism, belief in one god, while acknowledging the possible existence of other gods.

Heresy, any belief or opinion contrary to orthodox religious doctrine.

Holy, a wholly subjective term used to designate some object or idea which is considered to be sacred and/or specially derived from a deity.

Holy Bible, the holy book used by the majority of Christian sects and denominations.
Comment: The book you are reading now references the King James Version of the Bible, and is abbreviated as "KVJ" throughout. Despite it being challenged often for its possible mistranslations, this version is still the most widely used Bible in the English-speaking world. It's the one with all the "thee's," "nigh's," and "lo's."

Holy Spirit, the third part of the Trinity (Father, Son, Holy Spirit). It is also invisible, like Yahweh, the Father.
Comment: Despite many theological attempts, it has never been adequately made clear how this invisible Holy Spirit is separate from the invisible Yahweh, and why it is necessary for it to be that way. It appears as though Jesus has a special function, but separation of the Holy Spirit from Yahweh is ambiguous and vague due to the fact that Yahweh is also supposedly invisible and possesses the same powers and attributes as the Holy Spirit.

Hypothesis, in science, a proposed possible explanation for a phenomenon that merits further investigation.

Ignosticism, the idea that most theological positions fail to define their god concept prior to arguing for the existence of their god, and when asked to do so, cannot adequately demonstrate its falsifiability. (See **Problem of Induction**)

Immaterial, not made of matter and outside the realm of space and time. Often used by interchangeably by theists with the words spiritual, and or, incorporeal. (See **Spiritual, Incorporeal**)

Impossibility of the Contrary, the Christian apologist idea that the contrary, or the opposite, of God existing is impossible.

Comment: It makes little sense to claim that the contrary of something is impossible when everything being claimed defies logic, reason, and even physics. The Christian doctrine thrives on an impossible god. The contrary of an impossible god is the possible: no god at all.

Incorporeal, having no body. The theistic notion that a mind or soul can exist without a body, or outside a body. It is the basis for claims of an afterlife.
Comment: A soul, if it existed, outside the body and with no brain to inhabit, would be quadriplegic, blind, deaf, dumb, and unable to taste, smell or feel anything. Its existence would be worthless.

Inductive Reasoning, (Bottom-Up Logic), reasoning that assembles or evaluates general conclusions that are based on specific examples. Inductive reasoning allows for the *possibility* that a conclusion is false, even if all of the premises are true. With inductive reasoning, the premises seek to provide strong evidence for (not absolute proof of) the truth of the conclusion. While the conclusion of a deductive argument is supposed to be certain (in a logical sense, not as an absolute), the truth of the conclusion of an inductive argument is supposed to be *probable,* based upon the evidence given. Simply put: Inductive reasoning is specific-to-general, whereas deductive reasoning is general-to-specific.
Comment: Please note that Christian apologists claim they use only deductive reasoning for their arguments for their god, not understanding that a conclusion can be true in a logical sense, but not certain in the absolute sense. They further contend that because science (which is apparently evil) uses inductive reasoning, it can only arrive at what is probable, unlike their side, which has absolute certainty regarding the existence of an all powerful being. And they proudly state that this certainty was derived, amazingly, through the use of a logical syllogism. No real evidence needed. (!)

Infinite, boundless, unbounded, unlimited, limitless, never-ending, interminable; subject to no limitation or external determination.
Comment: For theists, this a word used to describe both their chosen deity and the time allotment believers will spend with that same deity "someday." Always, forever, and "for an eternity" is not only a long time, it is all the time there is. It's a concept that is often quoted by religionists, but barely understood by them – as you would expect for finite beings. Expecting to live infinitely long in a place that isn't even part of the universe, with a being you can't show exists, is infinitely beyond absurd.

Inquisition, the former organization within the Roman Catholic Church responsible for finding and punishing people for the "crime" of heresy. (See: **Heresy**)

Intelligent Design, (See: Creationism).

Ipse dixit, an arbitrary dogmatic statement which is expected to be believed at face value, without argument or inquiry.
Comment: The statements, "God exists" and "Jesus loves you" are ipse dixit statements.

Islam, the Muslim religion; a monotheistic faith that worships the god, Allah, as revealed to its adherents through a prophet named Muhammad.

Jihad, struggle or war; within Islam, the struggle or war against the non-believer (kafir), or against one-self for falling away from Islam.

Justified True Belief, believing something is true based on the verifiable facts.
Comment: For many of the devoutly religious, the word "justified" doesn't have to point to demonstrable evidence. It simply means anything the religious person feels is a good reason for wanting it to be true – an interpretation which nullifies the word entirely, dispossessing them of any real justified true belief.

Kafir, in Islam, the lowest form of human being; a non-believer, atheist or doubter; any non-Muslim.

Kalam's Cosmological Argument, an Islamic-sourced variation of the cosmological argument. (See **Cosmological Argument**).

Kill, to put an end to a life.

Knowledge, facts; information; reasonable certainty about a subject, idea, concept, or tangible person, place, or thing, which is also supported by a reasonable amount of evidence.

Judaism, the religion of the Jews founded sometime during the Late Bronze Age or Early Iron Age by Abraham of Ur, in present-day Iraq. Jews worship the non-corporeal god Yahweh (also known as El).

Laws of Logic, the three basing principles necessary for reasoning. They are: 1. The Law of Identity: "Whatever is, is." 2. The Law of Non-Contradiction: "Nothing can both be and not be." 3. The Law of the Excluded Middle: "Everything must either be or not be."

Lie, a false statement that is (usually) intentional.

Littlewood's Law, states that an individual can expect to experience "miracles" at the rate of about one per month. A miracle is defined as a "one in a million" event which is considered exceptional or containing special significance to the individual experiencing the event.

Logic, philosophy that is concerned with the principles of valid reasoning.

Mahdi, in Islam, the future savior-like being who will usher in a new era of peace for the world. After this era ends, Judgment Day occurs.
Comment: Oddly enough, Jesus will be at the Madhi's side, as his assistant. Apparently, some messiahs need a sidekick, the same as talk show hosts.

Materialism, philosophical idea that all things in existence are composed of matter. (See: **Physicalism**)

Matter, physical substance in general; that which occupies space and possesses mass.

Misotheism, hatred of a god, or gods.
Comment: Misotheism can only be experienced by believers in a god or gods. Atheists, by definition, cannot be misotheists. Hatred for something that does not exist has no rational basis.

Moral relativism, philosophical construct that recognizes and accepts the differences in moral judgments of different people and cultures.

Morality, standards or principles defining correct human behavior which are derived from a particular philosophy, religion, or culture.

Münchhausen Trilemma, an epistemological reference that invokes the impossibility of proving anything at all in math or logic. The trilemma demonstrates this via the shortcomings of the circular, regressive, and axiomatic arguments. Because all three fail, certainty about anything is impossible.

Naturalism, the philosophical viewpoint that everything arises from natural properties and causes, and supernatural or spiritual explanations are excluded or discounted.

NDE, or Near Death Experience, a profound psychological event that may occur to a person on the brink of death, giving the person a feeling of being separated from their body and moving toward a light or a tunnel of light.
Comment: There's a reason it's called a "near" death experience. It's not actually death. If the person actually died, it would be labeled "Death Experience" and the person could claim resurrection. NDE's are falsely used to proclaim "proof" of an afterlife.

Nihilism, the philosophical doctrine that argues that life has no meaning, purpose, or value.

Non-sequitur, literally means "it does not follow"; a logical statement followed by an illogical, irrational, or irrelevant statement.

Objective, the state or quality of being true outside of a subject's individual biases, interpretations, feelings, and imaginings.

Occam's Razor, a principle of parsimony designed to keep investigation and its conclusions less complex. For example, in modern usage, one might hear: "Out of several choices, the simplest explanation usually the correct one." Or, "After all other possibilities have been eliminated, what remains is most likely correct." Both are adulterations of the original, and are often expanded and applied very differently than what its creator, 14th Century philosopher William of Ockham originally proposed. The Razor is used in a variety of ways to justify many different conclusions in science, philosophy, religion, and math.

Onanism, the practice of disengaging the penis from the vagina prior to ejaculation. Named after the character, Onan, in the Old Testament.
Comment: Coitus Interruptus, or "pulling out" at the last second, resulted in an early death sentence for Onan, a demise dispatched directly from Yahweh himself. Yahweh made sure Onan died young for the horrible crime of removing his penis from a vagina before ejaculating. Perhaps this is the real *reason men don't live as long as men! As a footnote: Yahweh also murdered Onan's older brother, but the Bible doesn't give any specifics other than "he was wicked."*

Pantheism, the belief that all of Nature and the Universe is god, or that the divine is in all things.

Paradox, a statement, argument, or proposition that appears self-contradictory or absurd yet expresses a possible truth.

Parthenogenesis, asexual reproduction; reproduction without fertilization.

Pascal's Wager, the argument that it is in one's own best interest to behave as if God exists, since the possibility of eternal punishment in hell outweighs any advantage of believing otherwise.

Physicalism, the philosophical concept that everything is physical, or that everything is wholly dependent on, or is necessitated by the physical. This is an expansion from the more simple concept of Materialism.

Plato, (428 – 348 BCE), one of the early founders of western philosophy. He was a student of Socrates and a teacher of Aristotle.

Polytheism, a belief in multiple gods.

Premise, a proposition supporting or helping to support a conclusion; either of the first two propositions of a syllogism from which a conclusion is drawn.

Presupposition, a supposition made prior to having knowledge (as for the purpose of argument); an implicit assumption during discourse wherein the truth of the supposition is taken for granted.

Primacy of Existence, the awareness of reality; the idea that existence exists, and the universe exists independent of any consciousness. Consciousness is the mode in which human beings are capable of perceiving that which exists, and through this process may gain knowledge of reality by looking outside the self.

Proselytize, to actively attempt to win converts to a particular religion or belief system.

Proof, any evidence that establishes or helps to establish the truth, validity, quality, etc, of something.

Proving a negative, the fallacious idea that one can shift their burden of proof for a belief or claim onto someone else. Normally, the obligation of proof lies with the one making a claim, for example: "I think X exists, and here's why..." If the one making the claim shifts their burden for proving X by stating, "Prove me wrong," they have asked someone to "prove a negative."

Pseudepigraphical, questionable, apocryphal, or potentially sacred religious texts which are not included in the official canon of Christian scripture.

Qur'an, the holy writ of Islam, allegedly given to an illiterate prophet, Muhammad, by the angel Gabriel, and transcribed by Muhammad's closest followers.

Randomness, the lack of a pattern, or a lack of predictability in events. For something to be truly random, all outcomes must be unpredictable. For human beings, randomness is subjective because what appears to be unpredictable to one, may not be unpredictable to another.

Reality, the state of things as they actually exist; that which exists objectively and in fact.

Red Herring, anything that deliberately leads someone to a false conclusion.

Religiosity, inappropriate, excessive, and obsessive devotion to the rituals and traditions of a religion.

Resurrection, the coming back to life of something that was dead. (See: **Zombie**)

Rock-Paper-Scissors, a hand game where one item is superior to a second item, and the second item is superior to a third item, and the third item is subsequently superior to the first item.

Sabbath, the holy "Day of Rest" for Judaism, Christianity, and Islam (each of which fall on different days of the week). Other religions also have their "rest days."

320

Sacrifice, in a religious context, the (usually) ritualized taking of an innocent life in an effort to make a god happy. (See: **Causality**)

Satan, a lesser god of the Old and New Testaments, and the Qur'an. Formerly, a "good" angel. He rebelled against Yahweh and became "evil." Satan is the adversary of Yahweh, Jesus, and Allah. Also known by various names such as, Lucifer, The Devil, the Evil One, etc.
Comment: Satan is also a long-term employee of Jesus and/or Allah, as he guards the gates of Hell and administers punishments as dictated by the judgments of Jesus and/or Allah.

Savior, a person sent to rescue someone from harm; hero or heroine; messiah or christ.

Savour, the quality in a substance that is perceived by the sense of taste or smell; to relish or enjoy.
Comment: This word is repeated several times in Leviticus and elsewhere in the Bible. Apparently, the invisible Yahweh had a functioning nose, and the smell of burning flesh upon the altar made him hungry. Or, would a more likely scenario be something more sinister? Were the priests running the show, duping the people who were making animal sacrifices into cooking meals for them?

Science, the process by which humanity organizes knowledge in the form of testable explanations and predictions about the universe.

Scientific Method, the process used by science to gain knowledge. The process includes: the formulation of a question, an hypothesis, a prediction, testing, and analysis.

Scientific Theory, an explanation of some aspect of the universe which has been derived through use of the scientific method. A scientific theory is based on facts and must be testable (falsifiable). A scientific theory is the pinnacle of scientific thought and inquiry.

Scripture, writings (usually from antiquity) considered sacred and holy by religions and religious sects or denominations.

Secular, that which is non-religious in nature; not affiliated with any religion or religious doctrine.

Secular Humanism, the philosophy that proposes the idea that humans can be ethical, moral, and responsible without the need for god or religion.

Self-evident, obvious or apparent; a truth that does not need to be demonstrated or explained.

Self-refuting, an idea or statement in which the logical consequence of holding such a view, or expressing such a statement inherently makes the view or statement untrue or contradictory; a logical contradiction and self-defeating statement. (Examples: "Don't obey me!" or "I can't speak any words in English.")

Servant, commonly known as a "domestic worker." A servant, unlike a slave, freely chooses to work as a servant and can quit at any time.
Comment: Christian apologists will often attempt to rename slaves in the Bible "servants," as a way to justify Biblical slavery.

Slave, a human kept as property by someone else, without the ability to escape.

Socrates, (469 – 399 BC), one of the great founders of western philosophy. He taught Plato, who later taught Aristotle. He is the creator of the Socratic Method which played a part in the eventual development of the Scientific Method.

Soul, an ethereal, non-material, but conscious portion of the human being that (allegedly) exists after death.

Soundness, the condition of containing truth; a way to judge whether or not an argument contains truth. An argument is only sound if the argument is valid and all its premises are true.

Special Pleading, a logical fallacy that argues a position as being an "exception to the rule" without providing justification for the exception.

Spirit, any ethereal, non-material, but conscious entity that (allegedly) exists outside the material world. (See **Soul**)

Straw Man, a fallacy that attempts to discredit an opponent's position by deliberately restating that position in a false or distorted manner.

Subjective, not necessarily self-evident or factual; a personal perspective based on feelings, beliefs, or desires.

Subjectivism, the philosophical position that one's own mental activity is the only unquestionable fact of our experience, and that there is no underlying true reality that exists independently of this perception.

Syllogism, a form of deductive reasoning in which a conclusion is derived from two (valid or invalid) premises.

TAG, (Transcendental Argument for the Existence of God), the argument that logic, morals, and science ultimately presuppose a supreme being, and that God must be the source of all logic, morals and science.

TANG, (Transcendental Argument for the Non-existence of God), the argument that "if something (logic) is created by or is dependent on God, it is not necessary – it is *contingent* on God. And if principles of logic are contingent on God, they are not logically necessary." – Michael Martin (1997). TANG shows that an all-powerful God could suspend the laws of logic, morals, and science on a whim. Such acts of God are violations of logic, morals and science, meaning that if logic, morals and science are real and true, as we know them to be, God cannot be real.
Comment: The very fact that such an argument exists in a valid form, demonstrates the weakness of the TAG argument. (Remember, TAG argues for the "impossibility of the contrary" when invoking the certainty of their position.)

Teleological, attributed to the study of any given thing's purpose. Used by creationists as an argument for a designer of the universe.

Theory, the pejorative term for one's opinion; a wild guess. (For the definition of **Theory,** as it is used in science, see **Scientific Theory,** above.)

Torah, the first five books of Moses, and the first portion of the Tanakh (the Hebrew Bible) used by Jews as the main foundation and focus for Judaism.
Comment: The majority of Christians use the Torah and the entire Tanakh as the precursor of the New Testament. However, the Christian interpretation of what the Tanakh means is quite different from the Jewish version, as Christianity perceives the Hebrew canon as consistently referring to Jesus Christ.

Transcendent, coming from God; above and beyond the physical realm.

Trilemma, a choice that proposes only three possible logical outcomes. Similar to a dilemma which proposes only two possible logical outcomes. (See **False Dilemma**)

Trust, firm belief in the dependability, truth, capability, or strength of something or someone, most often based on some prior evidentiary rationale.
Comment: Trust and Faith are often used interchangeably, but they do not actually have the same meaning. (See **Faith**)

Truth, the true or actual state of a matter; conformity with fact or reality; a verified or indisputable fact, proposition, principle, or the like.

Unfalsifiable, that which cannot be proved false due its lack of testability. (See **Falsifiable**)

Uniformity of Nature, the scientific observation that the natural laws and processes that operate in the universe now have always operated in the universe in the past and that these processes apply everywhere in the universe.

Universe, everything that exists, including earth and beyond.

Van Til, Cornelius, (1895 – 1987) Popular U.S. theologian and Christian presuppositional apologist.

Watchmaker Argument, a teleological argument in the form of an analogy, featuring a "found watch" which *must* have had a designer. It states that because a watch is complex, it must have been designed, and concludes, by way of analogy, that all things complex (such as the universe) must also have a designer.
Comment: The analogy conveniently leaves out the fact that, being more complex than a watch, the designer of the watch must also have a designer, and that designer's designer must have a designer as well. Each designer of a designer must be more complex than the one that came before, and so on, ad infinitum, i.e., "Who designed God?" and "Who designed God's designer?"

Woozle Effect, the effect of misleading others with false information by repeatedly citing half-truths, urban legends, and/or dubious sources. It derives from an imaginary weasel-like creature in the children's book, *Winnie The Pooh,* by A. A. Milne. In the book, the Woozle is talked about but never seen.

World View (also worldview), an individual's general point of view about the universe which directs and influences the individual's thoughts, actions, and life.

Yahweh, (also known as **El**), the main god of the Old Testament who is most frequently invisible, but not always. He was an ancient male Canaanite war god who first appeared in the Levant during the Late Bronze Age or early Iron Age, (approximately 3200 years ago), with his consort/wife Asherah. He is the supposed creator of the universe. Known by Muslims as "Allah," and by Christians, as "God."
Comment: It is interesting to note that this god is unknown and/or completely uninvolved with humans prior to a mere 3200 years ago! Certainly there were humans living on earth before this time period. Who discovered this god? Or, perhaps we should say, who invented him?

Zombie, a reanimated corpse, brought back to life by supernatural means.
Comment: Zombies, as depicted in books and films, never come back to life better than they were before they died – with the exception of Jesus, Lazarus, a widow's son, a little girl, and various unnamed "saints" in the Bible. If resurrections were real, a power like that should have had millions of people requesting a similar re-animation for their own friends and relatives immediately! Why weren't there tens of thousands of people coming day and night to Jesus so their own relatives could be resurrected?

Zone of Avoidance (ZOA), the area of the night sky obscured by the Milky Way.
Comment: This book refers to the ZOA as that area of the human mind obscured by religious thought.

A SHORT LIST OF ATHEIST ORGANIZATIONS
IN NORTH AMERICA

American Atheists
PO Box 158
Cranford, NJ 07016
www.atheists.org

American Humanist Association
1777 T Street, NW
Washington, DC 20009-7125
Phone: (202) 238-9088
Toll free: (800) 837-3792
americanhumanist.org

Canadian Atheist (blog)
www.canadianatheist.com

Canadian Secular Alliance
802 – 195 St. Patrick Street
Toronto, ON M5T 2Y8
Phone: (416) 402-8856
www.secularalliance.ca

Centre for Inquiry Canada
55 Eglinton, Ave E, Suite 307
Toronto, ON M4P 1G8
Phone: (647) 391-2342
www.centreforinquiry.ca

The Clergy Project
www.clergyproject.org

Freedom From Religion Foundation
PO Box 750
Madison, WI 53701
Phone: (608) 256-8900
www.ffrf.org

Military Association of Atheists & Freethinkers
888 16th St NW Ste 800
Washington, DC 20006
Phone: (202) 656-6223
www.militaryatheists.org

National Center for Science Education
420 40th Street Suite 2
Oakland, CA 94609-2509
Phone: (510) 601-7203
www.ncse.com

Rational Response Squad
www.rationalresponders.com

Richard Dawkins Foundation for Reason and Science
1012 14th Street NW, Suite 209
Washington, DC 20005
Phone: (202) 733-5275, Ext. 202
www.richarddawkins.net

ADDITIONAL RESOURCES

Americans United for Separation of Church and State
1901 L Street NW, Suite 400
Washington, DC 20036
Phone: (202) 466-3234
www.au.org

Committee for the Scientific Investigation of Claims of the Paranormal
Committee for Skeptical Inquiry
Box 703
Amherst, NY 14226
Phone: (716) 636-1425
www.csicop.org

Ex-Muslims of North America
www.exmna.org

SELECT BIBLIOGRAPHY

Azumah, John Alembillah. *The Legacy of Arab-Islam In Africa: A Quest for Inter-religious Dialogue.* London: Oneworld Publications, 2014.

Bostom, Andrew G., M.D. *The Legacy Of Jihad: Islamic Holy War And The Fate Of Non-muslims.* Amherst, New York: Prometheus Books, 2005.

Cochran, Gregory & Harpending, Henry. *The 10,000 Year Explosion, How Civilization Accelerated Human Evolution.* New York: Basic Books, 2009.

Damer, T. Edward. *Attacking Faulty Reasoning. A Practical Guide to Fallacy-Free Arguments.* Boston, Massachusetts: Wadsworth, 2013.

Darwin, Charles. *From So Simple a Beginning: Darwin's Four Great Books,* edited by Edward O. Wilson. New York: W.W. Norton, 2005.

Davis, Robert C. *Christian Slaves, Muslim Masters: White Slavery in the Mediterranean, the Barbary Coast and Italy, 1500-1800.* New York: Palgrave Macmillan, 2003.

Dawkins, Richard. *The God Delusion.* New York: Houghton Mifflin, 2008.

Gillette, Penn. *God, No!: Signs You May Already Be an Atheist and Other Magical Tales.* New York: Simon and Schuster, 2011.

Goldsmith, Donald & Tyson, Neil deGrasse. *Origins: Fourteen Billion Years of Cosmic Evolution.* New York: W.W. Norton, 2004.

Harris, Sam. *Letter to a Christian Nation.* New York: Random House, 2008.

Hitchens, Christopher. *God Is Not Great. How Religion Poisons Everything.* New York: Hachette Book Group, 2009.

Irwin, William & Jacoby, Henry. *House and Philosophy, Everybody Lies.* Hoboken, New Jersey: John Wiley & Sons, Inc., 2009.

Jordan, Michael. *Encyclopedia of Gods: Over 2,500 Deities of the World.* New York: Facts On File, Inc., 1993.

Khan, M. A. *Islamic Jihad: A Legacy of Forced Conversion, Imperialism, and Slavery.* Bloomington, Indiana: iUniverse, 2009.

Mills, David. *Atheist Universe. The Thinking Person's Answer to Christian Fundamentalism.* Berkeley, California: Ulysses Press, 2006.

O'Neill, John J. *Holy Warriors: Islam and the Demise of Classical Civilization.* Felibri Publications, 2009.

Pagels, Elaine. *The Gnostic Paul. Gnostic Exegesis of the Pauline Letters.* New York: Continuum International Publishing, 1992.

Pirie, Madsen. *How to Win Every Argument, The Use and Abuse of Logic.* New York: Bloomsbury Academic, 2013.

Robertson, J. M. *Pagan Christs.* New York: Barnes & Noble Books, 1993.

Scott, Emmet. *Mohammed & Charlemagne Revisited: The History of a Controversy.* Nashville, Tennessee: New English Review Press, 2012.

Seaman, Ann Rowe. *America's Most Hated Woman: The Life and Gruesome Death of Madalyn Murray O'Hair.* New York: Continuum International Publishing Group, 2006.

Voland, Eckart & Schiefenhövel, Wulf (Editors). *The Biological Evolution of Religious Mind and Behavior (The Frontiers Collection).* Germany: Springer, 2009.

Warner, Bill. *Mohammed And the Unbelievers. The Islamic Trilogy, Volume 1.* USA: CSPI Publishing, 2006

ABOUT THE AUTHOR

Edward Trillian is a graduate of Texas A&M University with a bachelor's degree in Political Science. His religious background has been quite varied and includes formerly held beliefs in Orthodox Judaism, Conservative Judaism, Evangelical Christianity, and Seventh Day Adventist Christianity. This is his first book on the subject of atheism. He currently resides in Dallas, Texas.

INDEX

A

abiogenesis, 226, 311

Abraham, 49, 120, 131, 168, 181-182, 211, 319

Afghanistan, 207

Affan, Uthman ibn, 182

Afterlife, The, 34, 39-40, 56-57, 151, 180, 244, 253, 287, 301, 303, 307, 311, 318, 320

agnostic, 20-23, 39, 84, 311, 313

angels, 17, 134, 137, 181, 184, 194, 262, 269, 295, 322-323

apriori knowledge, 81, 312

Arabic, 184, 195-196, 209, 216

Arabs, 182, 204, 208-209

astrophysics, 100, 210, 224, 226, 235, 246, 253, 282, 312

atheist,
    agnostic-atheist, 20, 22, 96, 311
    gnostic-atheist, 20-21, 23, 313

Azumah, John Alembillah, 208, 329

B

Bahá'íism, 258

Bahnsen, Greg, 76, 96

belief,
    justified true belief, 35, 88, 103-104, 315, 319
    without evidence, 29, 31, 33, 35-36, 38-39, 164, 183

Bible, The
    apocrypha, 137
    canon, 45, 136-138, 145, 161, 322
    and homosexuality, 130, 132, 165, 167-168
    pseudepigraphy, 136, 138, 322
    and rape, 127, 131-132, 149, 166-167, 269, 299
    and slavery, 129-130, 132, 149, 166-167, 170, 174, 275, 276, 324

Big Bang Theory, 212-213, 230, 237, 241, 244-245, 247, 249-250, 252, 269, 313

Brahma, 31, 259, 304

Bronze Age, 61, 112, 122, 161, 172, 252, 287, 319, 326

Buddhism, 258

Bukhari, al, 197-198, 200, 202

burden of proof, 14-15, 17, 23-24, 31, 37, 80, 86, 90-91, 93, 95-96, 103-106, 238, 271, 273, 284, 292, 302, 313, 322

C

certainty, 39, 79, 83, 87-90, 93-95, 99, 104-106, 223, 251, 278, 278, 313, 318, 320, 325

chaos, 58, 100, 225, 229, 237, 282

Charlie Hebdo, 202

Christianity,
    and the Crusades, 204
    vs. Islam, 219

circumcision, 68-69, 155

claims,
    extraordinary, 15, 23-24, 29, 109, 139, 305

Clergy Project, The, 290, 327

Colbert, Stephen
    quote, 109

coincidence, 67, 164, 240-241, 243-244, 280

Communism, 19, 59, 168

confirmation bias, 81, 164, 314-315

Confucius,
    quote, 257

Cosmological Argument, 50, 250, 314, 319

U

V

W

Z

Printed in Great Britain
by Amazon